TROUBLED WATERS

Troubled Waters

The Fight for the Boundary Waters Canoe Area Wilderness

by

Kevin Proescholdt
Rip Rapson
Miron L. Heinselman

NORTH STAR PRESS OF ST. CLOUD, INC.

Library of Congress Cataloging-in-Publication Data

Proescholdt, Kevin.
    Troubled waters : the fight for the Boundary Waters Canoe Area
Wilderness / Kevin Proescholdt, Rip Rapson, Miron L. Heinselman.
    352 p. 23 cm.
    Includes bibliographical references and index.
    ISBN 0-87839-100-2 (pbk.)
    1. United States.   Act to Designate the Boundary Waters Canoe Area
Wilderness, to Establish the Boundary Waters Canoe Area Mining Protection
Area, and for Other Purposes.   2. Boundary Waters Canoe Area (Minn.)
3. Wilderness areas—Law and legislation—Minnesota.
4. Wilderness areas—Law and legislation—United States.
I. Rapson, Rip, 1952-   . II. Heinselman, Miron L.   III. Title.
KF5646.B68P76 1995
346.7304´6782—dc20
[347.30646782]   95-37239
                                                                              CIP

Cover photo: Kevin Proescholdt

ISBN: 0-87839-100-2

All rights reserved. Printed in the United States of America by Versa Press, Inc.,
East Peoria, Illinois.

Published by: North Star Press of St. Cloud, Inc.
                 P.O. Box 451
                 St. Cloud, Minnesota 56302

Dedication

To Bud Heinselman,
whose vision, dedication, and warmth
inspire us still.

Table of Contents

About the Authors

Kevin Proescholdt has worked as the executive director of Friends of the Boundary Waters Wilderness for the past ten years, dealing with issues affecting the BWCA Wilderness and the broader Quetico-Superior ecosystem on a daily basis. He also is editor of the organization's newsletter.

Rip Rapson worked as a legislative aide to Congressman Donald Fraser during the time of the BWCA congressional battle. His chief assignment was Fraser's pro-wilderness BWCA legislation, and Rip worked with all the principal actors in Washington on planning strategy, writing legislation provisions, and working with the Friends and the national environmental community on passage of the BWCA law. He practiced law in Minneapolis, Minnesota, helped defend the 1978 BWCA Wilderness Act in federal courts, and chaired the board of directors of the Boundary Waters Wilderness Foundation.

Dr. Miron "Bud" Heinselman took an early retirment in 1974 from his position as forest ecologist with the U.S. Forest Service to work on saving the BWCA. He helped form the Friends of the Boundary Waters Wilderness in 1976 and served as its unpaid chairman for two and one-half years while working full time with a national grassroots network to pass the 1978 BWCA Wilderness Act. Bud was at the center of the Friends coalition and lived in Washington for most of that time, working with elected officials, staff, and the national environmental organizations on BWCA legislation. His major professional research involved studying and mapping the areas of virgin forest in the BWCA, involving nearly a decade of field research in the canoe country. He became one of the nation's foremost experts on the ecology of forests, peatlands, and the natural role of fire. Though he died before publication, his influence on *Troubled Waters* is evident.

Introduction

December 7, 1976. *A group of Minnesota environmentalists meet in a St. Paul home to discuss the future of the Boundary Waters Canoe Area. A federal appeals court has recently permitted the logging of BWCA virgin timber to resume. The timber industry has refused a plea for a voluntary logging moratorium, and has stated plans to resume cutting any day. A lawsuit to ban snowmobiles from the area awaits an impending court decision. Congress is considering opposing bills that would address these and other BWCA issues, but has taken action on neither.*

Bud Heinselman is obviously frustrated: "We have to do something, Chuck!" *He paces nervously in front of the fireplace, fidgeting occasionally with a piece of firewood and running his fingers through his hair.* "They're going back any day to start logging the forest we've been fighting for years to save!"

"Bud, I agree, we have to do something," *Attorney Chuck Dayton responds.* "But we don't have too many options left."

Dayton pauses a moment. "We don't have any good legal options. We've exhausted them. But I think we should try something slightly different. It's legal to go winter camping in the BWCA, right? Why don't we camp in the middle of the road to the Sunnydale sale? I know it could be thirty below zero," *he continued,* "but I would be surprised if the logging trucks would run over our tents and sleeping bags with us in them. We notify the media, we organize support teams and enough bodies to go in to the timber sale road, and we physically block the machinery from going in."

The group sits silently, contemplating the proposal. They agree: they will do it.

* * *

August 5, 1978. *Residents near the Boundary Waters Canoe Area are livid. They resent a process that threatens to tell them how they could and could not use the lakes and forests in their own backyard. They have resolved to do something about it.*

On this Saturday morning, one of the busiest of the summer, they blockade six of the busiest entry points to the Boundary Waters from early in the morning until late afternoon. They don't let anyone in and they don't let anyone out. Local county sheriff's deputies stand by and watch as one ugly confrontation followed another.

One blocked canoeist explodes. "You're punishing me for going into the wild," a woman who had traveled from Ohio yells at Ely resident Jay Salerno. "You're infringing on my rights." "This is the last chance we've got," Salerno replies. "All we want is to keep the BWCA open to everyone."

His answer infuriates the visitor all the more. She hadn't come all that way for nothing: "I can't believe you will take my day away from me to prove something to the government. It's totally irrational. I've never had another citizen do this to me in fifty-three years."

They avert an escalation when she walks away to look for another place to enter. But the threat of violence remains in the air. "I hate to say this," local resident Sue Scufsa observes, "but if we lose the election this fall, you're never going to see anything like it. There's going to be utter destruction. We have the feeling that if we can't use the area, nobody can."

* * *

Two incidents separated by two years of legislative and political wrangling. Not atypical of the confrontations that have plagued the BWCA for much of this century. It is an area that inspires passion and generates controversy in equal doses. What follows is the story of the most recent examples of both, of the events that led to the protection of the Boundary Waters Canoe Area Wilderness in 1978.

Stretching over a million acres along the Minnesota-Ontario border, the Boundary Waters Canoe Area Wilderness is a web of a thousand crystalline lakes, cascading rivers, and meandering streams embedded in emerald green forests and majestic cliffs. Red and white pines dating from the 1600s help provide the habitat for wolves, moose, bear, bald eagle, and hundreds of other less imposing species.

The only lakeland wilderness in the nation, the BWCAW is the largest wild land east of the Rockies and north of the Everglades. Together with Ontario's adjoining Quetico Provincial Park, it forms a wilderness ecosystem of more than two million acres, an area of incomparable ecological value to both nations.[1] The BWCA's thousands of visitors compile over one million "visitor days" of use annually, making it the most heavily visited wilderness in the United States.

The early human history of the area is only dimly known and best pieced together through the archaeological record. Faded red pictographs on cliff faces

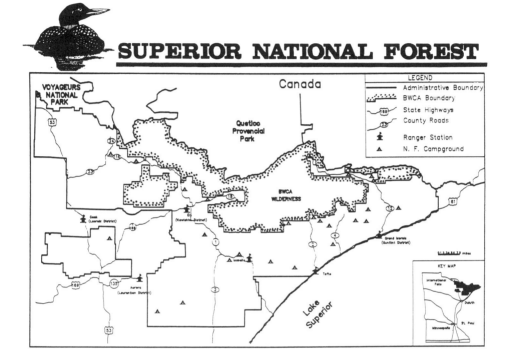

Regional setting of Superior National Forest and BWCA Wilderness. (*Map courtesy of U.S. Forest Service.*)

attest to the early native inhabitants, and both the Dakota and Ojibwa peoples have lived in the area in more recent times.[2] The area was the highway of the fur trade, the birchbark canoes of the French voyaguers passing through its lakes and portages long before white settlers pushed up from the south.[3] It would later witness the logger and the fisherman, the mining prospector and the resorter.

Since the beginning of the twentieth century, the human history of the BWCA has been one of battle after battle between those who would dam, log, mine, or motor and those who would preserve the area's wilderness character.[4]

The conservation effort to protect the border country wilderness can be traced to at least as early as 1902, when Minnesota's chief fire warden, Christopher C. Andrews, successfully convinced the federal General Land Office to withdraw from sale 500,000 acres of public domain land in northeastern Minnesota.[5] This and subsequent land withdrawals formed the nucleus of the Superior National Forest, established by President Theodore Roosevelt in 1909.[6] Despite this designation, early management provided only minimal caretaking. In addition, privately owned properties remained inside the area, seemingly isolated and undevelopable.

The Boundary Waters Canoe Area contains over 1,000 lakes, many with islands. (*Photo by Kevin Proescholdt*)

In 1919, the Forest Service hired a young landscape architect, Arthur Carhart, to produce recreational development plans for national forests throughout the country. In Colorado's White River National Forest, Carhart surprised his superiors by recommending that the Forest Service not develop the Trapper's Lake area for cabin sites but instead preserve it in its natural state. In 1922, he produced a similar surprise by suggesting a recreation plan for the Superior National Forest that emphasized wilderness canoeing:

> [T]he scheme of developing the human use within the Superior
> National Forest will be based on a demand now existing, and which in
> the future will be of greater magnitude, for human contact with typical
> lake-land wilderness.[7]

In the early 1920s, the infant Izaak Walton League of America helped defeat a good portion of an ambitious Superior Forest road-building plan proposed by the Forest Service and backed by local commercial interests. Their work led Agriculture Secretary William Jardine to designate a large part of the forest in 1926 for wilderness recreation—the second such wilderness area designated in the country and the first coming from as high an authority as the secretary.[8]

Jardine promised to retain "as a wilderness" as much of the Superior National Forest as possible and to "leave not less than 1,000 square miles of the best canoe country in the Superior without roads of any character."[9]

Although the Jardine decision rejected several road proposals—the most serious of which proposed connecting the Gunflint Trail with the Fernberg Road

The million-acre BWCA is the only significant lakeland unit in the National Wilderness Preservation System where visitors travel primarily by canoe. (*Photo by Kevin Proescholdt.*)

across the heart of the canoe country—it did allow construction of the Fernberg Road east from Ely, the extension of the Gunflint Trail from Gunflint Lake to Seagull Lake, and, later, the creation of the Echo Trail northwest from Ely to Buyck.[10]

About the same time Carhart was developing his ideas on a canoe wilderness and Jardine was limiting road construction, an entrepreneur and timber baron named Edward Wellington Backus proposed building a series of dams along the international border lakes to generate hydroelectric power. He also planned to log the area's shoreline timber.[11]

Led by Ernest Oberholtzer, conservationists opposed Backus' plans and convinced Congress to pass the Shipstead-Newton-Nolan Act in 1930, which prohibited logging within 400 feet of lakeshores and barred further alteration of natural water levels.[12] The law was an effective antidote to the likes of Backus but failed to protect against logging away from lakeshores.

The Backus threat made clear to the emerging conservation community that it needed a more formal and powerful forum in which to raise issues concerning the wilderness. In 1934, concervationists persuaded President Franklin Roosevelt to create the President's Quetico-Superior Committee.[13] Oberholtzer and Charles Kelly were among the three private conservationists appointed; one of the two government slots was filled by Bob Marshall, who with Oberholtzer and others would found the Wilderness Society the following year.[14]

By the mid-1940s, dozens of resorts serviced by pontoon-equipped airplanes had sprung up on privately owned properties in the interior of the Superior Roadless Areas, as the wilderness was then called. The resorts and the burgeoning air traffic dramatically changed the character of the wilderness. Ely wilderness proponent Sigurd Olson wrote that he had seen seven planes fly in, land, and take off in the time it had taken him to paddle across Agnes Lake.[15] A friend of Olson's, Frank Hubachek, tallied thirty-eight planes that had flown over his cabin on Basswood Lake in a single day.[16] Ely had become the largest inland float plane base on the continent.[17]

Olson and others took their case to Washington. In 1948, Congress passed the Thye-Blatnik Act, authorizing monies for the purchase of privately owned fly-in resorts and cabins in the Roadless Areas.[18] The following year, President Truman signed an executive order establishing an unprecedented air

French-Canadian voyageurs once portaged their canoes around Curtain Falls on the international border. (*Photo by Kevin Proescholdt*)

Glaciers once scoured the BWCA, leaving a rocky, forested landscape. (*Photo by Kevin Proescholdt*)

space reservation above the roadless areas, preventing float planes from landing.[19]

The new law and executive order were powerful tools. But they were severely limited in their effectiveness by the absence of condemnation authority and by inadequate funding. As a result, acquisition of private properties dragged through the 1950s and even into the 1960s.[20]

The Forest Service also moved forward with its own agenda. In 1948, it produced a management plan for the roadless areas that, for the first time, sought to regulate the use of motorboats. Although the Forest Service never issued motorboat regulations, the agency had articulated a management approach that would limit motorboats to routes on which they had become well established. The plan also formally established a 362,000-acre No-Cut Zone along the international border in which logging was prohibited.[21]

Outside the No-Cut Zone, however, logging continued. By 1958, the Forest Service changed the area's name to the Boundary Waters Canoe Area, recognizing that its maze of logging roads crisscrossing the area had rendered the term "roadless" a misnomer, despite Jardine's vow some thirty years earlier to keep the wilderness free of roads.[22]

In 1964, Congress established the National Wilderness Preservation System. The BWCA was included, but singled out for special treatment: logging and motorized use would be permitted to continue.[23]

This book takes up the story there, setting the stage for, and then focusing on, the intense period of activity from 1975 to 1978. It was a period of controversy unsurpassed in the intensity of its politics and in the reach of its implications for local and national wilderness policy.

The BWCA provides one of the few safe havens in the lower forty-eight states for the federally threatened bald eagle (top), and (bottom) is home to a variety of large mammals, including the moose. (*Photos by Kevin Proescholdt*)

Notes

1 For information on Quetico's conservation history, see Gerald Killan and George Warecki, "The Battle for Wilderness in Ontario: Saving Quetico-Superior, 1927 to 1960," in Roger Hall, William Westfall, and Laurel Sefton MacDowell (eds.), *Patterns of the Past: Interpreting Ontario's History* (Toronto and Oxford: Dundurn Press, 1988):328-355; George Warecki, "The Quetico-Superior Council and the Battle for Wilderness in Quetico Provincial Park, 1909-1960," master's thesis, University of Western Ontario, 1983; George Warecki, "Protecting Ontario's Wilderness: A History of Wilderness Conservation in Ontario, 1927-1973," Ph. D. thesis, McMaster University, 1989; Bruce Litteljohn, "Quetico: Great Park or Forest Industry Asset?" *Canadian Audubon* 32 (May/June, 1970):79-83; Bruce Litteljohn, "Quetico: Great Park, or Timberman's Reserve?" *Naturalist* (Winter 1970):26-33; and Bruce Litteljohn, "Battlefield of Conservation," *Naturalist* (Winter 1973):1-7.

2 See, for example, Selwyn Dewdney and Kenneth Kidd, *Indian Rock Paintings of the Great Lakes,* (Toronto: University of Toronto Press, 1962); also Emerson S. Coatsworth, *The Indians of Quetico,* (Toronto: University of Toronto Press, 1957); and Gordon Peters, *The Archeology of Northeast Minnesota,* (Duluth: Lake States Interpretive Association, 1985).

3 See Grace Lee Nute, *The Voyageur's Highway,* (St. Paul: Minnesota Historical Society, 1941); Grace Lee Nute, *The Voyageur,* (St. Paul: Minnesota Historical Society, 1955); J. Arnold Bolz, *Portage Into The Past,* (Minneapolis: University of Minnesota Press, 1960); Eric Morse, *Fur Trade Canoe Routes of Canada: Then and Now,* (Ottawa: National and Historic Parks Branch, 1969); Sigurd F. Olson, "White Water Yields Relics of Canada's Voyageurs," *National Geographic,* Sept. 1963, pp. 412-435.

4 The efforts of conservationists who worked to save the canoe country, particularly during the period from the 1920s to the 1950s, are well chronicled and documented in Newell Searle, *Saving Quetico-Superior: A Land Set Apart* (St. Paul: Minnesota Historical Society Press, 1977). See also David Backes, *Canoe Country: An Embattled Wilderness* (Minocqua, Wisconsin: NorthWord Press, 1991).

5 Christopher C. Andrews to General Land Office Commissioner Binger Hermann, May 10, 1902; Binger Hermann to C.C. Andrews, June 30, 1902; both letters found in Chief Fire Warden of Minnesota, Eighth Annual Report, 1902, pp. 38-40.

6 See Theodore Roosevelt, Presidential Proclamation No. 848, Feb. 13, 1909. Other presidents later expanded the boundaries of the national forest. William H. Taft, Presidential Proclamation No. 1215, Sept. 19, 1912; Calvin Coolidge, Presidential Proclamation No. 1800, Apr. 9, 1927; Franklin D. Roosevelt, Presidential Proclamation No. 2213, Dec. 28, 1936; John F. Kennedy, Executive Order No. 11072, Dec. 28, 1962.

7 See Arthur Carhart, "Recreation Plans: Superior National Forest," May 1922, 111 pp., at p. 14. Carhart soon left the Forest Service and began writing more forcefully and eloquently for preservation of the Superior's wilderness. See, for example, Arthur Hawthorne Carhart, "Our Superior Forest," *Field and Stream,* June 1927, p. 42. For a treatment of

The BWCA contains a characteristic maze of lakes and waterways. (*Photo by M. L. Heinselman*)

Carhart's early recreation plan, see David Backes, "Wilderness Visions: Arthur Carhart's 1922 Proposal for the Quetico-Superior Wilderness," *Forest & Conservation History* 35 (July 1991), pp. 128-137.

8 The Forest Service's Aldo Leopold sparked the establishment of the first wilderness area in 1924 on the Gila National Forest in New Mexico. Leopold had promoted the Gila Wilderness Area since October 1922 in his position as chief of operations in the district office (now called regional office). District Forester Frank Pooler implemented Leopold's Recreational Working Plan and established the Gila Wilderness Area on June 3, 1924, five days after Leopold left New Mexico for Madison. See Curt Meine, *Aldo Leopold: His Life and Work*. (Madison: University of Wisconsin Press, 1988), pp. 211-228.

9 William Jardine, "The Policy of the Department of Agriculture in Relation to Road Building and Recreational Use of the Superior National Forest, Minnesota," Sept. 17, 1926, 9 pp.

10 *Ibid.*

11 See Newell Searle, *Saving Quetico-Superior: A Land Set Apart* (St. Paul: Minnesota Historical Society Press, 1977), pp. 60-89.

12 Public Law 71-539, 46 Stat. 1020. In 1933 the State of Minnesota enacted similar legislation, popularly referred to as the Little Shipstead-Newton-Nolan Act, dealing with

state-owned lands in the same area; see Minnesota Laws 1933, p. 411; Minn. Stat. 92.45 and 110.13 (1984). In 1934, the International Joint Commission ruled against Backus and his proposal—at least for the moment—finally ending the battle. Backus died later that same year.

13 Franklin D. Roosevelt, Executive Order No. 6783, June 30, 1934.

14 For information on Marshall, see generally Sigurd F. Olson, "Quetico-Superior Elegy," *Living Wilderness*, Spring 1948, pp. 5-12; James M. Glover, *A Wilderness Original: The Life of Bob Marshall* (Seattle: The Mountaineers, 1986); Jim Vickery, *Wilderness Visionaries* (Merrillville, IN: ICS Books, 1986); Kevin Proescholdt, "How Wilderness Returned to Brule Lake," *Minnesota Volunteer*, Jan.-Feb. 1987, pp. 25-31. For some of Marshall's official Forest Service work on the Superior's wilderness, see Lyle F. Watts, regional forester, to Forest Service chief, Jan. 7, 1938; Robert Marshall to Lyle Watts, Jan. 13, 1938; R.U. Harmon, forest supervisor, to Lyle Watts, regional forester, Mar. 2, 1938; Robert Marshall to Lyle Watts, Mar. 21, 1938; Lyle F. Watts to Forest Service chief, Mar. 8, 1938; R.U. Harmon to Lyle F. Watts, Apr. 2, 1938; Robert Marshall to Lyle Watts, June 17, 1938; Lyle F. Watts to Forest Service chief, June 20, 1938; Robert Marshall to Lyle Watts, July 6, 1938; copies in possession of authors.

15 Sigurd F. Olson, *Open Horizons* (New York: Alfred A. Knopf, 1969), p. 203.

16 Frank Hubachek to Charles S. Kelly, July 15, 1946, Control of Use of Airplanes file #2, Quetico-Superior Council Papers, Minnesota Historical Society Archives.

17 Sigurd F. Olson, *Open Horizons* (New York: Alfred A. Knopf, 1969), p. 203.

18 Public Law 80-733, 62 Stat. 568. In passing the law, Congress followed the example set by the Izaak Walton League Endowment, which had purchased significant numbers of key private holdings within the roadless areas for eventual re-sale to the Forest Service.
    Some owners willingly sold their resorts or properties to the federal government. One example was Florence and Pete Peterson, who sold their Basswood resort to the Forest Service and remained stalwart wilderness advocates. One property purchased on Trout Lake under the Thye-Blatnik Act was sold by Iowa fishing tackle entrepreneur Berkley Bedell, who later became an Iowa congressman and co-sponsored the BWCA wilderness legislation in 1977.

19 Executive Order 10092, December 17, 1949; *Federal Register*, December 22, 1949, 14 FR 7637.

20 Congress subsequently strengthened the Thye-Blatnik Act with several amendments. In 1956, it extended the Thye-Blatnik Act to cover the entire BWCA and increased the total maximum appropriation to $2.5 million. P.L. 84-607 (70 Stat. 326). In 1961, it added another $250,000 for acquisitions, P.L. 87-122 (75 Stat. 258), deleted the condemnation restriction from the Thye-Blatnik Act, P.L. 87-351 (75 Stat. 772) and increased the authorization to $4.5 million, P.L. 87-351 (75 Stat. 772). In 1976, it bumped the Thye-Blatnik authorization to $9 million, authorized funds from the Land and Water Conservation Fund for use in similar BWCA acquisitions, and authorized these appropri-

ations for payment of court judgements in condemnation actions. P.L. 94-384 (90 Stat. 1123).

21 Superior National Forest, "Plan of Management, Superior Roadless Areas," February 13, 1948.

22 See Richard E. McArdle (Forest Service chief) to E.L. Peterson (assistant secretary), Jan. 27, 1958. Peterson approved the name change the following day.

The Boundary Waters Canoe Area was only the most recent name change for the wilderness in Superior National Forest. After Jardine's 1926 designation, it was known as the Superior Wilderness Area. In 1939, with approval under the 1929 Forest Service Regulation L-20, the name changed to Superior Roadless Primitive Area and then in 1948, under 1939 Forest Service Regulation U-3(a), the three wilderness units (Little Sioux, Superior, and Caribou) were re-named collectively as the Superior Roadless Areas. See, for example, Superior National Forest, "Plan of Management, Superior Roadless Areas," February 13, 1948, p. 11.

23 Public Law 88-577, 78 Stat. 890, 16 U.S.C. 1131-1136.

Chapter One

The Roots of Controversy

The origins of the great wilderness controversy that swept over the Boundary Waters Canoe Area in the 1970s first took root two decades earlier during the national public debates over whether to create a national wilderness system. Senator Hubert Humphrey, Minnesota wilderness advocates, and the BWCA itself played critical roles in that debate.

The earliest wilderness protections for the area came in 1926, when Secretary of Agriculture William Jardine designated 1,000 square miles of the canoe country as wilderness. Though some logging did occur in the BWCA, about 540,000 acres of virgin forest remain, the largest block east of the Rockies. (*Photo by Kevin Proescholdt*)

Hubert Humphrey and the Early
Politics of Wilderness Preservation

If there is a legislative godfather of the national wilderness preservation system, it is Hubert Humphrey. But his paternity was not without controversy. Humphrey believed strongly that wilderness needed to be preserved through federal stewardship. He struggled throughout his senate career with home-state pressures to keep wilderness lands available to pre-existing and long-standing commercial and recreational uses.

Humphrey's balancing of his belief in a wilderness ethic and his desire to accommodate the politics of multiple use led him to forge one of the most consequential political compromises of his career: a brief paragraph in the 1964 Wilderness Act that would set the stage for all of the ensuing wilderness battles of the 1970s.

That compromise had been building for more than a decade.

Propelled into national prominence by his fiery civil rights speech at the 1948 Democratic National Convention, Humphrey won a seat in the senate in the fall of that year and took office in 1949. At the same time, Minnesota conservationists were waging a battle to restrict flights over the Superior Roadless Areas, as the BWCA was then called. The airspace restrictions sought to prohibit float planes from landing on BWCA lakes, a practice that enabled visitors to patronize resorts tucked deep within the wilderness and to gain easy access to remote lakes that had not yet been fished out.

The conservationists convinced Humphrey that such effortless penetration of the area's most fragile and secluded lakes by motorized means made a mockery of wilderness. Humphrey's support of airspace restrictions was instrumental in securing a Presidential Executive Order in December of 1949 banning flights below 4,000 feet.[1]

The local tensions that accompanied the air flight ban over the BWCA paralleled the growing debate in Washington over whether to establish wilderness areas that would be protected by federal statute, and thus much more protected than the administrative wilderness designations in place by the Forest Service.[2] In 1949, for example, the Library of Congress issued a sobering report on the status of wilderness preservation efforts. The report concluded that before many years "original wilderness . . . will have disappeared entirely. . . . If then, there is reason for preserving substantial portions of the remaining wilderness, it must be decided upon before it is too late."[3]

As the national wilderness debate evolved, Humphrey's friendships with several well-known wilderness proponents in Minnesota, particularly William Magie and Sigurd Olson, powerfully influenced Humphrey.

Humphrey had met Magie in 1949 when the senator and his wife Muriel visited the Magie home in Hibbing just prior to President Truman's signing of the airspace reservation order. Magie's organization, Friends of the Wilderness, was among the most active in Minnesota in promoting the airspace reservation and, later, passage of the Wilderness Bill.[4]

Humphrey also met Sig Olson of Ely during the airspace reservation controversy. During the 1950s, Olson would emerge as an influential thinker, leader, and wilderness activist in several national conservation organizations.[5] Humphrey knew Olson well enough to describe him to his colleagues on the senate floor as "truly one of the nation's leading conservationists. He is a very dear friend of mine." Humphrey elaborated: "If any of my colleagues would like to have a good duck dinner, and I do not mean one of those tame grocery store ducks, but a duck in the northern Minnesota style, I think I could arrange it with Sig Olson."[6]

These experiences and relationships prepared Humphrey to play a leading role in early efforts to develop national wilderness policy.[7] An unlikely event spurred him into taking on such a role: a speech given in 1955 by Wilderness Society Executive Director Howard Zahniser.[8] As he had for a number of years, Zahniser called for a statute that would codify federal principles of wilderness protection. Humphrey was taken with the concept, inserting Zahniser's remarks in the Congressional Record a week later.[9]

Sigurd F. Olson. His friendship with Hubert Humphrey played a key role in including the BWCA in the 1964 Wilderness Act. (*Photo by Bruce Litteljohn*)

The federal wilderness statute Zahniser envisioned took form a short year later, with Humphrey as the chief Senate sponsor.[10] Humphrey remarked upon introduction of the measure:

It is indeed fortunate that after the centuries we have spent in developing this continent we do still have some large areas of wilderness. It is doubly fortunate that many of these areas are federally owned and are also included in parks, forests, or refuges, or other kinds of reservations within which the wilderness has so far been preserved in keeping with the purposes of the reservations.[11]

Humphrey included with his remarks a number of letters of support for the Wilderness Bill, including one from Sig Olson, then President of the National Parks Association.[12]

In an article written for his Minnesota constituents, Humphrey explained his hopes for the wilderness legislation:

If the Wilderness Bill . . . is enacted, we who prize our wonderful canoe country will have won a great victory. We will be assured that the irreplaceable primeval area with which we are blessed will be protected for the enjoyment of ourselves, our children, and for the generations to come. . . . The communities of northern Minnesota bordering the wilderness have a great asset for a permanent future prosperity which exceeds anything that a short-lived exploitative boom might bring. As Americans increase in number, their need for outdoor recreation will expand many fold, and a bit of wilderness will prove to be a unique attraction to millions. We need the wilderness. . . .[13]

It is unlikely, however, that Humphrey anticipated the torrent of criticism his bill would unleash from residents of those communities in northeastern Minnesota.

Perhaps he should have.

Northeastern Minnesota had been settled largely by Scandinavian and Eastern European immigrants. The economic backbone of the region came from its iron mines and forests, its politics from the working class that emerged from those mines, logging camps, and sawmills. It created a highly individualistic, get-your-knuckles-dirty political environment, one that would resist anybody, particularly someone from Washington, D.C., telling them what they could and could not do with their lakes and their forests.

The "Iron Rangers" also had ample historical reason to distrust those who would impose outside values on the local economy. Iron mining on the Vermilion Range at Tower and Ely had already begun by the 1880s. Mining began on the nearby Mesabi Range in 1892 and by 1916 produced half the nation's iron ore. Changes or innovations in the industry often resulted in loss of jobs or periods of unemployment over which the miners had no control. Over the years, a culture of anger and suspicion developed between the miners and the mining companies, a culture stoked by local politicians as a way of generating support for heavy taxation of the mines and commercial property. At its height, this taxing strategy resulted in mining companies paying as much as eighty percent of local taxes, while exercising little control over local politics.

In the early part of the century, iron range towns had become lavish spenders, thriving on a political patronage system. In one ten-year period, the town of Hibbing, with a population of 15,000, spent more than the city of Duluth, with its population of 100,000.

But the vicissitudes of the industry and the onset of the Great Depression changed dramatically the fortunes of northern Minnesota. By the 1930s, Hibbing stood three million dollars in debt, a plight shared by most northeast Minnesota counties. Many townships became dependent upon county and state aid. In 1932, in an extreme example, residents of three northern St. Louis County townships paid $658 in county and state taxes, yet received more than $25,000 in county and state aid.

To ease the counties' plight, state and federal governments created four new state forests and expanded Superior National Forest by a million acres as a way of taking property off the tax roles in exchange for payments in lieu of taxes. But this action also increased local animosity toward outside control, and the Superior Roadless Areas, as the wilderness was then called, became a favorite target for local citizens who felt they no longer controlled their own destinies.[14]

Prior to the late 1940s, much of northeastern Minnesota had supported efforts to protect the wilderness character of the Quetico-Superior area. Those efforts had posed little threat to the ability of the local communities to use the lakes, harvest the forests, or create a resort economy inside the wilderness. The 1948 Thye-Blatnik Act and the air ban of 1949 changed all that. These actions cut off ready access to many resorts in the interior of the BWCA, forcing them to sell out to, or later be condemned by, the government.

The tenacious fight waged by a small group of local businessmen against the air ban illustrated how dramatically the stakes had changed.

Immediately after President Truman's creation of the airspace reservation, an Ely-based organization called "Outdoor America, United" and led by Virginia float plane pilot Ray A. Glumack formed in Ely to fight it.[15]

On May 1, 1950, Outdoor America wrote to Forest Supervisor Galen Pike conveying its opposition to Pike's proposed regulations "in their entirety" for implementing the airspace reservation.[16] Although its efforts did not change the Forest Service's course and the organization dissolved soon after it was formed, Outdoor America set a tone of opposition to the air ban and other wilderness restrictions that would endure for the next half century.

Implementation of the air ban dragged on for years. The government sued local resort owners and float plane operators. The owners and pilots fought back.[17] When the dust settled in 1952, Federal Judge Gunnar Nordbye had upheld the ban.[18]

Undeterred, the resorters continued to fly in guests and supplies during the 1953 summer tourist season as Forest Service rangers, Minnesota game wardens, federal marshals, and FBI agents gathered evidence of illegal flights. On July 2, state and federal authorities brought events to a head. They seized two float planes owned by local pilot Elwyn West, took another pilot into custody at Ely, and arrested West himself in a third plane at an interior resort. The sting made national news and left dozens of vacationers stranded at remote resorts with no way out. Judge Nordbye fined the two pilots a total of $3,000 for violating his injunction.[19]

Two resort owners embarked on their own course of guerrilla resistance. Joe Perko and William Zupancich refused to sell their resorts on Crooked Lake to the federal government while seeking an alternative way of bringing in their guests than the long motorboat route they had been forced to use when the fly-ins stopped. In 1954 and 1955, Perko and Zupancich began the arduous process of creating a land route by upgrading and extending an abandoned 1915 railroad grade, the Cloquet Line. Breaking locked gates and gouging several miles of rough trail from Gun Lake north to Sunday Bay of Crooked Lake, the two men carved out a route passable by a World War II vintage all-terrain "weasel."

The courts were not impressed with either their creativity or their perseverance. In 1955, a permanent injunction barred Perko and Zupancich from using the "road" they had created. Zupancich's resort at Curtain Falls on Crooked Lake was finally condemned in 1963, and he was ordered to vacate by early 1966. He subsequently established a new resort on Canadian property on the western portion of Lac La Croix, a stone's throw across the international border from the BWCA.[20]

By the mid-1950s, these disputes, together with the systematic federal purchases of resorts within the roadless area, had fueled the misgivings that northern Minnesota residents felt about the heavy hand of the federal government. It was an attitude that would shape their reaction to Senator Humphrey's proposed wilderness legislation.

Congress had done little with the first wilderness bill.

Humphrey re-introduced it in essentially the same form in February of 1957. The bill's first hearing occurred in June; Humphrey himself testified in favor of the measure.[21]

But the bill met with resistance from the very agency the local residents viewed as the enemy: the United States Forest Service.

Forest Service Chief Richard McArdle opposed the Wilderness Bill, but offered an alternative. He proposed to treat the wilderness area in the Superior

National Forest not as a pure wilderness, but as an area open to a variety of economic and recreational uses. He called for the continuation of logging and the maintenance of the road network necessary to support that activity.[22] He proposed re-naming the area the "Boundary Waters Canoe Area" since so many logging roads had been built in the wilderness that the "roadless" name could no longer truthfully apply. And, in a phrase that would re-emerge again and again in the battles to come, he proposed that the Forest Service manage the area for "the general purpose of maintaining, without unnecessary restrictions on other uses including that of timber, the primitive character of the area, particularly in the vicinity of lakes, streams, and portages."[23]

Shortly after the Washington hearing, two Ely men ignited a storm of protest against Humphrey's bill. Their actions would dramatically alter the course of efforts to bring full wilderness protection to the BWCA.

Around July 10, 1957, Ely City Attorney Willard Domich spoke at a local banquet and harshly condemned Humphrey's bill; radio station WELY in Ely repeated his statements in several separate broadcasts.[24]

On July 18, Ely Miner editor Fred Childers followed suit, penning a front-page editorial blasting the Humphrey bill:

> A bill that vitally affects the future economic life of Ely, one that, in part, curtails future development, restricts present operations, and in some instances cancels out entirely three of our major industries—mining, lumbering, and tourist business—was introduced into the legislature last February by Senator Hubert H. Humphrey.[25]

Childers compared Humphrey to Brutus or Judas for introducing the bill and concluded with the plea that "everyone from this area write to Sen. Humphrey protesting the passage of this bill, which bans the outboard motor, and curtails lumbering and mining in this area." The editorial was followed over the next three months by a weekly series of articles and editorials by Childers condemning one aspect or another of Humphrey's legislation.[26]

Humphrey's two principal Minnesota wilderness allies, Sig Olson and Bill Magie, alerted Humphrey to the growing ferment in northeastern Minnesota.[27] Olson subsequently left for a month-long canoe trip, leaving Magie to organize local support for the bill.

On July 20 Humphrey wrote a memo to his aide Herb Waters telling him to work with Zahniser in organizing Minnesota supporters "to go to bat for us right now" on the bill:

> I will need their help on this issue, and I want a concentrated dose of it. This fellow Childers is a reactionary editor in Ely. He hates my guts,

and he has been after me for years. He feels he has a good issue now, so I want to take him on—head-on—so let's give it to him.[28]

Humphrey also wrote a letter to Childers on July 22 responding to Childers' allegations.[29]

Magie responded to Humphrey's call for support with a three-page statement on behalf of the Friends of the Wilderness. In a quote picked up by newspapers, radio stations, the Associated Press in New York, and CBS News' "World Today" newscast, Magie wrote:

> A small but noisy minority, living in Ely, parts of Lake and Cook County, some of them county employees, have been crying in their beer and their buttermilk for so many years over their thwarted efforts to exploit and destroy the Wilderness Canoe Country, that the boundary waters are becoming salty from their affluent tears.[30]

Humphrey wrote back to Magie and said, "Dear Bill: How can I thank you enough, my friend? When William H. Magie makes a statement, people listen . . . ."[31]

Meanwhile, Humphrey was moving on his own to contain the controversy. A July 22nd version of the bill had not only picked up changes suggested in the June hearing, but had incorporated the Forest Service's language permitting logging in the Superior wilderness area, a point Zahniser emphasized a day later in a letter to Childers.[32]

The revisions did not end there. Humphrey aide Howard Haugerud drafted a new sentence to the July 22nd version providing that "nothing in this act shall preclude the continuance within these roadless areas of any of the already established use of motor boats." Haugerud explained in a undated memo to Humphrey,

> This is an amendment that Mr. Z and I have talked over. He has sent the proposal to Sig Olson and asked him to ok it. I think it goes a long way to assure the people of the Ely area that we are not trying to fool them and at the same time does not weaken the bill. As yet, Mr. Z does not have approval from his organization so I will not use it in any letters.[33]

On the 25th of July, Humphrey issued a press release that made clear the purpose of this new language:

> The Wilderness Bill will not ban motorboats from the Superior National Forest, and any such claim is just a scarecrow to frighten people.

Nothing in this bill would stop present use of motorboats in the Caribou, Little Indian Sioux, and Superior Roadless Areas of northern Minnesota. The bill does not in any way jeopardize, threaten, or remove any rights that any person now has under present law relating to recreation, mining, forestry, land use, grazing privileges, mineral exploration. . . . The bill specifically states that present rights and property rights are fully protected and honored. We are . . . trying to maintain the primitive character of some areas without unnecessary restrictions on other uses, including that of timber.[34]

This flurry of activity during these few days of July forever altered the BWCA's future.

The compromise sponsored by Humphrey—to appease the Forest Service on timber harvesting and his Ely critics on motorboating—planted the seeds for repeated confrontations over whether the BWCA would remain open to a variety of recreational and commercial uses or be managed consistently with principles of wilderness preservation.

It was a Faustian exchange. On one hand, Humphrey's new language would usher the BWCA into the national wilderness system. On the other, it carved into federal law—for the first time and apparently in perpetuity—the permissibility of carrying on uses such as logging and motorized travel within wilderness areas.

Humphrey's approach had the grudging approval of Minnesota's wilderness proponents, though they personally found it distasteful. Zahniser, Magie, and Olson went along with the bill revisions because, as Olson told Congress twenty years later, "[Although] I didn't like the change, nor did any of the rest of us . . . we accepted it because we wanted the wilderness bill to pass."[35]

Despite the compromises, opposition in northeastern Minnesota continued to simmer.

On July 30, Two Harbors Mayor David Battaglia approved a City Council resolution opposing the bill.[36]

Ely Chamber of Commerce Executive Secretary Stan Pechaver sent a vitriolic letter to Humphrey on August 3 blasting the Izaak Walton League, the Quetico-Superior Council, and the Wilderness Society as "high pressure fanatic wilderness groups" who use "high-handed, steam-rolling tactics."[37] Pechaver singled out Sigurd Olson for particular scorn:

Sig Olson (of Ely, we're sorry to say), is not a member of any organization active in local affairs. I understand he even (and quietly at that) revived a chapter of the Izaak Walton League here just to give him some Ely prestige that he does not have. He does not speak for any of our organizations.

Grand Marais Chamber of Commerce President Ted Wynn wrote Humphrey on August 5 that the wilderness bill was "a disguised octopus whose tentacles will continue to reach farther and farther with nefarious purpose cloaked in a theme designed to capture public fancy and assure public lethargy."[38]

Humphrey waited for things to cool down before responding. In December, he convened an informal hearing on the bill in St. Paul, bringing with him a printed draft containing the new compromise language on logging and motorboats.[39]

Humphrey opened the hearing by complaining that he had suffered undeserved criticism from northeastern Minnesotans over his bill. His plea failed to mollify the bill's opponents. They set out a laundry list of demands to protect motorboats, logging, mineral prospecting, mining, and the storage of boats within the BWCA. They vigorously opposed any additions of land to the area. They were so adamant about obtaining iron-clad guarantees that Ely City Attorney Domich hired a court reporter to document every word said at the hearing.

Humphrey was anxious not to leave the hearing without a meeting of the minds. After persistent questioning, Humphrey told the crowd that "your existing rights are maintained; such as motorboating rights or mineral rights, they are maintained; your forestry rights are all maintained." When this failed to stem the mounting tensions, Humphrey stated bluntly: "[T]here was no intention in the bill to alter the motorboating situation at all. [T]he intention was to protect the rights of the motorboating."[40]

That seemed to turn the tide. The bill's critics left feeling that they had extracted the concessions for which they had come. A number of them acknowledged that Humphrey had taken "practically all the wind out of their sails."[41] The press ran the headline: "Hubert's Wilderness Bill Critics Retreat."[42]

Humphrey referred to the informal hearing when he re-introduced the wilderness bill in 1958, noting the need to protect "the business enterprises so vital to the economy" in the Superior National Forest. "We were able to meet some of these objections," Humphrey reported. "We conferred, clarified, and revised."[43]

Humphrey incorporated his compromise language for the BWCA into the Wilderness Bill. For reasons unrelated to the BWCA provisions, however, the bill failed to pass not only in the 1958 congressional sessions, but in subsequent sessions until 1961.[44] The measure passed the Senate in 1961 and again in 1963, but the House did not pass it finally until 1964. President Lyndon Johnson signed that bill into law, creating the National Wilderness Preservation System—a wilderness system including the Boundary Waters Canoe Area—on September 3, 1964.[45]

The Local Flashpoint: Logging

While conservationists worked for passage of the Wilderness Bill at the national level, an almost completely separate effort began in Minnesota to re-examine the management policies for the BWCA. The most controversial of these involved logging.

Logging began in the BWCA about 1895 during the height of the big-pine logging. Logging companies used rafts and stream-drives to move the great virgin timber across lakes and along rivers to local sawmills or railheads. Much of this logging occurred in the central section of the wilderness: the Basswood Lake, Knife Lake, and Kekekabic Lake areas. By 1930, approximately one-fourth of the BWCA had been cut over.

These practices would appear almost quaint in comparison with the high-powered pulpwood logging that began after World War II. Pulpwood logging involved clearcutting large tracts of timber using skidders, bulldozers, and other heavy mechanical equipment. Such heavy-duty activity required an extensive network of gravel haul roads to carry out the pulpwood on trucks.[46]

These techniques opened an era of vastly accelerated harvesting of the BWCA forest.[47] In 1940, logging in the Superior National Forest totaled 9.1 million board feet. By 1945, harvest volume had increased to 45.0 million board feet, and by 1952 had increased to 97.5 million board feet, a ten-fold increase since 1940.[48]

To further accommodate the new demand for logging, the Forest Service also moved to delete lands from the Superior Roadless Area. As early as 1942, Forest Supervisor Clare Hendee proposed deleting lands around the Silver Island Lake area to facilitate logging.[49] But he issued a word of caution: "[T]here is a definite danger, if this elimination is made, that the interests advocating complete preservation of the roadless area may use such elimination to strengthen their stand for restricting cutting on the remainder of the area." The Roadless Area deletion, finalized in 1947, removed over 30,000 acres and excised Silver Island Lake, the Island River, parts of Brule and Homer Lakes, and part of Isabella Lake from the roadless area boundaries.[50]

These logging practices created a rift within the conservation community. Some organizations, such as the Izaak Walton League, or individuals like Ely canoe outfitter Bill Rom, wanted to end the damage and stop the logging of the wilderness. Others, such as the President's Quetico-Superior Committee, felt that a complete logging ban was politically unachievable and that pressing for one might risk an erosion of wilderness protections already in place.[51]

The Izaak Walton League assumed a particularly active role.[52] Around 1960, the League's Wilderness Committee[53] began regular meetings with

Superior National Forest Supervisor Larry Neff to discuss such logging issues as "accidental" BWCA accesses created by new logging roads, the failure to remove existing roads following logging, and the length and size of timber-sale contracts.[54]

In early 1964, a collection of nine groups formed a new coalition called Conservation Affiliates to work on wilderness issues in Minnesota.[55] The leaders of the Affiliates came primarily from the Twin Cities area and included many well-known business people as well as leaders of conservation organizations. Dr. Clayton Rudd, president of the Minneapolis-based Natural History Society, became the chairman. Minneapolis insurance executive Paul Clement, an outspoken member of the President's Quetico-Superior Committee and former national president of the Izaak Walton League, served as secretary.

Conservation Affiliates publicly questioned the Forest Service's BWCA policies and called for the area's reclassification as an official wilderness to prohibit logging and motorized travel.[56] The organization produced several glossy brochures in the spring of 1964, showing through aerial photographs the extensive clearcuts within the BWCA and through ground photographs the logging roads and logging camps along or near canoe routes within the wilderness. Conservation Affiliates charged that some of this logging violated federal laws and Forest Service policies.[57]

The success of the Conservation Affiliates in bringing the BWCA issues into a public debate spurred the Forest Service's boss, Secretary of Agriculture Orville Freeman, into action.

In May of 1964, former Minnesota Governor and then-Secretary Freeman established the Boundary Waters Canoe Area Review Committee to probe the most vexing issues of BWCA management—particularly logging, motorboating, and mining—and to provide him with recommendations that would put those issues to rest.[58] He appointed as the committee's chair Dr. George A. Selke, a consultant to the Secretary of Agriculture and the Commissioner of Conservation during the Freeman governorship.[59]

The Selke Committee and Freeman Directives

The two-year life of the Selke Committee, as it was to become known, and the subsequent Freeman Directives would be tumultuous. The committee's recommendations and the regulations based on them would both provoke controversy and create the basis for the major BWCA battles a decade later.

The parallels between the 1964 to 1965 Selke era and the 1975 to 1978 BWCA wilderness fight era remain striking.

Many of the most prominent local advocates on both sides of the Selke disputes were to re-emerge a decade later.[60]

Minnesotans dominated the national political scene in both eras. During both, a Minnesotan served as Vice President (first Hubert Humphrey and then Walter Mondale) while another Minnesotan served as Secretary of Agriculture (Orville Freeman and later Robert Bergland).

The political process worked much the same way in both times. Conservationists appealed to the area's national constituency and sought resolution from the national government; local area residents argued about impacts to the local economy.

And finally, the controversial issues themselves were virtually indistinguishable.

Environmentalists wanted to end logging in the BWCA, preclude the threat of mining, and eliminate motorized use.[61] Local residents sought to continue patterns of existing use, citing a threat to local jobs, an erosion in the local resource-based economy, a "locking up of timber resources," an imposition of insensitive federal controls on access to the area, and a reduction in the freedom to use the area for multiple recreational purposes.

These issues would burn on high heat from the very day that Freeman appointed the Selke Committee.

In fact, the very next day, May 22, 1964, a day-long conference called the Quetico-Superior Institute convened in St. Paul to explore the management controversies swirling around the BWCA.[62] Jointly sponsored by the President's Quetico-Superior Committee and the Quetico-Superior Foundation[63] and attended by George Selke, the Institute revealed deep divisions not only between wilderness advocates and advocates of multiple use, but within the conservation community itself.[64]

On an organizational level, the split came between those who sought to end timber harvesting in the area—the Conservation Affiliates and the Izaak Walton League—and those who backed the Forest Service approach of some controlled logging—especially, the President's Committee on the Quetico-Superior.[65]

On a personal level, the split was symbolized by the growing divisions among four old friends: Bill Magie; Charles Kelly, the chair of the President's Committee; Frank Hubachek, Kelly's law partner; and Ernest Oberholtzer, the architect of the original Quetico-Superior wilderness program that dated from 1927.

Magie ardently advocated for an end to logging in the canoe country.[66] He and his close friend Bill Rom formed a two-man reconnaissance unit, checking out logging areas on the ground, conducting fly-overs to observe timber sales from the air, and photographing logging cuts and logging roads across portages.

Kelly and Hubachek, perhaps because the President's Committee worked so closely with the Forest Service, had always been reluctant to publicly criticize the agency's forest management practices in the wilderness.[67]

Oberholtzer, though, now almost eighty years old and no longer active in the President's Committee, had evolved in his views beyond the early wilderness policies he had helped create four decades before:

> I don't think we are short of timber anywhere in this country, and I am not convinced that the economic loss from stopping logging in the BWCA would be an important one, though it would be a blow to the pride of the Forest Service. It is inevitable that they must handle the area as a wilderness and there is nothing whatsoever in the Forest Service policy to prevent them from designating a true wilderness for the health and enjoyment of people.[68]

One person might have bridged these differences. Sigurd Olson served as wilderness consultant to both the Ikes and the President's Committee; he was the author of several wilderness books and a close friend of all these men. But indicating the growing polarization over these issues, Olson could not find common ground among the old friends; he himself spoke out at the institute in favor of complete wilderness.[69]

The Institute suggested, therefore, just how difficult the Selke Committee's work would be. The Committee soon received a number of reminders of that fact.

During July the Committee held public hearings in Grand Marais, Ely, Orr, Duluth, and St. Paul. A majority of those who testified at the four northeastern Minnesota hearings favored "multiple use" as opposed to wilderness. The story reversed itself in St. Paul, however, where eighty percent of those who testified wanted logging stopped and motorboats, snowmobiles, and houseboats eliminated.[70]

The public hearings signaled to the timber industry that they would have to go to work to protect their logging activities in the BWCA. Their formidable public relations machinery shifted into high gear. It had plenty of fuel to power the effort.

In addition to the usual arguments of jobs, economics, and the "let the professionals run the forest" line, the industry rested much of its argument on a 1963 National Park Service report concerning the management of wildlife and vegetation in national parks. Called the Leopold Committee for its chair A. Starker Leopold (son of famed naturalist Aldo Leopold),[71] the report contained a sentence that was often quoted by the industry: "Management may at times call for the use of the tractor, chainsaw, rifle, or flame-thrower but the signs and sounds of such activity should be hidden from visitors insofar as possible."[72]

The industry also enlisted academic experts in its cause. Dr. Frank Kaufert, Dean of the University of Minnesota's School of Forestry, was prominent among them. Citing the Leopold report, he became a staunch and frequent defender of the need to log the forest in order to manage it properly:

> [The Report] condemns the hands-off, no disturbance, complete fire protection management practices [as] mismanagement . . . .[T]he BWCA needs the logger more than the logger needs the BWCA.[73]

Coupled with the fact that parts of the BWCA forest had been logged for generations and that logging provided a mainstay for the local economy, the credibility of these arguments seemed overwhelming.

But wilderness proponents found a powerful antidote in an unlikely package: a bespectacled, wispy-haired, self-effacing Forest Service forester and ecologist named Bud Heinselman.[74]

Breaking ranks with the vast majority of his forestry colleagues,[75] Heinselman stunned the industry with remarks he delivered in June 1964 to a special session of the Society of American Foresters convened to discuss the BWCA controversy.

Heinselman called for an end to logging in the BWCA. But where others rested the argument on general principles of wilderness character, Heinselman raised in public for the first time the ecological and scientific value of protecting the virgin forests of the BWCA:

Forest Service ecologist Bud Heinselman began urging an end to BWCA logging in the 1960s. Bud is shown here (left) with Trish Record (right) of the Sierra Club. (*Photo by M. L. Heinselman*)

[T]here is still another value in our wilderness areas, and this is a "practical" one. I refer to the scientific value of large scale natural communities. . . . [W]e can hardly imagine the possible values that future generations of scientists may uncover in these "islands of the natural world," that hopefully we may save . . ."[76]

The argument took the industry by surprise. Heinselman was asked to give a special closed-door presentation on these novel arguments to the Selke Committee on September 17, 1964.[77]

In a bold move, Heinselman also contacted the members of the Leopold Committee in early 1965 about Frank Kaufert's use of their report, expressing concern that Kaufert's propensity for selective quotation served to mischaracterize the report's basic findings. Committee Chair Leopold confirmed to Heinselman that Kaufert and others had quoted the report out of context and wrote to Kaufert to inform him personally. Kaufert, to his credit, stopped citing the report.[78]

Heinselman continued his assault on the timber industry's public relations campaign by taking his ecological arguments into the professional forestry journals. In a 1965 Journal of Forestry article, Heinselman described the broader scope of the Leopold Committee report and challenged his colleagues as a matter of professional integrity to rise to the challenge of wilderness management.[79]

The logging controversy was also being played out in the forest itself.

When he appointed the Selke Committee, Secretary Freeman also requested the Office of Inspector General to conduct an investigation into the timber management practices within the BWCA. This request came about in large part to allegations by the Conservation Affiliates that the Forest Service had violated the Shipstead-Newton-Nolan Act and the 1948 Management Plan by allowing logging of no-cut zones and of shoreline timber.

In a tactical error, the Conservation Affiliates cited a road and logging operation near Phantom Lake in the Little Sioux unit of the BWCA as a case in point. It turned out, however, that the operation occurred on state, not federal, land and lay just outside the area protected by the Shipstead-Newton-Nolan Act. The Inspector General cleared the Forest Service of any wrong-doing in August 1964, soon after the Selke Committee's public hearings.[80]

The clean bill of health turned out to be premature. In the fall of 1964, conservationists discovered yet another logging road—the Finn Lake Road—that vividly illustrated the kind of violations they had alleged in conjunction with the Phantom Lake sale.

Logging companies had built the Finn Lake Road west of the Gunflint Trail by bulldozing road fill into and across the narrow west end of Finn Lake. Not only did the road violate the protected 400-foot strip around the lake, but it blatantly damaged the lake itself and divided it into two segments.

The incident galvanized the conservation community. In a twelve-page photo story on the incident, *Naturalist* magazine wrote:

> A more brutal, devastating, disregard for the sensitivity of dedicated Conservationists fighting for the rights and privileges of millions of Americans seeking inspiration and enjoyment in a unique wilderness area could not be devised than this road bulldozing its way through a wilderness dear to the hearts of Americans.[81]

All the while, the Selke Committee continued meeting, gathering information and deliberating. It submitted its report to Freeman in December 1964.[82] In its major recommendations, it gestured in the direction of both conservationists and proponents of multiple use.

Multiple use proponents could take solace from the Committee's recommendations that logging continue in the BWCA outside the no-cut zone[83] and that three recreation zones would be recognized—a Large Motor Zone, a Small Motor Zone, and a No-Motor Zone.

Wilderness proponents could similarly be pleased at a number of recommendations:

• Approximately 150,000 acres would be added to the no-cut zone along prime canoe routes or in areas of old-growth forest, and another 35,000 acres in the Crane Lake-Namakan Lake area not adjacent to the BWCA would be continued in no-cut status for at least another decade.

• An additional 22,000 acres adjacent to the BWCA would be given special recognition and management to "protect their particular features and complement the management of the BWCA."

• Visitor registration and permits would be initiated.

• Snowmobiles and houseboats would be prohibited.

• The "mechanical portages" (commercial operations that used trucks or jeeps to haul boats) at Prairie Portage and Four Mile Portage would be closed upon acquisition of remaining private rights.

• Current mineral exploration permits would be rescinded, future permits would not be granted, and private mineral rights would be acquired.

• A research program on forest ecology in the BWCA would be conducted by the Forest Service.[84]

Any celebrating the conservation community might have wanted to do was forestalled by Secretary Freeman's decisions in January 1965.[85] This set of decisions came to be called the Freeman Directives.[86]

The Freeman Directives fell into three categories:

First were those that reinforced the wilderness protection recommendations of the Selke Committee: enlargement of the no-cut zone,[87] set-aside of the special management areas,[88] and limitation of motorboats of certain sizes to designated routes.

Second were those that retreated from the Selke Committee's recommendations (and some which retreated from Freeman's recommendations), particularly those that permitted snowmobile use on those routes designated for motorboats.[89]

Third were those that were missing: there were no restrictions on the storage of boats within the BWCA as a means of evading motorboat restric-

In 1965, proponents for multiple use in the BWCA held a parade in Ely, Minnesota. Logging trucks (top), an argument for continued logging in the BWCA, and snowmobiles and motorboats (bottom) were included in the parade. (*Photos by M. L. Heinselman*)

tions,[90] no controls over the "accidental" access points to the BWCA created by logging roads,[91] and no guidelines for how the no-cut zones outside the BWCA were to be managed or acquired.

The biggest problem to emerge from the Freeman Directives lay not in any of these three categories, however, but in the extraordinary manipulation of the directives by the Forest Service in preparing the regulations to carry them out.

The Forest Service took almost a year to develop the regulations to implement the Freeman Directives. During that time, the agency altered the directives virtually beyond recognition.

Part of the explanation was politics.

Local residents ratcheted up their pressure after the Freeman Directives were issued. Perhaps the most visible and vocal among these efforts was the Boundary Waters Resource Committee, formed to fight the directives. Among its activities, the Committee organized a protest parade when Freeman and Lynda Bird Johnson dedicated the Forest Service's new Voyageur Visitor Center in Ely in the summer of 1965.[92]

But part of the explanation had to do with the professional culture of the Forest Service itself, and its inherent proclivity to accommodate local interests.[93]

In June, the Forest Service released Draft Regulations that suggested the power of that culture. The concept of motor-size zones was eliminated in favor of merely a listing of routes on which motorboats would be permitted. Snowmobiling would be continued at least one more winter to accommodate lodge reservations made well in advance and to minimize enforcement problems.[94] The Prairie and Four Mile mechanical portages would remain open.[95] Logging could continue in the areas set aside for the 1975 additions to the No-Cut areas.[96] And although mining would be banned, exploration for minerals would be permitted.

The final regulations issued in December of that year watered down the directives even further.[97] It was as if the Forest Service had been further emboldened by having been able to weather the adverse reaction to their already-weakened June draft regulations.[98]

This blatant dilution of the Freeman Directives stunned the conservation community. It taught wilderness advocates an important lesson about the consequences of leaving the future of the wilderness to administrative discretion.[99]

Mounting Controversies: 1966-1977

The Forest Service regulations served more to muddy the water than to set in place a regulatory framework for the BWCA. The Selke Committee's deliberations had raised the visibility of the controversies surrounding logging, motorboating, snowmobiling, mining, and land additions. If the Freeman Directives had stoked those controversies, the draft and final regulations poured gas on them.

This resulted in a decade-long string of challenges to the Forest Service's management policies and practices. With each new challenge, it became increasingly clear that a long-term, permanent solution could only come from statutory changes that would take matters out of the realm of the inherently unstable Forest Service rule-making apparatus. That realization would have to wait, however, until the administrative trench warfare over mining, logging, and snowmobiling had run its course.

Mining and Mineral Exploration

The Forest Service's failure to prohibit the issuance of mineral exploration permits opened the possibility that mineral exploration would occur within the BWCA. With the enormous financial stakes involved, that possibility quickly became a reality.

In June of 1966 International Nickel Company (Inco) signed twenty-year federal mining leases with the Forest Service for the right to extract copper-nickel ore from a 5,000-acre tract of land just outside the BWCA southeast of Ely near the South Kawishiwi River.[100]

Although these leases covered minerals outside the wilderness, their signing sparked national interest in the area's mineral potential. That interest intensified with the publication by the Minnesota Geological Survey of a detailed geologic map that showed not only Inco's deposits but other potential "target" areas as well.[101] Two other mining companies quickly announced their interest in exploring the area, contingent only upon seeing the lease terms of forthcoming state rules.[102]

The State of Minnesota wasted no time in approving rules covering leases for copper, nickel, and associated minerals on state lands. After a hearing in July 1966 and adoption of final rules in November, leases covering 88,000 acres with thirteen corporations were awarded in December.[103]

The Minnesota Legislature was the next to jump in. In its 1967 session, the Legislature passed legislation reducing the taxes on copper-nickel mining.[104]

All of these actions set the stage for the inevitable: a mining operation within the BWCA.

By the summer of 1969, an entrepreneur named George W. St. Clair, a northeast Minnesota native who had relocated to New York City, had begun prospecting for minerals within the BWCA itself.[105] St. Clair owned "severed" mineral rights—sub-surface rights that had been disconnected from surface rights.

So even though someone else, typically a jurisdiction of government, owned the land or water, St. Clair could extract minerals from below the surface.[106]

St. Clair's crew prospected by canoe in the Howard Lake region west of the Gunflint Trail near Gabimichigami Lake. This kind of prospecting did not require a Forest Service permit.[107] In December 1969, however, this relatively modest operation threatened to take a new turn with the use of heavy, diamond-drilling equipment.

The Forest Service drew the line. Forest Supervisor Craig Rupp vowed to fight the drilling, announcing that if St. Clair's crew tried to enter the BWCA, "we will be there to stop them physically."[108] But despite this stern tone, Rupp and the Forest Service were not confident that they had the legal grounds to block the operation.

The Izaak Walton League moved to lend its support to the Forest Service. The national arm of the Ikes was well-positioned to be an ally. They had a long-standing interest in the BWCA.[109] They had also recently completed an analysis of land and mineral ownership and acquisition in the BWCA,[110] retaining Ray Haik, a member of the Selke Committee and an officer with the Ikes organization, to conduct the research.[111]

On December 23, the Ikes sought a permanent injunction against mineral exploration in the BWCA.[112] The Ikes again retained Haik, now the Ikes national president, this time as chief counsel.[113]

The injunction was first heard in January 1970 before Federal

The Sierra Club staged a mid-winter rally along the Gunflint Trail to protest mining in the BWCA. (*Photo by M. L. Heinselman*)

District Judge Philip Neville. The suit named St. Clair, the Forest Service, and the State of Minnesota as defendants, despite the sympathetic position the latter two had assumed.[114] The complexity of mineral laws, mineral ownership, and the number of parties to the suit,[115] extended the proceedings over three years. Judge Neville ruled on January 5, 1973. Concluding that wilderness and mining are incompatible, he granted the injunction:

> Mineral development thus by its very definition cannot take place in a wilderness area; else it no longer is a wilderness area. To create wilderness and in the same breath to allow for its destruction could not have been the real Congressional intent, and a court should not construe or presume an act of Congress to be meaningless if an alternative analysis is possible.[116]

The decision was appealed. A year later, the Eighth Circuit Court of Appeals overturned Neville's ruling on procedural grounds.[117] The case was remanded to District Court.

The Court of Appeals had re-opened the door to BWCA mineral exploration and development, but it would fall to others to take advantage of this opportunity. George St. Clair had died of cancer in February 1972.[118]

The conservation community did not wait for others to take up where St. Clair had left off. They sought to build an alliance with the state to prohibit by statute a repeat of the St. Clair experience.

In 1975, Lieutenant Governor Rudy Perpich asked freshman DFL legislator Bud Philbrook to introduce the "BWCA Protection Act," a bill to protect the BWCA from commercial exploitation.[119] The bill prohibited both logging and mining in the BWCA by prohibiting "the development, exploitation, removal or adulteration of a natural resource" within the BWCA.[120]

The bill received a wide hearing. Subcommittee hearings were held in August, September, and October, including one in Ely. Perpich, Philbrook, Senate author John Milton, and Bud Heinselman toured the state to drum up support for the bill throughout the fall.[121]

State Representative Doug Johnson (DFL-Cook) waged a vigorous and successful opposition to the logging ban, which was ultimately dropped from the bill. But wilderness opponents failed to remove the mining provisions. The act passed the legislature on April 7, 1976, with the mining prohibition intact.[122]

The victory was, however, precarious. The conservation community, the state, and local residents all sensed that the fight would likely surface again.[123] It did, but the venue had shifted to Washington. In the meantime, the logging controversy was also boiling.

Logging

Following the Selke and Freeman recommendations, logging took a back seat to other BWCA controversies. That all changed in 1971, not by a act of the Forest Service or the legislature, but by an act of nature.

In the middle of May, a fire began from slash-burning logging operations in the Little Sioux area just outside the BWCA south of the Echo Trail. The Little Sioux fire spread quickly, consuming some 15,000 acres during its four-day life. It blackened extensive areas along the Echo Trail and in the Ramshead and Nina-Moose Lakes areas of the BWCA.[124]

Fire on such a scale presented both a spectacular and frightening spectacle. The Forest Service came under considerable pressure to enter the burned-over area and clean it up. But voices emerged to pursue a different tack.

Dr. Herbert Wright, Jr., Director of the Limnological Research Center at the University of Minnesota, was the first to challenge the Forest Service. He made a fervent public plea to use the Little Sioux fire to study the ecological processes of a virgin forest ecosystem, "rather than entering the virgin forest with chain saw and bulldozer to 'clean up the damage.'"[125] His plea, though, fell on the deaf ears at the Forest Service.

That fall Susan Kline, a researcher with the Minnesota Public Interest Research group (MPIRG), became an unintended accessory to Wright's cause.

During a canoe trip, Kline came across a parcel owned by U.S. Steel that lay within the Little Sioux burn area just outside the wilderness. The company was doing salvage logging at the Moose River BWCA access. Kline was stunned that this kind of activity could take place in a federal wilderness and began to investigate.

The more she looked, the more she was troubled. She soon discovered Herb Wright's work.[126] She was able to convince MPIRG's research director, attorney Charles Dayton, that MPIRG had to make BWCA logging practices a high priority.[127]

The results of their inquiry shocked them. The salvage operations were just the tip of the iceberg. In a twenty-five-page report, MPIRG laid out the extent of timber sales inside the wilderness. It was a sobering and disturbing list.

In November 1971, speaking on behalf of a broad environmental coalition, MPIRG demanded that the Forest Service put an immediate halt to BWCA logging.[128] Undersecretary J. Phillip Campbell denied the request in January of the next year, deciding that all fifteen existing BWCA timber contracts, covering 15,500 acres, would be honored.[129]

But the environmentalists also knew of some discussion about forcing the Forest Service to prepare a new management plan for the BWCA. That plan would revisit federal logging policies and practices.

The environmentalists sought to take advantage of the opening. They enlisted the help of Minneapolis Congressman Don Fraser in convincing Russell Train, chair of the Council on Environmental Quality, to involve the public more fully in the preparation of the management plan.[130] They in turn convinced Fraser to seek a moratorium on logging within the National Forests pending additional study.[131] The Forest Service again declined.

Pending completion of its new management plan, the Forest Service proposed in October a variety of options for dealing with logging but stopped short of suspending any of the active timber contracts. MPIRG concluded that the Forest Service was trying to have it both ways: "While we're studying the alternatives, logging will proceed as before," MPIRG's Chuck Dayton argued.[132] They decided to wait no longer.

In November 1972, MPIRG filed suit in federal district court to halt logging in the BWCA.[133] Dayton prepared and litigated the action, which claimed that the Forest Service had violated the National Environmental Policy Act by failing to complete an environmental impact statement. The Forest Service denied that an EIS was required. The trial began in January 1973.

Just as with the mining lawsuit, the logging lawsuit would raise technical issues and require complex professional testimony. MPIRG realized that the enormous resources of the timber industry could place them at a severe disadvantage. Their hope lay in the same unlikely figure who, almost a decade earlier, had urged the Selke Committee to re-examine BWCA logging practices: Bud Heinselman.

The problem for Heinselman centered on his employer—he still worked for the Forest Service. Articulating his principles of wilderness preservation would put him at odds with official agency policy. Herb Wright brokered the solution. He invited Heinselman and Dayton to meet each other at the Wright home. Then came a meeting between Dayton and Heinselman at the latter's home. Heinselman spread out his maps of the BWCA and ran through his research on the fire and logging history of the canoe country and the importance of the area's virgin forests. Dayton was so impressed that he wanted Heinselman to testify at the trial. He pointed out that the plaintiffs could (and ultimately did) formally subpoena Heinselman, forcing the Forest Service to permit him to testify whether the agency liked it or not. Heinselman agreed. He would become MPIRG's chief witness.[134]

The suit ran during most of January 1973 and was tried in front of Federal Judge Miles Lord.

When Heinselman took the witness stand, it was as if the cumulative frustrations of twenty years of working for the Forest Service had been stripped away. He talked of the uniqueness of the BWCA forest ecosystem, of its dependency on fire, of the cataclysmic changes in the natural succession brought about

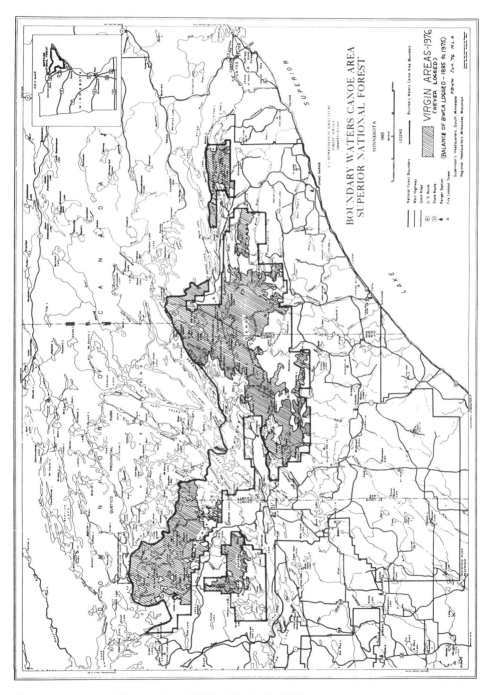

Virgin forests (unlogged forests) of the BWCA. (*Map by M. L. Heinselman*)

by logging, of the irreplaceable qualities of the BWCA's virgin timber stands. The story poured out of him for ten days of testimony. When he left the stand, he had single-handedly overcome the reams of testimony that had been offered by the Forest Service and forest industry.[135]

On April 16, 1973, Judge Lord handed the conservationists a huge victory, granting an injunction halting the logging on the seven active timber sales of virgin forest pending completion by the Forest Service of a new BWCA Management Plan and an environmental impact statement:

> [I]t is abundantly clear, and has been abundantly clear since NEPA [National Environmental Policy Act] became law, that the Forest Service should have prepared an impact statement on logging in the BWCA. Where there is conflict between maintaining the primitive character of the BWCA and allowing logging or other uses, the former must be supreme.[136]

On appeal, the Eighth Circuit Court of Appeals agreed with the trial court, upholding the injunction on June 10, 1974.[137]

In compliance with Lord's ruling, the Forest Service released its new draft BWCA Plan and Environmental Statement for public comment in August 1973 and its final EIS and Management Plan on June 28, 1974. The EIS proposed six management alternatives for logging in the BWCA, only one of which ended the logging. It therefore complied technically with the court order. But in a bizarre circumvention of the spirit of the court's ruling, the final plan opted for an alternative that permitted the logging to continue.[138]

MPIRG, joined by the Sierra Club, immediately hauled the Forest Service back into court. Whereas the first suit had been tried on procedural grounds— the failure to undertake an EIS—this suit claimed the conclusions of the EIS were contrary to the protections of the 1964 Wilderness Act.[139] The second logging trial, which began on November 4, 1974, was again tried before Judge Lord.[140]

In a replay of his earlier ruling, Judge Lord issued a permanent injunction in August 1975 against further logging of virgin forest in the BWCA. He concluded that the Forest Service's EIS ignored the Wilderness Act's implicit prohibition of logging of virgin timber:

> [A] restriction upon timber harvesting is "necessary" within the meaning of the Wilderness Act whenever timber harvesting interferes with the maintenance of the primitive character of the BWCA . . . . The Forest Service has chosen a policy alternative for managing the BWCA which by its own estimates will not preserve the primitive condition of the BWCA to as great an extent as would other alternatives.[141]

August 15, 1975 editorial cartoon in the *Minneapolis Star*. (*Reprinted with permission of* Minneapolis Star Tribune)

But on appeal, the Eighth Circuit Court of Appeals disagreed, overturning his injunction on August 30, 1976. It was one thing to require an EIS; it was another to overturn the administrative discretion of the Forest Service based on an expansive reading of the Wilderness Act:

> We hold that the Wilderness Act does not prohibit commercial logging in the virgin areas of the BWCA's Portal Zone and that the EIS . . . is procedurally and substantively adequate under NEPA.[142]

The appeals court lifted the logging ban in November 1976 after the United States Supreme Court refused to hear the case.[143] The logging operations started to gear up for renewed activity.

Snowmobiles

By ignoring the Selke Committee's recommendation to eliminate snowmobile use in the BWCA, the Forest Service invited a third set of controversies that would end up in federal court. The size and the ardor of the snowmobile constituency grew with each passing year.

In 1972, President Richard Nixon signed an Executive Order prohibiting off-road vehicles within designated wilderness areas or primitive areas.[144] The Superior National Forest Service office, however, equivocated. Claiming uncertainty about the Order's application to the BWCA, the Forest Service announced that they would seek public comment. The reaction in northern Minnesota reaffirmed the Forest Service's caution. In a comment that appeared to capture the prevailing mood, Ely Chamber of Commerce official Duane Krause stated:

> What [the environmentalists are] doing is an effort to turn the Boundary Waters into a preserve is creating an economic Appalachia in northeastern Minnesota. . . .[145]

Soon after, the Forest Service began to prepare its 1974 BWCA Management Plan. The Plan called for terminating snowmobile use in the area, but not until after the 1979/1980 winter season.[146] The Sierra Club and the Minnesota Federation of Ski Touring Clubs ("MINNTOUR") challenged the phase-out by filing administrative appeals with the Forest Service.[147]

The Forest Service agreed with the challenge and banned snowmobiles in May 1975, effective to the previous season.

Local residents and snowmobile manufacturers erupted in anger. They launched a series of high visibility protests.

They picketed Ely canoe outfitters Bill Rom and Jon Waters, who supported the ban, and blocked entry to their businesses during the busy opening weekend of the fishing season. Rom, a long-standing supporter of wilderness, was a particular target—the picketers carried such signs as "RUN THE BUM 'ROM' OUT OF TOWN" and "ROM GET OUT OF TOWN WE DON'T WANT YOU."

The snowmobilers also picketed at the Forest Service's Voyageur Visitor Center and along the highway leading into Ely, asking people to stop and sign petitions protesting the snowmobile ban.

The pressure paid off. Senator Humphrey sent a letter to Forest Service Chief John McGuire requesting an extension of snowmobile use. In November, the Forest Service relented, extending snowmobile use for one more year pending appeals to the Secretary of Agriculture.[148]

In February 1976, Secretary of Agriculture Earl Butz let stand the Forest Service's temporary ban. But Butz also announced that there would be another public hearing, in April, to solicit public comment. He would then review the entire case to determine "the scope of wilderness uses" that would be allowed.[149]

On the eve of the April public hearings in Duluth, two ski touring groups filed a lawsuit in federal district court to ban snowmobiles. Minntour and the

United States Ski Association claimed that the Forest Service had no discretion to decide whether to ban snowmobiles, but rather was required to ban them under the 1964 Wilderness Act and Nixon's 1972 order. Again, Chuck Dayton represented the environmentalists.[150]

The public hearings, which covered two days, quickly turned rancorous. A dummy marked "Sierra Club" was hung in effigy. Local political leaders, particularly Eighth District Congressman Jim Oberstar and State Senator Doug Johnson, stirred the crowd's fury. Snowmobiler after snowmobiler traveled to the microphone to criticize this assault on the local economy and lifestyle. Although environmentalists dutifully spoke in support of the ban, the day belonged to the louder voices.[151]

Secretary Butz weighed the arguments for almost five months. On September 8, 1976, he surprised and infuriated local residents by re-affirming the ban.[152]

Despite Butz' ruling, the court actions continued. The two ski organizations, fearing never-ending administrative appeals and reversals, decided to press forward for a decision that the Secretary had no discretion to either allow or prohibit snowmobiles in the BWCA—the Wilderness Act and Nixon's Executive Order mandated such a ban.

Snowmobilers and snowmobile manufacturers intervened in the lawsuit as plaintiffs, seeking to invalidate the ban as arbitrary and capricious. The snowmobilers claimed that the Forest Service was pressured into initiating the ban by "a small band of elitists"— environmentalists—who seldom used the BWCA in winter.[153]

Judge Donald Alsop ruled against both sets of parties in January 1977, deciding that the secretary did possess discretion to regulate snowmobile use and that his exercise of that discretion had not been arbitrary and capricious. "It is unfortunate," he wrote, "that the language of the Wilderness Act is such as to foster continual litigation regarding the appropriate use of this natural resource." His ruling had the effect, therefore, of leaving the snowmobile ban intact.[154]

Condemnation and Motorboating

From the time of the Truman airspace ban in 1949, the threat of condemnation had hovered over residents who had owned land, homes, or resorts within the BWCA. The sight of condemned resorts burning or landowners being evicted stirred the passions of local residents. But perhaps no condemnation proceeding became more symbolic of local frustrations than that of the fleet of houseboats on Basswood Lake owned by James and Jacob Pete. Starting in the 1960s

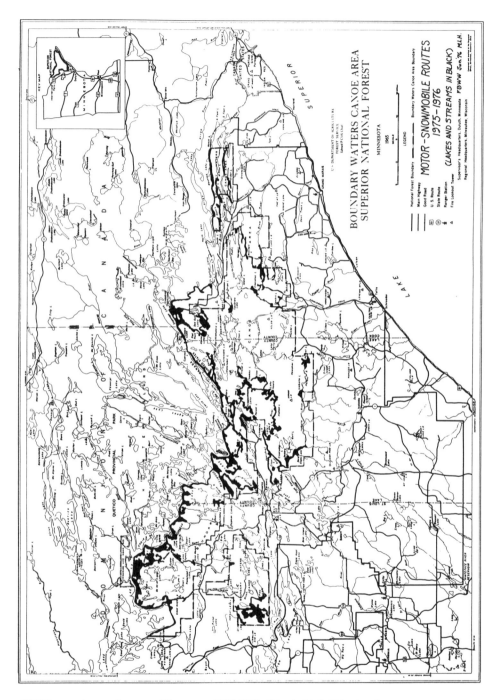

BWCA motorboat and snowmobile routes, 1975-1976. (*Map by M. L. Heinselman*)

and dragging into the 1970s, these proceedings clogged the courts and elevated the Petes into near-mythical figures in the local press.[155]

Motorboating was similarly a slow-boiling issue.

Motorboat use in the BWCA had grown steadily since enactment of the 1964 Wilderness Act. Motorboat routes monopolized the biggest lakes and best routes inside the wilderness, covering sixty-two percent of the BWCA's water surface.[156]

In its 1974 administrative appeal of the Forest Service's EIS and Management Plan, the Sierra Club sought to roll back this level of motor use. The appeal argued that the level of permissible motorboating should be tied to the use levels present in 1964. The Sierra Club also contended that to permit such extensive motorboating elevated the uses of a minority—motorboaters—above all other uses. But Forest Service Chief John McGuire ruled against the challenge on both counts.[157]

The Sierra Club challenge did, however, set the stage for the Forest Service to consider limiting certain routes to certain sizes of motors, which had been a key recommendation of the Selke Committee.[158]

In 1977, the Forest Service segregated the motor routes into routes of up to twenty-five horsepower and routes of up to ten horsepower.[159]

This hierarchy of use did little to reduce the tensions among the increasingly large number of BWCA visitors. By 1974, the BWCA had more visitors than any unit of the National Wilderness Preservation System—over one million "visitor days" annually.[160] Motorboaters and paddlers increasingly conflicted with each other in the wilderness—with particularly negative impacts on wilderness paddlers. One study found that nine out ten canoeists found contacts with motorboats destructive of their wilderness experience.[161] It was becoming increasingly clear that motorboat use and canoeing co-existed in a most unstable balance.

A Congressional False-Start

Mining. Logging. Snowmobiling. Condemnation. Motorboating. All had required the wilderness advocates to seek judicial or administrative intervention to quell the controversy. Each had served to escalate public polarization, complicate Forest Service management, and leave all parties involved with a distaste for solutions that appeared neither complete nor final.

On July 27 and 28, 1974, a small group of national and local environmental advocates convened in Ely at Bud Heinselman's cabin to strategize on the crises converging around the canoe country.[162] To introduce the national members of the group to the area, the group took a field trip to the periphery of the

BWCA and visited Sig Olson at his Burntside Lake cabin, immortalized as the "Listening Point" in one of Olson's popular books about the northwoods.

A number of strategies emerged, but the most important among them entailed enlisting Eighth District Congressman John Blatnik in an effort to attach a BWCA protection amendment to a pending legislative proposal called the Eastern Wilderness Act.[163]

Everything pivoted on Blatnik. Blatnik had served in Congress for almost thirty years, rising to the chairmanship of the powerful House Public Works Committee and establishing a reputation for delivering in the old style for his constituents. He knew the BWCA controversies as well as anyone. He had sponsored the Thye-Blatnik Act in 1948, which authorized the Forest Service to acquire private inholdings inside the BWCA, and was a personal friend of several key BWCA activists, including Sig Olson and Bill Magie.

The problem, in part, was one of timing. Blatnik had announced that he would not seek re-election in November of 1974, leaving less than six months in which to pursue the Eastern Wilderness Act strategy with him.

On September 8, a carefully selected group met with Blatnik over lunch in Chisholm, the congressman's home town.[164] Blatnik gave the group a guarded commitment to offer the amendment. He asked Olson to send proposed language.

Olson followed up with a letter a week later:

> This letter confirms our conversation concerning legislative protection for the Boundary Waters Canoe Area during our luncheon with you and your son in Chisholm, September 8, 1974. John, all of us see this amendment as a chance for you to cap-off your long and successful career as a supporter of important conservation legislation.
>
> I have just returned from four days with the National Advisory Board studying Voyageurs National Park, as beautiful a stretch of country as exists along our border. When I think of the magnificent part you played in its creation, the long battle to preserve the BWCA, which you made possible, the Grand Portage National Monument at the Lake Superior end, almost 300 miles of the most beautiful lake country on the continent and possibly in the world, we are all proud and happy to have had the privilege of working with you. Fifty odd years have gone into this struggle and it is high time that the eternal controversies over BWCA management be ended once and for all through the simple medium of a few slight changes in the Eastern Wilderness Act. You saw the logic and wisdom of it immediately.[165]

Blatnik called Olson in mid-October to discuss legislative tactics. The next day Sig followed up with a letter outlining the specific strategy and proposed language.[166]

Blatnik followed through with his commitment. On November 26, he wrote to Representative John Melcher of Montana, chair of the House Interior Committee's subcommittee handling the bill, asking for the inclusion of the BWCA in the Eastern Wilderness Act:

> This would have the effect of administering the BWCA in the same manner as the other wilderness areas subject to the act and thus assure equal treatment for all these unique and irreplaceable wilderness areas. I feel very strongly that before I leave Congress I would like to see this accomplished in my own District.[167]

Blatnik had set the stage for subcommittee action in early December.

The environmentalists prepared two amendments. The first banned both logging and motorized use in the BWCA, and the second ended logging only.[168]

A Minnesota environmental delegation (Chuck Dayton, Bill Rom, and Bud Heinselman) spent early December quietly lobbying House Interior Committee members.[169] They were joined by a powerful trio from the national environmental organizations: Ernie Dickerman of the Wilderness Society, the Izaak Walton League's Maitland Sharpe, and Brock Evans of the Sierra Club.[170]

Such a forceful effort could not go unnoticed, however. The Minnesota timber industry and economic development interests caught wind of the proposal and flew three lobbyists of their own to Washington to meet with Melcher and Blatnik.[171] They argued less on the amendment's merits than in its procedural unfairness. They drove the point home that the complexities of these issues could not be done on the sly, but required, at the very least, a public hearing.

With time running out, these procedural arguments carried the day. Blatnik and Melcher agreed to withdraw the BWCA amendment.[172]

The setback came as something of a mixed blessing to the Minnesota environmental community. On one hand, they felt frustrated at having come so close to seeing a legislative end to the timber (and perhaps motorboat) controversies. On the other hand, they had weathered their first legislative battle since the Wilderness Act, an experience that would prepare them for the more complex, protracted, and difficult fight that would come next.[173]

Notes

1 Executive Order 10092, Dec. 17, 1949; Federal Register, Dec. 22, 1949, 14 FR 7637.

2 The long and controversial history of the wilderness canoe country in northern Minnesota, where wilderness designation itself or wilderness management policies could be changed at the whim of each Forest Supervisor, had helped shape this national debate. For a history of the early administratively-designated wilderness areas, see James P. Gilligan, The Development of Policy and Administration of Forest Service Primitive and Wilderness Areas in the Western United States, Ph. D. Dissertation, University of Michigan, 1953.

3 Humphrey knew of the Library of Congress report and submitted it as an exhibit with his testimony favoring the Wilderness Bill during a congressional hearing in 1957. See C. Frank Keyser, Legislative Reference Service, Library of Congress, "The Preservation of Wilderness Areas (An Analysis of Opinion on the Problem)" Sept. 1949; "Hearings on S. 1176 before the Senate Committee on Interior and Insular Affairs," 85th Congress, 1st Session, p. 23 and 30 (subsequently cited as "1957 Hearings"); and The Living Wilderness No. 52, p. 29, (Spring-Summer 1955).

4 Magie apparently met Humphrey sometime after Sept. 29, 1949, when Magie received a very exasperated, curt, and formal reply from Humphrey to one of his letters. But by the end of the year, the relationship between the two men had warmed to a first-name basis. See Sen. Hubert H. Humphrey to William H. Magie, Sept. 29, 1949, and Humphrey to Magie, Dec. 29, 1949; Friends of the Wilderness Papers, Box 2, Minnesota Historical Society.

5 Among the organizations with which Olson was involved included the National Parks Association (he served as President in the mid-1950s), the Izaak Walton League of America (Sig acted as the "Ikes" wilderness consultant), the Wilderness Society (he served on the organization's governing council), the Sierra Club (where he gave a number of speeches at the Club's Biennial Wilderness Conferences in the 1950s and 1960s), and the President's Quetico-Superior Committee (as a consultant).

6 Congressional Record, Jan. 24, 1956, at A728-A729.

7 The early efforts to create national wilderness legislation were driven largely by the national Wilderness Society, which embarked upon an effort to establish a statutory wilderness system following its meeting in June 1947 in the Quetico-Superior wilderness. The meeting was organized by Minnesota's Ernest Oberholtzer, long active in Quetico-Superior wilderness battles and a co-founder of the Wilderness Society in 1935.

Howard Zahniser of the Wilderness Society led the discussion of a statutory wilderness system at the Sierra Club's First Biennial Wilderness Conference in 1949, and the Society and other conservation groups began immediately building support for such a concept throughout the country. See 1957 Hearings, p. 195. See John C. Hendee, George H. Stankey, and Robert C. Lucas, Wilderness Management, Second Edition, (Golden, Colorado: North American Press, 1990), pp. 102-104; and Roderick Nash, Wilderness and the American Mind, 3rd Edition, (New Haven: Yale University Press, 1982), pp. 220-226.

8 The speech was given in May 1955 to the National Citizens Planning Conference on Parks and Open Space for People.

9 *Congressional Record*, June 1, 1955, pp. A3809-A3812. See McCloskey, Michael, "The Wilderness Act of 1964: Its Background and Meaning." *Oregon Law Review*, Vol. 45 (1966), pp. 297-298.

      Humphrey received a number of favorable responses to Zahniser's speech, which he later inserted in turn in the *Congressional Record*. *Congressional Record*, February 29, 1956, pp. 3551-3554.

10 S. 4013, 84th Congress, 2nd Session. He was joined by eight co-sponsors.

11 *Congressional Record*, June 7, 1956, pp. 9772-9783.

12 "Dear Hubert," Olson had written from his Ely home in April, "I have worked closely with Howard Zahniser and others for some time on this measure . . . . I feel strongly that this is the last chance to preserve the wilderness on this continent for we are on the verge of an era where the pressures to destroy or change it will become greater than anything we have ever experienced." *Congressional Record*, June 7, 1956, pp. 9772-9783.

13 *Naturalist* (Natural History Society, Minneapolis) 8(4) 1957, pp. 144-150.

14 Paul H. Landis, *Three Iron Mining Towns: A Study in Cultural Change* (Ann Arbor, Michigan, 1938), cited in David James Backes, "The Air Ban War: Sigurd F. Olson and the Fight to Ban Airplanes from the Roadless Area of Minnesota's Superior National Forest,"(University of Wisconsin-Madison, M.S. Thesis, 1983), pp. 92-94.

15 The organization had as its mission "that no bureaucratic regulation be made effective to prohibit any mode of travel that prohibits the entire use of all recreational facilities within our national forest." Outdoor America, United membership card; copy in possession of author. See *Ely Miner*, Feb. 23, 1950, p. 1, "Wilderness Group Formed Here Sunday"; *Mesabi Daily News*, March 7, 1950. Ely's John A. Smrekar served as secretary.

16 Letter from John A. Smrekar (Outdoor America, United) to Galen Pike, May 1, 1950. Copy in possession of author. Smrekar listed six reasons for his organization's opposition and concluded that the airspace reservation "is unnecessary, unwarranted and without merit."

17 Resort owners Joseph Perko and Martin Skala, pilot Elwyn West, and, later, resorter William Zupancich transformed federal lawsuits that had been brought against them for violating the air ban into counter-attacks on the airspace reservation itself.

18 *United States v. Perko*, 108 F.Supp. 315 (1952). The Eighth Circuit Court of Appeals upheld Nordbye's decision on appeal in May 1953. *Perko et al. v. United States*, 204 F.R. 2d 446; *New York Times*, May 29, 1953, "Court Upholds Ban on Forest Flights;" see also Searle, pp. 178-86.

19 *Minneapolis Star*, July 3, 1953, p. 1, "2 Accused of Flights Into Forest"; *Duluth News-Tribune*, July 3, 1953, "Plane Seizures Strand Tourists"; *New York Times*, July 4, 1953,

"Campers Stranded as U.S. Seizes Planes Violating Ban in Minnesota"; *New York Times*, July 5, 1953, "200 in Woods Face Rough Trip Home"; *New York Times*, July 6, 1953, "Forest Unit Flies Some Out of Woods"; *Duluth News-Tribune*, July 8th, 1953, "Air Ban Figure Plans to Sell Out"; *Duluth News-Tribune*, July 14, 1953, "Judge Stern With Pilots"; *New York Times*, July 14, 1953, "Two Forest Fliers Enter Guilty Plea"; *Ely Miner*, July 16, 1953, "Ely Flyers Are Fined $3000 on Monday in Duluth Federal Court."

20 Both Zup and Perko, like John Smrekar, remained involved through the 1970s in the continuing fight against wilderness regulations. In 1955, Perko and Zupancich hired as their attorney William W. Essling, the former assistant federal attorney who had represented the federal government against the resorters in previous litigation. The resorters sued both Northwest Paper Company (owner of much of the Gun Lake road) and Forest Supervisor Galen Pike in federal district court in May 1955 and sought an injunction to prevent the defendants from preventing the resorters from using the Gun Lake road. Judge Nordbye denied their request. See *Perko v. Northwest Paper Company*, 133 F. Supp. 560 (D. Minn. 1955). The federal government then successfully sought an injunction against the resorters. *United States v. Perko and Zupancich*, 133 F. Supp. 564 (D. Minn. 1955); *United States v. Perko and Zupancich*, 141 F. Supp. 372 (D. Minn. 1956). See *Duluth News-Tribune*, Nov. 20, 1965, "U.S. Court Refuses Appeal by Zupancich;" and Searle, pp. 186-192.

21 S. 1176, 85th Cong., 1st Sess.; *Congressional Record*, February 11, 1957, pp. 1892-1906; 1957 Hearings, pp. 17-90.

22 McArdle stated:
> We wanted very much, and the wilderness people wanted very much, to have this particular area, these three roadless areas—when I say 'roadless' I mean permanent roads—in Minnesota included in the wilderness area and managed as wilderness. And we want to do it, too, but since there are temporary logging roads in there which are plowed up and blocked after logging, we could not include those in the other definition. We would be precluded from having them managed as wilderness under the proposed legislation unless you took special action. And that is why those areas are mentioned. And these roads are purely temporary. They are not permanent roads.

1957 Hearings, p. 100.

23 1957 Hearings, pp. 13, 276 (emphasis added). The compromise language thus protected already established uses and specifically authorized the continuation of logging. This language was modeled on the language of the 1948 Management Plan for the Roadless Areas. The 1948 language sought to maintain the primitive character of the areas "without unnecessary restrictions on other uses including that of timber." *Superior National Forest*, "Plan of Management, Superior Roadless Areas," February 13, 1948, pp. 1, 16.

24 Willard S. Domich to Hubert H. Humphrey, May 10, 1957; Hubert H. Humphrey to Willard S. Domich, May 17, 1957; both found in Hubert H. Humphrey Papers, Senatorial

Files 1949-1964, Correspondence on S. 1176, Jan.-May 1957, Minnesota Historical Society Archives; copies in possession of author. See Sigurd F. Olson to Howard Zahniser, July 17, 1957; found in Hubert H. Humphrey Papers, Senatorial Files 1949-1964, Correspondence on S. 1176, 1957-1958, folder 2, Minnesota Historical Society Archives; copy in possession of author.

25 *Ely Miner*, July 18, 1957, p. 1, "Humphrey Bill Threat to Ely's Economic Life."

26 *Ely Miner*, July 25, 1957, p. 2, "Will Ely Become a 'Ghost Town'?"; *Ely Miner*, Aug. 1, 1957, p. 1, "Humphrey Protests Miner Editorial"; *Ely Miner*, Aug. 8, 1957, p. 1, "Mining Permit Blocked"; *Ely Miner*, Aug. 15, 1957, p. 1, "Wilderness Craze"; *Ely Miner*, Aug. 22, 1957, p. 1, "Double Talk"; *Ely Miner*, Aug. 29, 1957, p. 1, "Humphrey Bill Termed 'Vicious Legislation'"; *Ely Miner*, Sept. 5, 1957, p. 1, "Legal Opinion Is Given on Humphrey's Bill"; *Ely Miner*, Sept. 12, 1957, p. 1, "Sig Olson Refutes Robb Legal Brief," and "'Humphrey Ill Advised' Says North Shore Unit"; *Ely Miner*, Sept. 19, 1957, p. 1, "Some Comments on the Humphrey Bill"; *Ely Miner*, Sept. 26, 1957, p. 1, "More Comments on the Humphrey Bill"; *Ely Miner*, Oct. 3, 1957, p. 1, "Public Meeting Held on Humphrey Bill"; *Ely Miner*, Oct. 10, 1957, p. 1, "Ely Jaycees Oppose the Humphrey Bill," and "Comments on Humphrey's NWPS Bill"; *Ely Miner*, Oct. 24, 1957, p. 1, "Ely Rod and Gun Club Opposes Humphrey Bill."

27 Sigurd F. Olson to Senator Hubert Humphrey, July 17, 1957; William H. Magie to Hubert H. Humphrey, July 21, 1957; Hubert H. Humphrey to William H. Magie, July 22, 1957; Hubert H. Humphrey to Sigurd F. Olson, July 25, 1957. All found in Hubert H. Humphrey Papers, Senatorial Files, 1949-1964, Correspondence on S. 1176, 1957-1958, folders 1 and 2, Minnesota Historical Society Archives; copy in possession of authors (subsequently cited as Hubert H. Humphrey Papers, Minnesota Historical Society Archives).

28 Memorandum from Senator Hubert H. Humphrey to Herb Waters, July 20, 1957; Hubert H. Humphrey Papers, Minnesota Historical Society Archives.

29 Hubert H. Humphrey to Fred C. Childers, July 22, 1957; Hubert H. Humphrey Papers, Minnesota Historical Society Archives. See *Ely Miner*, Aug. 1, 1957, p. 1, "Humphrey Protests Miner editorial."

30 Statement from Friends of the Wilderness in support of the National Wilderness Preservation Act of 1957—Senate Bill S-1176, Aug. 5, 1957. Magie noted that his organization had voted in 1950 to oppose any change in the present use of outboard motors in the Superior National Forest, and "[w]e still see no need to change the law in this regard in the Wilderness Areas of the Superior Forest."

31 Hubert H. Humphrey to William H. Magie, Aug. 15, 1957; Hubert H. Humphrey Papers, Minnesota Historical Society Archives.

32 Zahniser also noted that, like logging, motorboat use would be permitted in national forest wildernesses in those areas in which they had become well-established. He wrote: "[In national forest areas the use of aircraft or motorboats may be permitted by the Chief

where these practices have already become well established.] This simply means continuing things as they are. No one is trying to use this bill to curtail motor boating." Howard Zahniser to Fred C. Childers, July 23, 1957; Hubert H. Humphrey Papers, Minnesota Historical Society Archives.

33 Haugerud included a handwritten note at the bottom of the memo: "The critical mail from Minn has about stoped [sic] but we are still receiving favorable national mail." Both the memo and July 22nd draft bill are found in the Hubert H. Humphrey Papers, Minnesota Historical Society Archives.

34 "Senator Humphrey Refutes Misleading Charges on Wilderness Bill," Hubert H. Humphrey Press Release, July 25, 1957, in Hubert H. Humphrey Papers, Minnesota Historical Society Archives. See *Mesabi Daily News*, July 31, 1957, p. 1, "Look to the Wilderness: Will Proposed Measure Hurt Ely?" This article was the first in a series of page one articles of the same title that the Virginia, Minnesota, newspaper ran about the pending Wilderness Bill. See *Mesabi Daily News*, Aug. 1, 1957, interviewing *Ely Miner* editor Fred Childers who opposed the measure; Aug. 2, 1957, featuring Ely City Attorney Willard Domich who opposed the bill; Aug. 3, 1957, depicted Forest Service ranger Bill Trygg supporting the bill; Aug. 5, 1957, interviewed Chamber of Commerce official Stan Pechaver opposing the Wilderness Bill; Aug. 6, 1957, showed Ely Mayor Dr. J.P. Grahek opposing the bill; Aug. 7, 1957, interviewed Bill Magie supporting the bill; Aug. 8, 1957, showed miner Frank Chernivec supporting the bill. Prominent Ely resident Sigurd Olson was not interviewed for the series, because he was away on a three-week canoe trip in northern Saskatchewan. See *Mesabi Daily News*, Aug. 10, 1957, p. 1, "Elyite Member of Wilderness Canoe Party."

35 Subcommittee Hearing Transcript, July 8, 1977, p. 359. Humphrey also received assurances of support from the influential President's Quetico-Superior Committee, which had long supported both wilderness and other uses within the BWCA. Charles S. Kelly, a friend of Olson's and a long-time Quetico-Superior conservationist who chaired the Quetico-Superior Committee, responded to Humphrey's review request in November 1957 by telling Humphrey that his original bill conflicted with the original multiple-use program adopted and defended by the committee for nearly twenty-five years. Despite the conscious effort "to minimize the conflict" between Humphrey's general wilderness bill and "the more precise, tailor-made regulations which have been worked out for the wilderness areas in Minnesota," Kelly wrote, Humphrey's original bill with its proscriptions on motorized use and logging "has threatened to alienate the support of important groups who have actively endorsed the Quetico-Superior program." Charles Kelly to Hubert Humphrey, Nov. 1, 1957, September-December 1957 folder, Box 105, Quetico-Superior Council Records, Minnesota Historical Society.

36 Two Harbors Resolution, July 29, 1957; see also Hubert H. Humphrey to David Battaglia, Aug. 15, 1957. Hubert H. Humphrey Papers, Minnesota Historical Society Archives.

37 Stan Pechaver to Hubert Humphrey, Aug. 3, 1957; see also Hubert Humphrey to Stan Pechaver, Aug. 15, 1957. Hubert H. Humphrey Papers, Minnesota Historical Society Archives.

38 Ted Wynn to Hubert Humphrey, Aug. 5, 1957; see also Hubert H. Humphrey to Ted Wynn, Aug. 14, 1957. Hubert H. Humphrey Papers, Minnesota Historical Society Archives.

39 The draft bill, Committee Print No. 1, included the Forest Service's language for timber harvest within the roadless areas and a refined version of the provision allowing motorboats. Committee Print No. 1 of the Wilderness Bill, Dec. 4, 1957; Hubert H. Humphrey Papers, Minnesota Historical Society Archives.

40 "Senator Hubert H. Humphrey's Informal Hearing on Senate File No. S. 1176, Known as the Wilderness Bill," December 10, 1957, pp. 15-16, p. 38, and p. 43.

41 *St. Paul Pioneer Press*, Dec. 11, 1957, p. 11, "Hubert's Wilderness Bill Critics Retreat."

42 *St. Paul Pioneer Press*, Dec. 11, 1957, p. 11, "Hubert's Wilderness Bill Critics Retreat." See *Ely Miner*, Dec 12, 1957, p. 1, "Use of Motor Boats Is Assured By Humphrey."

43 S. 4028, 85th Congress, 2nd Session; *Congressional Record*, June 18, 1958, pp. 11551-11558. Humphrey's new version of the Wilderness Bill in 1958 included the compromise section from the December Committee Print No. 1. This section, with slight revision, became Section 4(d)(5) of the 1964 Wilderness Act. The final language provided for management "without unnecessary restriction on other uses, including that of timber," and also stipulated "that nothing in this Act shall preclude the continuance within the area of any already established use of motorboats." 1964 Wilderness Act, P.L. 88-577; 78 Stat. 890-96; 16 U.S.C. 1131-36.

      For a brief moment, however, all that conferring, clarifying, and revising appeared to come unravelled. At the 1958 Senate hearings on the wilderness bill, former federal attorney William Essling, representing a new organization called the "Ely Citizens Committee," brought forward resolutions from all three local county boards of commissioners opposing the legislation. The impact was minimized by a line of questioning from Senator Neuberger. Neuberger asked whether a great many of the earlier objections had not been met. Essling replied, "Yes, I agree with you, Senator. Those relating to mining, lumbering, and prospecting, and the use of outboard motors. I am authorized by the governing bodies of these communities and counties to say that they are very pleased that those measures have been met." Hearings on S. 4028 Before the Senate Committee on Interior and Insular Affairs," 85th Congress, 2nd Session., July 23, 1958, pp. 67-78; subsequently cited as "1958 Hearings."

44 Humphrey continued sponsoring the bill throughout, although Senator Clinton Anderson took the Senate lead after assuming the chairmanship of the Senate Interior Committee in 1961.

45 For a thorough discussion of the Wilderness Act's long legislative history, see Michael McCloskey, "The Wilderness Act of 1964: Its Background and Meaning." *Oregon Law Review*, Vol. 45 (1966), pp. 288-321.

      Minnesota conservationists had supported a wilderness bill even before the introduction of Humphrey's first bill in 1956. Sig Olson and Bill Magie, in particular, actively promoted the Humphrey bill, testifying at hearings, writing letter after letter, and drumming up support locally and nationally. Olson testified at the first hearing in 1957, and both he and Magie submitted written statements. Olson's testimony is found in the 1957 Hearings, pp. 318-25; Magie's statements and letters are found in 1957 Hearings, pp. 421-23 and 1958 Hearings, pp. 159-60, 181-83, and 196-97.

See, as an example of later support, Bill Magie's letter to Congressman Wayne Aspinall on Feb. 22, 1962, supporting passage of the Wilderness Act, S. 174. Magie tells of his meeting with President Kennedy in March 1963 about the Wilderness Act and describes the two of them lobbying Wayne Aspinall in David Olesen (ed.), *A Wonderful Country: The Quetico-Superior Stories of Bill Magie* (1981, Sigurd Olson Environmental Institute), pp. 174-176.

As noted earlier, although Minnesota conservationists did not want Humphrey's compromise language for the BWCA included in the Wilderness Bill, they were unsure about how far they could push the issue. For example, intense discussions took place at the 1963 Minnesota Izaak Walton League convention in Bemidji, particularly among Sig Olson, Ikes national Executive Director Joe Penfold, and others, whether to seek removal of the section that became § 4(d)(5). Concluding that an all-out effort to remove § 4(d)(5) on the floor of the House or Senate might kill the chances of passing the Wilderness Bill, Olson and Penfold decided not to push for its removal.

46 Miron L. Heinselman, "Crisis in the Canoe Country," *The Living Wilderness*, Jan./Mar. 1977, pp. 14-15.

47 This acceleration was mirrored at the national level. Timber sales from the national forests increased over seventy-five percent through the war years, from 1.552 billion board feet in 1941 to 2.732 billion in 1945. The pace quickened after the war. From 1950 to 1952, sales jumped from 3.195 billion board feet to 4.516 billion, nearly triple the level of 1941. David A. Clary, *Timber and the Forest Service* (Lawrence, Kansas: University of Kansas Press, 1986), pp. 110-125.

48 The timber harvest figures come from a U.S. Forest Service document, "Superior National Forest, Harvest and Sold Volume in MBF/Year, FY 1940 to FY 1989."

49 By the end of 1946, the Acting Forest Supervisor urgently requested approval from the Regional Office for the Silver Island deletion since "[o]ur Silver Island access road construction project is already operating within the boundaries of the Roadless Area" and a separate railroad "spur is being built in connection with our Isabella Block (Ontanagon Fibre Company) sale which will be logged in conjunction with the Tomahawk Sale." The Regional Forester immediately wrote to the chief saying that "technically we may be violating existing policies"; the chief gave his grudging approval in early January 1947 and final approval in April.

50 Clare Hendee to Regional Forester, Mar. 31, 1942; K.W. Udd, Acting Forest Supervisor to Regional Forester Jay Price, Dec. 19, 1946; Jay Price to Lyle F. Watts, Forest Service Chief, Dec. 27, 1946; Lyle F. Watts to Jay Price, Jan. 3, 1947; Lyle F. Watts Order, Superior Roadless Area Boundary Adjustments, April 15, 1947; copies in possession of author. The Timber-Frear chain of lakes just west of Silver Island Lake also was part of

the roadless area as of the 1938 L-Classification, but the Forest Service deleted it, too, at the time of the U-Classification of 1939. "Our primary purpose here [with the proposed elimination] was to make available a small chain of lakes for the use of the low salary-bracketed class of people in an effort to appease to some extent the criticism of the primitive area, which has been defined as an exclusive area for the wealthy." Lyle F. Watts, Regional Forester, to Forest Service Chief, Jan. 7, 1938; copy in possession of author.

51 Outfitter Bill Rom, for example, wrote to Frank Hubachek of Chicago early in 1951 about logging. Rom asked Hubachek where the President's Quetico-Superior Committee, chaired by Hubachek's law partner Charles S. Kelly, stood on the issue of logging. "It appears to me that the Committee has given up hopes of preserving the canoe country as a wilderness, that they have conceded to the Forest Service desire of logging all mature timber in the Roadless Areas outside of the no-cut area," Rom wrote. The letter sparked a feisty reply. Rom's desire to designate the entire roadless area as no-cut, Hubachek fired back, "is a sound objective, if there is hope of attainment, but it overlooks entirely the number one job of getting private property into public ownership. . . .[W]e are all pulling in the same direction," Hubachek continued, "and . . . the differences are principally questions of expediency and differences in method rather than in what we really want. Apparently some of us draw the line differently as to how far short of our ideals it is prudent to draw the line in order not to block our own progress." Bill Rom to F.B. Hubachek, Jan. 29, 1951; F. B. Hubachek to Bill Rom, Mar. 12, 1951. Letters found in Friends of the Wilderness Papers, Box 12, Minnesota Historical Society; copies also in possession of authors.

Rom replied with an eloquent description of his personal experiences with the wilderness and a plea for its protection. "This highly-valued recreational area is a public asset, the property of the people. There is no doubt in my mind that if the people were given a fair voice in its government it would remain an untouched wilderness. . . . There is no compromise in preservation of wilderness. If we give one inch the wilderness is destroyed." Bill Rom to F. B. Hubachek, Mar. 15, 1951. Letter found in Friends of the Wilderness Papers, Box 12, Minnesota Historical Society; copies also in possession of authors.

Rom later made his plea in a state-wide newspaper. He charged the Forest Service with failing "to admit that the wilderness will be destroyed if the timber is cut"and concluded that "[w]ilderness is to be left alone." See *Minneapolis Sunday Tribune*, April 29, 1951, p. 3, "He Would Ban Timber Cutting in Wilderness."

52 The Izaak Walton League played a catalytic role for the BWCA during these years, as it had in earlier times. An organization highly regarded by the Forest Service for its major role in the purchase of private lands within the BWCA, the Ikes had members nation-wide and was one of few conservation organizations active throughout the nation at that time. The Ikes passed resolutions calling for full wilderness protection for the BWCA on many occasions and often struck a more militant tone than the President's Quetico-Superior Committee.

53 The Wilderness Committee was primarily composed of members from the Ike's Grand Rapids Chapter, including Adolph Anderson, Arnold Bolz, Bud Heinselman, Morris Patterson, and others.

54 One such huge sale, the Tomahawk Sale, began in 1948 and continued for a quarter-century until the mid-1960s.

55 The Conservation Affiliates comprised the Izaak Walton League of America, Friends of the Wilderness, Minnesota Conservation Federation, the Natural History Society, Citizens Natural Resources Committee, National Campers and Hikers Association, the Nature Conservancy, National Wildlife Federation, and the Wilderness Society. *Minneapolis Sunday Tribune*, March 22, 1964, p. 10H, "Nine Groups Protest Handling of State's Border Canoe Region"; *Minneapolis Tribune*, April 19, 1964, p. 1H, "Conservationists Seek Official State Wilderness"; and *Minneapolis Tribune*, April 19, 1964, p. 7H, "Logging Called Canoe Area Peril"; *Naturalist*, Spring 1965, p. 1.

56 *Ibid.* See three undated brochures (apparently from spring 1964) by Conservation Affiliates; copies in possession of the authors.

57 Other individuals, like Ike leader Tom Dustin of Indiana, tried to give national visibility to the logging issue. Dustin produced and distributed a brochure describing the logging problems, in part to counter a booklet produced by Burton Atwood of the Izaak Walton League of America Endowment, which dismissed any claims of logging impropriety and supported the Forest Service's multiple use perspective. "Controversy In the Boundary Waters Canoe Area," a study by Burton H. Atwood, Secretary-Treasurer, Izaak Walton League of America Endowment, 17 pp. See "the boundary waters canoe area" brochure, Izaak Walton League of America, 1965; copy in possession of the authors.

58 The committee was appointed on May 21, 1964. John Blatnik, Hubert Humphrey, and Eugene McCarthy to Orville Freeman, April 11, 1964; Orville Freeman to John Blatnik, Hubert Humphrey, and Eugene McCarthy, May 7, 1964. Both letters cited from J. Wesley White, "The Selke Review Committee," *Historical Sketches of the Quetico-Superior*, Vol. X (May 1972), pp. 1-2.

59 Freeman would later ask Selke to play a similar role in attempts to settle a dispute over logging in the national forest lands of Washington State's Cascade Mountains, an area later to be designated as North Cascades National Park.

　　The other members of the Selke Committee included: Raymond A. Haik, an attorney and Vice-President of the Minnesota Division of the Izaak Walton League of America; Rollie G. Johnson, News Director of WCCO-TV in Minneapolis; Wayne H. Olson, Commissioner of Conservation for the State of Minnesota; John E. Vukelich, a member of the Board of Commissioners for St. Louis County; and David J. Winton, the conservation-minded President of the Winton Lumber Company in Minneapolis.

60 For example, Bud Heinselman, Sig Olson, Doc Grahek, and John Smrekar. Others, like reporters Al McConagha and Dick Conlon, were less visible, but nonetheless maintained a long and personal involvement. See, e.g., Al McConagha's articles during this time in the *Minneapolis Tribune*, and Dick Conlon, "Wilderness Area Roads Proposed," *Duluth News-Tribune*, June 19, 1960, p. 1.

61 Conservationists from the Twin Cities began to play a more active role in the BWCA controversies during the Selke era. Prior to 1964, the pro-wilderness movement had been

dominated by the northern part of Minnesota. The northern-based Friends of the Wilderness, for example, formed in May 1949 and had widespread support and leadership from the Iron Range and northeastern Minnesota. By the 1960s, Twin Cities activists increasingly shared the stage with such northern figures as Olson, Magie, Rom, Adolph Anderson, Heinselman, Morris Patterson, Wes Libbey, and Milt Stenlund.

62 Among the speakers were Dr. Frank Kaufert, the highly respected Dean of the College of Forestry, and representatives from the Forest Service (Forest Supervisor Larry Neff, Regional Forester George James, and Deputy Chief Arthur Greeley), the timber industry (William MacConnachie, Jr.), local residents (Cook County Commissioner Jean Raiken and Minnesota Arrowhead Association President John Smrekar), and conservation organizations (represented by Clayton Rudd, Sig Olson, Bill Magie).

63 The Quetico-Superior Foundation was established in 1947 by the late Frederick S. Winston, a long-time Quetico-Superior activist and former chairman of the Quetico-Superior Council's Executive Committee. In 1964, the Foundation was chaired by Henry McKnight.

64 See Quetico-Superior Foundation and President's Quetico-Superior Committee, "Quetico-Superior Institute." Proceedings of the Institute, 108 pp.; and Al McConagha, "Multiple Use for Canoeing Area Debated," *Minneapolis Tribune*, May 23, 1964, p. 12.

65 The President's Committee backed the so-called "Quetico-Superior program," which had originated in the late 1920s. This program (and the 1930 Shipstead-Newton-Nolan Act) permitted timber harvesting in the wilderness backcountry away from lakeshores and canoe routes. The President's Committee did not oppose BWCA logging if done beyond the 400-foot lakeshore screen mandated by the Shipstead-Newton-Nolan Act.

66 Quetico-Superior Institute, pp. 87-90.

67 Kelly did indicate his openness to "a fresh look at the Forest Service Plan of Management and [the possibility] that this Plan of Management should be substantially revised. I [want to] emphasize, however, that it is the program rather than the Forest Service which should have this fresh look." Quetico-Superior Institute, p. 20.

   For profiles of Kelly and Hubachek, see Kevin Proescholdt, "Tall Pines and Wilderness: The Legacy of Frank B. Hubachek," BWCA *Wilderness News*, Winter 1987, pp. 6-7; and Kevin Proescholdt, "Just What We Did Nights': Charles Scott Kelly and the President's Quetico-Superior Committee," BWCA *Wilderness News*, Autumn 1987, pp. 6-7.

68 *Minneapolis Tribune*, Jan. 10, 1965, p. 1H, "He's Lived 45 Years on Island."

69 Falling out with his long-time friends Kelly and Hubachek, Olson told the conference that logging and motorboat use could not be tolerated in the BWCA:

   Personally, and I am not speaking for the other conservation groups, or the President's Committee, or any organizations, but I feel that if it were possible to give this area wilderness status, in view of its uniqueness, it would be the wise thing to do. . . . There is nothing quite like it, and so, to me it is mandatory that

it be given wilderness status. . . . I would like to see all motors banned. I would like to see all mechanized use taken out of the wilderness.
Quetico-Superior Institute, pp. 84-85.

In recognition of his unique standing at the Institute, Olson was lobbied hard by all sides. Prior to the conference, for example, one member of the Conservation Affiliates sent Olson a one page letter with only the word "Wilderness" written on it dozens of times. Olson called Bud Heinselman and expressed his irritation at such heavy-handed lobbying from his wilderness allies at a time when he anticipated the need to make the personally painful split with Kelly and Hubachek: "Bud, I don't need this." Miron L. Heinselman, personal recollections.

Olson and Kelly exchanged letters after the Institute. Kelly felt that the Conservation Affiliates' accusation that the President's Committee and the Forest Service defended logging and motorboat use within the wilderness was "an irresponsible attack" that might destroy the President's Committee and the international cooperation it had achieved. Olson wrote back to Kelly to explain his position: "After all I had written and said over the years, plus my long connection with the League . . . I simply could not refuse to stand up and be counted among those who plead for wilderness." Olson expressed the hope that the differences he had with Kelly and Hubachek would not break up "the old triumvirate." After all these years," Olson continued, ". . . you and Hub are a part of my life and loyalty and though we may differ, it will never change my feelings for you." Olson to Kelly, May 27, 1964; Kelly to Olson, July 20, 1964; Olson to Kelly, July 24, 1964. Letters located in records of the President's Quetico-Superior Committee, BWCA Controversy, Sig Olson folder; quoted from Searle, pp. 222-23.

70 *Minneapolis Tribune*, July 15, 1964, p. 25, "Foes Outnumber Backers at Canoe Area Hearing"; *Minneapolis Tribune*, July 16, 1964, p. 43, "2nd Canoe Area Limits Hearing Finds Opposition"; *Minneapolis Tribune*, July 22, 1964, p. 15, "Forest Fires Called Better Than Loggers." See J. Wesley White, "The Selke Review Committee," *Historical Sketches of the Quetico-Superior*, Vol. X, 1971.

71 The committee also included four other respected experts: ecologist Stanley Cain from the University of Michigan; Clarence Cottam, president of the National Parks Association; Thomas L. Kimball, executive director of the National Wildlife Federation; and Ira N. Gabrielson, president of the Wildlife Management Institute.

72 Leopold Committee Report (1963). Conservationists felt that lifting this quotation from its context was highly misleading since the thrust of the entire report was "to maintain or create the mood of wild America." The report was printed in full in *Living Wilderness* 83, Spring/Summer 1963, pp. 11-19.

73 Dr. Frank H. Kaufert, "The Issues of the Boundary Waters Canoe Area Controversy," Quetico-Superior Institute, May 22, 1964, pp. 3-4; Statement by F.H. Kaufert before the Secretary of Agriculture's Review Committee on the Boundary Waters Canoe Area, July 21, 1964, pp. 3-4; Letter to Editor by F.H. Kaufert, "National Park Report Applies Equally Well to Canoe Country," *Minneapolis Tribune*, August 23, 1964, p. 3C.

74 Dr. Miron L. ("Bud") Heinselman, to whom this book is dedicated, passed away before the manuscript was completed. A modest and selfless man, he would have blanched at the descriptions of him contained in the text. He was, however, without question the person most responsible for the 1978 legislation's passage. As subsequent chapters will show, it is impossible to overstate his importance to the preservation of the BWCA.

75 Heinselman was himself a former student of Dean Kaufert.

76 M.L. Heinselman, "Wilderness in the Boundary Waters Canoe Area? A Challenge to our Profession," June 12, 1964. See Al McConagha, "End Urged to Tree Cutting in Canoe Area," *Minneapolis Tribune*, June 13, 1964, p. 16. For an excerpt of Heinselman's speech see also M.L. Heinselman, "Wilderness Values," *Naturalist* (Spring 1984):25-26.

77 Heinselman's Forest Service superiors, including his immediate supervisor, Zigmund Zazada, and Dr. Kaufert, also attended the private session.

78 See correspondence between Miron L. Heinselman, Starker Leopold, and others in the files of Miron L. Heinselman.

79 M.L. Heinselman, "Vegetation Management in Wilderness Areas and Primitive Parks," *Journal of Forestry* (June 1965), pp.:440-445.

80 Brief of the Inspector General's Report, found in the supplemental reports with the Report of the Boundary Waters Canoe Area Review Committee, December 15, 1964.

81 *Naturalist* 15(3) (Fall 1964). Another violation of the No-Cut reserve occurred at this time along Maniwaki Creek, where a road went right through an arm of the no-cut reserve. See Bill Rom Interview, March 25, 1987.

82 Report from Boundary Waters Canoe Area Review Committee to Orville Freeman, December 15, 1964.

83 The committee was, however, critical of the Finn Lake Road incident: "The road fill in Finn Lake is an example of the thoughtless destruction of the Area's aesthetic qualities which should never be tolerated."

84 This project was conducted through the agency's North Central Forest Experiment Station. The ecologist who took the assignment was Dr. Miron L. Heinselman. He worked from 1966 to 1974 as principal plant ecologist for the station studying the BWCA's forests, logging history, and fire ecology.

85 Statement by Secretary Freeman on the Report of the Review Committee for the Boundary Waters Canoe Area, January 12, 1965. Orville Freeman Statement, December 16, 1965; *Federal Register*, December 21, 1965, 30 FR 15738-9; 36 CFR Section 251.85.

86 Although Freeman announced his directives in January, the Forest Service did not issue final regulations to implement them for eleven months, or not until December 1965, during which time the agency continued to weaken the regulations.

87 Freeman called for the addition of 150,000 acres immediately, with another 100,000

acres to be added to the No-Cut Zone no later than 1975.

88 The 35,000 acres in the Crane Lake-Namakan Lake area would later be designated as part of Voyageurs National Park. The other land designated by the Freeman Directive would become the nucleus of the 1978 legislation's additions to the BWCA: Fowl Lakes-McFarland Lake area, the South-North-Little Gunflint area, the North Kawishiwi River, and the Fourtown-Horse-Tin Can Mike area.

89 The strained justification was that snowmobiles were nothing more than winterized motorboats.

90 Known as "boat-stashing," this involved the mooring of boats to posts driven into lakes just offshore from portage or boat landings. Because the State of Minnesota retained authority over the state's lakes and lake beds, the federal Forest Service officials were reluctant to enforce motorboat regulations without state approval.

91 These additional accesses broke up long, formerly remote, canoe routes with additional entry points and accesses. For example, the remoteness and solitude of the single-access Perent River-Isabella River route was soon broken up by new, logging road accesses at Kawishiwi Lake, Hog Creek, the Perent River, Isabella Lake, Isabella River, Snake River, Gabbro Lake, and other points.

A quarter (twenty-one) of the BWCA's current eighty-seven official entry points began as accidental accesses from logging roads, including: Snake River, Little Isabella River, Bog Lake, Lake Isabella, Little Gabbro, South Kawishiwi River, Kawishiwi Lake, Hog Creek, Moose River South, Pow Wow Trail (Perent R.), Pow Wow Trail (Pose L.), Island River, Ball Club Lake, Morgan Lake, Swamp Lake, Rib Lake Trail, Crocodile River, Portage Lake, Norway Trail, Cummings Trail-Coxey Pond, and Blandin. See the Affidavit of Kevin Proescholdt regarding Below-Cost Timber Sales in *Friends of the Boundary Waters Wilderness et al vs. F. Dale Robertson et al*, United States District Court, District of Minnesota, Civil No. 4-90-8.

92 *Minneapolis Tribune*, July 25, 1965, p. 1A, "Freeman Boundary Area Policy Protested in Ely"; and *Minneapolis Tribune*, July 25, 1965, p. 1A, "The Migration of Lynda Bird." Freeman and Johnson, the President's elder daughter, also took a highly publicized canoe trip in the BWCA prior to the dedication.

93 In a revealing statement concerning the Draft Regulations in June, the Forest Service Press Officer stated:
> The [Forest Service] recommendations are a very liberal interpretation of the report released last January by George Selke and a lot of people will be surprised because the recommendations are not so strict as those in the Selke report.

Comment by Rod Leonard, USDA press officer announcing the Draft Regulations. See "Freeman Endorses Regulations." *Duluth Herald*, June 30, 1965, p. 1.

94 Forest Supervisor L.P. Neff Press Release, January 26, 1965, quoted in J. Wesley White, "Brief History of Snowmobile Use in the Superior National Forest," *Historical Sketches of the Quetico-Superior*, Volume X (May 1972), pp. 12-13.

95 The Regional Forester, George James, explained his reasoning in a letter to the Chief of the Forest Service:

> [There must be] a more reasonable solution so that all water-oriented wilderness interests may be served equitably. The use associated with Basswood Lake historically has included big boats, small boats and canoes. Some of us believe big boats should be permitted for all time. The logical conclusion then is that mechanical portages must be a part of the scene.

George S. James, Regional Forester, to Chief of the Forest Service, May 24, 1965; copy in possession of the authors.

96 When these areas were added to the BWCA in 1975, approximately ninety percent had been logged.

97 For example, the Final Regulations added seven motorboat routes to those proposed in the Draft Regulations. They did eliminate one motor route that had been proposed in the Draft Regulations, as well as four other lakes from three other routes.

98 For example, after acknowledging that ninety-five percent of the 1,336 letters it had received on the Draft Regulations favored more stringent wilderness protection for the BWCA, the Forest Service announced that the agency would disregard the number of letters it received. *Duluth News-Tribune*, "Tighter BWCA Control Favored by Many Groups," Oct. 17, 1965, p. 3.

This announcement prompted an angry letter to the editor from Paul Clement of the President's Quetico-Superior Committee and Conservation Affiliates, charging that the Forest Service "set about to interpret the orders of the secretary of agriculture in a manner to completely undo the work of the Selke committee and the orders to save the Boundary Waters Canoe Country." *Minneapolis Tribune*, "Will Bureaucrats Ruin Wilderness?" Nov. 3, 1965, p. 4.

99 For other examples of the Forest Service culture and behavior, see Herbert Kaufman, *The Forest Ranger: A Study in Administrative Behavior*, (Baltimore: John Hopkins University Press, 1967), pp. 75-80; and Kevin Proescholdt, *After the Shouting Stopped: Implementation of the Boundary Waters Canoe Area Wilderness Act* (Minnesota Audubon Council, 1984), pp. 37-45, concerning the Forest Service's implementation of BWCA motorboat quotas following passage of the 1978 Act.

100 The tract lay along the so-called "Duluth gabbro contact."

101 J.C. Green, W.C. Phinney, and P.W. Weiblen, "Geologic map of Gabbro Lake quadrangle, Lake County, Minn.," Misc. Map M-2, Minn. Geol. Survey, 1966.

102 Paul K. Sims, "Copper and Nickel Developments in Minnesota." *Mining Congress Journal* (March 1968), pp. 29-31. See *Minneapolis Tribune*, June 15, 1966, p. 1, "Copper, Nickel Mining Set for Ely Area," and *Minneapolis Tribune*, June 19, 1966, p. 5C, "2 more Firms Interested in State Copper." See *Minneapolis Star*, Jan. 26, 1967, p. 7D, "Ore Discovery at Ely May Spur Land Survey."

103 Sims, pp. 30-31. See Minnesota Rules 6125.0100-6125.0700. The Minnesota Department of Conservation offered leases covering about 120,000 acres. The Executive

Council approved the new rules on Nov. 8, and received 617 bids from seventeen different companies in December. See *Minneapolis Tribune*, July 14, 1966, p. 10, "State to Offer 120,000 acres for Copper and Nickel Mining"; *Minneapolis Tribune*, Dec. 21, 1966, p. 9, "State opens 617 Bids on Mining Rights"; and *Minneapolis Tribune*, Dec. 30, 1966, p. 12, "State Leases 88,000 acres to Mining Interests."

104 Minnesota Laws 1967, Chapter 671, codified as Minn. Stat. 298.51-298.67 (1984). See Sims, p. 31, and *Minneapolis Tribune*, Oct. 29, 1967, p. 17B, "'U' Expert Urges State to Mine Wilderness Ores." Without this new legislation, copper-nickel ores would have been taxed under the same provisions as natural iron ores.

105 St. Clair's family had long been involved with mineral exploration and development in northern Minnesota. George's father had been active in mining circles through St. Clair Exploration Co., and his grandfather (G.A. St. Clair) had begun purchasing mineral rights within the BWCA before the turn of the century. *St. Paul Dispatch*, Dec. 23, 1969, p. 13, "Rich Nickel-Copper Lode Predicted in Canoe Waters Area."

106 In the BWCA, the federal or state governments owned most of the surface rights but not necessarily the mineral rights. St. Clair himself claimed mineral rights on 30,000 to 33,000 acres of land in the BWCA. See *St. Paul Dispatch*, Dec. 23, 1969, p. 13, "Rich Nickel-Copper Lode Predicted in Canoe Waters Area."

107 *Minneapolis Tribune*, Aug. 17, 1969, p. 1A, "Boundary Waters Area Prospected."

108 Superior National Forest News Release, Dec. 17, 1969; *Minneapolis Tribune*, Dec. 18, 1969, p. 1, "Canoe Area Mineral Fight Looms"; *Minneapolis Tribune*, Dec. 19, 1969, p. 1, "U.S. to Block Planned Drilling in Canoe Area"; *Minneapolis Tribune*, Dec. 21, 1969, p. 1A, "Drilling Plan Reopens Boundary Waters Battle." See the editorial in *Minneapolis Tribune*, Dec. 21, 1969, p. 2C, "Let's Save the Boundary Waters Area."

109 The Ikes noted in the ensuing court proceedings that they had spent nearly $400,000 through their endowment to purchase over 7,000 acres of land within the BWCA.

110 This research had been prompted in part by a state statute that had established a moratorium on federal land acquisition in the Superior National Forest until July 1, 1967. Minnesota Laws 1965, Ch. 553.

111 Raymond A. Haik to Izaak Walton BWCA Task Force Committee, April 12, 1966; May 4, 1966; June 10, 1966; and August 23, 1966. Copies in possession of the authors.

112 Izaak Walton League of America v. St. Clair, 313 F. Supp. 1312 (D. Minn. 1970)(Civil Docket No. 5-69-70).

113 *Minneapolis Tribune*, Dec. 24, 1969, p. 26, "Walton League Sues to Block BWCA Drilling"; *Minneapolis Tribune*, Dec. 29, 1969, p. 8, "Conservationist Haik Says BWCA is 'Zoned' as a Wilderness"; See Cutler, Malcom Rupert. "A Study of Litigation to Management of Forest Service Administered Lands and Its Effect on Policy Decisions. Part Two: A Comparison of Four Cases." (unpublished Ph.D Thesis, Department of Resource Development, Michigan State University, 1972), pp. 317-407.

114 The Forest Service had already seized gear the St. Clair crew had stashed in the BWCA. *Minneapolis Tribune*, Jan. 22, 1970, "U.S. May Seize Gear in BWCA"; *Minneapolis Tribune*, Jan. 28, 1970, "U.S. to Oust Gear of Crew in BWCA"; and *Minneapolis Tribune*, Jan. 30, 1970, p. 20, "Gear Impounded".

The State of Minnesota would later join the Ikes as a plaintiff. *Minneapolis Tribune*, Jan. 15, 1970, p. 1, "Senator: State May Drill in Boundary Waters Area"; *Minneapolis Tribune*, Jan. 16, 1970, "U.S. Stand on BWCA Questioned."

115 See, for example, *Izaak Walton League of America v. St. Clair*, 55 F.R.D. 139 (1972) (State of Minnesota did not have standing to challenge fraudulently procured land patents); *Minneapolis Tribune*, May 17, 1972, "Judge Rules State can't Dispute mine claims in BWCA."

116 *Izaak Walton League of America v. St. Clair*, 353 F. Supp. 698 (D. Minn., 1973). See *Minneapolis Tribune*, Jan. 6, 1973, p. 1A, "Judge Bans Mining in Canoe Area."

117 *Izaak Walton League of America v. St. Clair*, 497 F. 2d 849 (8th Cir. 1974). The Court of Appeals ruled that the case was not ripe: the Forest Service had not yet had the opportunity to act on the St. Clair application for the mining permit. See *Minneapolis Tribune*, May 18, 1974, p. 1A, "Appeals Panel Reverses BWCA Prospecting Ban."

118 *Skillings' Mining Review*, March 25, 1972, p. 23.

119 Perpich had campaigned for Lt. Governor in 1970 in part on preventing mining in the BWCA; see Rudy Perpich letter to Fellow DFLer, June 16, 1970; copy in possession of authors. See Burnham Philbrook, "Portfolio of Papers Relating to State and Federal Legislation Affecting the Boundary Waters Canoe Area," Plan B Paper, Humphrey Institute of Public Affairs, University of Minnesota, Spring, 1981, p. v.

120 News Release, State Senator John Milton and Rep. B.J. Philbrook, Feb. 11, 1975; *Minneapolis Tribune* editorial, Feb. 17, 1975, "Closing the Door on the BWCA"; H.F. 922, 69th Session, Minnesota Legislature, March 13, 1975.

121 They visited Duluth, Bemidji, Morris, Alexandria, Mankato, Northfield, St. Cloud, Marshall, Rochester, Winona, and Moorhead, covering nearly 2,500 miles. See the following press releases from Rep. B.J. Philbrook: " Lt. Governor Perpich Testifies in Support of Philbrook-Milton Bill," Sept. 17, 1975; "Philbrook Bill Passes Subcommittee," Oct. 23, 1975; and the untitled press releases dated Nov. 19, 1975, and Dec. 17, 1975. For Philbrook's statement in Ely, see "Testimony by Rep. Bud Philbrook to the Recreation and Open Space Subcommittee, Aug. 11, 1975." See Lt. Gov. Rudy Perpich press release, Oct. 22, 1975; and *Minneapolis Tribune*, Oct. 17, 1975, "State Panel Backs BWCA Logging Ban."

122 H.F. 1644, 69th Session, Minnesota Legislature, Apr. 17, 1975; 1976 Minn. Laws Ch. 322, codified at Minn. Stat. 84.523 (1984).

123 Despite the new state law, concern over the development of copper-nickel mining in northeastern Minnesota led the environmental community to maintain their vigilance

through the Copper-Nickel Coalition. The State of Minnesota also embarked upon a lengthy study of the potential impacts of the development of a mining industry in the Arrowhead region.

124 *Minneapolis Tribune*, May 16, 1971, p. 1A, "Forest Fire Rages at Ely"; *Minneapolis Tribune*, May 17, 1971, p. 1A, "Forest Fire Remains Unchecked"; *Minneapolis Tribune*, May 18, 1971, p. 2B, "Canoe Country Fire Yields to Men and Rain." See *Naturalist* (Winter 1971), Wilderness Research following the Little Sioux Fire."

125 H.E. Wright, "BWCA Fire: Chance to Restore an Ecosystem," *Minneapolis Tribune*, May 30, 1971, p. 7A.

126 Dr. Wright had independently continued to raise concerns about U.S. Steel's salvage logging. He also sought to draw attention to Potlatch Corporation's logging operation inside the BWCA at the Sunnydale Sale. See Herb Wright's letter to the editor in *Minneapolis Tribune*, Sept. 23, 1971, p. 19A, "Cutting BWCA Trees"; and *Minneapolis Tribune*, Sept. 23, 1971, p. 1A, "Logging near BWCA Assailed."

127 Charles K. Dayton to Kevin Proescholdt, Feb. 12, 1991.

128 The coalition included the Sierra Club, Minnesota Environmental Control Citizens Association, Minnesota Canoe Association, Rovers Outing Club, the Natural History Society, and the Northern Environmental Council.

    The MPIRG coalition claimed, among other things, that no environmental impact statements (EIS) had been conducted for the timber sales as required by the National Environmental Policy Act.

    MPIRG also requested that U.S. Steel halt its logging operations in the BWCA. U.S. Steel declined the offer. *Minnesota Daily*, Oct. 7, 1971, "MPIRG Achieves First Victory, U.S. Steel Agrees to Stop Logging"; *Minneapolis Tribune*, Oct. 9, 1971, "U.S. Steel Denies agreeing to Curb Logging in BWCA".

129 MPIRG also raised the issue of below-cost timber sales from the Superior National Forest (claiming that timber sales cost the Forest Service more than the revenues produced by the sales). "'In effect,' said Susan Kline of the MPIRG staff, 'we are subsidizing private companies to take one of the last remaining virgin wilderness areas in this country and make it into toilet paper and turpentine.'" *Minneapolis Tribune*, Jan. 4, 1972, "Halting of Logging asked in State BWCA Wilderness." See *St. Paul Pioneer Press*, Jan. 4, 1972, "Logging Will Continue in BWCA"; *Minnesota Daily*, Jan. 5, 1972, p. 2, "MPIRG asks end to BWCA Timber Cutting"; and Sue Kline's article in *Minnesota Daily*, Jan. 12, 1972, pp. 5-6, "Clearcutting in BWCA: Barking the Wrong Trees."

130 *Minneapolis Tribune*, Feb. 17, 1972, p. 1A, "BWCA Logging Review Pledged."

131 *Minneapolis Tribune*, Mar. 10, 1972, "Fraser Seeks 2-year Halt on Clear-cutting in National Forest Areas."

132 *Minneapolis Tribune*, Oct. 4, 1972, p. 1A, "BWCA Logging Options Outlined."

133 *MPIRG v. Butz*, 358 F. Supp. 584 (D. Minn. 1973). See *Minneapolis Tribune*, Nov. 26, 1972, "MPIRG asks Court to Halt BWCA Logging Operations."

134 Charles K. Dayton to Kevin Proescholdt, Feb. 12, 1991, pp. 2-3.

135 Ibid. See *Minneapolis Tribune*, Jan. 20, 1973, "'U' Dean Backs Logging in BWCA"; *Minnesota Daily*, Jan. 29, 1973, p. 3, "Forestry Dean Testifies Against MPIRG attempt to halt BWCA Logging"; *Minnesota Daily*, Feb. 1, 1973, "Final Arguments were heard in MPIRG BWCA Logging Suit." See also Charles K. Dayton to Kevin Proescholdt, Feb. 12, 1991, pp. 2-3.

136 *MPIRG v. Butz*, 358 F. Supp. 584 (D. Minn. 1973); see *Minneapolis Tribune*, Apr. 17, 1973, p. 1B, "Judge Predicts Ban Likely on BWCA Logging"; Herbert E. Wright, Jr., "The Boundary Waters: Wilderness at Stake," *The Living Wilderness*, Spring 1974, pp. 21-31.

137 *MPIRG v. Butz*, 498 F. 2d 1314 (8th Cir. 1974).

138 USDA Forest Service, *Superior National Forest*, "Boundary Waters Canoe Area Plan and Environmental Statement," Aug. 15, 1973; USDA Forest Service, *Superior National Forest*, "Boundary Waters Canoe Area Management Plan and Environmental Statement," June 28, 1974. See *Minneapolis Tribune*, July 8, 1974, p. 1B, "New Land-Use Plan Proposed for BWCA."

139 The suit was filed on August 19, 1974. *Minneapolis Tribune*, July 29, 1974, p. 1B, "Research Group to Renew BWCA Antilogging Action"; *Minnesota Daily*, July 29, 1974, "MPIRG to Renew Attack on Logging in BWCA"; *Minneapolis Tribune*, Aug. 20, 1974, "MPIRG asks Judge Lord Prevent Logging in BWCA"; *Minneapolis Tribune*, Aug. 29, 1974, "Sierra Club asks to Intervene in BWCA Lawsuit."

140 *Minneapolis Tribune*, Nov. 5, 1974, p. 8B, "Ruling on Intent of U.S. Environmental Law asked as new BWCA Trial Opens"; *Minnesota Daily*, Nov. 5, 1974, p. 18, "Judge Lord inclined toward Boundary Waters Logging Ban."

141 *MPIRG v. Butz*, 401 F. Supp. 1276 (D. Minn. 1975). See *Minneapolis Tribune*, Aug. 8, 1975, p. 1A, "Judge Lord Orders Permanent Halt of Logging in BWCA."

142 *MPIRG v. Butz*, 541 F. 2d 1292 (8th Circuit, 1976). See *Minneapolis Tribune*, Feb. 8, 1976, p. 1B, "Appeals court will consider another Lord decision—BWCA logging case"; *Minneapolis Tribune*, Feb. 9, 1976, p. 1A, "Both sides worry about losing timber in BWCA"; *Minneapolis Tribune*, Aug. 31, 1976, p. 1A, "BWCA ban on logging overturned."

143 See *Minneapolis Tribune*, Oct. 1, 1976, p. 1B, "U.S. court won't alter logging decision"; *Minneapolis Tribune*, Nov. 9, 1976, "High court denies ban on logging in BWCA."

144 Executive Order 11644, "Use of Off-Road Vehicles on the Public Lands," February 8, 1972.

145 *Minneapolis Tribune*, Mar. 15, 1972, "Snowmobile ban may cover BWCA."

146 1974 Management Plan, P-33 to P-35. See *St. Paul Dispatch*, Dec. 28, 1973, "Locals Dislike BWCA Boat, Snowmobile Plans."

147 "Sierra Club Request for Administrative Review," October 15, 1974; "Minnesota Federation of Ski Touring Clubs Request for Administrative Review," October 15, 1974.

Both documents are found in the Charles K. Dayton Papers, Box 13, Folder 4, Archives /Manuscripts Division of the Minnesota Historical Society. See *Minneapolis Tribune*, Oct. 17, 1974, "2 groups ask BWCA snowmobile ban" and *Minneapolis Tribune* editorial, Oct. 21, 1974, p. 8A, "Snowmobiling in the BWCA."

148 *Duluth News-Tribune*, May 7, 1975, p. 1, "Snowmobile use ended in BWCA"; *Minneapolis Tribune*, May 7, 1975, p. 1B, "Forest Service reverses self, bans snowmobiles in BWCA"; *St. Paul Pioneer Press*, May 7, 1975, "2 groups claim BWCA closed to snowmobilers"; *Mesabi Daily News*, May 7, 1975, "Snowmobile Ban Ordered for BWCA." See *St. Paul Pioneer Press*, May 14, 1975, "Snowmobilers plan blockade at Ely"; *Minneapolis Tribune*, May 17, 1975, p. 1A, "Snowmobilers go fishing for support"; *Duluth News-Tribune*, May 17, 1975, p. 1, "Ely residents line roads to gain voice in BWCA"; *Ely Echo*, May 21, 1975, p. 1, "Snowmobile Protest Only Tip of Iceberg." On Humphrey's involvement, see *Minneapolis Tribune*, June 7, 1975, "HHH questions snowmobile ban" and *Minneapolis Tribune* editorial, July 25, 1975, "Humphrey's questionable stand on the BWCA." For the Forest Service reversal to allow snowmobiles another year, see *St. Paul Pioneer Press*, Nov. 4, 1975, "BWCA snowmobiles on again—for awhile" and *Minneapolis Tribune*, Nov. 4, 1975, "Snowmobile trails in BWCA to be reopened."

149 *Minneapolis Star*, Feb. 18, 1976, "Butz upholds banning snowmobiles in BWCA."

150 *Minneapolis Tribune*, Apr. 21, 1976, p. 1B, "Ski groups sue for snowmobile ban in BWCA"; *Duluth News-Tribune*, Apr. 22, 1976, "Skiers seeking BWCA use cut."

151 *Duluth Herald*, Apr. 22, 1976, p. 1A, "Oberstar plugs own bill"; *Duluth News-Tribune*, Apr. 23, 1976, p. 1A, "Motor bans opposed for BWCA"; *Minneapolis Tribune*, Apr. 24, 1976, p. 1B, "Snowmobile use in BWCA debated"; *Duluth News-Tribune*, Apr. 24, 1976, p. 1, "Forest Service 'disastrous' for BWCA business."

152 USDA "Decision of the Secretary," September 8, 1976, regarding Requests for Administrative Review, Boundary Waters Canoe Area. See *St. Paul Dispatch*, Sept. 10, 1976, "Snowmobiling Ban is Upheld"; *Minneapolis Tribune*, Sept. 10, 1976, "Snow vehicles banned in BWCA"; *Duluth News-Tribune*, Sept. 11, 1976, p. 1, "Ely in a Stew Over Snowmobile Decision."
Local reaction was, literally, incendiary: "People up here feel, if we can't use it, nobody can. There are people . . . that could start a fire [and burn down the BWCA] because they don't like this deal."

153 *Minneapolis Tribune*, Nov. 5, 1976, "Snowmobile clubs fight BWCA ban."

154 *Minnesota Federation of Ski Touring Clubs et al. and Coalition of Minnesota Snowmobile Organizations et al. v. John Knebel and John McGuire*, D.C. Minn., No. 4-76 Civ. 169, Jan. 19, 1977.
Attorney Dayton stated: "We lost a battle but we're winning the war." *Minneapolis Tribune*, Jan. 20, 1977, p. 1B, "Judge upholds ban in BWCA."

155 See *United States v. 967.905 Acres of Land, etc., Cook Co., Minn.*, 305 F. Supp. 83 (D. Minn. 1969); *United States v. 967.905 Acres of Land, etc., State of Minn.*, 447 F. 2d 764

(8th Cir. 1971); *Pete v. United States*, 531 F. 2d 1018 (8th Cir. 1976). See *Duluth Herald*, Feb. 14, 1968, "Pete's Holdout in BWCA Like a Storybook Crusade" and *Duluth Sunday News-Tribune*, Dec. 17, 1969, "Ely Man Fights to Keep Houseboat Fleet."

156 The State of Minnesota adopted regulations dealing with the BWCA on December 31, 1970, as NR 1000, limiting motorboat use to the same nineteen routes as designated in the Secretary's 1965 Regulations. These state rules banned "boat-stashing" (the mooring of boats just off shore) and aroused considerable controversy in northeastern Minnesota. Commissioner of Natural Resources Jarle Lierfallom, a conservative Republican who himself canoed in the BWCA, finalized the rules just before leaving office. See Minnesota Rule NR 1000, recodified at Minnesota Rules Chapter 6140.

157 See Request for Administrative Review, Sierra Club, Oct. 15, 1974, in Charles K. Dayton Papers, Box 13, File 5, Minnesota Historical Society.

158 The Selke Committee recommended a large motor zone, a small motor zone of under four horsepower, and a no-motor zone.

159 See Order of the Regional Forester Restricting the Use of the Boundary Waters Canoe Area, *Superior National Forest*, Minnesota, March 30, 1977.

160 A visitor day is nation-wide Forest Service measure—the equivalent of one visitor staying one twelve-hour period. So a party of six traveling five full days would account for sixty (not thirty) visitor days.

161 See David W. Lime's "Sources of Congestion and Visitor Dissatisfaction in the Boundary Waters Canoe Area" in Proceedings, The Quetico-Superior Foundation 1975 Institute on the BWCA. Duluth, Minnesota, May 9, 1975, pp. 68-82.
    Another wilderness research study in 1973 recommended a ban on motorcraft in the BWCA to increase the area's visitor carrying capacity. See George H. Stankey's "Visitor Perception of Recreation Carrying Capacity," USDA Forest Research Paper INT-142, 1973. (Intermountain Forest and Range Experiment Station, Ogden, UT 84401).

162 The meeting included: Bud Heinselman, Chuck Dayton, Walt Pomeroy of the Northern Environmental Council (NOREC), Dr. Darby Nelson of Minnesota Environmental Control Citizens Association (MECCA), Brock Evans and Doug Scott of the Sierra Club's Washington D.C. office, Jonathan Ela from the regional Sierra Club office in Madison, Ernie Dickerman with the Wilderness Society, Dick Flint of the Sierra Club's North Star Chapter, Adolph Anderson, Arnold Bolz, Al Buchholz, Paul Toren (all four from the Minnesota Ikes), Chuck Kahler of the Natural History Society, and MPIRG lawyer Jerry Seck. Attendance Sheet, Discussion on Boundary Waters Canoe Area Management Plan, Ely, Minnesota, July 27-28, 1974; copy in possession of authors.

163 The group decided to pursue three other strategies as well: (1) file an administrative appeal of the just-released BWCA EIS and Management Plan; (2) return to federal district court to halt logging; and (3) to introduce independent congressional legislation on the BWCA should the attempt to latch onto the Eastern Wilderness Act fail. *MLH Chronology*, July 27-28, 1974.

164 The group included Heinselman; Olson; Veda Ponikvar, a long-time Blatnik friend and editor of the Chisholm newspaper; and Arnold Bolz, a Grand Rapids doctor, writer, photographer, and Ike member.

165 Sigurd F. Olson to John A. Blatnik, Sept. 17, 1974; copy in possession of authors; *MLH Chronology*, Sept. 17, 1974.

166 Olson wrote: "What we need now is language in the E. Wilderness Bill which will protect our great wilderness canoe country and give it the status it deserves: a true wilderness." Sigurd F. Olson to John A. Blatnik, Oct. 14, 1974; copy in possession of authors.

The language read: "Notwithstanding the permissive language of the Wilderness Act of 1964, the BWCA of the Superior National Forest in Minnesota shall be managed in the same way as all other wilderness areas subject to this act."

167 John A. Blatnik to John Melcher, Nov. 26, 1974; copy in possession of authors; *MLH Chronology*, Nov. 26, 1974.

168 The first amendment in effect repealed § 4(d)(5) of the Wilderness Act. The second provided: "Notwithstanding any provision of law to the contrary, the Boundary Waters Canoe Area, Superior National Forest, Minnesota shall be managed in the same manner as all other wilderness areas with respect to timber cutting." BWCA Amendment, Dec. 9, 1974; copy in possession of authors.

169 Dayton, Rom, and Heinselman traveled the congressional hallways. *MLH Chronology*, Dec. 8-10, 1974. Bill Magie telegrammed his longtime friend Blatnik to shore up Blatnik's resolve:

Having known you since our CCC days in 1934 . . . I ask of you and this will be my last request I ever make to you as my congressman, kindly testify before the Committee Monday in favor of . . . the amendment putting a complete stop to logging, mining and mechanical uses in the Boundary Waters Canoe Area. You have had a great part in its preservation and as you leave your post this winter you will leave with glory.

William H. Magie Mailgram to John A. Blatnik, Dec. 8, 1974; copy in possession of authors.

170 *MLH Chronology*, Dec. 8-10, 1974.

171 The three were: Thomas Smrekar, director of public affairs for Potlatch and a son of Ely's John Smrekar; Harold E. "Andy"Andersen, the former Superior National Forest Supervisor who now headed the Arrowhead Regional Development Commission; and Robert Babich, the executive director of the Northeastern Minnesota Depvelopment Association (NEMDA).

172 *Duluth News-Tribune*, Dec. 11, 1974, p. 1, "Timber Industry Ax Fells BWCA Cutting Ban"; *Ely Echo*, Dec. 18, 1974, p. 1, "Quarterback Blatnik Tries Sleeper Play"; *MLH Chronology*, Dec. 10, 1974.

173 As Olson wrote to Magie in January: "Chuck Dayton and Bud Heinselman and others did a magnificent job on the E. Wilderness Bill Amendment plus Ernie Dickerman of

the Wilderness Society. We'll win yet in spite of temporary defeats." Sigurd F. Olson to Bill Magie, Jan. 28, 1975; copy in possession of authors.

Chapter Two

The Fight Begins

The false start at the end of the 1974 Congress left the door open to further legislative maneuvering. John Blatnik's retirement from Congress created a large uncertainty, however, about what direction that maneuvering would take: despite his backpeddling on the Eastern Wilderness Act, Blatnik had proved a reliable friend of the environmental community throughout his tenure. There was no guarantee that his successor would bring that same sensibility to the job.

An Emerging Political Force

The race for Blatnik's job was hotly contested.

The leading contender was state Senator Tony Perpich, the brother of Lieutenant Governor Rudy Perpich. Together with a third brother, George, who also served in the Minnesota senate, the Perpich family had long been a political powerhouse on the Iron Range. But they had been engaged in running warfare with John Blatnik since 1962, when Blatnik had backed an opponent of Rudy in a state senate race.

Therefore, as a surprise to no one, the Blatnik camp weighed in against Tony Perpich. Indeed, Perpich's strongest competition for the seat was Jim Oberstar, Blatnik's administrative assistant.[1] A native of Chisholm, Oberstar had served as Blatnik's chief of staff from 1963 to 1974 and as administrator of the Public Works Committee from 1971 to 1974. He was known as a tough, hardworking, smart capitol-hill veteran, someone who would both hit the ground running and fit well into the rough and tumble world of eighth-district politics.

And rarely had it been more rough and tumble than the 1974 election season. The race quickly became divisive, bitter, and plain nasty, beginning in the spring, when the Eighth District DFL convention went through thirty ballots before awarding the party's endorsement to Perpich. Casting party unity to the winds, Oberstar announced that he would ignore the endorsement and challenge

Perpich in the September primary.[2]

Things only got worse. At the height of the campaign, the state DFL party went to court to bar Oberstar from using sample ballots that the party felt suggested that Oberstar had received the party's endorsement.[3] Not to be out-done, Oberstar launched a last-minute advertising campaign that blamed Perpich for the closing of a Duluth steel plant.[4]

Whether that twelfth-hour ad made a difference was unclear, but Blat-nik's endorsement of Oberstar and a substantial anti-Perpich Republican cross-over vote certainly did. Oberstar won the September primary in a walk, capturing all eleven counties and piling up a victory margin of nearly two to one.

The primary election was no more successful in closing party ranks than the endorsing convention had been. Perpich complained bitterly about the unfairness of Oberstar's last-minute ad campaign. Brother Lieutenant Governor Rudy refused to endorse Oberstar in the general election.[5] The Perpich/Blatnik rift had proved itself remarkably enduring. It was not, however, enough to derail Oberstar, who won the November general election handily.

As Oberstar prepared to take office, the BWCA controversies were high on his agenda.

All sides to those controversies saw in Oberstar a potential ally. Local res-idents had taken heart from Oberstar's campaign position that logging should continue in the area within the BWCA known as the Portal Zone. Conservationists were guarded in their optimism; many saw hope in Oberstar's association with Blatnik, while others were concerned about his close ties to the politics of the Iron Range.[6]

The conservationists wasted no time in giving the newly-elected con-gressman an opportunity to prove himself.

They began by approaching Hubert Humphrey, whose authorship of the nettlesome language of the Wilderness Act had contributed to so many of the ambiguities about how the area would be used and managed.[7] In a letter to the senator, Bill Magie asked Humphrey to pick up where Blatnik had left off by offer-ing an amendment that would "stop it all, the bickering, the logging and the snowmobiles and outboard motors. . . ."[8]

Humphrey responded by suggesting a more moderate course. Arguing that administrative actions might accomplish just as much as legislation, Humphrey suggested that Magie start with a meeting with the state attorney gen-eral and DNR commissioner to explore just how much protection could be gained without federal intervention.[9] Nothing came of the suggestion.

Conservationists realized that they would also need to cultivate Oberstar directly. In January, Oberstar visited the Sig Olson home in Ely with Governor Wendell (Wendy) Anderson and Idaho Governor Cecil Andrus. Although they discussed no BWCA business, Olson reported that "Jim seemed friendly." There was also a telling moment: "Andrus seeing the big beautiful Idaho book on my table told us looking at the Salmon River shot 'No one will touch that timber as long as I'm in power.' I hope Anderson and Jim got the parallel."[10]

Encouraged by Oberstar's visit to Olson, a dozen conservationists met with the congressman in early April to discuss the BWCA. They proposed an end to logging in the BWCA through the designation of the BWCA's Portal Zone as wilderness.[11] Oberstar listened carefully, stated his desire to still the controversy, but gave them no commitments.[12] Whatever his plans might have been, he kept them close to his vest.

It soon became clear exactly what those plans were.

Oberstar was not the kind of leader who waited on events. At the very time he was meeting with the environmentalists, he was formulating a strategy that would guarantee his imprint on the BWCA's future. His principles were straight forward: mixed-use needed to be accommodated, management needed to be simplified, and the controversies needed to be put to bed.

He quietly traveled throughout the country to visit other national wilderness areas and national recreation areas. A concept began to take shape in his mind for which he requested the Forest Service's technical and drafting help. A draft bill was ready by July.[13]

But still he kept it under wraps. Forest Chief John McGuire was scheduled to make a final decision that fall about the snowmobile ban. Oberstar wanted to beat him to the punch.[14] That left little time for public hearings, discussions, or negotiations.

In fact, there were none. Instead, Oberstar unveiled his bill on October 14 at separate meetings with Superior National Forest staff, local residents, and environmentalists. He held a press conference at day's end to announce the bill to the general public.[15]

The action caught the environmental community off-guard. The bill was complex, thorough and a dramatic retreat from the expanded wilderness protection that conservationists sought.

The major innovation of the bill was to create two zones, one to be managed as wilderness, one to be managed largely as a multi-use recreational and economic activity area.

The Boundary Waters Wilderness Area consisted of 625,000 acres in which logging, mining, and mechanized travel would be prohibited.

The Boundary Waters National Recreation Area (NRA) carved out 527,000 acres in which logging and mechanized travel would be allowed. It included such favorite BWCA lakes as Seagull, Saganaga, Basswood, Brule, Isabella, Bald Eagle, Trout, Rose, Mountain, and Lac La Croix.

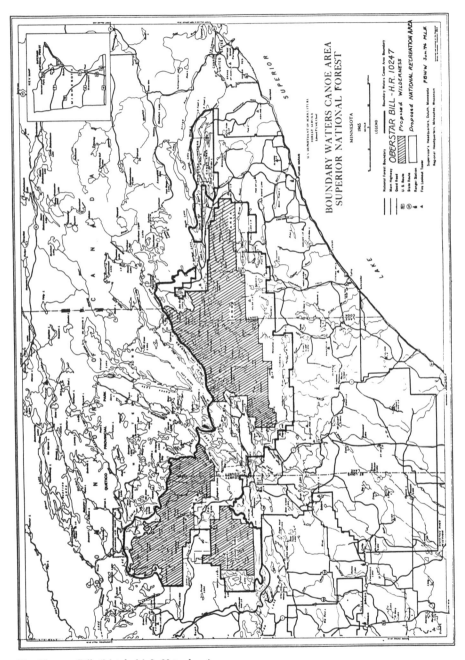

The Oberstar Bill. (*Map by M. L. Heinselman*)

'I'LL TRADE YOU 626,700 ACRES OF WILDERNESS
FOR SOME SNOWMOBILES AND A FEW MOTORBOATS — WHADAYA SAY?'

October 20, 1975, *Minneapolis Star*. (*Reprinted with permission from the* Minneapolis Star Tribune)

Oberstar formally introduced his measure in Congress as H.R. 10247 on October 20, 1975.[16] He explained that the bill was intended to resolve "public confusion over the present status of the BWCA, uncertainty about its future, a growing divisiveness over its use, and emerging resentment of people in the northern area of the state against people in the other areas of the state and nation."[17]

He had concluded from his trips to other National Recreational Areas throughout the country that bifurcating use was prudent politics and sound management.[18] He was also realistic about the difficulties such an approach would encounter: "Reasonable people will differ over the details and, no doubt, the philosophy of this approach. But I hope the public will give it serious, careful consideration . . ."[19]

The timing of the bill's introduction also succeeded in buying northern Minnesota residents another season of snowmobiling. Forest Service Chief McGuire announced in early November that the snowmobile ban would be delayed until the following November.[20]

The environmental community collected its thoughts quickly. They understood that the bill's approach of segregating uses would be superficially appealing to those who sought a middle ground. But they also knew that the implica-

'OBERSTAR IS COMING!! OBERSTAR IS COMING!!'

April 23, 1977, *Minneapolis Star* cartoon. (*Reprinted with permission from the* Minneapolis Star Tribune)

tions of this approach would be far-reaching both for the BWCA itself and for the national wilderness preservation movement.

Nineteen environmental leaders sent Oberstar a letter on October 24 that urged him to reconsider:

> We have . . . a philosophical concern over the precedent-setting aspect of declassifying portions of an established Wilderness. . . . The new N.R.A. designations outside the B.W.C.A. are appealing to many on both sides of this issue, but declassifying portions of the B.W.C.A. as Wilderness is a serious matter that deeply troubles the members of our organizations.[21]

Oberstar responded to each of the signatories with a polite letter, leaving the door open for further discussions.[22]

Those discussions proved fruitless. Bud Heinselman carried the environmentalists' message to Oberstar on December 5 and again in March of the next year. He returned discouraged. It was clear that Oberstar would not reconsider carving a National Recreation Area out of the existing BWCA.

One environmentalist understood early on the futility of talking Oberstar out of an NRA. Herb Johnson, an engineer and the CEO of a small Twin Cities computer company, took a slightly different route: "Your plan for the BWCA greatly interests me because it resembles a plan that has evolved in my own thinking of what is best for that area," Johnson wrote Oberstar in November. He proceeded to outline his own plan, which called for preserving the BWCA as wilderness at its current size and surrounding it with an NRA-like zone outside the wilderness.[23] Although Oberstar chose to stick to his own course, Johnson's concept would later play an important role.

The State of Minnesota was the next to weigh in. Commissioner of Natural Resources Bob Herbst[24] appointed a department review team in early 1976 to analyze the Oberstar bill. The team released its recommendations in March.

The Department of Natural Resources (DNR) sharply criticized Oberstar's NRA concept, proposing that the BWCA's existing boundaries be fully contained within the National Wilderness Preservation System. The department also proposed that the Interior Zone, in which logging was forbidden, be enlarged from 618,000 acres to 746,000 acres.[25]

It was not clear that the DNR's position would be any more persuasive with Oberstar than the environmentalists' position had been. Oberstar gave no indications that he was prepared to budge.[26]

The Environmentalist's Antidote

The environmentalists had run into a wall. Oberstar had been thorough in his preparation, had gauged the political climate effectively and had proved an unmovable negotiator. His effectiveness gave them little choice but to switch tactics.

The tactic they chose carried long odds. They proposed to have another member of Congress carry an antidote bill, one that would negate Oberstar's on every point: no bifurcation, no mining, no logging, no motorboating, no snowmobiling. Pure wilderness.

It was risky on a number of counts.

First, it would be characterized as an extreme response when the situation required a more modulated middle ground.

Second, it would challenge the most sacrosanct of congressional conventions: deference to a congressional member's discretion to guide events in his or her home district.

Third, it would pit someone from outside the district against not only the elected representative of that district but many of the residents of the area.

And fourth, it would ensure that a bill would emerge, if at all, only after protracted, polarizing, and potentially politically-charged legislative deliberations —normally a recipe for legislative procrastination.

But the environmentalists preferred long odds to no odds at all. They selected as their champion a member of Congress who had little experience with national environmental issues: Don Fraser of Minneapolis.

Donald M. Fraser had won his first election to Congress in 1962, following eight years in the Minnesota state senate. A thoughtful, principled legislator, the liberal Fraser embodied much of the best from the progressive wing of the Democratic-Farmer-Labor party. In 1973, he was also elected to lead the liberal Americans for Democratic Action (ADA), and chaired the Democratic Study Group in the Congress from 1969 to 1971. He often received voting ratings in the ninety-to-one-hundred-percent range from organizations like the ADA, the League of Women Voters, organized labor, consumer groups, and the League of Conservation Voters.[27]

Though he had compiled an excellent voting record on environmental matters, Fraser had not been noted for his leadership in this area. Rather, he had carved out expertise on such disparate policy areas as international affairs and the District of Columbia.

During one of the BWCA logging lawsuits in the early 1970s, Chuck Dayton and Bud Heinselman had run into Fraser in the cafeteria of the Minneapolis Federal Building, where Fraser had his congressional district office and where the logging trial was being held. When the conversation turned to the BWCA, Fraser told them to let him know if he could ever be of help.

It was not until early 1976 that the environmentalists took Fraser up on his offer. By that spring, particularly after their visits with Oberstar following his bill announcement, the conservationists had become convinced that Oberstar was unlikely to address their concerns. They asked Fraser to introduce a bill that would be the antidote to Oberstar's. Fraser agreed.

The Fraser bill was introduced at the end of June.[28] "The bill I am introducing today is brief and simple in concept," Fraser told his House colleagues:

> It will lay to rest the endless controversies over this area by protecting its remaining virgin forests and allowing the restoration of areas already damaged by logging and roadbuilding, by ending the needless conflicts over mechanized versus compatible wilderness recreational uses, and by protecting the area from mining or mineral exploration activities inside its borders.[29]

Fraser avoided a confrontational posture. He soft-peddled the tensions inherent in having introduced a bill at odds with the home district congressman's

Congressman Don Fraser , who introduced legislation to save the BWCA as wilderness. (*Photo from Don Fraser*)

legislation: "In an effort to give Congress the opportunity to consider several alternative plans for the BWCA, I am introducing a bill which places greater emphasis on protection of the wilderness features of the BWCA."[30]

Fraser's introductory statement did, however, draw a bright line between legislation that was driven by a short-term desire to find a middle ground and legislation that took a longer term view:

> If this bill is enacted it will preserve this last great remnant of the old 'northwoods' for all of our children—both for today and for generations yet unborn. Let me remind you that if only one of the many battles to preserve the splendid Superior-Quetico Wilderness had been lost, there would be no BWCA program to debate in Congress today. . . . Let us commemorate the historic contributions of the canoe country's waterways to the development of both nations by preserving this splendid example of primeval America for all time.[31]

Despite the conciliatory tone, therefore, the lines were drawn.

The Show-Down

As 1976 came to close, and with it the 94th Congress, neither the Oberstar nor the Fraser bill drew additional attention. That would change immediately in the new, 95th Congress.

Fraser moved first, introducing his bill on January 31, 1977. His "purist" approach to wilderness became even purer with a new provision that would add to the BWCA fifteen parcels totalling almost 35,000 acres.[32]

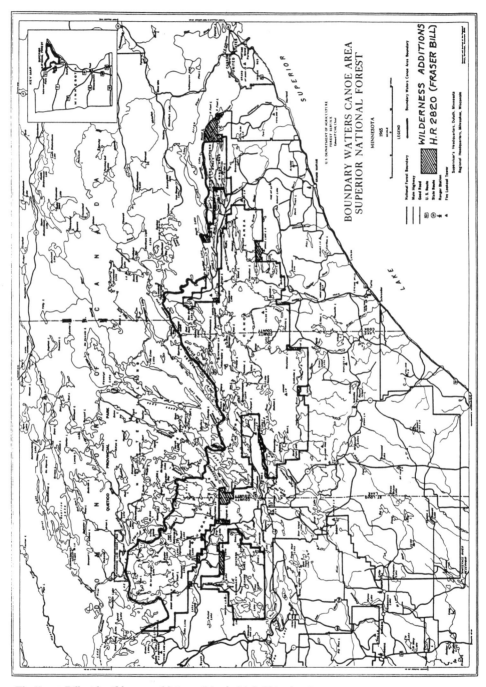

The Fraser Bill with wilderness additions. (*Map by M. L. Heinselman*)

Fraser explained that, unlike the 94th Congress, the 95th Congress would be under the gun to act:

> The voluntary suspension of logging of virgin timber will expire this September; the courts have urged that legislation be enacted to remove the ambiguity of the Wilderness Act; the Forest Service, caught in the middle, would welcome clarification of its management responsibilities. I am introducing this legislation in the hope that this body will have the vision to take the steps necessary to insure that this irreplaceable national treasure will be spared further despoilment and will be maintained and restored for the enjoyment and enrichment of those to whom it will be bequeathed.

Fraser's tactics this time around underscored the heightened stakes.

He attempted to transform the issue from a locally based recreation discussion to a nationally significant, land-use controversy that carried implications for the entire wilderness system. Working closely with national environmental organizations, he ultimately assembled more than one hundred House co-sponsors. He also began lining up support in the Senate, convincing highly respected Iowa Senator Dick Clark to carry the bill in that body.

Fraser also went to work elevating the stakes in Minnesota. He assigned his legislative aide Rip Rapson to work full time on the wilderness bill and to gear up for a prolonged and intense state-wide effort. Rapson would from that point forward establish Fraser's Washington office as BWCA Central, coordinating media contacts, environmental lobbying efforts, political strategy, and information exchange. With Fraser taking on the difficult public politics of the bill, Rapson was given the charge of handling the behind-the-scenes, day-to-day work.

Oberstar's tactics were the mirror image of Fraser's: providing little public fanfare, seeking a moderate middle ground, focusing on local ramifications, and retaining to himself all responsibility for daily work on the bill.

Waiting until April to introduce his bill, Oberstar almost seemed to down play the event, providing no introductory statement.[34]

His new bill differed in several significant respects from his previous bill. In a clear gesture to the environmental community, the bill increased the size of the wilderness area by 25,000 acres, reduced the size of the national recreation area by 28,000 acres, prohibited logging of virgin forest even within the NRA, and strengthened restrictions on mining.[35]

From the time he introduced his first bill in 1975, Oberstar hammered away against the Fraser argument that the BWCA debate should be seen in state-wide or national terms. He built strong coalitions with local residents, businesses, and organizations in shaping his new approach. He never missed the opportunity

(Reprinted with permission from the Duluth News-Tribune)

to remind the public that local residents had the greatest interest in the outcome of the BWCA: they lived in the area year-round, knew most intimately the area and its problems, and should not be bullied by Twin Cities or Washington outsiders.

(*Reprinted with permission from the* Minneapolis Star Tribune)

In Congress, this argument took the form of local-member prerogative. Oberstar never sought co-sponsors for his bill, underscoring that the BWCA issue was his alone to resolve.

Oberstar further made it clear that he would personally master the details of his bill and chart its strategic direction. In Tom Reagan, his administrative assistant, and John O'Connor, his legislative aide, he had strong and competent support. He nevertheless made all important BWCA appearances himself and made all the critical decisions on the issue.

In a telling remark that was perhaps symbolic of the contrast between Fraser's choice to delegate substantial responsibility to staff and Oberstar's desire to manage personally every aspect of the BWCA issue, Oberstar sarcastically told Rapson when the two were walking back from the Capitol that it must be nice for Fraser to be able to conduct his United States Senate campaign in Minnesota while Rapson did his BWCA work for him in Washington.[36]

The Citizen Teams

Behind the principals in the Congress, two very different coalitions formed to push the BWCA issue in opposite directions. The Friends of the Boundary Waters Wilderness organized as a response to the negative provisions in the first Oberstar bill. Congressman Oberstar himself created the Boundary Waters Conservation Alliance to rally support for his own legislation.

Friends of the Boundary Waters Wilderness

The Friends of the Boundary Waters Wilderness formed soon after Oberstar introduced his first bill in October 1975.

On May 7, 1976, a veritable who's who of the warriors from recent BWCA battles met at Tobies Cafe in Hinckley.[37] They made two key decisions. First, they settled on the tactic of approaching Don Fraser to carry the wilderness bill.[38] Second, they decided to constitute themselves formally as the "Friends of the Boundary Waters Wilderness," selecting Bud Heinselman as the organization's first chair.[39]

The Friends' first order of business was to draft a legislative proposal for Fraser's consideration. During the last half of June, Chuck Dayton and other Friends members worked closely with Minnesota DNR attorney Phil Olfelt and Antoinette Kassim of Fraser's office to develop a bill.[40] The drafting was completed by month's end, and Fraser formally introduced H.R. 14576 in the House of Representatives.[41]

The Friends' work then began in earnest. They immediately faced daunting logistical issues: how to build an organization, raise money, and position the issues on the national stage.

Although a number of Friends members would emerge as key leaders,[42] Heinselman was the linchpin.

Heinselman had been involved with BWCA controversies since the 1950s, when he had worked with the Ikes Wilderness Committee. But it was his work as a forestry professional that had drawn him into the Selke Committee discussions in the 1960s and the logging lawsuits of the early 1970s.

Until 1974, Heinselman had been employed as a forest ecologist for the Forest Service. His research had focused on mapping the remaining BWCA virgin forest, constructing detailed forest-stand-origin maps of the region, and reconstructing the BWCA's fire history dating to the year 1595.

His professional calling had become his personal passion. Opponents once said of him, only partly facetiously, that he was on a first name basis with every tree over the age of fifty in the entire BWCA. His field research brought him to places his personal canoe and winter camping trips did not. His knowledge of the area was a blend of personal observation, forestry research, and ecological analysis. Nobody knew the area as well as he did. Nobody was as passionate about its future.

But because of his employment with the Forest Service, Heinselman had been forced to limit his public involvement in BWCA conservation and management issues. That increasingly became a source of frustration for him. As he watched the mining, logging, motorboat, and snowmobile controversies simmer in the early 1970s, he concluded that he simply could not stand on the sidelines. In June 1974, Heinselman took early retirement from the Forest Service in order to throw himself into efforts to save the Boundary Waters. By the time the Friends formally constituted themselves almost two years later, Heinselman was working on BWCA issues sixteen hours a day.

The Friends soon realized that their local organization would have to be supplemented by a national network of support capable of educating and bringing pressure on Congress.[43]

This approach was best illustrated by the Friends work with the Iowa Public Interest Research Group (Iowa PIRG).

After reading an article in the *Des Moines Register* about the Fraser bill, Iowa PIRG Executive Director Eva McGinnis asked the Friends for a slide-tape presentation to show to groups on the Iowa State University (ISU) campus. But the real push to get Iowans interested in the congressional debate came from an ISU student who directed a small BWCA canoe-camping program based in Ames.

In the fall of 1976, Kevin Proescholdt had just completed his third summer guiding BWCA canoe trips when he learned of Iowa PIRG's interest in the BWCA issue. He quickly arranged with McGinnis to become the organization's BWCA chairperson.[44]

The impact was dramatic.

Iowa PIRG helped organize a large turnout for a presentation by Heinselman in December on the Iowa State campus, began a letter-writing campaign to newspapers and congressmen throughout the state, organized a petition drive supporting the Fraser bill that eventually garnered 15,000 names,[45] sold BWCA T-shirts, sponsored raffles and fundraising concerts, and showed the Friends slide presentation on college campuses throughout the state.[46] As a result of this work, the entire Iowa congressional delegation, even arch-conservative Chuck Grassley, ended up sponsoring the Fraser bill.[47]

Other efforts throughout the country were less dramatic, but nevertheless contributed to the fire of interest that was spreading in congressional districts nationwide.[48]

In the Chicago area, a graduate student named Paul Nachman took the lead in generating Friends support. He organized a large gathering at Northwestern University to hear Heinselman, wrote letters to the editor, engineered favorable editorials in the Chicago newspapers, and ultimately went to Washington to testify at hearings and lobby members of Congress.

In suburban Virginia, an engineer named Terry Royt formed the East Coast Advocates of the Boundary Waters Wilderness. Unlike his midwest counterparts, Royt's network was built on the strength of well-known environmental advocates such as Seymour Fishbein of National Geographic, forest ecologist F.H. Bormann of Yale, ecologist Simon Levin of Cornell, author Paul Brooks of Massachusetts, George Woodwell of the Marine Biological Laboratory at Woods Hole, and George Collier of Rutgers. The East Coast Advocates organized letter-writing and telephone-call campaigns on the East Coast, and kept wilderness supporters there informed of the latest developments.[49]

These national networks built centers of support for the BWCA. The Friends sought to reinforce these centers by taking their show on the road.

They produced a slide-tape presentation on the BWCA crisis that was sold and loaned to teachers, clubs, groups, colleges, and anyone else who would listen. They also developed a second presentation entitled "The Seasons of Sigurd F. Olson's Singing Wilderness," which featured Olson reading from his popular book against a color slide backdrop of the scenes he described.[50]

The Friends also produced several brochures featuring full-color photos, a plea for contributions and letters to Congress, and the cover slogan "The Boundary Waters Wilderness. Speak up for it now or forever hold your peace."[51] They also produced a collector's item button that appealed particularly to young congressional staffers: under a shadow of a canoeist, it bore the slogan "I Like It Wild."

But the Friends' most successful bit of Madison Avenue guerilla warfare came with a full-color poster by nationally known wilderness photographer Gerry Brimacombe. Featuring a beautiful sunset over a wooden canoe resting on the rocks of a BWCA lake, the poster read, "The Boundary Waters Wilderness— Take a Long Last Look before It Vanishes." The Friends sent the poster to every congressional office in Washington and to key supporters around the country. It increasingly popped up in congressional offices, libraries, storefront windows, and student dormitories—one was even spotted in the White House.

What the Friends needed the most, however, was a way of expanding beyond their centers of support into a broader national constituency.

One key was to tap into the tens of thousands of people who had recently visited the BWCA.

Using a Freedom of Information Act request filed by the Sierra Club, the Friends were able to obtain from the Forest Service the BWCA visitor list.[52] They then assembled the "dirty dozen," a group led by Bud and Fran Heinselman, to spend several tedious days in the basement of the Duluth Forest Service office laboriously hand-copying the names and addresses of every canoeist who had obtained a BWCA travel permit over the previous two years.

The hard work paid off. In the fall of 1976, the Friends sent their first mailing—a sixteen page book of text and illustrations calling attention to the threats to the BWCA, describing the Fraser and Oberstar bills, and urging people to write their elected officials in support of the Fraser bill—to 30,000 people.[53] More than twenty thousand of those names had been taken from the Forest Service visitor list. Response to this "Educational Note No. 1" gave the Friends the basis for a highly reliable mailing list of some 10,000 supporters.[54]

A second key to building a broad base of national support was to tap into the organizational sophistication of other environmental organizations. By January 1978, the Friends had compiled an extensive list of organizations endorsing full wilderness status for the BWCA, including thirteen national environmental organizations, eleven Minnesota environmental organizations, and almost ninety organizations without an environmental focus, fifty-five from outside the state.[55]

The Friends could also call on some of the most respected elder statesmen of the environmental movement to help elevate the importance of the BWCA controversy within the priorities of national environmental groups. Sig Olson, Chuck Stoddard, Bill Magie, and many others threw themselves into the effort.[56]

The Friends had, in the course of less than a year, built a formidable organizational structure. Their very success, however, spawned a mirror image organization that would work equally aggressively on behalf of the Oberstar bill.

Boundary Waters Conservation Alliance

The early organizing success of the Friends impressed on Oberstar the need for an organized coalition to work the other side of the issue.

On May 17, 1977, twenty-five local residents, resort owners, public officials, and others gathered in Duluth at Congressman Oberstar's office to form the Boundary Waters Conservation Alliance.[57] The group established five committees: fundraising, public speaking, media, letters and resolutions, and legislation.[58] It incorporated two months later with a three-person board of directors: James Saranpaa of Virginia, Vi Lahtonen of Babbitt, and Bruce Kerfoot of Grand Marais.[59]

From its inception, the group was tied closely to Oberstar.[60] Bob Buckler left his job as the congressman's legislative aide to become the first executive director of the Alliance; Buckler's successor, Ed Zabinski, interned in Oberstar's

"Why save the wilderness for canoeists? They just camp in it and don't spend no money."

August 25, 1978, *Des Moines Register* cartoon. (*Copyright 1978 Des Moines Register and Tribune Company. Reprinted with permission.*)

office and subsequently worked on Oberstar's campaign staff.

The Alliance was funded primarily by the timber industry initially, which provided a $20,000 start-up investment. The Alliance was, however, careful to avoid giving the impression that it was just a front for timber interests.[61] No timber industry representatives, for example, sat on the Alliance's board of directors. And the Alliance worked hard to raise money from other sources—membership dues, bake sales, and other local events.

The Alliance's constituency was in fact far broader than the timber industry. Local resort owners and canoe outfitters, area residents, local elected officials, and organized labor—particularly the steelworkers—all had high stakes in the BWCA dispute. But that very breadth also meant that multiple, sometimes diverging, interests would have to be accommodated. Just how difficult that might prove to be was suggested by the attitude of resort owners.

Many resorts located on the edge of the BWCA had built up businesses and attracted customers based on motorized access to the BWCA. The five resorts on Moose Lake near Ely, for example, extensively used motorboat access to the Moose Lake chain and Basswood Lake. As a result, the owners of these resorts were among the most vocal Fraser bill opponents: Ron Stockdill of Canadian Border Lodge, Ted Cleys of Tanglewood Trail Resort, Bill Burley of Kirk's Lodge, and Don Beland of Moose Lake Lodges and North Country Lodge.

But their antipathy to Fraser's closing of motorboat routes did not translate into support for Oberstar's bill. Because Oberstar also proposed to change the general regulatory environment without compensating local business for possible loss and because his bill also called for the closing of some of the secondary motorboat routes, resorters' attitudes toward the Oberstar bill ranged from lukewarm at best to openly hostile.[62]

To some degree, BWCA area resorters faced problems felt throughout the resort industry in Minnesota. By the mid-1970s, the Minnesota resort industry found itself in a critical transition. In the heyday 1920s and 1930s, the resort industry had flourished as a fishing-camp style operation. But it had reacted slowly to the changes in recreational trends and demands following World War II. It was difficult for most BWCA resorts, which were mainly small, family-owned operations, to keep pace with the need to invest in maintenance, modernization, and marketing.[63] By the mid-1960s and early 1970s, almost one hundred resorts per year were closing throughout the state.

These trends sharpened the threat BWCA resorters felt from the Fraser and Oberstar bills. Closing major routes, as Fraser proposed, was unthinkable. But so too might any restrictions on motorboat use be the straw to break the resorters' backs. If the number of available routes was reduced or if their ability to haul canoes to remote lakes by high-powered "tow-boats" was curtailed, the resorts might become that much less competitive.[64]

No less than resort owners, local residents and community leaders were united by an opposition to a new regime of regulations and restrictions. This segment of the Alliance quickly became the organization's loudest and most recognizable voice.

Mayor Doc Grahek of Ely was a legend. A medical doctor, he had many of the qualities of a Wild West hero. Plain-spoken, tough, and committed completely to his community, he was seen by many as the embodiment of the town over which he presided as mayor. When people talked about Iron Range politics, Doc Grahek was part of the conversation.

At the eastern end of Superior Forest and the southern end of the Gunflint Trail, Mayor Richard Humphrey of Grand Marais cut a less imposing figure than Doc Grahek, but brought the same passion to the fight. If Doc Grahek summoned an image of nineteenth-century Wichita, Mayor Humphrey seemed to walk out of an early twentieth-century logging camp. Short, muscled and bearded, he moved quickly to the point, leaving niceties for someone else to pick up later.

But the most intriguing character of all was a five-foot engine of raw energy, will-power, and *chutzpah* named Justine Kerfoot. Kerfoot defied easy categorization. She had lived along the Gunflint Trail since the late 1920s. She had visited as many countries as BWCA lakes. She could as easily charm an audience with her eloquence as she could embarrass a sailor with her vernacular. She had faced down bears, county commissioners, and anybody else who got in her way. Even environmentalists begrudgingly admitted their fascination with her.[65]

Kerfoot also understood the power of the press. She wrote a regular column in the local weekly newspaper. She consented to a widely watched public television feature of her life and philosophy. She and her son, Bruce, who became the Cook County leader of the Alliance, were regular media commentators on how the controversy affected long-term residents of the area.

In Grahek, Humphrey, and the Kerfoots, the Alliance possessed strong, respected voices of the local community. But others within the organization were equally as vocal and sometimes considerably more shrill.

Frank Salerno, Joe Skala, and Shirley Klaesges had no time for the Oberstar bill and never missed a beat in drumming that message home. "The Oberstar bill is embroiled in ambiguities," Salerno complained. "I don't like the idea of having these two bills force fed to us. It's like having the option of being shot or being stabbed."[66]

The real venom, though, was reserved for the environmentalists. In a typical tone and style, Klaesges directed the following sentiments to Ikes President David Zentner in an open letter printed in the *Ely Echo*:

> You have the utter gall to accuse the people of Ely of being rude, ugly, selfish and irresponsible—we who have been harassed by your well-heeled purists for years; we who are not only fighting for our homes and businesses but for the right of all citizens, young, old, middle aged, handicapped and even you, to enjoy a wilderness experience; we who

have gone to hearing after hearing and testified—have written our Congressmen, gone to Washington; we who have protested peaceably, formed committees, we who have watched our rights dwindle, our business shrivel and our area become congested with youth groups who have been brainwashed by pressure groups through out the country; we who have been fed lip service by our representatives, lied to by the Forest Service, ignored by the Dept. of Agriculture; we who have been fined for using snowmobiles on routes the Forest Service themselves cut; we who have been told when, where and how to live, and when to enter here and when not to enter there; we who have out numbered and out testified you time and time again only to end up with the short end of the stick. HOW DARE YOU![67]

Organized labor—especially the steelworkers from the Iron Range—added another ingredient to the Alliance's mix. Their interests were both direct and indirect: curtailment of mining and logging hit them in their pocketbooks, and recreational limitations affected their leisure time and their sense of ownership of what they considered their backyard. Their experience with organizing and their strong ties into the state and national political networks made them valuable allies for the Alliance.[68]

The large timber companies—Potlatch, Boise Cascade, and others interested in BWCA softwood pulp for paper manufacture—stayed behind the scenes, content to provide funding, share information, and call on their national political network. Smaller timber companies assumed a more visible presence within the Alliance's activities.

One of those companies, run by the Kainz brothers of Ely, was positioned to symbolize the plight of the small logger. The Kainz operation had special interest in large pine sawlogs from virgin BWCA timber. The Kainz' plea was simple: block us from those saw logs, and you eliminate an historic and economically important part of the Ely economy.

Positioned between the giants and the Kainz' were the middle-sized operations: Hedstrom Lumber Company of Grand Marais, which relied primarily on saw logs, and Harry Fisher of Northern Forest Products, who had contracted to cut two of the enjoined BWCA timber sales.[69]

Resorters. Local public figures. Unions. Big business. Small business. Some had worked together previously, but most had not. Not only had the Crane Lake resorters not worked with the Vermilion Lake resorters who had not worked with the Gunflint Trail resorters, they viewed themselves as competing for the same narrow tourist dollar. Similar tensions percolated throughout the coalition. It promised to be an uneasy marriage.[70]

All the more so given the very different attitudes Alliance members had

'Nobody here but us wild animals'

March 26, 1976, *Minneapolis Star Tribune* cartoon (*Reprinted with permission from the* Minneapolis Star Tribune)

about their purpose. Some thought that Oberstar's bill and Fraser's bill deserved the same treatment. Others found Oberstar's bill the best way of putting the controversies to bed. Others still hoped that a third path could be found.[71]

The only thing that unified everybody was opposition to the Fraser bill. It was not a long road from this opposition to a piece of legislation to the demonization of the man himself. As it became increasingly clear that some legislation would be taken up by Congress, Alliance members developed a growing sense of impotence and rage. This was in turn redirected toward Fraser and the political process.[72]

All of this internal churning and frustration did not get in the way of the Alliance putting together a sophisticated campaign to affect the congressional deliberations.

Calling on many of the same techniques as the Friends[73] (letter-writing campaigns,[74] resolutions of support from other organizations,[75] direct lobbying in Washington,[76] presentations to countless groups,[77] petition drives[78]) the Alliance grew its base dramatically: by one estimate, from a handful of members in June 1977 to 800 a year later and to 4,000 by the fall of 1978.[79]

And like the Friends, the Alliance began packaging their cause for popular consumption. Where the Friends "liked it wild," the Alliance wanted to "Keep the BWCA Open to Everyone." One effective advertisement showed a boy and his grandfather in a canoe with a small outboard motor, accompanied by the slogan, "We're fighting for the Spirit of '64," (i.e., no changes from the BWCA provisions of the 1964 Wilderness Act).

The Alliance was perhaps most effective in using rallies and demonstrations to call attention to its message. Its first demonstration came in October 1977, when steelworkers picketed Fraser's Minneapolis office. Subsequent demonstrations became increasingly creative and media-friendly. A snowmobile protest ride into the BWCA in January 1978. The eviction of the U.S. Forest Service from the district ranger's office in Grand Marais in April. A blockade of BWCA entry points in August.[80]

As the debates in Congress began, therefore, both Fraser and Oberstar had in their corners advocacy organizations that were highly motivated, sophisticated and effective.

Broadening Circles of Interest

Both the Alliance and the Friends effectively broadened the circles of interest in the dispute. In short order, national environmental organizations, Minnesota's congressional delegation, the federal government's executive branch, and the State of Minnesota would all join the fray.

The National Environmental Organizations

No element was more important to the Friends strategy than drawing in as active participants a half-dozen of the most influential national environmental organizations: the Wilderness Society, the Sierra Club, the Izaak Walton League, the National Audubon Society, and others. Their value lay less in each group making the BWCA its highest priority than in all of the groups making a commitment to pooling resources. Where one organization might place an article in a key newspaper, another might contact a crucial committee member, and another yet might organize a targeted mailing.

The Friends accordingly hoped to identify one person within each organization who could command the resources of his or her organization, who was connected to the rest of the national environmental network, and who was willing to make the BWCA a high personal priority.

They began with a pitch to everybody at once. On February 23, 1977, the Wilderness Society pulled together leaders of the national groups to hear a pitch for support from Bud Heinselman and Chuck Dayton. Heinselman and Dayton kept their request simple: help in distributing a new color brochure to members across the nation, and a commitment to make the BWCA issue a high priority for each of the groups.[81] Nobody balked.

With that toe hold secured, the Friends could press forward with their strategy of solidifying the personal support of key individuals.

They began with the Wilderness Society. Although the society was probably the most ideological and ardent of the national organizations on the BWCA issue, the BWCA dispute could not have come at a more difficult time. The Wilderness Society was undergoing dramatic internal reorganization, running short of money, and stretched to the limit in covering the brewing congressional debate over the Alaska wilderness bill.

Helped along by the prodding of two Friends members who also happened to be former presidents of the Wilderness Society, Sig Olson and Chuck Stoddard, the society took a gamble and put its full resources behind the BWCA effort. It called on one of its top field workers, Steve Payne, to open a Wilderness Society office in Duluth.[82]

Payne immediately focused on the fight that would be waged in the legislative anterooms. He conducted what amounted to a legislative strategy boot camp for the Friends' volunteers—or at least as much of a boot camp as the gentle, deeply reflective environmental activist could muster. He then walked the halls with Friends members, calling on his vast network of friends throughout the capitol.

If the Wilderness Society brought the greatest passion among national organizations to the dispute, the Sierra Club brought the most influence. It could draw on membership lists in every congressional district in the country. It was amply endowed. It was accustomed to mobilizing for unpopular causes.

Like the Wilderness Society, the Sierra Club was concerned about the demands the huge Alaska wilderness dispute would place on its Washington, D.C., staff. But also like the Wilderness Society, the Sierra Club realized that the stakes in the BWCA dispute demanded the skills of a senior strategist and was able to commit that person to the BWCA effort.

Brock Evans, the director of the Sierra Club's Capitol Hill office, was on every environmentalist's top-five list in the someone-you-want-in-your-corner-when-things-get-tough category. He was on a first-name basis with virtually every member of Congress. He was equally respected by Democrats and Republicans for his bedrock integrity and a first-rate intellect. He was tenacious but pragmatic, a true believer who knew his organization could not afford to burn bridges. Like Payne, he patiently taught the green Friends volunteers the nuts and bolts of lobbying on the Hill.[83]

The Izaak Walton League of America was an older and generally more cautious organization than either the Wilderness Society or the Sierra Club. But its membership was filled with hunters and fishing enthusiasts, groups not generally found in the membership lists of the latter two organizations. Bringing that segment of the conservation community into the BWCA coalition was a high priority for the Friends.

In Dave Zentner, the Ikes national president, they found the person to do that. Zentner was a Duluth native, long active on BWCA issues. He went to bat within the organization to secure its commitment to the Friends' struggle. That effort paid off. The Ikes authorized their legislative director, Maitland Sharpe, to join with Payne, Evans, and others in developing a national environmental coalition on behalf of the BWCA.[84]

Other national environmental organizations also came on board.

Brock Evans, director of the Sierra Club's Washington, D.C., office. (*Photo by Kevin Proescholdt*)

The National Audubon Society, with an enviable network of grass-roots chapters around the country.[85] Friends of the Earth, with 25,000 members and extensive connections into the scientific community.[86] The National Wildlife Federation, the largest of all the national environmental groups. The National Parks and Conservation Association, well-versed in the politics of fighting for the future of public space.

These organizations brought to the Friends table not only staff, but mailing lists, grass-roots chapters filled with activists, and exposure to millions of people through the organizations' periodicals.[87]

The Congressional Delegation

The environmental organizations could advocate, but the task of legislating remained with the Congress. How the Minnesota congressional delegation would become involved in the BWCA dispute accordingly created more than passing interest.

The dean of the Republican delegation was Al Quie, a soft-spoken, moderate Republican from southern Minnesota farming country. As the ranking minority member of the House Education and Labor Committee, Quie had carved a reputation for thoughtful pragmatism. He was an architect of the Vocational Education Act and countless other pieces of legislation that affected quietly, but profoundly, the daily routines of many Americans. Tall, lanky, with sculpted, tan features, he could be mistaken for having escaped from the back lot of a Hollywood set, until your eyes reached the floor and the signature cowboy boots—a short-hand for his passion for horses and the outdoors. Both sides to the dispute eyed Quie as a pivotal vote to be won over.

The other Republican members of the delegation were pigeonholed as allies of the Alliance. Tom Hagedorn from the southwestern part of the state, Arlen Stangeland from the northwest, and Bill Frenzel from the western suburbs of Minneapolis were all seen as sympathetic to the concerns of the timber industry, resort owners, and local residents.

On the democratic side of the aisle, the question was whether two young members, freshman Bruce Vento from St. Paul and Rick Nolan from St. Cloud, would sit out the battle or join up sides. Nolan, an unabashed liberal in a conservative district, seemed a likely Fraser ally. Vento, who had been assigned to the House Interior Committee, where the bills would begin their legislative journey, was a less certain commodity.

The democrats held both Minnesota senate seats, but the state-wide political pressures that come with the job made predicting their behavior on the BWCA controversy impossible.

Senator Wendell Anderson had arrived in the Senate in 1976 with considerable fanfare. A highly popular governor, Anderson had stepped down from that post when Walter Mondale had been elected as Jimmy Carter's vice president. The current governor, previously lieutenant governor, Rudy Perpich then turned around and appointed his former boss to the vacated seat.

The so-called self-appointment played poorly within the state. The governor, whose picture on the cover of *Time* holding a fish he had just hooked had come to symbolize the good life in Minnesota, became the object of widespread derision.

It did not help matters much that his senior partner in the Senate was revered by friends and respected by foes: Hubert Humphrey.

Humphrey was accustomed to taking charge of a situation. In other circumstances, predictably, he would have taken hold of the BWCA controversy, brought the combatants together and hammered out a way of resolving the issues. Circumstances prevented this from playing out, however. Tragically, he had been diagnosed in early 1977 with terminal cancer.

But Humphrey resolved to carry on his public duties in his inimitable fashion. That applied to the BWCA.

Humphrey could not help but believe that the issues were susceptible to reasoned resolution, particularly the question of timber, which for him was the most serious of the disputes. In March, he requested the Library of Congress' Congressional Research Office to study the BWCA timber question and offer some recommendations.[88] Anticipating that these recommendations would spring the impasse loose, Humphrey called a meeting of the entire congressional delegation on March 31, 1977.

The meeting was vintage Humphrey. He presided as would a father calming a dispute among unruly children. He was clear that the group should not leave the room until it found common ground. He talked passionately about the unseemliness of elected representatives of the citizens of Minnesota quarreling when they should be leading. He presented the Congressional Research Office study as a way to reconcile the interests of timber harvesting and conservation.

But this was one time that the Humphrey magic failed to do the trick.

Part of the reason was undoubtedly the late date of his intervention. The parties had been solidifying their positions for a long time, and the stakes had been raised quite publicly.

Another reason was Humphrey's failure to appreciate how complex the issues were and how the sides had lined up.

At one point, when Oberstar was trying to make his case, Humphrey pulled out the latest issue of the Wilderness Society's magazine and asked Oberstar whether he had read the article on the BWCA: "Have you read this article by Meeeron Heinselman?" Upon hearing the responding laughter, Humphrey concluded with an unknowing understatement, "I take it you have heard of him."[89]

Humphrey's detachment from the current BWCA issues went much further than not recognizing Bud Heinselman's name. The Congressional Research Office study in which Humphrey had placed so much stock represented an old-line set of timber industry arguments, arguments the environmentalists had spent twenty years trying to debunk. The study, more fundamentally, did not even attempt to address the complex layers of recreation, land-use, wilderness management, or economic issues that were driving the positions of both sides.[90]

Fraser's aide Rapson, who had presented the Fraser bill to the delegation, finally broke the ice. Rapson told Humphrey that the BWCA controversy went far beyond a discussion about those areas where logging could be justified. He noted that a national constituency now pushed for full wilderness status for the BWCA and that that constituency deserved a voice beyond any compromise that the Minnesota delegation might consider.[91]

There was an agonizing silence. Humphrey flushed noticeably. He leaned forward in his chair and informed Rapson that he did not need a lecture in the politics of wilderness protection, particularly not from someone who was not old enough to remember when these issues really began. Rapson sat down, but the air had been let out of the balloon. The meeting ended soon after, with no detectable progress having been made.[92]

The Executive Branch

Because no one could bridge the deep fissures within the congressional delegation before the legislative process began further playing out, the Executive Branch assumed a greatly heightened importance.

The administration of the newly elected President Carter sent a breath of fresh air to the environmental community.

Carter himself had campaigned with sensitivity to national environmental issues. His vice-president, Walter Mondale, a politician who went to the lakes and woods to get his bearings, had developed an intimate familiarity with the BWCA disputes.

Even more crucial were two key appointments in the Department of Agriculture, the agency with jurisdiction over the BWCA. Carter chose as his Secretary of Agriculture another Minnesotan: Bob Bergland, who had represented the northwest part of the state in the House. Although the Friends were concerned that Bergland's attitudes toward the BWCA might be shaped by his having represented large snowmobiling manufacturers and avid recreational users of the BWCA, they were encouraged by his reputation for open-mindedness and accessibility.

They were even more encouraged by the appointment of Rupert Cutler as the Assistant Secretary of Agriculture with oversight authority of the Forest Service. Cutler's doctoral dissertation had included an analysis of the recent mining dispute within the BWCA. The national environmental groups assured the Friends that they would be impressed with Cutler's grasp of and sensitivity to wilderness values.[93]

It would take that kind of attitude to offset what the environmental community perceived to be an antagonistic Forest Service.

The Forest Service relationship with the environmental community had always been tense. Through years of managing national forest lands, it had developed a close—some would say cozy—relationship with the timber industry.[94] Because it also managed only one wilderness area in Minnesota—the BWCA– it felt most comfortable with a wilderness management model that emphasized recreation and multiple uses. And the agency's foresters on the Superior National Forest had years invested in managing the BWCA as it had been in the past: complete with logging, motorboating, snowmobiling, and mineral exploration.

The Lobbying Heats Up

By the beginning of 1977 the tableau was in place. Oberstar and Fraser were squared off. The Friends and the Alliance were consolidating their spheres of influence. The new federal administration was taking form. The maneuvering was systematic and deliberate.

But a crisis was brewing that would shatter that slow and steady pace.

At the end of 1976, a number of pending, but dormant, BWCA timber sales threatened to come to life. Winter is high season for BWCA loggers, who can use the iced-over lakes and frozen bogs as temporary roads to remove timber. The Friends looked for some way to prevent a resumption of the harvesting, at least until Congress had had the opportunity to take up the issue.

Their first strategy, requesting the logging companies with pending contracts to enter into a voluntary moratorium, fell on deaf ears and was rejected formally on December 6, 1976.[95]

The second strategy, an approach to the Superior National Forest Service staff to impose an administrative moratorium on the sales, was equally fruitless.

A third recourse, civil protests such as a mid-winter camp-in on the timber sales, presented high uncertainties and risks. Although the Friends had tentatively adopted it as a last-ditch strategy, some felt it too extreme.

The Friends were out of ammunition.[96]

Relief came from an unlikely source: Oberstar. Recognizing the public relations disaster that would accompany clearcutting hundreds of acres of virgin forest when Congress was poised to begin its consideration of BWCA legislation, the congressman announced just before Christmas 1976 that he had engineered an agreement among the timber contractors, the Forest Service, and his office to impose a voluntary moratorium on renewed cutting.

The Friends, who had been left completely outside the discussion, praised Oberstar's "important and statesmanlike act."[97] They recognized, however, that Oberstar had turned the tables. By appearing conciliatory and reasonable and by establishing himself as the only person able to broker competing interests, Oberstar had neutralized the considerable progress the Friends had made in the preceding months in raising the specter of an opposition that was narrowly self-interested. The Friends' tentative plan of a mid-winter camp-in seemed all the more marginal.

Oberstar's stock was accordingly high as the 95th Congress opened a few weeks later. Oberstar sought to take advantage of that situation in an early procedural skirmish.

Forest Service bills are normally handled by the House Agriculture Committee. Wilderness bills are normally handled by the House Interior Committee. Fraser had assumed that both his and Oberstar's bills would be sent to Interior. Oberstar requested, however, that his bill be referred to Agriculture.

What appeared to be a mundane squabble over procedure was in fact a crucial tactical ploy by Oberstar.

Once in Agriculture, Oberstar's bill would be shaped by committee members steeped in the management philosophy of the Forest Service—the kind of multiple-use philosophy that underlay Oberstar's legislation. An Agriculture referral would virtually guarantee that Fraser's bill would never emerge or that it would be amended so thoroughly as to be indistinguishable from the Oberstar bill.

In contrast, if one or both bills could be sent to Interior, the bills would be hammered out by committee members far more familiar with the kind of wilderness management philosophy that the Fraser bill represented.

The political profiles of the committee members were important as well.

The Agriculture Committee was home to a large number of conservative midwestern and southern members who were not about to embarrass a well-liked, moderate colleague by favoring an extreme approach championed by one of the most liberal members of the House. They could be counted on to cut Oberstar a wide swath in promoting his legislation.

The Interior Committee, on the other hand, was chaired by Morris Udall of Arizona, a dyed-in-the-wool liberal who was a kindred spirit and good personal friend of Fraser. The key subcommittee was similarly headed by liberal powerhouse Phil Burton from San Francisco, who personified the tradition of progressive democratic politics of northern California.

Fraser's office and the national environmental coalition made an all-out assault on the referral question. Rapson and Evans made sure that daily calls from every nook and cranny of the Washington conservation community went into House Speaker Tip O'Neill's office.[98] Fraser enlisted the support of Udall and Burton. Friends members generated letters to the House Rules Committee.

But the key pressure point was Oregon Congressman Jim Weaver, who chaired the Agriculture subcommittee that would have heard the bills. Drawing on Weaver's close personal relationship with Tom Harkin and his strong professional relationships with the national environmental community, the Friends mounted a campaign within a campaign to win him over. They briefed him, had constituents call him, sent colleague after colleague in to bend his arm. It ultimately worked. Weaver consented to waive his possible jurisdiction and to permit the bills to be heard in Interior only. And so they were.

If the committee referral fight was the little-noticed opening battle of the BWCA legislative wars, the escalation of the two sides' public relations campaigns was the highly visible, protracted war of the trenches.

It broke out first in the sedate pages of the *Congressional Record*, the official daily record of congressional deliberations. In a section of the *Record* called "Extension of Remarks," members of Congress would "extend" remarks they might have made on the floor by inserting a longer version of those remarks in the written record compiled at the end of each congressional workday. Members would often append to those remarks newspaper articles, transcripts of radio interviews, proclamations, or any other document susceptible of being put into writing. It was a handy device to call their colleagues' attention to an issue, to showcase the accomplishments of a constituent, or to have an easily reproducible position statement that could be sent to voters in the district.

Fraser's office used this device to make sure that hardly a week went by in which the BWCA was not highlighted. Rapson laid out a twelve-month plan in which he mapped out every argument that might be raised to support or criticize the Fraser bill, identifying for each a possible article, study, or other document that could be inserted in the *Record*. Most of these were submitted under Fraser's name, but others were prepared for submission by other members, creating the impression of widespread interest in the issue. Coming from a variety of legislators, the BWCA pieces—some twenty-five of them in the period from February 1977 to October 1978—helped demonstrate wide support in the House for Fraser's bill.[100]

Oberstar followed suit, although at a less frenetic pace. He placed a dozen inserts in the *Record* in the space of a year—all under his own name. Oberstar's inserts described his series of BWCA bills, announced endorsements from groups like special education directors or the VFW and described favorable news articles and columns.[101]

The *Congressional Record* wars certainly raised the visibility of the BWCA controversy within the Washington beltway. That visibility was further extended by the increased attention paid to the controversy over time in papers throughout the country.

As the congressional deliberations began and the Friends coalition stoked its editorial contacts, commentaries and editorials started to crop up in the *Chicago Tribune, Chicago Daily News, Milwaukee Journal, Milwaukee Sentinel, Fort Wayne (IN) Journal-Gazette, Des Moines Register, New York Times,* and many others.[102] This was complemented by a steady stream of feature articles in publications of national circulation.[103] This barrage from around the country sent a message to Congress that people outside Minnesota were concerned and watching.

Back in Minnesota, this attention likely had a marginal impact. But the local press coverage clearly took up where the national media's sphere of influence left off.

There were, in turn, two worlds of local reporting: the Twin Cities papers and the papers of greater Minnesota.

The two Minneapolis papers, the evening *Minneapolis Star* and the morning *Minneapolis Tribune,* framed the controversy for most Twin Cities residents.[104] The BWCA became an increasingly familiar topic on the editorial and news pages

Piranha .... in Minnesota

March 4, 1976, *Minneapolis Tribune* cartoon. (*Reprinted with permission from the* Minneapolis Star Tribune)

alike. On the editorial side, the papers were consistently supportive of Fraser's wilderness approach. But it was through its columnists and news reporters that the most complete picture of the controversy took form.

With a raspy voice and gruff questioning style, the *Star* and *Tribune's* Washington correspondent Al McConagha was everyone's image of an old-school beat reporter. And environmental politics was a beat that fit McConagha perfectly. He had reported on the BWCA since at least 1964.[105] He had canoed solo around Lake Superior and the full length of the Minnesota-Canadian border waters.

In Minnesota, Dean Rebuffoni picked up the BWCA beat for the *Tribune*. Rebuffoni had covered environmental issues for the Minneapolis papers for more than five years, reporting on the early BWCA mining, logging, and snowmobiling issues.[106]

A number of columnists weighed in on particular aspects of the BWCA controversies. But none among them wrote with such consistent personal passion as Jim Klobuchar. Klobuchar had grown up in Ely, where his mother still lived. He was a canoist and cross-country skier. He was unapologetic for his eloquent and hard-hitting columns in support of wilderness values.[107]

Coverage of the BWCA controversies in the *Duluth News-Tribune*, the largest newspaper in northeastern Minnesota, provided a fascinating glimpse into the ambivalence many northern Minnesotan residents felt about the issue.

The paper initially adopted an editorial position in strong opposition to Fraser's bill,[108] contrasting it with the carefully developed approach of the Oberstar legislation.[109] Fraser's was an "extreme proposal," "the typical idealistic impracticality of a liberal Democrat."[110] Oberstar's, on the other hand, evinced "a barrelful of political guts" and was "a well conceived, thoroughly prepared plan which should be supported by anyone who can see the forest for the trees."[111]

Nonplussed, Friends members Jan Green and Dave Zentner met with the editors in February 1977 to encourage them to revisit the issue.[112] The trip apparently had an effect. By July, the newspaper had reversed field and set the stage for local congressional field hearings by endorsing the Fraser bill in a long, carefully crafted editorial.[113] Six months later, in January 1978, the paper ran a second editorial, proposing that "one use is enough" and that "it's time all parties involved in the BWCA controversy recognized that the days of 'multiple use' must come to an end."[114]

The weekly newspapers in the vicinity of the BWCA did not share the *Duluth News-Tribune's* ambivalence. The *Ely Echo*, the *Ely Miner*, and Grand Marais' *Cook County News-Herald*, grew more ferocious in their opposition to changes in management as the controversies progressed.

The lone exception was Dennis Anderson of the *Miner*, who sought to bring a semblance of balance to his coverage. In a highly controversial move, for example, Anderson complemented a long interview with Alliance Director Bob Buckler with an equally long interview a week later with Friends Chair Heinselman.[115]

But Anderson's attempts at evenhandedness were more than compensated for by the *Echo*. Editor Bob Cary took on the BWCA dispute as a personal journalistic crusade.[116] For almost two years, Cary launched weekly grenades into the opposing camp, sometimes drawing return fire, but most often content to shake things up.

Due east, Cary had his counterpart in Justine Kerfoot, whose weekly column in the *Cook County News-Herald* provided a good reading of the temperature of local sentiments in any given week. Like Cary, Kerfoot was a born provocateur. In December 1977, for example, she informed her readers that "the Fraser forces" intended "to buy out the entire holdings on the Gunflint Trail. What have you done to keep the pot boiling? Have you written your congressman, your senator?"[117]

The strength of Cary and Kerfoot's written voice not only served to give vent to frustrations among local residents, it also served to dampen dissent. When the director of a local canoe base along the Gunflint Trail challenged the idea that the entire "Gunflint community" opposed greater protections for the area, Kerfoot did not miss the chance to call him out by name as someone who would turn against the survival of his neighboring businesses.[118]

A number of voices in northeastern Minnesota refused to be intimidated. Perhaps most prominent among them were Veda Ponikvar of the *Chisholm Free Press* and Alan Zdon of the *Hibbing Daily Tribune*, both of whom went on record in favor of wilderness protection at critical times during the debate.[119]

The heightening media interest joined with the solidification of the lobbying alliances to focus attention on the real center of activity: the House of Representatives. In that body, the starting point was the National Parks and Insular Affairs Subcommittee of the House Interior Committee. And in that Subcommittee, one person, and one person only, counted: Chairman Phillip Burton.

Notes

1 Oberstar announced his candidacy within days of Blatnik's retirement announcement. *Minneapolis Tribune*, Feb. 16, 1974, p. 12A, "Oberstar Candidate for Blatnik House Seat."

2 *Minneapolis Star*, June 14, 1974, p. 8A, "Oberstar Says He Has the Backers."

3 *Minneapolis Tribune*, Sept. 5, 1974, p. 1B, "U.S. Judge Orders Oberstar Sample Ballot Revised."

4 *Minneapolis Star*, Sept. 18, 1974, p. 1E, "Perpich is Angry About Ads."

5 *Minneapolis Tribune*, Sept. 12, 1974, p. 1A, "8th District Election Draws Mixed Reactions"; *Minneapolis Tribune*, Oct. 19, 1974, p. 7B, "Rudy Perpich Won't Endorse Oberstar."

6 See, e.g., Bill Magie to Hubert Humphrey, Jan. 20, 1975:

> I havent heard from John Blatnik for quite some time—we were all sorry that he backed down at the last moment on the amendment to the Eastern Wilderness Bill that would have put an end to logging and mining in the BWCA. I had a lot of letters and phone calls about it. We don't trust Jim Oberstar; he is too close-ly connected with the Grahek and Ely crowd. . . .

Copy in possession of authors.

7 This approach was suggested by Chuck Dayton. Sigurd F. Olson to Chuck Dayton, Jan. 24, 1975; copy in possession of authors.

8 Bill Magie to Hubert H. Humphrey, Jan. 20, 1975; copy in possession of the authors.

Magie continued, "You know if [it] had not been for a lot of good Conservationists like myself, the area would have been logged off, resorts and roads into every lake. I have traveled the Canoe Country more than any living or dead person–Last summer I made 15 trips and since my retirement, I have made over 150 trips."*Ibid*.

9 Humphrey stated:

> [I]t may be possible for the Forest Service to do a number of significant things administratively that would reduce the need for legislation. I prefer this approach when the existing authority is already adequate. If it is your view that adequate administrative authority does not exist, it may be necessary to make legislative changes.

Hubert H. Humphrey to Bill Magie, Feb. 24, 1975; copy in possession of authors.

Humphrey proposed that the meeting with the state representatives focus on three areas: first, an update of the Selke Committee recommendations to show what had happened to the committee's proposals since 1964; second, an outline of the effects of pending Minnesota legislation on the BWCA; and third, the development of draft lan-guage for Humphrey to use for federal legislative changes. Humphrey concluded the let-ter by reaffirming his commitment to wilderness values:

> I am much interested in the BWCA. When it comes right down to it this is the real original wilderness area. It is unique because nature and man treated so

much of it harshly, yet it came back, and its great system of lakes and streams give it a special character. If with wise and prudent management we can make appropriate provision for the use of its resources while assuring that its priceless characteristics are amplified, then we ought to search for that combination.

Ibid.

10 Sigurd F. Olson to Charles K. Dayton, Jan. 24, 1975; copy in possession of authors.

11 Those who attended included Bill Magie of Friends of the Wilderness, Chuck Dayton of the Sierra Club, wilderness photographer Arnold Bolz, Adolph Anderson of the Minnesota Izaak Walton League's Wilderness Committee, Audubon's Jan Green, aquatic biologist Darby Nelson of MECCA, Milt Pelletier of the Minnesota Conservation Federation, Walt Pomeroy of the Northern Environmental Council, Dr. Herb Wright of the University of Minnesota, and Dave Zentner, the Ikes National Vice President.

12 See also Herbert E. Wright, Jr., to James Oberstar, Apr. 9, 1975; James Oberstar to H.E. Wright, Jr., May 9, 1975; Walter Pomeroy to James Oberstar, May 23, 1975; in Herbert E. Wright, Jr. Papers.

13 Oberstar's draft bill referenced a Forest Service map dated July 1975 for the Boundary Waters National Recreation Area and Wilderness. Oberstar was quick to underscore the purely technical nature of the Forest Service's assistance: "The Forest Service acted as my agent in this process. It's my bill, not theirs, [but] their general reaction has been 'we like your bill; we like your idea,' because it gives them clear directives for management of the area." *Minneapolis Tribune*, Oct. 16, 1975, p. 1A, "Oberstar Proposes Bigger BWCA."

14 "I would have loved to have had more time with the people, but I knew the Chief was coming to the point of making a decision," Oberstar stated. "I had to get my bill on the public shelf before he got to that point. I also knew the wilderness crowds were here in Washington peddling a total wilderness bill . . . if I didn't move first, then we would be on the defensive." *Ely Echo*, Nov. 5, 1975, p. 1, "Forest Service Chief Lifts Snowmobile Ban."

15 *Ibid.*

16 H.R. 10247, 94th Congress, 1st Session.

17 *Congressional Record*, Oct. 20, 1975, H10116 and E5453-54.

18 Robert Buckler Interview, Dec. 22, 1987.

19 H.R. 10247, 94th Congress, 1st Session; *Congressional Record*, Oct. 20, 1975, H10116 and E5453-54.

20 *St. Paul Pioneer Press*, Nov. 4, 1975, p. 13, "BWCA Snowmobiles on Again—for Awhile"; *Duluth News-Tribune*, Nov. 4, 1975, p. 1, "Snowmobilers get BWCA Extension"; see also the editorial cartoon in the *St. Paul Dispatch*, Nov. 6, 1975, p. 8.

21 S. Stephen Chapman and eighteen others to James Oberstar, Oct. 24, 1975. See also *Minneapolis Tribune*, Nov. 4, 1975, p. 1B, "Oberstar BWCA Proposal Criticized by 16-unit Coalition."

22 James L. Oberstar to Charles K. Dayton, Oct. 31, 1975; copies in possession of authors.

23 Herbert C. Johnson to Rep. James Oberstar, Nov. 12, 1975; Herbert C. Johnson, "Plan for Creating a Quality Recreational Area Surrounding the BWCA While Preserving and Improving the BWCA Itself," Nov. 10, 1975. This proposal marked Johnson's first active involvement with BWCA wilderness activists, and he remained involved from that point on.

24 Herbst was a former executive director of the Izaak Walton League of America and a close friend of Hubert Humphrey.

25 Minnesota DNR, "Review of Current Plans for Changes in the Boundary Waters Canoe Area," Feb. 26, 1976; Minneapolis Tribune, Mar. 2, 1976, p. 8A, "DNR Urges Changes in BWCA Bill"; St. Paul Dispatch, Mar. 1, 1976, p. 1, "DNR Plan for BWCA Presented."

26 The Izaak Walton League's Wilderness Committee also continued to work on Oberstar. The committee, including Sig Olson, Bill Magie, Arnold Bolz, Dave Zentner, and Paul Toren, met in Duluth at the end of February, 1976, to discuss the Oberstar bill and the DNR proposal. At the League's annual Minnesota convention in early May, the group adopted a resolution to re-name the BWCA as the Superior Wilderness Area and to provide it with full wilderness protection. Minneapolis Tribune, May 3, 1976, "League favors changing BWCA name to Superior Wilderness Area"; Ely Echo, May 12, 1976, p. 15, "BWCA Name Change." See also minutes from the Wilderness Committee meeting, Feb. 29, 1976, copy in possession of authors.

27 See, for example, Michael Barone, Grant Ujifusa, and Douglas Matthews, The Almanac of American Politics 1976, pp. 446-447.

28 H.R. 14576, 94th Congress, 2nd Session, June 28, 1976.

29 Congressional Record, June 28, 1976, pp. 21056-59.

30 Ibid.

31 Ibid.

32 Proposed Additions to the Boundary Waters Canoe Area Wilderness (Fraser Bill, 95th Congress), Dec. 28, 1976; copy in possession of authors.

The additions included de facto wilderness areas, some of which, such as 9,100 acre Moose-Fowl Lakes addition at the far eastern tip of the BWCA, the Selke Committee had identified back in 1964 as areas to be managed like the BWCA. Other additions included South and North Lakes, Brule, Isabella, Duncan-Daniels Lakes, the Fourtown-Range River area, the Hegman Lakes, and portions of rivers such as the Sioux, Moose-Portage Rivers, Stuart, and North Kawishiwi.

33 H.R. 2820, 95th Congress, 1st Session; Congressional Record, Jan. 31, 1977, H 621-624.

34 H.R. 5968, 95th Congress, 1st Session, April 4, 1977; *Congressional Record*, Apr. 4, 1977, p. 10308.

35 *Ibid.* The bill also incorporated the airspace reservation into statutory law rather than merely authorizing the president to create a new one over the wilderness and NRA.

36 Rapson Recollections, December 1983. Fraser was then running for the seat vacated by Hubert Humphrey. See discussion below.

37 The group included Chuck Dayton, Bud Heinselman, Jan Green, Herb Johnson, Dick Flint, Paul Toren, Fern Arpi, Steve Payne, Chuck Stoddard, Dan Engstrom, Herb Wright, Jack Mauritz, Dick Wyman, and others who had participated in the BWCA logging, mining, or snowmobile controversies.

38 The Friends Executive Committee met again on June 1st at Tobies and on June 9th at the Heinselman home in St. Paul before a formal meeting with Fraser at his Minneapolis office on June 12. At this meeting the Minneapolis congressman formally agreed to sponsor a BWCA wilderness bill. Antoinette Kassim to Donald M. Fraser, May 13, 1976; *MLH Chronology*, May 15, 1976; June 1, 1976; June 9, 1976; and June 12, 1976.

39 Friends of the Boundary Waters Wilderness Press Release, June 3, 1976; *MLH Chronology*, May 7, 1976; Dan Engstrom Interview, Nov. 17, 1987. The Friends proposed to rename the BWCA as the Boundary Waters Wilderness to underscore their approach and hence the organizational name.

40 The drafting was complicated because of the highly technical nature of the mining and mineral exploration section. The drafters were forced to work around section 4(d)(5) of the Wilderness Act—which contained the Humphrey clause permitting existing uses to continue in the BWCA—in order not to diminish the precedential value of the Izaak Walton League's court decision on mining.

41 *MLH Chronology*, June 13-27, 1976.

42 A biological consultant named Dan Engstrom operated the Friends' Duluth office as Northern Vice Chair and soon became the Friends' unsalaried, but primary, staff person. Engstrom began by organizing support in northern Minnesota for the Friends' position. He instituted a speakers bureau to make presentations to Rotary, Kiwanis, and other civic organizations. He coordinated contacts with key wilderness supporters in northeastern Minnesota. He shuttled by train to the Twin Cities, where he would work several days each week from the Friends office there; his responsibilities later evolved into coordinating activities in Washington, D.C. Interview with Dan Engstrom, Nov. 17, 1987.
An associate professor of genetics and cell biology at the University of Minnesota named Bill Cunningham served as the Friends' Southern Vice Chair for the first year of the organization's existence. Cunningham had traveled the BWCA since the early 1940s as a boy of ten. He initially staffed the Friends office in the Twin Cities. See also *Ely Echo*, May 18, 1977, p. 1 "Echo Interviews 'Friends of the BWCA.'"
    Frances Heinselman, wife of Bud, served as the unofficial full-time secretary of the Friends. From the Heinselman home in St. Paul, she kept membership records, han-

dled correspondence, and organized mailings of newsletters, alerts, and posters.

Two volunteers, Erika Sitz and Barb Bader, took over the small Friends Twin Cities office in the Midland Bank Building in 1977, when Sitz succeeded Bill Cunningham as the Southern Vice Chair. Sitz increasingly served as the national BWCA clearinghouse, coordinating the growing number of contacts from around the country.

Darby Nelson, an aquatic biologist and professor at Anoka-Ramsey Community College, was the Friends' treasurer, bailing out the organization on a number of occasions early in its existence with his own money.

43 The Friends, while trying to nationalize the BWCA issue, also developed and maintained a number of ties with residents in northeastern Minnesota who would be key contacts in the local area: Harry Drabik of Hovland, owner of Pigeon River Outfitters in the Grand Marais area; Bill and Barb Rom of Ely, who had just retired from Bill Rom's Canoe Country Outfitters; Bob and Janice Conklin of Cook; Jon and Dan Waters of Canadian Waters outfitters in Ely; Jim Cherry, Director of Wilderness Canoe Base on Seagull Lake at the end of the Gunflint Trail; Fern Arpi of Virginia; Fred and Pam Thompson of Brimson; and Sig and Elizabeth Olson of Ely.

44 See Tom Harkin, "National Significance of the Boundary Waters Wilderness Act," *Congressional Record*, May 19, 1978, p. 14724 (describing Proescholdt and the Christou Canoe camping program).

45 A similar petition drive by the Minnesota Public Interest Research Group netted 11,000 signatures. *Minnesota Daily*, June 2, 1977, "11,000 Petition for Fraser BWCA Bill."

46 See, for example, Iowa PIRG alert, Jan. 19, 1977; Iowa PIRG alert, June 20, 1977; Iowa PIRG alert, July 12, 1977; Iowa PIRG alert, July 27, 1977; Christou Canoe alert, Aug. 8, 1977; Iowa PIRG alert, Jan. 19, 1978; Iowa PIRG press release, Feb. 10, 1978; Iowa PIRG Action Alert, Apr. 24, 1978; Iowa PIRG update, Oct. 1978; Iowa PIRG alert, Nov. 4, 1978. See also Kevin Proescholdt, "Boundary Waters Needs Help," *Iowa PIRG Gazette*, Mar. 1977, p. 2; Kevin Proescholdt, "Boundary Waters Update," *Iowa PIRG Gazette*, April/May 1977, p. 1; *Iowa State Daily*, Sept. 20, 1977, p. 1, "Expect Bill to 'Save' Boundary Waters"; Kevin Proescholdt, "Boundary Waters Protection Near," *Iowa PIRG Gazette*, Fall 1977, p. 1; Kevin Proescholdt, "Congress Moves on BWCA Bill," *Iowa PIRG Gazette*, May 1978, p. 2; Kevin Proescholdt, "New Threat Dampens BWCA Victory," *Iowa PIRG Prairie Fire*, Jan. 1979, p. 1; Iowa PIRG BWCA petition; Iowa PIRG BWCA flier, fall 1976; Iowa PIRG BWCA fundraiser flier, March 14, 1977. Copies in possession of authors.

Iowa PIRG also raised money for the Friends, sent a delegation to a Friends strategy workshop in the Twin Cities in April 1977, testified at BWCA congressional field hearings and lobbied in Washington, D.C.

47 One Iowa co-sponsor of the Fraser Bill was Berkley Bedell, a fishing tackle manufacturer who had once owned a cabin on Trout Lake; that cabin was purchased and removed from the BWCA under the Thye-Blatnik Act.

48 The Friends also used rallies and demonstrations as means of publicizing the BWCA issue and gaining public support. For example, the environmentalists held two rallies on

the steps of the State Capitol in St. Paul, the first in July 1977 in conjunction with the congressional field hearing, and the second the following May, featuring congressmen Don Fraser and Bruce Vento and octogenarian wilderness advocate Paul Clement. On April 21, 1978, 200 Friends protesters also picketed a John Denver concert at the St. Paul Civic Center, which was a fund raiser for Senator Wendell Anderson's Senate campaign. *Minnesota Daily*, May 22, 1978, "BWCA Defenders Rally for Burton-Vento"; *Minneapolis Tribune*, Apr. 22, 1978, p. 1A, "200 Picket Denver for Backing Anderson."

49 See, for example, the East Coast Advocates of the Boundary Waters Wilderness newsletters of Sept. 1, 1977; Oct. 25, 1977; Jan. 30, 1978; and May 18, 1978; copies in possession of authors.

    Some of the affiliates of the East Coast Advocates had emerged from a special mailing from Herb Wright and Heinselman in 1977. Wright and Heinselman had written to several hundred scientists who were members of the Ecological Society of America, describing the ecological value of the BWCA's virgin forests, explaining the need for federal legislation, and asking for their support. See M.L. Heinselman and H.E. Wright, Jr., to Fellow Ecologist, May 2, 1977; copy in possession of authors. This mailing produced support well beyond the east coast. Among those who lent their support to the Friends were: Dr. Estella Leopold (a daughter of Aldo Leopold) and Dr. Harold C. Fritts, a professor of dendrochronology at the University of Arizona-Tucson.

50 Both presentations were developed by a professional film-maker named Fred Thompson, who also happened to be a Friends member. Thompson himself marketed the Olson tape extensively in schools and toured the East Coast at his own expense to generate support for the bill.

51 Friends 1977 brochure, copy in possession of authors. This brochure was produced as a contribution by the Martin-Williams advertising firm.

52 Candace Luecke, North Star Chapter of the Sierra Club, to Forest Supervisor James Torrence, May 14, 1976; Curtis L. Smith, Acting Regional Forester to Candace Luecke, May 28, 1976; copies in possession of authors.

53 "Your Boundary Waters Canoe Area Wilderness Needs Help, Now!" Friends of the Boundary Waters Wilderness, Educational Note Number One, Aug. 1976.

54 The Forest Service reacted to this use of the Freedom of Information Act request by dropping the address box from their permit form the following year. They later reinstated the request for visitor addresses, however.

55 "List of Organizations and Groups Endorsing the Fraser Bill or Advocating Full Wilderness Status for the Boundary Waters Canoe Area," Jan. 30, 1978.

56 The Friends highlighted and honored many of these influential wilderness "elders of the tribe" at a well-attended St. Paul party in December of 1977.

    The wilderness elder statesmen also drew in a younger generation of activists. Perhaps the best example was the Bill Rom family of Ely. Bill Rom, Sr., had fought for wilderness all his life with Sig Olson and Bill Magie; his children Bill, Jr., Becky, and Roger all testified at hearings and lobbied in Washington with the Friends. See *Minneapolis Tribune*, Dec. 14, 1975, p. 1F, "Canoe outfitter slips into quieter waters."

57 Among those who attended were: Laurel and Gladys Bennett, former resort owners of Canadian Border Lodge; resort owners from the Grand Marais area; Loren Filter, president of the International Snowmobile Association; Herb Anderson, St. Louis County Grants-in-Aid Coordinator; and Ruth Ericson of the Northeastern Minnesota Environmental Economic Council. *Ely Echo*, June 1, 1977, p. 1, "Oberstar Supporters Organize to Fight For BWCA Bill"; *Ely Miner*, June 15, 1977, p. 1, "An Interview With Former Oberstar Aid Bob Buckler"; *Duluth News-Tribune*, June 16, 1977, p. 2A, "Foes of Friends Unite"; Zabinski Paper, p. 12; Zabinski Interview, Dec. 21, 1987.

58 Zabinski Paper, pp. 13, 18.

59 Articles of Incorporation, Boundary Waters Conservation Alliance, July 25, 1977.

60 Zabinski Paper, p. 12; Zabinski Interview, Dec. 21, 1987.

61 In the words of Zabinski, the second executive director, "Neither the Alliance nor the industry wanted the organization perceived as a front for the industry." Zabinski Paper, pp. 12, 18.

62 The Oberstar bill closed both Sucker and Ensign Lakes to motorboats, two routes favored by the Moose Lake resorts. *Ely Miner*, July 6, 1977, p. 1, "Pending BWCA Bills Embitter Moose Lake Resorters."

63 See Uel Blank, Larry Simonson, and Dayton Larsen, "Minnesota's Resort-Tourism in Critical Transition," *Minnesota Tourist Travel Notes* 15(2), Fall 1977, pp. 1-12; *Duluth News-Tribune*, July 31, 1977, p. 1B, "Resorting: Lifestyle, Not a Living."

64 *Ely Miner*, July 6, 1977, p. 1, "Pending BWCA Bills Embitter Moose Lake Resorters." For a treatment of the motorboat issue, see James Gladden, *Boundary Waters Canoe Area: Wilderness Values and Motorized Recreation* (Ames: Iowa State University Press, 1990).

65 Heinselman once remarked: "It's hard to stay mad at Justine—she's the real item." Rapson Recollections, December 1983.

66 *Duluth News-Tribune*, July 3, 1977, p. 5D, "In Ely, Neither Smacks of Popularity"; *Ely Miner*, July 6, 1977, p. 1, "Disagreements Surface at 'Alliance' Meeting."

67 Shirley Klaesges letter to the editor, *Ely Echo*, Aug. 3, 1977.

68 The steelworkers organized a picket of Fraser's Minneapolis office in October 1977 and utilized political connections within the AFL-CIO in an attempt to influence key members of Congress. Zabinski Interview, Dec. 21, 1987.

69 *Duluth News-Tribune*, Feb. 10, 1978, p.1, "Ely Man May Cut Trees on BWCA Land." The Kainz brothers were Norman, Leo, and Ray; Norman wrote an outspoken column for the *Ely Echo*. The two sales contracted by Northern Forest Products were the East Tofte and West Tofte Sales, both within the BWCA.

70 Zabinski Paper, pp. 12, 14. The selection of Lake County Board Chair Lenore Johnson to head the Alliance's key legislative committee (she later served as Alliance president) was a careful choice in this regard. The Alliance hoped that she, as an impartial public official not tied to either Ely or Grand Marais, would show no favoritism to any one community.

71 Zabinski Paper, pp. 13-14.

72 On the eve of the July field hearings in Ely, for example, the Echo reported "an air of resigned futility in town." *Ely Echo*, July 6, 1977, p. 1, "U.S. Congressmen in Ely Friday for BWCA Hearings." Local residents, the paper noted, felt that appearing before the subcommittee would change very little: "What is most frustrating to the people in the area is that they feel neither bill addresses the current problems of the Boundary Waters Canoe Area. And the people of Ely are getting very tired of being labeled 'local, selfish interest' opposed to wilderness management." *Ely Echo*, July 6, 1977, p. 1, "U.S. Congressmen in Ely Friday for BWCA Hearings."

73 Unlike the Friends, the Alliance did not begin a regular newsletter to its members until the summer of 1978. See, for example, the Boundary Waters Conservation Alliance brochure, circa spring 1978; "Voices In The Wilderness," Boundary Waters Conservation Alliance newsletter for June 1978, July 1978, Aug./Sept. 1978, Oct./Nov. 1978, Nov./Dec. 1978.

74 Resorters and outfitters also often asked their customers, some of whom came from all over the country, to write letters on their behalf. See "Future for the Boundary Waters Canoe Area: A Look in Perspective," statement by Edward M. Zabinski at the Wisconsin Park and Recreation Association, Nov. 2, 1978, p. 4.

The Alliance relied heavily on form letters. See, for example, Form Letter to Bruce Vento; copy in possession of authors.

75 The Alliance sought resolutions of support from local governmental units, Chambers of Commerce, labor union locals, veterans groups like the 8th District American Legion and VFW, Minnesota special education directors, and seniors groups like the Minnesota Senior Federation. See, for example, *Duluth Herald*, Jan. 25, 1977, "Oberstar BWCA Bill Supported by Legion"; *Duluth Herald*, Mar. 23, 1977, p. 2A, "State Seniors Back Oberstar on BWCA Bill"; Duane Googins, President of the Minnesota Administrators of Special Education, to Cong. James Oberstar, Apr. 11, 1978, found in *Congressional Record*, Apr. 25, 1978, p. 11516-11517; Frank Volk, VFW Commander for the Eighth District of Minnesota, to Minnesota Senators and Representatives, May 28, 1978, found in *Congressional Record*, May 31, 1978, p. 15832.

76 The Alliance's lobbying strategy was a powerful antidote to the appeals of the Friends. The Alliance was able to send to Washington those very people it claimed the Fraser bill would hurt. These personal testimonials were unquestionably effective.

77 For example, the timber industry produced a slide show, which it used for presentations around the state. The presentation included photos of rolls of toilet paper on a store

shelf (demonstrating the need to log the BWCA in order to keep paper products in adequate supply) and one of a burned deer (showing the need to "manage" forests in order to reduce fire hazards to wildlife).

78 One of the Alliance's most effective petition drives came during the opening weekend of fishing season in May 1978. Alliance activist Ted Young organized the drive to meet incoming fishermen along roads and highways in the Ely and Gunflint Trail areas. The Alliance secured almost 10,000 supporting signatures in this effort. *Ely Echo*, May 10, 1978, p. 2, "Alliance To Picket This Week"; *Ely Echo*, May 17, 1978, p. 1, "Highway Pickets Get 10,000 Signatures."

79 The estimates come from Ed Zabinski, the Alliance's second Executive Director (Zabinski, see footnote 74).

80 See *Minneapolis Tribune*, Oct. 6, 1977, p. 2B, "Rep. Fraser Picketed for Stand on BWCA"; *Duluth News-Tribune*, Jan. 15, 1978, p. 1, "15 Snowmobilers Face Charges after Protest Ride into BWCA"; *Minneapolis Tribune*, Apr. 15, 1978, p. 15A, "City Cuts Off Electricity to Protest BWCA Bill"; *Duluth News-Tribune*, June 4, 1978, p. 1, "BWCA Issue Sparks, Fails to Light"; *Minneapolis Tribune*, Aug. 6, 1978, p. 1A, "Angry BWCA Area Residents Block Roads, Vent Frustration"; *St. Paul Pioneer Press*, Aug. 6, 1978, p. 1, "Ely-Area Residents Block BWCA"; *Ely Miner*, Aug. 9, 1978, p. 1, "BWCA Lockout Stays Non-violent."

81 See Herbert E. Wright, Jr., to Jeffrey Knight (Friends of the Earth), Feb. 9,1977; in Herbert E. Wright, Jr., Papers.

82 Another Wilderness Society staffer, Dave Foreman, provided BWCA back-up for Payne during crucial occasions. Foreman would later form Earth First! (and eventually the journal *Wild Earth*) and become a nationally recognized leader in the preservation of wild lands.

83 Two staff members from the Sierra Club's Midwest regional office in Madison also played key roles. Jonathan Ela and Trish Record lobbied in Washington, testified at hearings, and kept the channels of communication within the Club filled with updates on the BWCA dispute.

84 The Izaak Walton League of America had maintained a decades-long presence on issues affecting the BWCA, going back to the very beginnings of the League in the 1920s and the roadbuilding and dam controversies.

85 The Minnesota chapters of the Audubon Society were particularly active. Jan Green and the Duluth Audubon Society sponsored a photographic exhibit on wilderness that traveled throughout northern Minnesota in the spring and early summer of 1977. See "Wilderness—as Friend and Enemy," brochure of the Duluth Audubon Society, March 1977; "Wilderness in Time and place," booklet of the Duluth Audubon Society, March 1977.

      Audubon's regional director Ed Brigham and Minneapolis members Marv Borell and Rick Glanz also helped galvanize grass roots Audubon support in Minnesota. In

Washington, staffer Steve Young helped with strategy and lobbying.

86 Herb Wright wrote to David Brower, president of Friends of the Earth, in December 1975 seeking the organization's support and involvement; the organization appointed him as the FOE's official representative on the BWCA. Dr. Wright quickly began representing the organization in a flurry of involvement and correspondence. See Herbert E. Wright, Jr., to David R. Brower, Dec. 30, 1975; and Chuck Williams (FOE) to Herbert E. Wright, Jr., Jan. 16, 1976; in Herbert E. Wright, Jr., Papers.

87 These included *Sierra* (the Sierra Club's magazine), *The Living Wilderness* (the Wilderness Society), *National Parks & Conservation Magazine* (National Parks and Conservation Association), *Outdoor America* (Izaak Walton League of America), *Not Man Apart* (Friends of the Earth), *Conservation News* (the National Wildlife Federation), *Audubon* (the National Audubon Society), and *Parks & Recreation* (National Recreation and Park Association). *Canoe*, *Outside*, and *Mariah*, other national outdoors magazines, also ran feature articles on the BWCA.

   See, for example, Patricia Record, "The Boundary-Waters Compromise," *Sierra Club Bulletin*, Oct. 1976, p. 47; Patricia S. Record, "The Question of Quiet Lakes," *Sierra*, May 1978, p. 37; Miron L. Heinselman, "Crisis in the Canoe Country," *The Living Wilderness*, Jan/Mar. 1977, pp. 12-24, plus Steve Payne's updates in *Wilderness Report*; Dean Rebuffoni, "Confusion at Boundary Waters Canoe Area," *National Parks & Conservation Magazine*, Jan. 1977, pp. 12-16, plus later shorter updates; Miron Heinselman and Michael Horn, "Boundary Waters In 1977," *Outdoor America*, Feb. 1977, p. 1, 6-7; Sigurd Olson, "Looking Back at Outdoor America," *Outdoor America*, April 1977, p. 14; "Boundary Waters Canoe Area," *Outdoor America*, June-July 1977, pp. 18-20, 28; Justin Isherwood, "Boundary Waters, A Romance," *Outdoor America*, Oct.-Nov. 1977, pp. 8-9; Carol Dana, "Congress Moves to Calm the Stormy Boundary Waters," *Parks & Recreation*, April 1978, pp. 30-36, 54; H.E. Wright, Jr., "The BWCA: A Wilderness Ecosystem in Need of Protection," *Conservation News* (National Wildlife Federation), May 1, 1977, pp. 1-5; Paul Brooks, "A Roadless Area Revisited," *Audubon*, March 1975, pp. 28-37; H.E. Wright, Jr., "Motors and Saws Threaten Boundary Waters Area," *Not Man Apart* (Friends of the Earth), Sept. 1976; H.E. Wright, Jr., "In Canoe Country," *Not Man Apart* (Friends of the Earth), May 1977, pp. 1-2; Karen Sonderegger, "BWCA: An Endangered Species," *Canoe*, May-June 1976, pp. 30-31, 34-35; Andrew Jaffe, "Outboard Politics In Canoe Country," *Outside*, Nov. 1977, pp. 68-75, with accompanying editorial by Jack Ford; Tom Gorton, "Getting to the Bottom of the Boundary Waters," *Mariah*, April-May, 1978, pp. 26-35; and Tom Gorton, "What shall be the fate of the Boundary Waters?" *Planning* (American Society of Planning Officials), Sept. 1977, pp. 10-16.

88 *Minneapolis Tribune*, April 1, 1977, p. 12A, "More land-use data sought on BWCA." Humphrey enlisted the help of an old friend within the Congressional Research Office, Robert Wolf, to prepare the study.

89 Rapson Recollections, December 1983.

90 Robert E. Wolf to Hubert H. Humphrey, Mar. 30, 1977, 4 pp.; Hubert Humphrey to Minnesota Delegation, Apr. 19, 1977; copies in possession of authors.

91 Rapson Recollections, December 1983.

92 Humphrey was not the only one whose attempts to broker a compromise fell flat.

The Environmental Balance Association, a timber industry-backed organization, attempted to interest the Friends in mediating the wilderness controversy. Robert Matteson, founder of Northland College's Sigurd Olson Environmental Institute and the last chairman of the President's Quetico-Superior Committee, approached Bud Heinselman in the spring of 1977 about the Environmental Balance Association on behalf of David Fradin, the association's executive vice-president. On May 25 the association sent the Friends a formal invitation to participate in a Fraser-Oberstar forum. Although neither Fraser nor the Friends attended, Rapson did. The forum, entitled "The Future of the Boundary Waters Canoe Area," was held on August 25 at the St. Paul campus of the University of Minnesota and included a panel discussion of university professors discussing economic and environmental impacts of the competing pieces of legislation. Nothing came of the discussion. *MLH Chronology*, Mar. 17, 1977; May 25, 1977; BWCA Issues Forum Program, Aug. 25, 1977. Matteson later resigned from the EBA, charging a lack of environmental input; see, for example, *Duluth News-Tribune* editorial, Feb. 9, 1978, p. 6D, "A Place for the EBA."

The Governor also tried to get into the act. Perpich's aide, Bud Philbrook, attempted in July 1977 to arrange a negotiating session between Oberstar, Fraser, and their supporters to develop a consensus bill on the BWCA. Philbrook indicated that Perpich could serve as an intermediary and threatened an effort by Oberstar, Humphrey, and the Minnesota legislature to kill the Fraser Bill if the Friends refused to cooperate. Again, all of this came to naught. *MLH Chronology*, July 13, 1977.

93 The Alliance would play on this theme over the next months. In one brochure, it stated that the Forest Service could not be trusted because "[t]he current head of the Forest Service, Assistant Secretary of Agriculture Rupert Cutler, is a past president of the Wilderness Society." Boundary Waters Conservation Alliance brochure, circa spring 1978; copy in possession of the authors. Though Cutler did work for the Wilderness Society at one time, he was never the organization's president.

94 This attitude was typified by former Superior Forest Supervisor Harold E. "Andy" Anderson, who opposed any changes in the BWCA's management that would involve curtailment of BWCA logging. A widely quoted Forest Service report prepared by the Superior Forest staff, for example, claimed that closing the Portal Zone of the BWCA to logging would mean a loss of 1,190 jobs and thirty million dollars. See letter of John R. McGuire to Phillip Burton, Sept. 12, 1977; copy in possession of authors. Although the Friends contested these conclusions, the Forest Service continued to refer to this report throughout the congressional debate.

95 *MLH Chronology*, Dec. 7 and 16, 1976. See *Duluth News-Tribune*, Dec. 7, 1976, p. 1, "Loggers snort at shutdown plea"; *Minneapolis Star*, Dec. 7, 1976, p. 2B, "BWCA logging

delay urged."

96 The Friends did turn to allies within Congress, but with equally disappointing results. For example, Congressman Tom Harkin of Iowa sought to convince a close friend on the House Agriculture Committee, Jim Weaver of Oregon, that the committee should act on the timber sales. Weaver declined to intervene.

97 *Minneapolis Tribune*, Dec. 21, 1976, p. 1A, "4 Logging Firms Agree to Delay Cutting in BWCA"; *Washington Star*, Dec. 21, 1976, "Minn. Wilderness Given Reprieve from Timbering."

98 Although the House Speaker never overtly took sides or formally weighed in on the referral question, there was widespread speculation among the environmentalists that he had made a friendly arrangement with Oberstar. If he did, it did not affect the outcome of this particular fight. Rapson Recollections, December 1983.

99 Even this was largely a formality—it was increasingly the practice that extensions of remarks could be included in the *Congressional Record* without having first made a floor statement.

100 Rapson ended up preparing some twenty-five of these inserts. Viewed as a group, they provide a good roadmap to the major issues of the controversy. See Donald M. Fraser, "The Boundary Waters Wilderness Act," *Congressional Record*, Feb. 23, 1977, E919-20; Donald M. Fraser, "The Boundary Waters Wilderness Act—The Need for Congressional Action," *Congressional Record*, March 28, 1977, pp. 9301-03; Donald M. Fraser, "The Boundary Waters Wilderness Act—The Problem of Access for Senior Citizens and Handicapped Persons," *Congressional Record*, Apr. 6, 1977, pp. 10814-17; Donald M. Fraser, "Crisis in the Canoe Country," *Congressional Record*, Apr. 26, 1977, H3612-16; Donald M. Fraser, "The Boundary Waters Wilderness Act," *Congressional Record*, June 7, 1977, pp. 17881-83; Donald M. Fraser, "In Canoe Country," *Congressional Record*, June 9, 1977, E3636-37; Donald M. Fraser, "The Boundary Waters Canoe Area: A Unique Wilderness' Uncertain Fate," *Congressional Record*, June 23, 1977, pp. 20671-72; Michael T. Blouin, "Boundary Waters Canoe Area," *Congressional Record*, Sept. 8, 1977, E5421-22; Donald M. Fraser, "Boundary Waters, A Romance," *Congressional Record*, Oct. 13, 1977, pp. 33752-53; Donald M. Fraser, "The Boundary Waters Canoe Area Controversy," *Congressional Record*, Oct. 26, 1977, p. 35364; Donald M. Fraser, "Handicapped Access to the Boundary Waters Canoe Area," *Congressional Record*, Oct. 27, 1977, pp. 35612-13; Donald M. Fraser, "The Boundary Waters Canoe Area: A Continuing Controversy," *Congressional Record*, Jan. 25, 1978, pp. 917-18; Donald M. Fraser, "The BWCA—A Wilderness Well Suited to Use by the Elderly and Handicapped," *Congressional Record*, Jan. 30, 1978; Donald M. Fraser, "The BWCA: A Summary of the Central Issues," *Congressional Record*, Feb. 2, 1978, pp. 2158-59; Donald M. Fraser, "Iowa Support for the Boundary Waters Wilderness Act," *Congressional Record*, Apr. 24, 1978, pp. 11262-64; Donald M. Fraser, "Illinois Support for the Boundary Waters Wilderness Act," *Congressional Record*, May 2, 1978, pp. 12281-82; Donald M. Fraser, "Wisconsin Support for the Boundary Waters Wilderness Act," *Congressional Record*, May

4, 1978, pp. 12718-19; Donald M. Fraser, "The Boundary Waters Wilderness Act—Sigurd Olson's Unique Role—Part I," *Congressional Record*, May 9, 1978, pp. 13123-24; Donald M. Fraser, "The Boundary Waters Wilderness Act: Sigurd Olson's Unique Role—Part II," *Congressional Record*, May 16, 1978, pp. 14002-03; Michael T. Blouin, "Misconceptions About the Boundary Waters Wilderness Act," *Congressional Record*, May 18, 1978, pp. 14533-34; Bruce F. Vento, "Use of the BWCA," *Congressional Record*, May 19, 1978, pp. 14717-18; Tom Harkin, "National Significance of the Boundary Waters Wilderness Act," *Congressional Record*, May 19, 1978, p. 14724; Donald M. Fraser, "The Boundary Waters Wilderness Act: Sigurd Olson's Unique Role—Part III," *Congressional Record*, May 23, 1978, pp. 15157-58; Jim Leach, "Protection for the Boundary Waters Canoe Area," *Congressional Record*, June 1, 1978, p. 16021; Bruce F. Vento, "Protection for Boundary Waters Canoe Area," *Congressional Record*, Oct. 11, 1978, p. 35933.

101 See James L. Oberstar, "The Boundary Waters Canoe Area: A Workable Solution," *Congressional Record*, Aug. 5, 1977, pp. 27765-67; James L. Oberstar, "Timber Harvesting in the BWCA," *Congressional Record*, Dec. 15, 1977, pp. 39635-37; James L. Oberstar, "What is at Stake in the BWCA," *Congressional Record*, Dec. 15, 1977, pp. 39741-42; James L. Oberstar, "Boundary Waters Canoe Area," *Congressional Record*, Jan. 26, 1978, p. 1193; James L. Oberstar, "Columnist Discusses Minnesota's Recreation Area," *Congressional Record*, Apr. 13, 1978, pp. 10185-86; James L. Oberstar, "Special Education Directors in Minnesota Support Oberstar BWCA Proposal," *Congressional Record*, Apr. 25, 1978, pp. 11516-17; James L. Oberstar, "Support for New BWCA Proposal," *Congressional Record*, Apr. 27, 1978, pp. 11841-42; James L. Oberstar, "Changes in BWCA Bill Narrow Differences," *Congressional Record*, May 18, 1978, pp. 14512-13; James L. Oberstar, "Strong Community Response to BWCA Legislation," *Congressional Record*, May 18, 1978, pp. 14515-16; James L. Oberstar, "Eighth District VFW Supports Oberstar Bill," *Congressional Record*, May 31, 1978, p. 15832; James L. Oberstar, "Ander-son-Humphrey Bill: Reasonable BWCA Proposal," *Congressional Record*, July 14, 1978, p. 21100; James L. Oberstar, "Spirit of Compromise Needed for BWCA," *Congressional Record*, July 28, 1978, p. 23311.

102 The *Milwaukee Sentinel* declared that "[t]here's nothing quite like the BWCA anywhere else in the world" and claimed that the Oberstar bill "would be another chip cut in the trunk as the BWCA slowly is chopped down."*Milwaukee Sentinel*, June 4, 1977, p. 10, "Preserve Unique Boundary Waters." The *Chicago Daily News* urged Congress to "keep the wilderness wild" and concluded that the BWCA "is for everyone who is willing to meet the wilderness on its own terms." *Chicago Daily News*, July 25, 1977, p. 12, "Keep the Wilderness Wild." The *New York Times* concluded that "no wilderness is enhanced by the internal combustion engine." *New York Times*, May 21, 1978, "Making Change: The Wild Ones." The *Chicago Tribune* cast its vote for "one unique, very special quiet wilderness." *Chicago Tribune*, April 18, 1977, Sec. 2, p. 4, "The Boundary Waters' Future."
      See also *Chicago Tribune*, July 19, 1978, Sec. 5, p. 2, "For One Quiet Wilderness"; *Milwaukee Journal*, March 30, 1978, "Preserving a Splendid Wilderness"; *Des Moines Register*, Jan. 6, 1977, p. 8A, "Delay on Logging"; Richard Liefer, "Boundary Waters Wilderness: Local vs. National Interest," *Des Moines Register*, July 23, 1977, p. 6A;

Des Moines Register, Jan. 2, 1978, p. 10A, "Compromise on BWCA"; *Des Moines Register*, April 8, 1978, p. 6A, "Plus for Preservation"; *Des Moines Register*, June 26, 1978, p. 6A, "Troubled Boundary Waters"; *Des Moines Register*, Oct. 9, 1978, p. 8A, "Compromise on BWCA"; *Des Moines Register*, Oct. 23, 1978, p. 8A, "Treasure Preserved"; and the editorial cartoon by Frank Miller in *Des Moines Register*, Aug. 25, 1978, p. 1A. For an example of other favorable coverage from Iowa newspapers, see, e.g., *Oelwein Daily Register*, Jan. 26, 1978.

103 See, for example, Thomas Love, "'Woodsman, Spare That Tree' Rings in Minnesota," *Washington Star*, Dec. 18, 1976; Phil Shabecoff, "Wilderness Plan Rouses Minnesota Lake Country And Poses Hard Questions About Land Use Policy," *New York Times*, July 28, 1977; Margot Hornblower, "Fate of a Unique Wilderness About To Be Determined" and "Turning Back the Clock to Primeval America," *Washington Post*, June 19, 1977, p. A16; *Time*, Sept. 11, 1978, pp. 64-66, "Storm Over Voyageur's Country"; Austin C. Wehrwein, "Minnesota Canoe Area Center of Ecology Debate,"*Christian Science Monitor*, Oct. 20, 1977, p. 12; Barth Falkenberg, "Storms over quiet waters," *Christian Science Monitor*, July 21, 1978; William Oscar Johnson, "Passionate Suitors for a Wild Paradise," *Sports Illustrated*, Oct. 10, 1977, pp. 50-58; Harold R. Kennedy, "A Noisy Environmental Fight Over A Quiet Wilderness," *U.S. News & World Report*, Oct. 31, 1977.

104 Across the river, the *St. Paul Pioneer Press* and the *St. Paul Dispatch* covered the BWCA frequently in editorials and news stories. But it was the Minneapolis reporters who most consistently developed the background stories that conveyed the fullest picture of events.

105 For an example of Al McConagha's early BWCA news stories, see the article he wrote on Bud Heinselman urging an end to BWCA logging during the Selke Committee debate, *Minneapolis Tribune*, June 13, 1964, p. 16, "End Urged to Tree Cutting in Canoe Area."

106 In addition to his news stories for the *Minneapolis Tribune*, Rebuffoni wrote in-depth articles on the BWCA for other publications. See, for example, Dean Rebuffoni, "Confusion at Boundary Waters Canoe Area," *National Parks & Conservation Magazine*, Jan. 1977, pp. 12-16.

107 As examples of Jim Klobuchar's columns on the BWCA in the *Minneapolis Star* in 1978 alone, see "Threats in the Canoe Dispute," Mar. 27, 1978; "A Calm Dialogue with Jeno," Apr. 11, 1978; "Short auditions his campaign speeches," Apr. 15, 1978; "The Land of Sky-Blue Hostages," Apr. 20, 1978; "The Wrong Numbers on the BWCA," Apr. 28, 1978; "No Bloodshed for Fraser at the Falls," May 8, 1978; "Not everybody is raging up north," May 12, 1978; "One way to buy loyalty for the DFL," June 1, 1978; "Anderson gives them what they want," June 5, 1978; "The pious season in political ads," June 13, 1978; "Republicans vs. bravery on the BWCA," June 26, 1978; "The senators tour the BWCA," July 14, 1978; "The Boundary Waters bleeds some more," Aug. 1, 1978; "A new friend of the wilderness," Aug. 4, 1978; "One way to define a tragedy," Sept. 14, 1978; "The dilemma of a young voter," Sept. 21, 1978; "The last days for a bill to save BWCA," Oct. 12, 1978; and "Should all politicians be toads?" Oct. 17, 1978.

108 *Duluth News-Tribune* editorial, June 29, 1976, p. 18A, "Fraser's Folly."

109 See *Duluth Sunday News-Tribune* editorial, Oct. 19, 1975, p. 46, "BWCA Compromise"(on the introduction of the first Oberstar bill).

110 *Duluth News-Tribune* editorial, June 29, 1976, p. 18A, "Fraser's Folly." The editorial page speculated that Fraser might be trying to do Oberstar an implicit favor by making Oberstar's proposal look so good.

111 *Duluth Sunday News-Tribune* editorial, Oct. 19, 1975, p. 46, "BWCA Compromise."

112 *MLH Chronology*, Feb. 12, 1977.

113 *Duluth News-Tribune* editorial, July 7, 1977, p. 8D, "New BWCA Law."

114 *Duluth News-Tribune* editorial, Jan. 4, 1978, p. 1B, "One Use is Enough." In addition, the paper would later editorially condemn the snowmobile protest ride and support the Burton-Vento compromise measure. See *Duluth News-Tribune* editorial, Feb. 10, 1978, p. 12B, "Bum Public Relations"; and *Duluth News-Tribune* editorial, March 18, 1978, p. 1B, "Good BWCA Bill."

115 *Ely Miner*, June 22, 1977, p. 1, "Bud Heinselman Says Wilderness Protection is Best for BWCA"; see also *Ely Miner*, June 15, 1977, p. 1, "An Interview With Former Oberstar Aid Bob Buckler."

116 Although even the *Echo* did have an occasional lapse. It did run an interview, for example, with Friends Southern Vice-Chair Bill Cunningham. *Ely Echo*, May 18, 1977, p. 1, "Echo Interviews 'Friends of BWCA.'" The interview was conducted by Doug Smith, however, not Bob Cary.

117 Justine Kerfoot, "On the Gunflint Trail," *Cook County News-Herald*, Dec. 1, 1977, p. 3.

118 Kerfoot wrote about Jim Cherry, Director of the Wilderness Canoe Base:
> Last fall, the Rev. James Cherry spent many hours trying to convince the Al Danielsons of Sea Gull, Don Enzenauer of Sea Gull River, homeowners on Sea Gull Lake, and anyone else he could buttonhole, that the Heinzelman-Fraser [sic] bill was the route everyone should take. . . . No mention was made on motor use on peripheral lakes, which means the survival or downfall of several resorts.

Ibid.

119 *Chisholm Free Press*, Feb. 9, 1978, p. 2, "Exploitation or Preservation!"; *Hibbing Daily Tribune*, Mar. 23, 1978, p. 10, "BWCA compromise."

Chapter Three

Shift to the House Subcommittee

The Chairman

Phil Burton was once likened to a cross between Lyndon Johnson, Cesar Chavez, and Chairman Mao. He was a master of political log rolling and infighting, deeply passionate about social justice, propelled by a single-mindedness of purpose that left little room for those who stood in his way.

He was a bear of a man, well over six feet tall, heavyset, with a deep booming voice. He could explode without notice, only to put his arm around you a moment later when he had made his point. In the words of one observer:

> [Burton is a] wily veteran of a thousand political intrigues [with] the body of an aging longshoreman and the instincts of a waterfront brawler. [Possessing] legendary anger and volcanic passion, [he is] one of the House's master legislators—a man whose relentless drive for power has roiled the Democratic leadership pot for years. [He is] a legislative titan who has engineered sweeping environmental, civil rights and other social legislation for over two decades.[1]

Phillip Burton ruled the Subcommittee on National Parks and Insular Affairs as a benevolent despot. (*Photo by Kevin Proescholdt*)

Burton represented the most

107

progressive slice of San Francisco. His politics were the politics of labor, the gay community, senior citizens. And it was the politics of the environmental community. With the Sierra Club's national headquarters located in San Francisco, Burton had developed close personal friendships with key Sierra Club leaders. It was one reason he had chosen his subcommittee assignment. It may have been the only reason: he would often joke that his version of a wilderness experience was having to get out of the car in Golden Gate Park to walk to the drinking fountain.

His exercise of power politics in the House was legendary. He horse-traded a concession here for a concession there, fashioning coalitions on an endless variety of issues. He used a prodigious memory to advantage. He took great pride, for example, in knowing the home congressional district of every major cotton producer and distributor in the South, the kind of knowledge that enabled him to find exactly the right trade necessary to bring conservative southern "Boll Weevils" into a coalition with their liberal colleagues from the North.

When he entered Congress in 1964, Burton went to work to demonstrate his election theme: "I'm a fighting liberal." He attacked the House Un-American Activities Committee. He openly opposed the Vietnam War well before others came to that view. He helped establish the cost-of-living adjustment for Social Security recipients, raise the minimum wage, and improve benefits for the elderly and people with disabilities. He fought for benefits for miners suffering from black lung disease, supported civil rights legislation, and became a recognized expert on welfare legislation such as food stamps.[2]

He took these issues on with a style that was direct and confrontational. He held intense personal loyalties and cultivated intense personal antagonisms. He earned a reputation for arrogance, suffering poorly or not at all people he regarded as enemies or idiots.

In a campaign that typified all these characteristics, Burton ran for House Majority Leader in 1977, when Tip O'Neill vacated that position to succeed Carl Albert as House Speaker.[3]

It was a crowded field: John McFall of California, the House Whip and favorite of Speaker-Elect O'Neill; Richard Bolling, a highly respected moderate from Missouri; and Jim Wright of Texas, like Burton, a horse-trading, story-telling infighter.

Burton led on the first ballot, with 106 votes to Bolling's 81, Wright's 77, and McFall's 31. Embarrassed by his inability to translate O'Neill's support into a stronger showing, McFall withdrew.

The scrambling for re-alignment was intense prior to the second ballot. The Bolling camp believed that if their candidate could knock off Wright on the second ballot, then Bolling could defeat Burton on the third ballot. Speculation abounded that Burton would divert some of his votes to Wright to defeat the more formidable Bolling and set up a final ballot between Burton and Wright.

The tally on the second ballot seemed to bolster the Burton conspiracy theory: Burton picked up only one vote, leaving the count at Burton—107, Wright—95, and Bolling—93, With the lowest vote count, Bolling was dropped from the third ballot.

Bolling's supporters were livid. They believed that they had been ambushed by Burton's Machiavellianism. On the third and final ballot, they swung their votes to Wright, giving the Texan a 148 to 147 victory. Burton's climb to the summit of House leadership had been stymied by a single vote.

Burton talked about that third ballot for years. Knowing that one vote would have forever changed his career, he maintained a mental list of every person who had voted with him and, perhaps most significantly, every person who had not.[4] Don Fraser was in the first category; Jim Oberstar was in the second.[5]

The Subcommittee on National Parks and Recreation

Burton was not the chair of the Subcommittee on National Parks and Recreation—he was the benevolent despot. A matter never came before the subcommittee without Burton knowing exactly what motions would be made and how every one of his twenty subcommittee members would vote on each. He did his deal-making in advance, leaving no room for surprise. He mastered every line of each bill of any significance, often reciting its language from memory. He determined when a bill would come before the subcommittee, for how long, and who would be heard. To the casual observer, the subcommittee was run in a leisurely, amiable way. To those who understood the inner workings, it was a highly choreographed extension of Burton's strength of will.

A ritualistic part of those inner workings were the private audiences Burton granted at the end of the working day. He would summon staff, friendly lobbyists, other House members, or whoever else struck his fancy to free-wheeling, closed-door working sessions in his office. There was always an agenda, it just took four or five hours to complete it. Armed with a stogie in his left hand and a glass of vodka in his right, Burton would plot strategies, lecture on the demise of liberal politics, thunder invectives about his political enemies, and otherwise proceed through the legislative business of the day to come.

The subcommittee enjoyed a broad jurisdiction, overseeing all public lands administered by the National Park Service. This included national parks, national monuments, historic battlefields, national trails, wild and scenic rivers, national lakeshore or seashores, and national recreation areas.

The subcommittee also pulled into its net matters of personal interest to

Burton. The BWCA was a prime example. Although the BWCA was administered not by the Park Service but by the Forest Service, Burton made the case that the committee's broad jurisdiction over conservation lands empowered it to hear the Fraser and Oberstar bills. Oberstar's attempts to refer the bills to the Agriculture Committee aside, nobody saw fit to challenge Burton's view.

Of the twenty members of the subcommittee, a handful played a role in forming its agenda.[6]

On the democratic side, Ohio's John Seiberling was the most ardent conservationist. He had been raised in a family that counted Sig Olson as a friend.[7] Chair of another powerful subcommittee, the General Oversight and Alaska Lands Subcommittee, Seiberling had extensive grounding in the politics and policies of wilderness preservation, particularly those of Alaska.

Paul Tsongas of Massachusetts had, in the few years since his 1974 election, established himself as an equally strong ally of the environmental community. The League of Conservation Voters, for example, rated Tsongas' voting record a perfect one hundred percent in 1977. His pet project was the establishment of the first urban national park in his hometown of Boston.

Like Tsongas, John Krebs from the California Central Valley had been elected in the post-Watergate democratic wave of 1974. His subcommittee assignment would permit Krebs to play a pivotal role in a complex controversy involving proposed recreational development in his district: the Mineral King project in the Sierra Nevadas at the southern edge of Sequoia National Park.[8]

The Republican delegation was the mirror image of these three: arch-conservatives like Steve Symms of Idaho and Don Clausen of California who were strongly aligned with western timber, mining, and property rights interests. An interesting exception to the rule was the ranking Republican member of the subcommittee, Keith Scbclius of Kansas, who consistently exhibited a moderate open-mindedness on conservation issues.

The BWCA bills landed in the subcommittee's lap at a busy time.

True to form, Burton created much of that activity by writing and sponsoring a bill to double the size of Redwoods National Park in California. In and of itself, this was guaranteed to create controversy among loggers, developers, and others with a vested interest in minimizing the federal government's presence in the forests of northern California. To add insult to injury, however, the park was located squarely in the district of subcommittee member Clausen, who bitterly opposed the measure. It had been a divisive, protracted battle and it was not yet over when the BWCA deliberations began.[9]

As difficult as the redwoods dispute was, it paled in comparison to two other Interior Committee matters.

The first was Burton's enormous Omnibus Parks bill, which bundled into a single $1.2 billion legislative package one hundred parks and preservation projects in forty-four states. Only Burton could have engineered such an unwieldy collection of "pork." On one hand, the bill was an unapologetic divvying up of political favors. On the other hand, however, it was a landmark step forward in expanded and improved protection for national park areas.[10]

The second came to be termed the environmental legislation of the century: the Alaska Lands bill.

By the spring of 1977, the Alaska Lands bill had the Interior Committee tied up in knots. Dealing with tens of millions of acres of the most pristine wilderness in the world, it dominated the energies of the committee members, their staff, and the national environmental organizations. How the Interior Committee sorted out the bill's complex land use, wildlife, and recreation issues would shape national wilderness politics for a generation.

The complexity, size, and significance of these two bills meant that it would be hard to focus attention, particularly Burton's, on the Boundary Waters. The Friends resorted to three close personal friends of Burton to register the BWCA on his radar.

The first was Dr. Edgar Wayburn, a key leader of the Sierra Club. Bud Heinselman wrote to Wayburn when it became apparent that Burton's role would be pivotal, asking him to raise the issue of the BWCA with Burton.[11] Wayburn agreed. It was Burton's first exposure to the issue.

The second was Dick Conlon, the director of the House Democratic Study Group (DSG), the research and policy development arm of House Democrats. Conlon had been its head since the 1960s.

Conlon was a native of northern Minnesota. He had worked as a reporter for the Duluth newspaper in the late 1950s and early 1960s, a beat which included covering BWCA issues. He had canoed throughout the BWCA and Quetico and had forged a close friendship with one of the strongest Canadian proponents of wilderness protection, Charles Carhart Ericksen. He had grown to love the BWCA, as a place and as an idea.[12]

Although Conlon could not use the official offices of the DSG to promote the BWCA issue, he could, and did, use his personal influence with Burton.

Fortunately for the champions of the Fraser bill, that influence was considerable.

Former Minnesotan Dick Conlon directed the House Democratic Study Group. (*Photo by Kevin Proescholdt*)

Conlon had forged close personal and professional relationships with three of his past DSG chairs: Phil Burton, Don Fraser, and Don Edwards of California. Of the three, Burton was the one with whom he was closest.[13] Both were intensely committed to the House as an institution. Both were iron willed and stubborn. Both were opinionated to the point of arrogance. And both were passionate. They were like brothers, each egging the other on, but always tempering their needling with a deep affection and respect.

Through Wayburn and Conlon, the Friends could gain access to Burton at a very personal level. Through Don Fraser, they could appeal to his love of good public policy.

Burton had a deep commitment to Fraser. Together with Edwards, Bob Kastenmeier of Wisconsin, Benjamin Rosenthal of New York, and Abner Mikva of Illinois, Burton and Fraser had formed an informal gathering of liberal House members called "The Group" that met to discuss issues and policy.

Burton viewed Fraser as the personification of an ideologically pure liberalism. Having risen through the ranks of street-tough Bay Area politics, Burton had shaped a give-and-take style that often left principle waiting on the back doorstep. In contrast, Fraser engaged little in day-to-day politicking, enabling him to protect the integrity of the party's philosophy and process.[14]

Burton both envied and respected these qualities in Fraser. He frequently remarked that he would put his reputation and career on the line if necessary to permit Fraser to carry on the work he did.[15]

Getting on the Subcommittee Agenda

With the subcommittee's agenda log-jammed with the redwoods, Omnibus, and Alaska Lands bills, rapid consideration of the BWCA legislation was out of the question. The question was how to begin the deliberations while the other matters worked their way through the system.

One answer was field hearings.

Field hearings have the advantage of gathering information about an issue on site, without tying up the Washington subcommittee machinery. They can be structured simply to take testimony, not to propose action. They also permit local members of Congress an opportunity to take a more visible leadership role than would be possible in Washington.

But field hearings are complicated, expensive, and unpredictable. Travel arrangements, hearing sites, court reporters, media coverage, and countless other details have to be coordinated with subcommittee members and staff, local citizen groups, elected officials, and many others. It was by no means certain that the subcommittee would be willing to take all of this on for the BWCA legislation.

It fell to Rapson of Fraser's staff to make the case.

Rapson first tried to enlist the support of Conlon and Staff Director Cleve Pinnix. His main argument was the need to diffuse the criticism that the subcommittee was intruding on the turf of the local congressman and on the prerogatives of local residents. What better way to demonstrate that Congress was proceeding deliberately and in good faith than to give the people of Minnesota a chance to be heard?

Conlon was reluctant. He feared that any field hearing, but particularly one in northern Minnesota, would inflame the controversy and discourage the subcommittee members from taking any action at all.

Cleve Pinnix was also cautious. He had just suffered through volatile hearings in northern California concerning the future of the redwoods. He recalled more than one logger having to be convinced to leave his pistol at the door.[16]

A turning point in the discussion came when Fraser was invited to meet with residents of the Gunflint Trail to talk about his bill. Rapson had been corresponding with a number of people in Grand Marais and along the Gunflint, including the owner of Jocko's Clearwater Lodge, Jocko Nelson. When Fraser was unable to attend, Nelson asked Rapson to come in his place.

Rapson, in turn, invited Bud Heinselman along. On May 2, 1977, Rapson made a forty-five minute presentation to a group of about fifty residents at a church at the foot of the Gunflint Trail. The reception was polite but muted. The questions came slowly at first, then in a barrage. Rapson and Heinselman responded for well over an hour. They agreed to make some technical adjustments in the bill and to remain open to further suggestions.

The tone was tense but courteous. Rapson felt the discussion had helped clarify differences without falling into rancor. The Gunflint contingent expressed satisfaction that Fraser's office was willing to hear them out.[17]

Rapson took the results of the meeting back not only to Fraser, but to Burton. Burton was fascinated. He saw in it the seeds of a possible working relationship with people of moderate views. He agreed with Rapson's view that field hearings, although potentially far more divisive than the Gunflint meeting had been, would be a prudent course to take.[18] He directed the subcommittee staff to set up two hearings in July, one in St. Paul and one in Ely.

Burton made it clear that he was not going to preside. The last thing he wanted was an outsider to be seen as driving the train. He looked instead to the young, first-termer from St. Paul, Bruce Vento. Although Vento did not sit on Burton's subcommittee, he did serve on the full Interior Committee. That was close enough for Burton, who directed, more than asked, Vento to be his stand-in.

Vento was a good choice. He was the only Minnesotan to serve on the Interior Committee. He had not yet carved out areas in which to make his mark. He was a quick study. And, perhaps most importantly for Burton, Vento had signed on as a co-sponsor of the Fraser bill.

Burton realized that if Vento was to conduct the hearings, Oberstar needed to be given a role. Not one to stand on ceremony, Burton had no trouble extending the courtesy of participation to Oberstar. Better to permit his voice to be heard than to be accused of stacking the deck.

That left Fraser. Burton decided to include him as well. With that the field hearing panel was complete. Vento would be in charge, but Oberstar and Fraser could contribute as they saw fit.

The Friends and the Alliance then went to work to choreograph the two events. The hearings would be open to whoever wanted to speak, but there was a quiet understanding that the Friends would have their day in St. Paul while the Alliance would have theirs in Ely. Working closely with the Friends and the Alliance, Pinnix became the clearinghouse to sort out the hundreds of requests for time. He assigned people to panels based on point of view and topic areas.

St. Paul

As the July 7th St. Paul hearing drew near, tensions heightened. Each side wondered if the other would pack the session. And it began to register on everybody that the event signalled the seriousness with which Congress intended to look at the issue.

On the morning of July 7, the auditorium of the Capitol's State Office Building auditorium was packed with cameras, microphones, tape recorders, and notepads—the event had clearly captured the media's attention. Outside, the Friends had organized a demonstration in support of the Fraser bill, complete with canoes, banners, bullhorns, and Friends members from as far away as Canada, Illinois, Nebraska, Indiana, Iowa, and Wisconsin. Inside, there was not an empty chair in the room.

The Friends organized their end of the event well. They packaged their testimony among key panels, mailed a hearing notice to thousands of their members, and prepared a special briefing sheet for each of the planned witnesses.[19]

Two key state legislators, Representative Phyllis Kahn of Minneapolis and Representative Willard Munger of Duluth kicked off the testimony.

Munger, a patriarch of the Minnesota conservation community and chair of the Environment Committee, spoke first. The BWCA "belongs to all the people of the United States," Munger stated. "In the end, national interests must supersede local concerns."[20]

Call of the wild!

June 30, 1977, *Chicago Tribune* cartoon. (© *copyrightd by Chicago Tribune Company. All rights reserved. Used with permission.*)

Representative Kahn, who chaired the House Recreation and Open Space Subcommittee and who had convened field hearings in Ely on proposed state legislation banning mining and logging in the BWCA, testified about the toll that motorized vehicles take on the wilderness:

> It is an undeniable conflict and above all it is a one-way conflict. It is the cross-country skier who expects tranquility and solitude both destroyed by the snowmobiler; as in the manner the canoeist's calm is broken by the presence of motorboats.[21]

Panel after panel made their way through the labyrinth of issues: ecology, resort and outfitter economics, timber economics, wildlife, recreation, education and youth groups, national environmental groups, midwest interests, Canadian interests, and many others.[22]

The testimony was often technical and narrow. Two moments helped lighten the proceedings.

The first came from an unlikely source. Pierce Butler III was a member of an aristocratic St. Paul family whose lineage included a United States Supreme

Court Justice. Assigned to a panel on recreational use, Butler became more and more exasperated as he worked his way through an explanation of the proliferation of snowmobile routes in the BWCA. He finally paused after a string of mind-numbing statistics and a particularly confusing explanation of a map with snowmobile trails marked in red. Groping to make his point, he stammered, "Well . . . well . . . They look . . . they look like a bunch of spaghetti!" When even Oberstar broke into laughter, Butler looked up in confusion, not realizing that he had made his point far more effectively than he could know.

The second break in the waves of detail was provided by wilderness photographer Les Blacklock. Where Butler had broken through with inadvertent humor, Blacklock broke through with personal eloquence:

> It is a thousand island-filled lakes, like strings of beads connected by tumbling streams. It is high cliffs and great boulders and gently sloping granite beaches by campsites. It's paddling into a good breeze with eyes wide open and never getting a speck of dust in the eye. It's sweet, soft, drinkable water by the pailfull right from the lakes, free of pollution and oil slicks. It's getting up at the crack of dawn for a silent paddling stalk along the shore before breakfast, slipping along as quietly as the fog itself, hoping to see mink, beaver, deer, or moose.[23]

The Alliance saved its ammunition. A contingent of resort owners and residents from the Gunflint Trail did step forward to express their reservations about both the Fraser and Oberstar bills.[24] Their testimony made the case that the Fraser bill would destroy resort operations, which depended on guests having a choice of canoe or motorboat travel: it would be "another stab in the back for free enterprise and the small businessman."[25]

The conservationists were buoyant at day's end. They had gotten in the first word, had brought a balance of personal and professional perspective into the debate, and had completely overshadowed the position of the Alliance.

That buoyancy was short-lived, however. The Ely hearing was not like anything the Friends had experienced.

Ely

Rapson knew that Ely would be different the minute he stepped out of his car the next morning in front of Ely High School.

The drive was jammed with huge log-hauling trucks, loaded to capacity, flatbed trucks carrying snowmobiles, pick-up trucks plastered with anti-Fraser, anti-Sierra Club placards, four-wheel drives with motorboats in tow.

As Rapson and Heinselman started to enter through the side door, they noticed dangling from the boom of one of the logging trucks an effigy identified as Sig Olson and Heinselman. Heinselman said nothing, but Rapson could see the color leave his face.

The temperature rose even higher inside the auditorium.

More than 1,000 people crushed into a space that could seat a fraction of that number. Loggers in their workboots, snowmobilers in their leather jackets leaned against every square inch of wall space. Signs, posters, and banners were plastered throughout the hall.

No less than the meticulous presentation of facts, figures, and arguments engineered the day before characterized the Friends organizing style, this more muscular organizing technique represented a well-honed style of northern Minnesota politics.

Throughout the long history of BWCA controversies, there had always been a fine line between rugged resistance to outside influences and vigilantism.

In the early 1930s, one C.R. "Dusty" Rhoades, an early bush pilot and local folk hero who trafficked in illegal beaver pelts poached from what is now the BWCA, was caught red-handed with fifty-five illegal beaver skins. He was, nonetheless, acquitted

At the Ely congressional field hearing, Sigurd Olson and Bud Heinselman were hung in effigy (top) while logging trucks lined the street (bottom). (*Photos by M. L. Heinselman*)

by a local jury.[26] Little wonder that many years later one Ely resident would pound his fist during a public hearing and shout: "We don't obey the laws of the United States or the state of Minnesota in Ely; we make our own law to suit our-selves."[27]

In the 1950s, Ely resorters and pilots flouted Truman's airspace reserva-tion and, later, a federal judge's injunction from continued flights into the wilder-ness. Later resorters smashed padlocked gates to drive machinery into the wilder-ness and illegally bulldoze an extension of the "Gun Lake Road."[28]

In 1965, the Ely Boundary Waters Resources Committee protested the newly announced Freeman Directives by staging a forty-five-minute "multiple use" protest parade in Ely during Agriculture Secretary Freeman and Lynda Bird Johnson's dedication of the Forest Service's Voyageur Visitor Center.[29]

The frustration of local residents often shifted from protests of govern-ment policy to pressure on individuals identified with wilderness causes.

Ely canoe outfitter Bill Rom had his home bombed one night in March 1949 because of his support of the airspace reservation over the wilderness.[30] Frank Hubachek received death and fire-bomb threats for the same reason.[31]

During the busy opening weekend of the fishing season in 1975, logging trucks and pickets blocked parking spaces in front of the outfitting businesses of Rom and Jon Waters in reprisal for the two men's support for the recently announced snowmobile ban.[32]

But perhaps the most poignant example of personal pressure was that applied to Sig Olson.

Olson had been identified with wilderness advocacy since the 1930s. The author of some of the most revered writings on wilderness and one of the elder statesmen of the national wilderness movement, Olson was perhaps the best-known resident of Ely. As the wilderness fights dragged on over the years, how-ever, he and his wife, Elizabeth, became *persona non grata* within their home com-munity.[33]

In the late 1930s and early 1940s, Olson was periodically threatened with termination from his position with the Ely Junior College if he refused to end his conservation activities with the Izaak Walton League. During the height of BWCA tensions, the Olsons were snubbed at social gatherings and were even occasionally refused service at the grocery store.[34]

It was through the prism of this checkered history of defiance and hostil-ity that Rapson, Vento, and Fraser viewed the crowd from their places on the stage.[35]

The tone was set immediately after Vento gavelled the hearing to order. State Senator Doug Johnson of Cook minced no words: "My people have com-promised. The preservationists are the most selfish people I have ever encountered." State Representative Bob Lessard of International Falls worked the crowd up further: "We can take care of our land. We can manage it without spoiling it."[36]

There was a short break in the tension when Bob Cary, editor of the *Ely Echo*, held up a two jars of water: one from the BWCA's Moose Lake, one from the Mississippi River. As he sipped from the Moose Lake jar, he asked the committee if they would be as comfortable drinking from the other jar. Twin Cities conservationists should go home and "save their own river" rather than getting into "some kind of a shin-kicking fight" with Ely "over how we are going to enjoy the lakes and woods up here."[37] The audience cheered and jeered.

But the brief interlude of humor didn't last. Next up was Norman Kainz, whose Kainz Lumber Company held one of the timber contracts that had been placed in abeyance by the congressional fight. Clearly nervous, Kainz rambled in a way that served to increase the tension in the hall. His concluding statements that Forest Service management of the area "makes me sick," drew cheers.[38]

Subsequent speakers built the anger to a crescendo.

Shirley Klaesges, owner of Timber Trail Resort, angrily attacked Fraser for having introducing a bill that was nothing more than Bud Heinselman's "personal, opinionated, and selfish conception of wilderness." She next turned on the committee "with disgust and mistrust" because of Vento's cosponsorship of the Fraser bill.[39]

A resort owner argued the need to use motorboats to spread canoeists deep into the wilderness.[40] A county assessor decried wilderness' impact on the tax base.[41] A disabled veteran claimed that without outboard motors, he and others from St. Cloud Veterans Hospital, whom he guided, would not be able to visit the BWCA.[42] A snowmobiler, one of the locally infamous "Ely 10" who had been arrested for violating snowmobile regulations, pointed out that just as he didn't mind "a little noise in the wilderness," nor should wilderness advocates, "since most [of them] are from the cities [and] a little noise shouldn't hurt them either."[43]

One by one they came forward until the audience was stomping their feet and cheering every sentence.

Unfortunately for the Friends, their witnesses came at the end of the parade. The Friends had decided to offer extensive testimony—their witness numbers actually exceeded those who opposed the Fraser bill. But their impact was largely lost in the raucous atmosphere that had been building and that met their appearances.[44]

Even the appearance of a pseudo-celebrity could not turn the tide. Jack Ford, son of the former president, had traveled to Ely to do a feature article on the BWCA for *Outside* magazine. His testimony was met with boos.[45]

One dramatic moment remained, however.

When Vento announced the name of the next witness, there was an immediate silence, followed closely by a cascade of hisses, shouting, and catcalls.

Sig Olson turned to a friend next to him, winked, and said wryly, "It's a good day to die."[46]

Olson, seventy-eight years old and in the early stages of Parkinson's disease, rose and slowly worked his way up the isle. Watching the old man's progress, the crowd again grew quiet. But with the words "My name is Sig Olson, my home Ely, Minnesota," the boos erupted again.

This time, they would not stop. For long minutes, wave after wave of boos and jeers rolled over the auditorium. An ominous stomping of boots began in the back. Sig sat and waited.

Vento gavelled. He threatened to terminate the hearing on the spot if the crowd continued. It only made matters worse. Vento turned to Rapson and told him to make sure there was a clear passage out the back in case violence erupted.[47]

But they stayed put. Finally, the crowd began to quiet. One voice refused to be silenced. Jacob Pete, an old nemesis of Olson's, continued to heckle from the rear of the auditorium, yelling out reminders of past incidents when Olson had used a motorboat on Basswood Lake. Oberstar, who until then had remained silent, intervened, admonishing the crowd to respect people's right to be heard. After a final few hisses, Olson began.[48]

His strong, clear voice echoed throughout the hall, drawing attention away from the persistent palsy in his right hand:

> I support the Fraser Bill whose purpose is to eliminate all adverse uses from the BWCA and give it complete wilderness status. . . . The time for action and immediate passage is now.
>
> I have crisscrossed the BWCA and its adjoining Quetico Provincial Park by canoe countless times since my early guiding days.
>
> This is the most beautiful lake country on the continent. We can afford to cherish and protect it.
>
> Some places should be preserved from development or exploitation for they satisfy a human need for solace, belonging, and perspective. In the end we turn to nature in a frenzied chaotic world, there to find silence—oneness—wholeness—spiritual release.[49]

Not a sound had interrupted him. He stood, turned, and waved to his Ely neighbors as he returned to his seat.

The rest of the hearing was anticlimactic. Vento closed the session without incident.

Ely political leader-
ship had had the foresight
and good grace to invite
Fraser, Vento, Oberstar, and
their staff to dinner following
the hearing. Not at the Holi-
day Inn, but at the home of
Mayor Grahek.

After stopping in at
the Heinselman cabin, where
the Friends had gathered to
wind-down and compare im-

Congressmen Bruce Vento (left), Don Fraser, and Jim Oberstar
(right) flew over the BWCA after the Ely field hearing. (*Photo
by Rip Rapson*)

pressions of the day's events, Fraser, Vento, and Rapson headed around Burntside
Lake to the Grahek's. Vento was fuming. It was past nine o'clock, his nerves were
still on edge, and the last thing he wanted to do was to spend a long evening with
many of the locals he had spent the day trying to gavel to order. And neither
Fraser nor Rapson particularly relished the prospect of polite conversation with
Oberstar.

Their dread was replaced with awe as they stepped out of the car and
were met by their host.

Under a full moon and cloudless sky, Victorian street lamps lit a long
boardwalk that hugged the waterfront all the way to an imposing log cabin.
Hearing the stirring of animals to their left, they turned to see dozens of eyes peer-
ing out of cages in a honeycomb up the hillside. Grahek explained that these were
his daughter's dogsled racing dogs—pure malamutes each one. A malamute,
Grahek explained, was half dog, half wolf. Nobody dared ask how that came
about.

As they approached the cabin, it became clear that this was not a garden
variety cabin. A roaring fireplace so large you could throw a log at it and not particularly care if you missed. An elegant bar. A study and library that would be the
envy of many small cities.

The table was filled with veal, fish, vegetables, wild rice, wine, and fresh-
ly baked pie. As people sat down, Grahek explained that this was to be a chance
to get acquainted and that the politics of the day were to be left at the door.

The evening provided the Washingtonians a chance to see the side of
Doc Grahek that had made him a fixture in the Ely community for many of his
sixty-seven years.

Jack Phillip Grahek was born in 1910 in an Ely that was a bustling mining, logging and tourist community. Two iron ore mines operated within Ely itself,
employing 1,500 men. There were seventy-five resorts in the area. As a youngster,

Grahek worked two summers as a packer for a canoe-outfitting business, assisting guides on canoe trips. After graduating from Ely High School, he went on to receive a medical degree from Marquette University in 1939. He returned home in 1940 to establish a family medicine practice.

After the war, Grahek became increasingly involved in the turbulent politics surrounding the air space ban and local defiance of it. He joined with a small group led by John Smrekar, Bill Zupancich of Curtain Falls resort, Bert Gustason of Skidway Borderline Lodge on Basswood Lake, and Chamber of Commerce Secretary Stan Pechaver to wrestle control from then-Mayor Matt Marolt, who supported the air ban.

Grahek quickly rose to prominence within the group. He was elected president of the Ely Chamber of Commerce in 1950 and Mayor of Ely in 1955. He and the Smrekar circle held the reins of power without interruption for the next twenty-five years.[50]

Nothing went on in Ely without Grahek being in on it. When baseball great Ted Williams vacationed at Gustason's resort, Grahek made sure that all Williams' hunting, fishing and leisure needs were facilitated.[51] As the influence of the Iron Range grew within the DFL party, Grahek was invariably counted among the handful who shaped Iron Range politics.

So it was no surprise that Grahek held court that night on the lake. Tensions dissipated as Grahek told story after story of his town, its people, and the great northwoods. Toasts were made all around. It was an equanimity that would not be achieved again.

The Subcommittee Moves Back to Washington

The field hearings had served to crystalize positions. They had also suggested to both sides that changes would have to be made in order to move the discussion off dead-center.

Oberstar met with the Alliance to prepare a new bill that would reflect some of the concerns that were raised by his supporters at the hearings. Rapson pulled together a series of meetings with Friends representatives to develop ways in which the claimed adverse effects on local businesses and residents could be softened. Governor Perpich assigned his aide Bud Philbrook to twist the arms of both sides in order to break the logjam.

Lest anyone forget, however, Phil Burton was still in charge. He scheduled a full subcommittee hearing in Washington for August 4. He was not particularly interested in taking in more testimony from either local residents or the environmental community. But he was interested in forcing the hand of the Forest Service. He let Vice President Mondale and Secretary Bergland's office

April 12, 1978, *Minnesota Daily* cartoon. (*Reprinted with permission from the* Minnesota Daily)

know in no uncertain terms that the August 4 session would be the Carter Administration's opportunity to shape the discussion.

The hearing was also calculated to give the Alliance its first real look at Phil Burton. Burton relished the idea of letting the local residents know that this was serious business—if they expected that Oberstar could simply wish the Fraser bill away, they were in for a shock.

In an attempt to diffuse in advance any negative impacts the hearing would have, Oberstar introduced his new bill the day before.[52] The bill gestured in the direction of the environmental community by prohibiting logging of virgin timber throughout the BWCA, but was fundamentally an attempt to convince the Alliance that the National Recreation Area would be managed permissively.[53]

Oberstar's preemptive move did not budge Burton an inch. The hearing set just the tone for which Burton had hoped.

Perched in high-backed, leather chairs on a pronouncedly elevated dais, the subcommittee members could not have cast a more different impression than had Fraser, Vento, and Oberstar sitting behind make-shift hearing tables on the stage of the Ely auditorium.[54]

Square in the middle, below the great seal of the United States, sat Burton. His welcome to the packed hearing room was a model of decorum. He explained that this was simply the first step in what could be many subcommittee sessions, that the bills would not be acted upon that day, and that he would adhere scrupulously to equal time for both sides.

He then introduced Oberstar, who, Burton explained, would be extended the same courtesy of subcommittee participation as he had enjoyed in the field hearings.

Oberstar opened with an explanation of his new bill. Burton seized immediately on Oberstar's willingness to cease the cutting of virgin timber—with a big smile, he announced that obtaining a logging moratorium was the foremost priority on the subcommittee's agenda.

Fraser came next. Like Oberstar, he had prepared a new approach.

After the field hearings, Rapson had asked Fraser for the authority to explore with the environmental community a series of accommodations that might make the bill less threatening to homeowners and resort operators near the BWCA. For the next four weeks, Rapson and Heinselman met non-stop with their allies and even some of their opponents to explore possible elements of a supplemental package.

The result was an eight-point amendment to the Fraser bill. In announcing the so-called "ameliorative measures," Fraser sought to focus the legislative debate on what could be done outside the BWCA, rather than inside.

If local residents were serious about wanting to preserve a wide variety of winter recreation options, Fraser said, the bill should provide the funding necessary to complete 110 miles of unfinished snowmobile trails outside the BWCA in the Superior National Forest.

If residents were intent on preserving the greatest number of summer recreation options, the bill should provide for the upgrading of accesses on twenty-nine lakes outside the wilderness, the building of remote campsites on lakes outside the BWCA to increase motor recreation opportunities, and the construction of more hiking trails inside the wilderness.

If local loggers legitimately were threatened by an end to logging in the BWCA, the bill should furnish funds to intensify forest management outside the BWCA and should offer alternative timber sales outside the BWCA to the four timber companies holding timber sale contracts within the wilderness.

And if local resort owners genuinely feared that the Fraser bill would destroy their businesess, the bill should fund, for the first time, the voluntary buyouts of resorts that no longer wished to operate. For those resorts that wanted to stay in business, the bill should make available grants and loans for upgrading facilities or converting them to a kind of business that would be more attractive to a wilderness-oriented clientele.

The resort purchase proposal arose from the resorters themselves. In a phone conversation with Seagull Lake resorter Kim Danielson, Rapson asked, "Would it help if we bought resort owners out?" "Yes," Danielson had replied. "Would you sell?" "Yes," came Danielson's reply again. "Would other resorters sell?" "Yes," came the reply a third time.[55]

And finally, if local residents were sincere in wanting to have a reasonable period in which to adjust, the committee should, Fraser suggested, "give serious attention to the possibility of extending to ten or fifteen years the motor-phase-out period for certain peripheral lakes and keeping other peripheral lakes permanently open to motors."[56]

Fraser's announcement took the audience by surprise. Members of the Alliance huddled in the back of the room to sort out what it might mean.

Burton seized on the momentary confusion to reinforce Fraser's testimony. He had recently traveled to the Grand Tetons, Burton said, some of the grandest country in the world. He and a dozen others were engaged in a high-energy conversation in Burton's hotel room, which overlooked a lake. Slowly the roar of a single motorboat a good three or four miles away drowned out the speakers. The conversation stopped until the motor passed out of hearing. Burton looked into the audience filled with "Keep It Open to Everyone" buttons and said that he did not need anyone to tell him that motorboats have no impact on the wilderness experience.[57]

Next was Vento. This was the first chance the subcommittee had had to hear a formal summary of the field hearings. After describing the testimony on both sides, Vento reiterated his support for the Fraser wilderness package.[58]

But more than Oberstar's logging concessions, Fraser's package of ameliorative measures, and Vento's summary of the July hearings, it was the testimony of the Carter Administration for which Burton was waiting. He would be kept waiting.

Forest Service Chief John McGuire explained to a visibly irritated Burton that the administration had not yet finalized its position. Instead, the Forest Service had developed seven alternative scenarios that would be presented to Assistant Secretary Cutler and Secretary Bergland. As McGuire walked through each of the seven, Burton became increasingly restless. He finally told McGuire that the subcommittee would reconvene a hearing in September, at which time he would expect not seven positions, not two positions, but one position from the secretary.[59] He declared the hearing adjourned.

After all the drama of the field hearings and all the pomp of the Washington hearings, it was revealing that the *Minneapolis Tribune's* Minnesota Poll showed the state still sharply divided on the BWCA question: 49% of state residents favored the Fraser bill's full wilderness approach, 46% favored the Oberstar bill's combination of wilderness and "multiple use."[60]

Maneuvering for Support

Burton's message to the Carter administration was not lost on the Friends or the Alliance. Both sides had a little less than two months to try to shape the views not just of Cutler and Bergland, but of Vice President Mondale, who would have a difficult time staying out of the controversy the longer it dragged on, and Bob Herbst, the former Commissioner of the Minnesota DNR and current Assistant Secretary of the Interior.

Both sides started with Herbst, reasoning that he had the greatest familiarity with the issue and might exercise the greatest influence over Mondale.

Oberstar wrote to Herbst in late July explaining why motors should be allowed on big lakes within the wilderness.[61] The Friends followed with a visit to Herbst in early August. They found him friendly, but non-committal.[62]

Unable to move Herbst, both sides shifted their attention to Cutler. As the person to whom the Forest Service reported, Cutler would likely have the most significant role in developing the Secretary's ultimate position.

And if anyone was qualified to shape that position, it was Cutler.

Cutler had cut his teeth in the national environmental movement. He had worked with the National Wildlife Federation and the Wilderness Society in the 1960s. While serving as the Society's principal lobbyist from 1965 to 1969, he

Dr. Rupert Cutler (center), with the Friends' Bud Heinselman (left) and Kevin Proescholdt (right), formulated the Carter Administration's BWCA position. (*Photo by Kevin Proescholdt*)

had developed a close relationship with Sig Olson, then president of the organization. Olson helped instill in Cutler an interest in the BWCA.

Perhaps in part because of Olson's influence, the BWCA figured prominently in Cutler's subsequent professional training. Cutler's doctoral dissertation focused on four lawsuits that highlighted the Forest Service's approach to land management; one of those was the 1970s BWCA mining lawsuit, Izaak Walton League of America v. St. Clair. As part of his research, Cutler visited Ely, flew over the BWCA with the Forest Service, and interviewed people like Bud Heinselman and Ikes attorney Ray Haik.[63]

Bergland had hand-picked Cutler for the position of Assistant Secretary in 1976. Bergland wanted a balance between solid professional training and hands-on experience with Forest Service management issues. He also wanted someone with rock-solid integrity and sound judgment. Cutler fit the bill. From the first interview, the two hit it off. Bergland made clear that he wanted an assistant secretary who was comfortable accepting a wide delegation of authority. On issues like the BWCA, he wanted Cutler to take the lead, marshall the arguments, and develop the department's preliminary position. Cutler welcomed the role.[64]

A line began to form outside his door the day after the August hearing.[65]

Oberstar met with Cutler to discuss the BWCA and the problems it was posing in his district. Rapson and Heinselman countered with their own meetings with Cutler and opened a daily telephone relationship with Pete Sorenson, Cutler's administrative aide.[66] In early August, Olson wrote to Cutler to rekindle their long-standing relationship. In an otherwise non-committal response, Cutler scribbled on the bottom "You'll like USDA's BWCA proposal."[67]

If the Friends were encouraged by Cutler's note, however, they were given pause by the renewed activity of the Perpich administration to pressure both Congress and the Carter administration to adopt a compromise position.

Perpich had deputized former state legislator Bud Philbrook to become the state's ambassador to Washington on BWCA issues. Philbrook, who now worked at the Department of Natural Resources, began a whirlwind of summer meetings and discussions with Friends leaders, Alliance activists, and anyone else who might have something to do with the resolution of the dispute.

In mid-July, Philbrook tried to convince Heinselman and Dayton that the only real option was a brokered political settlement. Philbrook proposed that Oberstar and Fraser participate in a negotiating session mediated by Perpich. He intimated that if the environmentalists refused to cooperate, Perpich would support an effort by Oberstar, Humphrey, and northern members of the Minnesota legislature to kill the Fraser bill.[68]

Heinselman and Dayton politely refused, explaining the need to permit the legislative process to continue on its course. Philbrook was irate. On July 22, he tried again, letting Heinselman and Dayton know in no uncertain terms that the governor held important trump cards.

First, Perpich was prepared to become more aggressive in his opposition to the Fraser bill, particularly on the Range. Second, the Governor was poised to raise legal arguments about the state's right to control use of surface waters in the BWCA. Third, he was willing to have his staff work hard to influence the debate in Washington.[69]

Heinselman and Dayton held their ground.

Philbrook tried circling around the issue. In early August, he prepared a memorandum for the governor, outlining six alternative strategies: doing nothing, supporting the Fraser bill, encouraging compromise, initiating compromise, making an alternative proposal, and initiating state action.[70]

The governor failed to jump at the chance to clarify his tactics. One reason may have been the emerging split within his administration about the best course. A number of the governor's staff, perhaps most prominently Ronnie Brooks, were becoming less reluctant to openly discuss the merits of the Fraser bill.

A second reason was the gradual emergence from within the administration of a logging position indistinguishable from that in the Fraser bill. Bill Nye, the commissioner of the Department of Natural Resources, had for months been preparing a logging proposal.[71] By the middle of August, the DNR surfaced the idea of banning logging within the BWCA and finding softwood outside the BWCA to compensate for the loss.[72]

Philbrook seized the event to try to engage the Carter Administration. He wrote letters to both Dave Bieging of Mondale's staff and Cutler explaining the governor's views about logging in the BWCA.[73]

But there was still the matter of motorboat and snowmobile use. And here, Philbrook had less to write from home about.

The DNR and the governor continued to favor limited motor use. The DNR suggested regulating the size of motors, permitting motorboat use only during the prime May and early June fishing season, closing some routes to motors, and limiting a motorboat's noise output and fuel consumption. Both the governor and DNR supported some snowmobile use in the BWCA.[74]

Philbrook found himself, finally, in a cul-de-sac. The environmentalists were not about to short-circuit the legislative process. The Carter Administration seemed unmoved by the endless string of overtures from the governor's office. Philbrook nevertheless pressed on, calling, writing, visiting. He could only wait for the September hearings to see whether his efforts would ultimately bear fruit.

He was not alone. If Mondale, Bergland, and Cutler had settled on a position, they weren't letting anyone know.

The Washington Hearings, Round II

No matter how the Carter Administration weighed in, a majority vote in the House would ultimately determine the fate of the Fraser and Oberstar bills. Both the Friends and the Alliance heightened their efforts to attract the attention of House members.

The Alliance resorted to the kind of politics it knew best: walking the halls, introducing themselves to the House members and staffs, and telling their stories as a reminder of the very personal stakes that were being played out.

But the epitome of the Alliance campaign of persuasion came the night of the September 12th hearing: a lavish old-fashioned, get-to-know-you-better wild game dinner to which all 535 House and Senate members and their staffs were invited. It was vintage Range politics, a reminder to Capitol Hill of northern Minnesota's hospitality, graciousness, and personal political style.[75]

Entering the large and ornate Rayburn Building reception room, the congressional guests were treated to a gastronomical spectacle that had people talking for weeks. Running the entire length of the left wall was table after table of venison, bear, moose, wild turkey, walleye, trout, muskie, wild rice, and vegetables. All from northern Minnesota. All flown in that morning. All steaming hot on silver serving trays.

In the seconds it took for people to take all of this in, they were greeted by a representative of the Alliance, offered a drink, and ushered to the food line. A second group of Alliance members served, explaining where the walleye had been caught or how the bear had been tracked.

It did not take long for the room to fill. More than eighty of the Senate's 100 members attended, as did hundreds of House members and staffers. The Alliance even made the enemy feel welcome. The moment he entered the room, Rapson, the one person from the Fraser camp whom Alliance members related well to, was met with a cordial but long line of Alliance members who proceeded to gently work him over for the next forty-five minutes.

The event could not have been more successful. It introduced to the Alliance scores of people who had little or no knowledge of the organization's issues or even of its existence. It also provided the Alliance with a certain cachet, as a group that had pulled off a memorable social event in a town accustomed to the point of callousness to grand events.[76]

The Friends' lobbying activities were less flashy.

Like the Alliance, they brought dozens of people to Washington during August and early September to meet with Interior Committee members and their staffs. They circulated to each Interior Committee member a packet that contained an information booklet, briefing sheets tailored to the congressman in question, and an "I Like It Wild" button.[77] Although the first two may have been the most educational part of the packet, it was the third that seemed to get the most attention. Fraser's racketball partner Ben Rosenthal remarked to Fraser after receiving a packet: "You're getting a pretty risque reputation, Don. All the women in my office are wearing 'I Like It Wild' buttons. Is there something you want to tell me?"[78]

On September 12, the hearing room in the Longworth House Office Building was packed with Alliance members, Friends members, staff, and media. Burton entered to take up his customary spot. He gavelled the session to order, explained that Oberstar would again have the participation privileges of a subcommittee member, announced that everyone who wanted to testify would be heard over the next two days, and proposed that the Alliance be heard first.[79]

Burton's statements were as savvy as they were considerate. By permitting Oberstar to ask questions, make points, and otherwise act as if he were a member of the subcommittee, Burton helped bolster Oberstar's image in front of an important group of constituents. And by making clear not only that the Alliance would start things off but that the subcommittee would remain in session until everyone had his or her say, he let the Alliance know they would have their full day in court.

The Alliance came prepared to take Burton at his word—they consumed the entire first day's testimony. They led with local officials: Grand Marais Mayor Humphrey, State Senator Johnson, Minnesota House Majority Leader Irv Anderson, Ely Mayor Grahek, and the chairs of the three local county Boards of Commissioners.[80]

Then came a string of panels focusing on particular subjects: logging, organized labor, Gunflint Trail resorts, Ely resorts, snowmobiling, motorboating, and access on the part of people with disabilities.

The panels made a powerful impression. Speaker after speaker emphasized that current management practices were working well, that people had made personal and professional adjustments to those practices, and that the dramatic changes embodied in the Fraser bill would disrupt lives and deliver a potentially fatal blow to local logging companies, resorts, and others.[81]

These themes were illustrated by the testimony of Luana Brandt, owner of Nor'wester Lodge on Poplar Lake. Brandt testified that she had experienced a fifty percent loss of winter business after the snowmobile ban. Visibly startled by such a stark statistic, Burton fired a series of tough follow-up questions. He was finally able to extract a concession that the loss had been two of Brandt's four winterized cabins during a three-month season.[82]

Despite Brandt's being caught in an embarrassing overstatement, by day's end the Alliance had engineered a considerable triumph. Their testimony had been personal, powerful and focused. Oberstar had skillfully orchestrated the sequence to keep things moving and to retain the subcommittee's attention. The subcommittee members were attentive and appeared supportive.

The Friends were frustrated and increasingly on edge. They had not expected this kind of treatment. The Alliance had had the first act to themselves and had performed well. Burton, whom they thought of as their champion, was being too solicitous, giving the appearance that the Alliance was eroding his resolve.

And then there was the uncertainty of the next day's session, during which the Carter Administration would announce its preferred position. Having heard absolutely nothing from Bergland or Cutler, the Friends feared that the next day would be worse than the first.

The Friends knew something unusual was up when they entered the hearing room the next day. As protocol would dictate, Cutler sat in the first row, ostensibly ready to start things off. But next to him sat Bergland. Whatever was to be unveiled apparently required the full political capital of the secretary himself.

Burton played the scene for its full effect, smiling as he acknowledged the presence of the secretary and asking him to begin. Chairs shuffled, necks craned, and the tension became virtually audible as a Forest Service staffer deliberately stepped forward to place on an easel a map showing the official position of the Carter Administration.

Gasps moved through the room as it became clear what the map showed.

It was, for all intents and purposes, the Fraser bill, only stronger.

It expanded the BWCA to pick up some 23,000 acres of prime wilderness lakes and terminated logging. It permitted motorboat use on only a few peripheral lakes (Saganaga, Lac La Croix, Snowbank, Moose, and Fall). And it stood Oberstar's idea on its head by establishing a Boundary Waters National Recreation Area *outside* the wilderness along the Gunflint Trail, Fernberg Road, and Echo Trail.[83]

The euphoria of the Friends was matched by the shock of the Alliance. Neither side had dreamed such an outcome to be possible. For the Alliance, it was the cruelest form of roller-coaster—from the high point of the previous day to this. For the Friends, it meant that an objective and powerful voice had spoken in their favor—it would be increasingly difficult to cast the Fraser bill as extremist.

Bergland's deference to Cutler during the hearing strongly suggested that Cutler had been the moving force in forging the department's position. That suspicion later proved to be the case.

Bergland had been genuine in his desire to invest his deputy with the authority to develop positions on those issues within Cutler's jurisdiction. Cutler had taken that charge seriously. After the August hearing in which the Forest Service's seven options were laid out, Cutler had taken the time to analyze each one of them. In the end, he had been given the latitude by Bergland to pick among them. He did, choosing the one that provided the "maximum wilderness" protection. He would later note that the entire process was done "without anyone [in the Carter Administration] raising any questions from any corner."[84]

If anything about this was a surprise, it was that Bergland and Mondale, two Minnesotans with deep ties into the state's political structure, would essentially sit on the sidelines. Cutler had the deepest respect for Bergland's restraint, believing that Bergland had elected to keep politics out of the department's process.[85] But he also concluded that both Bergland and Mondale "didn't want to touch the [BWCA issue] with a ten-foot pole."[86]

In the early stages of the Carter Administration's development of its BWCA position, Cutler had approached Mondale at a social event. Cutler asked the Vice President if he had any advice to offer about the BWCA. Mondale shrugged and said, "Some of my friends are for it, and some of my friends are against it, and I'm with my friends." He smiled, turned on his heels, and left.[87] Cutler, who had been sincere in trying to draw Mondale out, was irritated by Mondale's flippancy, recognizing the line as one often used by Hubert Humphrey.[88]

Cutler was clearly proud of having proceeded free of the customary political influence. As he left the hearing room, he tapped Rapson on the shoulder, gave him a grin, and whispered, "Not bad for a bunch of bureaucrats."[89]

The Carter Administration's testimony was a hard act to follow. But Minnesota's inimitable governor gave it a shot nonetheless.

Perpich and Nye started well enough. Nye testified that he favored a ban on logging and supported substituting timber outside the wilderness for timber inside the wilderness. He proposed limiting motorboat and snowmobile use.[90]

Had they stopped there, the State of Minnesota's position would have been relatively clear.

Perpich was not content to stop there, however. He launched into a desultory, often incoherent, monologue that was at first simply hard to follow, but ultimately had people gaping in disbelief. It would have been funny had the stakes not been so high.

In trying to get to the core of the disputes over motorboat use, the governor offered the following insight:

> I am in support of small motorboat use limited to certain areas. We are again issuing a proclamation of cleaning and clearing out the streams. This program will alleviate much pollution, because many of our rivers can and are considered wild and scenic. Some complain that motors dis-

'I WOULD GUESS THIS MEANS, GOV. PERPICH,
THAT YOU'RE IN FAVOR OF SOME SORT OF SNOWMOBILE ACCESS TO THE BWCA'

September 15, 1977, *Minneapolis Tribune* **cartoon.** (*Reprinted with permission from the* Minneapolis Star Tribune)

turb the wilderness. But so does my canoe. I am not a motorboat enthusiast. I think that I have probably scared as many wild animals out in the woods as anyone in a motorboat.[91]

It only got worse. But by then the subcommittee members and people in the audience were intrigued. Many had never been witness to such a performance.

The Alliance fared better. They picked up where they had left off the previous day, offering testimony on snowmobiling, motorboating, forest management, economic hardship to canoe outfitters and resort owners, and personal hardship on homeowners.[92]

When the final Alliance member finished, it was late in the day. It was the Friends' turn.

They came well prepared. As they had done for the Minneapolis hearings, the Friends had relied on Rapson to choreograph the sequence of presentations and to rehearse the key pieces of testimony.

First up was Heinselman. "Your reputation precedes you, Mr. Heinselman," Burton said as a visibly nervous Heinselman started.

Heinselman's forty-eight-page written testimony focused primarily on the forests of the BWCA—forest ecology, the impacts of logging, a description of the six BWCA federal timber sales, timber supply and demand in Minnesota, and alternatives to BWCA timber. Burton peppered him with questions, unnerving Heinselman, but bringing his complex testimony into sharper focus. And even Burton's crustiness was softened by Heinselman's closing statement:

> Now the hour of decision is upon us. Will we at last put an end to these interminable debates. . . .? Or will we forsake those who have gone before us, and allow the flood-tides of civilization to overwhelm this beautiful wilderness. I plead for the wilderness.[93]

The Friends followed with presentations on each of the major topic areas that added a deeper dimension to the discussions the subcommittee members had heard thus far.

Darby Nelson, an aquatic biologist, pointed out the destabilizing effects of snowmobiling on BWCA trout systems.[94] Janet Green documented the growing trend toward canoe use, the conflict between canoe and motor users, and the amount of lake surface area available to paddle-only and motor use.[95] Attorney Dayton pointed out how the hardships of resort owners had been accommodated in the past and could be accommodated in the future.[96]

Herb Wright, Regents' Professor of Geology, Ecology, and Botany at the University of Minnesota and a member of the National Academy of Science, underscored the BWCA's immeasurable scientific value, focusing on the origin and nature of the lakes, the sensitivity of the lakes to human influence, and the long-range history of the forest.[97]

Jack Maloney of the Minnesota Federation of Ski Touring Clubs (MINN-TOUR) reminded the subcommittee of the importance of winter wilderness use: "Essentially, the conflict over winter recreation in the BWCA is drawn between a widespread, growing national constituency of people who seek a quiet, primitive wilderness experience, and local ice fishermen who want to regain easy access to good meat fishing."[98]

The national environmental community showed up in force as well: the Wilderness Society, the Izaak Walton League of America, the National Parks and Conservation Association, the Sierra Club, Friends of the Earth, and the National Audubon Society all weighed in.[99] So too did a variety of citizen coalitions from throughout the country.[100]

But the testimony that most effectively captured the interest of the subcommittee was offered by Bill Muir, a blind professor of botany and environmental biology at Carleton College:

I am classified as a seriously handicapped person and am eligible for retirement on total disability. I am a severe diabetic, requiring two large injections of insulin daily, and I am totally and absolutely blind. I have advanced circulatory impairment, with my feet and lower legs being quite numb and atrophied, making it necessary for me to wear special support shoes. Yet, with my wife's help, I continue with my teaching. During five summers since 1971, my wife and I canoed two thousand miles in the Boundary Waters and Quetico. Thus, the area certainly is available now to many who are severely handicapped without the use of motorized vehicles.[101]

Muir noted that the only time his BWCA experiences had been danger-ous was when the wake of a large motorboat capsized his canoe on Basswood Lake. Although a storm was developing, the operator made no attempt to help.

With his simple and direct eloquence, Muir had brought the subcommit-tee back full circle to proposal the Carter Administration had advanced many hours before: the idea of creating and managing as a canoe wilderness a unique collection of lakes and forests.

Burton had delivered on his promise to hear everyone who wished to be heard. He adjourned the session just before 7:00 P.M.

The two days of hearings were a powerful indicator of where the debate was headed and who would shape it.

First, there was an emerging consensus that the life expectancy of BWCA logging had been shortened considerably. If there was a moment of focus in Perpich's testimony, it was the need to meet the state's timber needs from outside the BWCA's boundaries.

Second, Fraser had opened a new discussion about the possibility of cre-ating an overall northern Minnesota assistance package to buffer potential adverse effects on homeowners, local governments, resorts, and other small busi-nesses.

Third, the credibility of Fraser's wilderness position had been buoyed sig-nificantly by the Carter Administration's testimony.

Fourth, the Alliance had demonstrated an ability to marshall effectively its arguments and resources. They had made major inroads into the subcommit-tee's more conservative wing and appeared likely to hone their arguments in deal-ing with the broader House membership.

Fifth, Burton had stayed in tight control and gave every indication that he would continue to do so. The hearings had been an ideal vehicle for the Chairman to learn quickly and thoroughly. Few doubted that so armed, he would become the dominant force in the months ahead.

But the next phase would not be as neat and tidy as a subcommittee hearing. The discussion would move from the hearing room to the anteroom. Success would be measured in vote counts, not in the smoothness of formal testimony.

As the hearing adjourned, Burton asked Dayton and Wright of the Friends to join him for drinks. With that gesture, the next phase began.[102]

Notes

1 *Wall Street Journal*, Sept. 28, 1982, p. 1, "Phil Burton Has Cut Many Political Deals; Is It One Too Many?"

2 *Washington Post*, Apr. 11, 1983, p. A1, "Phillip Burton Collapses, Dies in San Francisco"; *New York Times*, Apr. 11, 1983, p. B6, "Rep. Phillip Burton, Democratic Liberal, Dies on Visit to California."

3 See 1977 *Congressional Quarterly Almanac*, pp. 5-9.

4 Burton's mental ability to juggle political numbers was like a sixth sense. When the State of California undertook its 1982 congressional redistricting plan, the California Assembly for all intents and purposes deferred completely to Burton to design the new boundaries of each of the forty-five congressional districts.

Burton used the opportunity in a way that gave new meaning to the proud tradition of gerrymandering. In order to create a democratically unassailable district for his brother and fellow-congressman John, Burton significantly weakened his own district by giving some of his strongest Democratic precincts to John. "[John's district] curls in and out like a snake," Burton said proudly. After all that work, however, John Burton announced just after the plan's completion that he would not seek re-election.

Burton's redistricting also threatened to cost California Republicans up to five House seats, including that of Burton's arch-rival, Representative John Rousselot. When asked if he drew his plan to unseat as many Republicans as possible, Burton laughed: had that been his intention, "'I might well have been able to get'—he paused in mid-sentence, his nimble brain calculating the possibilities—'two more seats.'" *Wall Street Journal*, Sept. 28, 1982, p. 1, "Phil Burton Has Cut Many Political Deals; Is It One Too Many?"

5 Had Burton won, of course, he wouldn't have chaired the subcommittee. See "The Majority Leadership," 1977 *Congressional Quarterly Almanac*, pp. 5-9.

6 Three members of the subcommittee staff also helped determine the subcommittee's approach and focus.

Cleve Pinnix headed the majority party staff for Chairman Burton. A former National Parks employee, Pinnix was an invaluable resource about how parks, wilderness, and public lands were operated.

Clay Peters directed the Republicans' minority party staff and worked particularly closely with Sebelius. He had an excellent working relationship with Pinnix.

Fran Sheehan worked for Mo Udall on the full Interior Committee staff. Although Sheehan did not officially work on the subcommittee staff, he functioned as a conduit between Chairman Udall and the subcommittee. He closely followed both the substance and politics of the subcommittee's agenda.

7 During the committee's consideration of the BWCA bill, Seiberling would speak of his father's friendship with Olson and the canoe trips which Olson had guided for his father.

8 The rest of the Democratic delegation comprised James Florio (NJ), Peter Kostmayer (PA), Robert Kastenmeier (WI), Jonathan Bingham (NY), Dawson Mathis (GA), Philip Ruppe (MI), Goodloe Byron (MD), Lamar Gudger (NC), Austin Murphy (PA), Bob Eckhardt (TX), and three territorial representatives: Antonio Won Pat (Guam), Ron De Lugo (Virgin Islands), and Baltasar Corrada del Rio (Puerto Rico).

9 Burton was fond of likening the redwoods dispute to the BWCA dispute. Both superseded the local interests of a few to take on national significance. Both were passionately playing out the tension between timber production and conservation. And both drew in the interests of organized labor.

10 In order to speed passage of the measure, avoid conference committee delays, and accommodate various senators, Burton eventually pushed the House not only to pass the Omnibus Parks bill, but to pass three separate versions of the measure, each the result of a different set of negotiations and deals with House and Senate members. With three House versions to choose from, Burton succeeded in shepherding the bill through the Senate in the final days of the 95th Congress and saw the measure enacted into law. P.L. 95-625; "Omnibus Parks Bill," 1978 *Congressional Quarterly Almanac*, pp. 704-07.

11 Miron L. Heinselman to Dr. Edgar Wayburn, April 7, 1977, and then met Edgar and Peggy Wayburn at a Sierra Club meeting in St. Paul soon after. See *MLH Chronology*, Apr. 7, 1977, Apr. 16, 1977.

12 See, for example, Richard Conlon, *Duluth News-Tribune*, June 19, 1960, "Wilderness Area Roads Proposed"; Richard Conlon, "Triumph Over the Wilderness," *Duluth News-Tribune*, Sept. 13-17, 1959 (an account of his 250-mile canoe trip along the border).

Conlon was killed in a sailing accident June 1988. For information on his life, see *Washington Post*, June 21, 1988, p. B6, "Hill Aide Missing After Sailboat Accident"; *Washington Post* (editorial), June 23, 1988, "Richard Conlon"; *Congressional Record*, July 12, 1988, H 5467, "Tribute to Richard P. Conlon"; and Kevin Proescholdt, " Dick Conlon: Congressional Leader and Wilderness Voyageur,"*BWCA Wilderness News*, Autumn 1988, p. 11.

13 Don Fraser remarked on the closeness of the two men: "With Burton, things didn't tend to remain just strictly professional. Sort of like Lyndon Johnson, who sort of tried to

absorb you. I know it was social outside [the working relationship], being the kind of intensely personal political person that Burton was."Fraser Interview, Oct. 25, 1991.

14 Fraser Interview, Oct. 25, 1991.

15 Rapson Recollections, December 1983.

16 Rapson Recollections, December 1983.

17 *Cook County News-Herald,* May 5, 1977, p. 1, "Fraser, Oberstar BWCA Bills Debated at Gunflint Meeting." This front-page commentary by Justine Kerfoot urged readers to write letters of support for the Oberstar bill.

18 *Ibid.*

19 The briefing paper explained the format of the hearings and relayed advice on testifying. Friends Field Hearings newsletter, June 1977; Friends of the Boundary Waters Wilderness to Potential Witnesses, June 20, 1977; Chuck Dayton Memorandum to Witnesses for the Fraser bill; copies in possession of authors.

20 Rep. Willard M. Munger, Testimony Before the Subcommittee on National Parks and Insular Affairs, July 7, 1977.

21 Rep. Phyllis Kahn, Testimony Before Subcommittee on National Parks and Insular Affairs, July 7, 1977;

22 Witness List, Subcommittee on National Parks and Insular Affairs, July 7, 1977.

23 Les Blacklock Testimony, July 7, 1977.

24 The resorters included Jocko Nelson of Jocko's Clearwater Resort, Jim Thompson of Borderland Lodge, Dave Tuttle of Bearskin Lodge, and Mark Janssen of Brule Lake's Sky Blue Water Lodge.

25 Mark A. Janssen Testimony, July 7, 1977. See also Jim Thompson Testimony, July 7, 1977; Jack A. Nelson Testimony, July 7, 1977; *Duluth News-Tribune,* July 8, 1977, p. 1, "BWCA's future debated by 200."

26 Julius Frederic Wolff, Jr., "Minnesota Conservation or Resource Management in Minnesota," Ph.d. Dissertation, University of Minnesota, July 1949, pp. 73-80.

27 *Minneapolis Star,* Aug. 23, 1978, p. 1A, ". . . Violence is Guaranteed."

28 See Chapter 1 and Searle, pp. 186-92.

29 *Minneapolis Tribune,* July 25, 1965, p. 1A, "Freeman Boundary Area Policy Protested in Ely."

30 Bill Rom Interview, March 25, 1987; Searle, p. 173.

31 Hubachek also became the target of a local smear campaign. Hubachek took the unusual step of printing a lengthy article in the *Ely Miner* to answer the charges made against him. *Ely Miner,* Aug. 25, 1949, p. 4, "F. Hubachek Makes Statement."

32 *Duluth News-Tribune*, May 17, 1975, p. 1, "Ely residents line roads to gain voice in BWCA"; *Duluth Herald*, May 19, 1975, "2 Ely firms kept targets of picketers."

33 In a bizarre sequence of events in the late 1940s, a man named Leo Chosa attacked Olson in the pages of the *Ely Miner*, accusing him of being a part of a grand conspiracy intended to front for the big timber companies. Chosa reasoned that Olson and others were advocating for the elimination of airplanes and tourism from the wilderness so that no one would know of the companies' logging operations. Implying in one letter that Olson was one of the timber companies' "paid hirelings and stooges," Chosa charged in another that Sig ignored the logging destruction "so a few farmer boys can paddle Sig's canoes in a primitive setting" and make Olson rich from his outfitting business. Cited from David James Backes, "The Air Ban War: Sigurd F. Olson and the Fight to Ban Airplanes from the Roadless Areas of Minnesota's Superior National Forest," master's thesis (Agricultural Journalism), University of Wisconsin-Madison, 1983, p. 111; subsequently cited as "Backes Thesis. See also Leo Chosa "Letters to the Editor," *Ely Miner*, June 17, 1948, p. 2; and Leo Chosa "Letters to the Editor," *Ely Miner*, Sept. 1, 1949, p. 9.

34 See generally Sigurd F. Olson to Kenneth Reid, Dec. 13, 1943 (not sent), Q-S files, Sigurd F. Olson Papers, Minnesota Historical Society.

35 See generally *Minneapolis Star*, Aug. 23, 1978, p. 1A, "' . . . Violence is guaranteed' in BWCA dispute"; *Minneapolis Star*, Aug. 26, 1978, p. 4, "Fear stalks the Ely 'resistance.'"

36 *Mesabi Daily News*, July 8, 1977, p. 1, "Ely's hearing on BWCA attracts crowd of 1,000."

37 Bob Cary Testimony, July 8, 1977.

38 Norman Kainz Testimony, July 8, 1977.

39 Shirley Klaesges Testimony, July 8, 1977.

40 Woods Davis Testimony, July 8, 1977.

41 Louise Leoni Testimony, July 8, 1977.

42 Ronald Harri Testimony, July 8, 1977.

43 *Ely Miner*, July 13, 1977, p. 1, "Emotions Surface at Subcommittee Hearings; 1,000 Attend."

44 The Friends had lined up a number of northern Minnesotans to testify in favor of the Fraser bill.

Mickie Scholtus, former writer for the Ely Echo, testified: "We must concede that there is a time to use and a time to preserve. The time to preserve is now, and the place is the BWCA."

Mike Link, of the Northwoods Audubon Center, stated: [I support the Fraser bill] with all my heart. This bill represents the love I have for the land and the spirit that is wilderness."

Izaak Walton League National President David Zentner pointed out the recent development of Jacob Pete's land on the Range River, within a proposed addition to the BWCA, as an example of the type of commercial exploitation of the wilderness which the Fraser bill would prohibit. Pete was a life-long Ely resident who formerly owned and operated a houseboat operation on Basswood Lake. He subsequently bought land along the Range River at the southwest end of Basswood Lake's Jackfish Bay and pushed a road to it from the Cloquet Line.

Mining engineer Robert Hautala of Virginia urged the subcommittee to disregard the home district deference to Oberstar because "this issue will have national precedence, and this wilderness must be preserved."

Fern Arpi, also of Virginia, presented a statement of sixteen reasons for supporting the Fraser bill. She told the subcommittee, "A heavy responsibility rests upon this committee. Gentlemen, you can either recommend fragmentation . . . or you can, before the opportunity is gone forever, finally grant to the Boundary Waters the Wilderness status it so richly deserves."

Mickie Scholtus Testimony, July 8, 1977; Mike Link Testimony, July 8, 1977; David F. Zentner Testimony, July 8, 1977; Robert Hautala Testimony, July 8, 1977; Fern Arpi Testimony, July 8, 1977.

45 *Echo* editor Cary later castigated the Ford group for legally flying in to Fourtown Lake to begin their canoe trip and for using the Four Mile truck portage and motorboats on Basswood Lake in order to get deep into the area. *Ely Echo*, July 27, 1977, "Why Did the Ely People 'Boo'?" Senator Johnson subsequently made the same criticisms at the Washington hearings. See Transcript of Proceedings, Hearing before Subcommittee on National Parks and Insular Affairs on H.R. 2820 and H.R. 5968, Aug. 4, 1977 and Sept. 12-13, 1977, pp. 724-725 (subsequently cited as "Hearing Transcript").

46 Recollections of Mike Link.

47 Cleve Pinnix later said that in his dozen years of public service, he had seen a rougher moment only once—in a redwoods hearing in Eureka, California, when members of the audience brought their guns into the hearing room

48 *Duluth News-Tribune*, July 9, 1977, p. 1, "BWCA Talks Spark Fiery Boos, Cheers"; *Ely Miner*, July 13, 1977, p. 1, "Emotions Surface at Subcommittee Hearing; 1,000 Attend."

49 Sigurd F. Olson testimony to the House Subcommittee on National Parks and Insular Affairs, July 8, 1977; see also edited presentation copy in Sigurd F. Olson Papers, BWCA 1974-1977 Folder, Box 6 (second series), Minnesota Historical Society.

A significant event unknown to the crowd also occurred with Olson's testimony. He carried with him a short statement written by Frank Hubachek addressed to the subcommittee, which was entered into the record.

For decades, Hubachek and his partner, Charles Kelly, had supported the position developed by the President's Quetico-Superior Committee in the late 1920s; this position protected the shoreline strips along canoe routes, while allowing logging in the backcountry. Thirteen years before the Ely hearing, Olson publicly supported an end to logging in the BWCA, parting company with his friends Hubachek and Kelly. But the letter from Hubachek that Olson carried contained a solid endorsement of the Fraser bill and publicly committed Hubachek to an end of logging and motorized use in the wilderness. Hubachek's letter reflected the strength of their fifty-year friendship and a healing of the earlier rift between the two over the logging issue. Recollections of Dr. Miron L. Heinselman.

50 See "Dr. J.P. Grahek Named Head of Ely Chamber of Commerce"; and *Who's Who in Minnesota—1958* (Waseca, Minnesota: Brown Printing Co., 1958).

51 See generally *Ely Miner*, Oct. 27, 1949, p. 1, "Knight 'Sir Ted,'"; and *Ely Miner*, Nov. 24, 1949, p. 1, "Still Holds 1.000 Average." See also *Ely Miner*, Jan. 12, 1950, p. 1; Backes Thesis, pp. 124-25, 136, 170.

52 H.R. 8722, 95th Congress, 1st Session.
    Oberstar met with the Alliance's Legislation Committee on July 15 to discuss their recommendations for his legislation. Following that meeting, Alliance official Lenore Johnson wrote to Oberstar recommending thirteen changes to the bill, eleven of which appeared in the August bill. Lenore Johnson to Congressman James Oberstar, July 22, 1977; copy in possession of authors.

53 The bill prohibited condemnation of private property within the NRA, expressly identified motorboat routes within the NRA, and adjusted the boundaries of the NRA and wilderness in various locations. H.R. 8722, 95th Congress, 1st Session. See also Hearing Transcript, pp. 600-630; "Statement on the Boundary Waters Canoe Area," Honorable James L. Oberstar, Aug. 4, 1977.

54 In addition to Burton, several other subcommittee members attended, including Krebs, Lagomarsino, Clausen, and Tsongas.

55 Rapson Recollections, December 1983.

56 Hearing Transcript, pp. 630-50; "News from Congressman Donald M. Fraser," Aug. 4, 1977; see also *Congressional Record*, Jan. 25, 1978, E 136.

57 Hearing Transcript, pp. 626, 641.

58 Vento did indicate, however, that he was "not insensitive to the local economic impact" of wilderness restrictions. Subcommittee Hearing Notes, Kevin Proescholdt, Aug. 4, 1977; see also Hearing Transcript, Aug. 4, 1977, pp. 651-664.
    The only other member of Congress to testify was Michael Blouin of Iowa. Blouin stressed the national significance of the BWCA, Iowa's closest wilderness, and mentioned the 10,000 Iowans who had signed Iowa PIRG's petition supporting the Fraser bill, as well as the 6,500 Iowa groups that had visited the BWCA in 1976. He told the subcommittee that he "strongly endorse[d] Mr. Fraser's approach and I urge the subcommittee to approve the Fraser Bill."Statement of Congressman Michael Blouin, Aug. 4, 1977.

59 The Administration's seven alternatives ranged from a Fraser bill approach at one extreme to an Oberstar bill approach on the other, with five alternatives in-between. With the exception of Alternative A, which would manage all 1,057,000 acres as wilder-

ness, each of the others contained National Recreation Areas of varying sizes and uses. Alternative G caught the environmentalists' attention: it proposed an expanded wilderness with no large lakes or international border lakes open to motors buffered by a National Recreation Area outside the BWCA along the Gunflint Trail, Echo Trail, and Fernberg Road. Statement of John McGuire, Chief, Forest Service, Aug. 4, 1977; Hearing Transcript, Aug. 4, 1977, pp. 708-15; Subcommittee Hearing Notes, Kevin Proescholdt, Aug. 4, 1977.

60 *Minneapolis Tribune*, Aug. 14, 1977, p. 1, "Minnesotans split over uses of BWCA." Residents of northern Minnesota favored multiple use over wilderness by a fifty-four to forty-two margin.

61 *MLH Chronology*, July 26, 1977.

62 Coincidentally, Herbst and Ikes leader Dave Zentner found themselves together on a summer rafting trip on Utah's Green River. Zentner also received a friendly, but neutral response about the BWCA issue. *MLH Chronology*, July 28, 1977; Aug. 1, 1977.

63 M. Rupert Cutler Interview, Oct. 5, 1986; see also Malcom Rupert Cutler, "A Study of Litigation Related to Management of Forest Service Administered Lands and Its Effects on Policy Decisions. Part Two: A Comparison of Four Cases," Ph.D. thesis, Michigan State University, 1972.

64 M. Rupert Cutler Interview, Oct. 5, 1986.

65 M. Rupert Cutler Interview, Oct. 5, 1986.

66 M. Rupert Cutler Interview, Oct. 5, 1986; *MLH Chronology*, July 26, 1977; July 27, 1977.
  A Forest Service recreation researcher named Bob Lucas talked with Cutler in early August and reported that Cutler seemed leaning towards the environmentalists' position. *MLH Chronology*, Aug. 11, 1977.

67 M. Rupert Cutler to Sigurd F. Olson, Aug. 16, 1977; found in Sigurd F. Olson Papers, BWCA 1974-1977 Folder, Box 6 (second series), MN Historical Society.
  Olson and Cutler had crossed paths a number of months earlier at the Sigurd Olson Environmental Institute at Northland College in Wisconsin, where Cutler gave a speech on the values of wilderness. *MLH Chronology*, May 14, 1977.

68 *MLH Chronology*, July 13, 1977.

69 See *MLH Chronology*, July 22, 1977; July 25, 1977.

70 Philbrook Paper, pp. 118-21.

71 Nye had built a good environmental record during his previous public service in Ohio and had received very positive support for his Minnesota DNR job from Sierra Club leaders. See *MLH Chronology*, Aug. 10, 1977.
  Nye was aided considerably in his task of preparing a logging position by Rod Sando, director of the Division of Forestry within DNR. Sando was convinced that alter-

native softwood was available to replace the wood that would be lost if logging were banned in the BWCA Portal Zone. He ultimately convinced Perpich and Nye that BWCA timber was not needed.

72 Memo to William B. Nye from DNR Staff (Barbara Clark, Bob Djupstrom, Wayne Hanson, Tim Jordheim, Erick Kurki, George Orning, Bud Philbrook, Rod Sando, Ken Wald, and Willard West) regarding "Analysis of Softwood Production Outside of the BWCA," Aug. 11, 1977; copy in possession of authors. See also *MLH Chronology*, Aug. 11, 1977.

73 Burnham Philbrook to Dr. Rupert Cutler, Aug. 19, 1977; Burnham Philbrook to David Bieging, Aug. 19, 1977; copies in possession of authors.

74 Memo to William B. Nye from DNR staff (Bob Djupstrom, Carroll Henderson, Robert Hodge, Frank Knoke, Jackie Kucher, Bud Philbrook, Rita Plourde, Steve Preston, and Richard Sternberg) regarding "Motor/Canoe Conflicts in the BWCA," Aug. 29, 1977; MN Department of Natural Resources, "Position Regarding Boundary Waters Canoe Area," 1977; copy in possession of authors.

75 According to one observer, the Alliance hoped to show "its hospitality and hopefully, that northern Minnesotans weren't such bad folks." Zabinski Paper, p. 20.

76 See generally *Ely Echo*, Sept. 21, 1977, p. 1, "80 Attend Hearings in Washington."

77 The information booklet was prepared by Friends member Herb Johnson. It contained photographs depicting logging practices, a map showing areas that could compensate for logging losses in the BWCA, and a variety of other visual depictions of the issues. Copy in possession of authors.

78 Rapson Recollections, December 1983.

79 To further put the Alliance at ease, Burton noted to a panel of Alliance members who were testifying that the Fraser bill would block access for them to the BWCA "I am not sure I could make that backpack into the wilderness country myself. My idea of exercise for a long hike is walking from the water cooler and back." Hearing Transcript, p. 832. A key member of the Alliance would say later that Burton had been fair in his treatment. Zabinski Paper, pp. 19-20.

80 Hearing Transcript, pp. 723-808; Agenda and Witnesses, Subcommittee on National Parks and Insular Affairs, Sept. 12, 1977.

81 See, for example, Testimony of Tom Smrekar and testimony of Wes Hedstrom. Hearing Transcript, pp. 808-983; Agenda and Witnesses, Subcommittee on National Parks and Insular Affairs, Sept. 12, 1977.

82 Hearing Transcript, pp. 854-58.

83 Administration Proposed Substitute Bill, Sept. 13, 1977; Statements of Bob Bergland and of M. Rupert Cutler Before the Subcommittee on National Parks and Insular Affairs, Sept. 13, 1977. Hearing Transcript, pp. 1010-71.

84 M. Rupert Cutler Interview, Oct. 5, 1986.

85 See M. Rupert Cutler Interview, Oct. 5, 1986.

86 *Ibid.*

87 *Ibid.*

88 *Ibid.* Minnesota Public Radio produced a documentary on Hubert Humphrey in 1988, ten years after his death. The full documentary included a segment in which Federal Judge Miles Lord attributes the quote to Humphrey. See "The Politics of Joy: A Radio Remembrance of Hubert H. Humphrey," Minnesota Public Radio, 1988.

89 Sig Olson wrote Cutler a letter a few days later, applauding his "courageous stand on the BWCA." "You are living up to the promise you made at Northland that the preservation of wilderness had high priority," Olson continued. "Your firmness and insight have been an inspiration to us all." Sigurd F. Olson to M. Rupert Cutler, Sept. 15, 1977; copy in possession of authors.

90 The state also supported improved educational efforts to lessen conflicts between canoeists and motorboaters, better distribution of users through techniques such as temporal zoning (time-of-year restrictions), and additional attention to the development of recreation resources outside the wilderness. Hearing Transcript, Sept. 13, 1977, pp. 1135-1172; Testimony of William Nye, Commissioner of the Minnesota Department of Natural Resources Before the Subcommittee on National Parks and Insular Affairs, Sept. 13, 1977.
    Nye and Philbrook had spent an hour and a half with Heinselman the day before discussing possible state moves to help alleviate the softwood timber supply if logging ended in the BWCA. *MLH Chronology*, Sept. 12, 1977.

91 Hearing Transcript, Sept. 13, 1977, pp. 1127-34.

92 Ed Junke and Loren Filter testified on snowmobiling; Bruce Kerfoot and Mark Janssen on outboard motors; Lee Hotaling on forest management; Robert "Jeep" Latourell and Bob Olson on canoe outfitters; and Justine Kerfoot and Frank Salerno on home owners concerns.
    Mark Janssen of Brule Lake's Sky Blue Waters Lodge told Burton that "our business is dependent on guests who use motor craft. It would be a gross injustice to ban motors and in turn the many who have come to enjoy the BWCA."
    Justine Kerfoot spoke on behalf of senior citizens and Gunflint Trail home owners; she told the panel that home owners "leave no trace with the melting snow and no worn path across the lakes. It is the canoe camper who leaves the impact on the land with the heavily used camp sites and gathering of wood for camp fires." Hearing Transcript, Sept. 13, 1977, pp. 1004-08; Written Testimony of Justine Kerfoot, Sept. 13, 1977.

93 Testimony of Miron L. Heinselman, Chairman, Friends of the Boundary Waters Wilderness, Sept. 1977. Hearing Transcript, pp. 1193-1226.

94 Darby Nelson, Statement for the Hearing Record in Support of HR 2820, and Hearing Transcript, pp. 1298-1308.

95 Green concluded:
> The time has come for full wilderness protection and the cessation of nibbling away at our last large remnant of an intact northern forest ecosystem. The setting aside of wilderness is an act of some humility by modern man. It is an attitude to be fostered if we are to gain the wisdom necessary to bring us into ecological balance with the natural world that sustains the mind and body of us all.

Statement by Janet C. Green before the House Interior Committee, Subcommittee on National Parks and Insular Affairs, Sept. 13, 1977. Hearing Transcript, pp. 1288-1291.

See also testimony of Tim Knopp, Subcommittee on National Parks and Insular Affairs, Sept. 13, 1977. Hearing Transcript, pp. 1256-59 (impact of motorboat use).

96 Dayton noted:
> It was as an accommodation to local interests and over the objection of wilderness advocates that the very road and boundary adjustments which made these resorts possible were developed. Local resort interests represent the only real claim of possible hardship in this controversy. They can be accommodated and can prosper without great change in their way of life and without sacrificing the wilderness character of the land.

Statement of Charles K. Dayton, House Subcommittee on National Parks and Insular Affairs, Sept. 13, 1977. Hearing Transcript, pp. 1292-96.

97 Statement in support of HR 2820, H.E. Wright, Jr., House Subcommittee on National Parks and Insular Affairs, Sept. 1977. Hearing Transcript, pp. 1311-12.

98 Maloney concluded: "[O]n behalf of all of the people who seek to experience the last vestiges of the great untrammeled wilderness that was once America—who go out into the four seasons of the year in search of places where the noise and haste of mechanized society are left behind—I urge your support for complete, uncompromised, unmutilated wilderness protection for the Boundary Waters Wilderness. . . ." Statement of Jack P. Maloney before the House Subcommittee on National Parks and Insular Affairs, Sept. 13, 1977. Hearing Transcript, pp. 1260-70.

99 See Statement of Charles H. Stoddard for the Wilderness Society, Sept. 13, 1977; Statement of Izaak Walton League of America (Maitland Sharpe), Sept. 13, 1977; Statement of T. Destry Jarvis, National Parks and Conservation Association, Sept. 13, 1977; Statement of Patricia S. Record regarding BWCA, Sept. 13, 1977; Testimony of Friends of the Earth, Sept. 13, 1977; Statement of Rick Glanz for the National Audubon Society, Sept. 12-13, 1977. Hearing Transcript, pp. 1175-89.

100 These included citizen activists from Illinois, Iowa, Virginia, New Jersey, and Virginia, as well as the Minnesota and national League of Women Voters. Testimony of Paul Nachman, Sept. 13, 1977; Testimony in support of the Fraser Bill by John C. McLaughlin, Sept. 13, 1977; Testimony on the BWCA by T. Robert Royt, Sept. 13, 1977; Statement of Martha E. Johnson, Sept. 13, 1977; Testimony by Mary Poppleton, League of Women Voters, Sept. 13, 1977. Hearing Transcript, pp. 1236-1255.

101 Testimony of William H. Muir before Subcommittee on National Parks and Insular Affairs, Sept. 13, 1977. Hearing Transcript, pp. 1271-81.

102 Hearing Transcript, pp. 1295, 1311-1312. See generally *Minneapolis Star*, Sept. 13, 1977, p. 1A, "Carter Team Says, 'Keep BWCA Wild'"; *Minneapolis Star*, Sept. 14, 1977, p. 1A, "BWCA Future Takes Shape"; *Duluth News-Tribune*, Sept. 14, 1977, p. 1, "U.S. Pushes Own BWCA Zoning Plan"; *Iowa State Daily*, Sept. 20, 1977, p. 1, "Expect bill to 'save' Boundary Waters"; *Ely Echo*, Sept. 21, 1977, p. 1, "80 Attend Hearings in Washington."

Chapter Four

The Legislation Takes Form

The September hearings had created an expectation that events would move quickly. But the intensity of the hearings gradually gave way to a long period of inactivity that frayed nerves and raised fears that the bills would die a quiet death. As Congress prepared to recess in early November, it became clear that nothing would be done in the subcommittee until lawmakers returned in January 1978.

Local Politics

The hiatus in Washington meant that the political focus would, for the moment, shift back to Minnesota.

That focus was in turn increasingly on the embryonic race for the United States Senate.

The State of Minnesota had watched with sorrow and admiration as Hubert Humphrey fought a dignified battle with cancer throughout 1977. Thinner by the week, Humphrey had been in and out of chemotherapy while courageously fulfilling his public service commitments.

The senator's declining health raised quiet speculation about the possibility that 1978 would see two elections: one for Wendy Anderson's seat and one for Humphrey's. Don Fraser was the subject of much of that speculation.

Fraser and Humphrey dated their relationship to the extraordinary post-World-War-II class of young DFLers: Humphrey, Mondale, Fraser, McCarthy, Freeman.[1] It was unthinkable that Fraser would consider running for Humphrey's seat as long as his old friend held it. But exploring a challenge to Wendell Anderson was an altogether different question.

By the fall of 1977, that was exactly what Fraser began to do.

After sixteen years in the House, Fraser was ready to move on to the next challenge.[2] The Senate would be an opportunity to lend another dimension to a life already defined by public service.

Challenging an incumbent senator from within the party was a risky and controversial business. Not something that a loyal and firm believer in the party, as Fraser was, would take lightly. But the bad taste of Anderson's "self-appointment" to the Senate had still not left Minnesotans' mouths. And Fraser had never been one to shy from risks.

In late October, Fraser mailed 36,000 cards to active DFLers around the state, asking their opinion about his potential candidacy. Eighty-six percent of the responses he received urged him to run, a staggering total even given the self-selecting nature of the respondents.[3]

The prospect sent chills up the collective spine of northern Minnesota residents. It was bad enough to have Fraser pushing his bill as one of 435 House members; it was quite another thing to imagine his influence as a senator.[4] Increasingly, the Alliance counted among its challenges the prevention of this from happening.

The Alliance's executive director, Bob Buckler, resigned in mid-November to work in public affairs for the forest products industry. A political veteran with close ties to Oberstar named Ed Zabinski took over the reins.[5] Zabinski had interned for Oberstar's office in 1975 and had worked part-time on Oberstar's campaign staff in 1977. He had lived in Ely since the age of six; he knew the area, its issues, and its people.[6]

Zabinski was instinctively more a creature of the political process than was Buckler. He immediately set to work increasing the Alliance's visibility and turning up the pressure on Fraser.

The Alliance began a concerted effort to get its word out through newspapers, radio, and television.[7] It also sought to create its own news.

In early October, the Alliance sent a busload of striking Iron Range steelworkers to picket Fraser's office in downtown Minneapolis. The steelworkers also took the opportunity to go door-to-door in blue-collar northeast Minneapolis gathering 700 signatures from Fraser's own constituents on a letter opposing Fraser's BWCA bill.[8]

Oberstar indirectly joined the effort. Borrowing a page from the logging experience, he wrote Bergland in mid-December, requesting that the BWCA snowmobile ban be lifted until Congress completed its deliberations. Speaking for the secretary, Rupert Cutler denied the request in February of 1978.[9]

A month before Cutler decided, Humphrey passed away. The day following his death, on January 14, a group of local snowmobilers headed by Alliance leader Ed Junke organized a protest ride in Humphrey's name. Leading somewhere between three and four hundred snowmobiles from Lake Vermilion to the BWCA entry point at Trout Lake, the group called the event the "Hubert Humphrey Memorial Snowmobile Protest Ride."

"THE SNOW IS ALWAYS WHITER..."

(*Reprinted with permission from the* Duluth News-Tribune)

By the time the protesters reached the Trout Lake portage, the snow machines covered an area 300 yards wide and half a mile long. Junke quipped, "You couldn't see the lake for the snowmobiles."[10] The snowmobilers stopped at the Trout Lake portage for a moment's silence in memory of Humphrey. They then roared across the portage and into BWCA territory.

The Forest Service patrolled the incident from the air. Junke complained that they "hovered over in their plane like vultures, Saturday, in order to catch the last few stragglers." After the main group turned back from Trout Lake to return to Vermilion, enforcement officers ticketed fifteen residents on the portage.[11]

The split in reactions in northern Minnesota reflected the polarizing effect the ride had on the entire state. The *Ely Echo* condemned "Jimmy Carter's USDA Airbourne Troops"—"The Forestry Fuzz"—for pouncing in the "Tower Blitz." But the *Duluth News-Tribune* editorialized, "Blatant disregard for law is usually a behavior reserved for children or the demented."[12]

The Alliance also sought to tap whatever influence the State of Minnesota might still have after the debacle of the fall hearings. Zabinski and nineteen other members of the Alliance traveled to the governor's mansion in March, meeting with Perpich, Iron Range state legislators, and State Senate Majority Leader Nick Coleman. Although Perpich reiterated his support of BWCA snowmobiling and softened his previous anti-logging position, he provided no specific strategies for affecting the congressional deliberations.[13]

The Friends dreaded the Alliance's resort to more intensively political tactics. If Congress perceived the BWCA bills as having become entangled with a local electoral fight, its inclination likely would be to let the political winds blow over and return to the BWCA another time. And the Alliance was increasingly and effectively fueling that perception.

The Friends' anxiety was compounded by the logjam building in the Interior Committee. The Alaska Lands legislation, Burton's Redwoods National Park bill, the gargantuan Omnibus Parks legislation—all were parked on the agenda with no immediate departure in sight.

The Friends decided on a three-part strategy to address both the Alliance's tactics and the impasse in committee.

First, they would keep the pressure on at the local level. Continuing the logging moratorium was the first order of business. In a rare show of solidarity, Vento and Oberstar were able to convince Forest Service Chief McGuire to suspend the six active sales until Congress had completed its deliberations.[14] The Friends also held a well-publicized fundraiser in St. Paul in early December[15] and increased the intensity of their letter-writing campaigns and public-speaking.

Second, they would begin informing House members beyond those who sat on the subcommittee.

The Heinselmans had rented an apartment across the street from the Cannon House Office Building that became the nerve center of the Friends' lobbying effort. Every morning a little before 8:00 A.M., Heinselman would bundle his maps, walk to check in with Rapson, and

Rip Rapson was at the center of countless strategy discussions with the Friends. (*Photo courtesy of Rip Rapson*)

head off on his rounds of appointments with House members and staff. He and Rapson had plotted out three tiers of priority: "friends," "convincibles," and "don't bother." Rapson wanted to buck up the first, concentrate on the second, and politely ignore the third. Heinselman insisted on trying to reach all three. It made for a lot of walking and talking. But for hours each day, from September through the winter, that is exactly what Heinselman did, sometimes with Rapson, sometimes with other Friends members, but most often by himself.

Rapson also mapped out a series of briefings that would reach larger clusters of key members and staff. The first was held in late September. Heinselman presented a slide show, and Rapson walked more than fifty congressional members and staff through the competing bills.

By the start of the new year, the Friends had reached well over one hundred offices, including some of the key senators.[16]

The third prong of the Friends' strategy was to work on Burton. Little did they realize that Burton had plans of his own along these lines.

A Smoke-Filled Room

The Alliance was exploring every possible channel to get to Burton.

Working through their national labor ties, the Alliance located a Californian named Carl Jones, a retired ranking official in the steelworkers union, president of the California Congress of Senior Citizens, and a close friend of Burton. The Alliance flew Jones and his wife to Ely in late January to get to know the Alliance better and to learn more about the BWCA. Jones left promising to speak with Burton.[17]

The Alliance's labor contacts also opened the door of House Speaker Tip O'Neill. O'Neill promised to speak to Burton about the BWCA when he attended a Burton fundraiser in San Francisco later that month.[18]

Burton was consummately political—he would hear out old friends and pay attention to the House Speaker. But he was also fiercely independent. And he had fixed on a course that neither these conversations, nor any other outside influences, would derail.

In October, Burton summoned Heinselman to a private audience in a small anteroom off of his main office. After swearing Heinselman to secrecy, Burton asked that he begin drafting yet another bill: the Burton bill. Burton explained that he believed Heinselman to be the one person whose motives were pure, who wanted to do what was right for the BWCA. Burton proposed that he and Heinselman work closely and intensively over the next few months to develop a bill that would combine the best aspects of everything that had been proposed up to that point. He made clear that he wanted Heinselman not to be a puppet, but to push him in directions Heinselman thought it wise to move.[19]

Heinselman began immediately, telling nobody except his wife, Fran, what he was doing.

He started with boundaries—evaluating which areas should be added to the BWCA. He necessarily drew in Forest Service officials, who provided specific technical assistance in the preparing of detailed Geological Survey topographic maps for all the possible wilderness additions.

Once Heinselman fixed on proposed boundaries, Burton called in Forest Service staff as a safeguard that Heinselman was not overreaching. The Forest Service staff and Heinselman spread the maps on the table and went through tens of proposed additions one by one. During the first vodka, Burton would let the Forest Service and Heinselman quarrel. With the second, he would pepper each with questions. By the third, he would indicate his decision by outlining with his socked right big toe which boundaries were acceptable. Heinselman would then trace the path of the toe onto the master copy of the map.

Although Cutler had directed the Forest Service to cooperate with Burton in all respects, they were more than a little uncomfortable with their role. During one particularly heated session, Bob Potter of the Forest Service had found himself on the losing end of an exchange about a particularly large addition to the wilderness. When Burton left the room to refresh his drink, Potter sputtered, "Bud, you've got to lay off. This is nothing but a damned land grab!"

Burton was anything but capricious, however. He intended to include all additions proposed by the Carter Administration, all of the few additions proposed by Oberstar, all of the additions proposed by Fraser, and any lands that the federal government proposed to add to wilderness through its review of national roadless areas.[20] He insisted that Heinselman outline on the topographic maps the existing and the proposed boundary for each addition. He grilled Heinselman on the rationale for each addition and on the kind of flak and counter-arguments he would encounter for each. By the time they were completed, the boundaries were as embedded in Burton's mind as a crucial vote count.

Once set, the boundaries provided the base for the rest of Heinselman's work. At that point, he drew in Rapson and a handful of others.[21] Just as before, Burton used Heinselman and now Rapson to develop ideas that he could mull over and critique. Unlike setting boundaries, however, the discussions about snowmobiles, logging, and especially motorboating were not amenable to taking the most expansive provisions of the Fraser, Oberstar, and Carter Administration bills.

The early sessions were philosophical. Burton asked Rapson how pure a wilderness would have to be to pass muster with Fraser and the environmental community. After Rapson identified some of the potential areas of compromise, Burton launched into a reflection on the rise and fall of progressive politics in

California, lamenting the ascendency of pragmatism and the disappearance of a politics of principle.

Two cigars, innumerable vodkas, and four hours later, he turned to Rapson and asked "So tell me what all of this has to do with some duck ponds in northern Minnesota." Before Rapson could offer an answer, Burton saved him the effort: "It has to do with sticking to your guns. It has to do with people like Don Fraser, who is risking his f— political neck because he thinks it's the right thing to do. It has to do with people like Heinselman here—people who understand that there is no compromise with the devil."[22]

That woke Heinselman up, who had dozed off on the couch. Burton looked over at him and said, "Goddammit, Bud, I love you." Still a little bleary-eyed, Heinselman didn't know what to make of the scene. He laughed nervously. "Well, Mr. Chairman, we really appreciate all that you're doing on this bill," Heinselman offered. "No, Bud," Burton interrupted. "I love you." Burton grinned, put his shoes on, and left Heinselman and Rapson staring at each other.[23]

The sessions continued into November. Burton decided early on that mining, logging, and snowmobiling had no place. The motorboats were trickier. Heinselman and Rapson had prepared a list of lakes on which the BWCA boundary ran through the middle of the lake. These were lakes on which homes and resorts were located. They were also lakes on which motorboating would always be permitted on that portion of the lake outside the BWCA boundary. Rapson made the case that a compromise that recognized the futility of banning motorboat travel on these lakes—even those portions inside the wilderness boundaries—might be seen as an accommodation to the homeowners and resorts on them. Heinselman was not entirely pleased at the prospect of permanent motorboat use within the wilderness, regardless of its limited scale. He agreed, however, that it was the least damaging potential compromise.

With Burton's agreement, the final details of the Burton bill fell into place by early November:

- a Boundary Waters Wilderness of about 1,065,000 acres;
- a Boundary Waters National Recreation Area similar to the one proposed by the Carter Administration;
- an end to logging, mining, and snowmobiling ;
- ten-horsepower motorboats permitted on Fall, Moose, Snowbank, East Bearskin, South Farm, North and Clearwater Lakes;
- ten-horsepower motorboats permitted on the east portion of Seagull Lake until 1992; and
- twenty-five-horsepower motorboats allowed on a channel along the eastern shore of Saganaga Lake north to Canada Customs.[24]

Heinselman was drained, but satisfied. By completing his work by November, Burton would have six weeks to make his preparations for bringing the new bill forward to the subcommittee in early January.

The Long Wait

When Congress reconvened in January, the Friends were anxious for quick action. They had no knowledge of the new compromise. They simply assumed that Burton would bring the Fraser bill up early and start the process in motion.

Before that happened, a number of political twists added to the uncertainty.

The first was the re-entry of Governor Perpich. In early January, Perpich had asked Heinselman to meet with him and DNR Commissioner Nye. Given Perpich's history of open meetings, Heinselman anticipated that the press would attend. He was correct. It ensured that the meeting would not move beyond broad platitudes. Heinselman did nevertheless tell Perpich and Nye that Burton would introduce a compromise bill soon. The Burton bill, Heinselman stated, would likely allow some motor use at the edge of the wilderness, but would prohibit logging, mining, and peat harvesting in the entire BWCA.

With the press' tape recorders spinning, Perpich said that he would support that kind of compromise bill: "That would take care of my major concerns —keeping mining, peat harvesting, and logging out of there. I'm not as concerned about snowmobiles and motorboats."[25]

A week later, on January 13, Hubert Humphrey's death took everyone's mind off the BWCA.

The nation's leaders honored his memory at a memorial service in Washington, including a rare joint appearance by President Carter and former Presidents Ford and Nixon. Vice President Mondale led mourners at the funeral service in St. Paul: "Hubert taught us all how to love, how to win, and how to lose. He taught us how to live, and, finally, he taught us how to die."

Humphrey's passing had several consequences for the BWCA debate. It introduced a new senator, Muriel Humphrey. It elevated the importance of Minnesota's former junior senator, Wendy Anderson. It changed Don Fraser's Senate plans. And it left a void at the heart of the Minnesota DFL party.

Humphrey's widow, Muriel Humphrey, was appointed by Perpich to serve the remainder of Hubert's Senate term. She made clear that she would not seek election to the seat. Muriel Humphrey was as opposite as opposite can be from her late husband. He craved the limelight; she shunned it. He exuded energy and confidence; she gave the impression of quiet assuredness. He lived and breathed public affairs; she thrived within a family context.

The new Senator Humphrey was largely an enigma to both sides of the BWCA dispute. She was free to fashion her own position—Hubert had made only very limited forays into the debate. She seemed beholden to very few.

One person for whom the new senator did feel a sense of responsibility was Wendy Anderson. Humphrey saw Anderson as one of Hubert's protégés who had been loyal to him during life and who would carry on his legacy.

For his part, Anderson was deeply affected by Humphrey's death. It was not only a personal loss, but a professional one. Anderson had been comfortable in his junior senator role, learning the ropes from a master. The tables were now turned—Anderson would be looked to to provide Senate leadership on the BWCA, with Muriel Humphrey taking her cues from him.

Muriel Humphrey's lack of interest in running for the Senate seat in a special election also freed Fraser from the need to run against Anderson. Despite the positive response he had received when exploring that possibility, Fraser was far more comfortable running for an open seat. He began making preparations to shift gears.

Humphrey's death also removed a potential wildcard. Where there had been the possibility of a senior, universally-respected statesman putting an imprint on the dispute once it arrived in the Senate, a void now existed. Anderson might rise to the challenge of the moment, but he would not be able to offer the kind of almost-paternal influence that was always a possibility with Humphrey.

Both sides had long speculated about what role Humphrey might play.

The Alliance had been confident that Humphrey would be an ally. They had been encouraged by the congressional delegation working session Humphrey had convened in March of the previous year. They also believed that Humphrey's authorship of the 1964 Wilderness Act language permitting logging, motorboating, and snowmobiling would lead him to fashion a compromise permitting those uses to continue. Finally, they suspected that the more political the debate became, the more Humphrey would enter the fray as the peacemaker.

On the other hand, the Friends had been hopeful that Humphrey's lengthy friendship with Sig Olson and Bill Magie, coupled with his basic belief in wilderness protection, would bring out the statesman in him. In the spring of 1978, Magie wrote Olson a letter that suggests that this faith may have been well-founded:

> I talked with HHH last fall twice, and he says to let them haggle over the bill in the House and he would introduce an amendment to the WILDERNESS BILL which would state in one paragraph, that THERE SHALL BE NO LOGGING, MINING OR MECHANICAL USE in the BWCA—He said that would end it once and for all. I am writing to Muriel to see if she would do what her late husband said he would do—

The trouble is he made those statements over the phone to me. Once he was in Washington, the other time he was home.[26]

The point was, of course, moot. But it suggested just how dramatically the political scenery had changed.

The third distraction from the subcommittee's timetable came from the Republican side of the aisle.

In late January, Al Quie traveled to Ely to attend the Ely Sled Dog Races. Quie's photo later appeared in the *Ely Echo* showing him riding a snowmobile— illegally—up the Moose Lake chain into the wilderness.[27] The message was clear: Quie was preparing to run for governor and needed to establish his bona fides on the BWCA dispute if he was to establish a base on the Range.

Quie was pivotal to both sides. His views would be highly influential within the Republican caucus, which had no particular desire to lend political support to Fraser, Oberstar, or Burton—all Democrats. His state-wide gubernatorial campaign would build visibility and support among moderate voters for whatever position he took on the BWCA.

Quie played his neutrality to full advantage. He permitted environmentalists to emphasize his past support of wilderness legislation[28] and his friendships with Olson, Magie, and other pillars of the conservation community.[29] But as the snowmobile ride demonstrated, he did nothing to discourage local residents from seeing him as sympathetic to the issues about which they were passionate.

After his return from Ely, Quie sought to become more centrally involved in the debate. He met with Heinselman, Dan Engstrom, and Rapson in early February to become more familiar with the options for discontinuing logging in the BWCA. Throughout February, he met individually with Fraser, Oberstar, Vento, and other members of the Minnesota delegation to explore whether a middle ground might be struck.[30] He kept his thoughts close to the vest, but was clearly preparing for a more active role.

The political eddies created by the Perpich intervention, the Humphrey succession, and the Quie exploration appeared to stall the subcommittee. By mid-February, there was no word from Burton about when the bill would be considered. The Friends' confidence gave way to a growing sense of panic. The bill had a very long way to go by the session's end in October, when the 95th Congress would adjourn and the slate would be wiped clean. The subcommittee had to mark up its bill. The Interior Committee had to make room in its crowded docket for hearings and its own markup. The House had to schedule floor time for full debate. And the entire process would have to be repeated in the Senate.

Heinselman was growing particularly distraught. He had a habit of groaning and running his hands through his few remaining wisps of hair when agitated. About this time, Rapson told him that he would wear entire layers of skin off the top of his head if he did not relax.

Heinselman finally arranged a meeting with Burton in late February by enlisting Raye Paige, a staff member of the Wilderness Society and a personal favorite of Burton. Heinselman and Paige were met with an uncharacteristically cool attitude; Burton remained noncommittal about when the bill would move. Heinselman was beside himself; he was convinced that somebody had gotten to Burton and that the bill was in trouble.

It was Rapson's turn to try. He met with Burton and Vento the next day.[31] The problem became clear five minutes into the conversation: Burton and Vento had secretly been charting a new strategy and developing their own version of the bill.

Burton and Vento had concluded that Oberstar could be convinced to accept a compromise provided it did not appear to be a capitulation to Fraser. They also wanted to redirect the controversy toward them to minimize the political fallout on Fraser's Senate bid. "Think of this as a tourniquet strategy: Don Fraser has already been slashed up—we have to stop the bleeding," Burton told Rapson.[32] The tourniquet strategy would require that the bill carry Burton and Vento's names, not Fraser's, and that it depart in important respects from Fraser's approach.

Burton knew that the strategy would be effective only if he were able to master every detail and become the bill's chief salesman. He and Vento had accordingly spent much of the previous week hammering out the key points and passing them to staffer Pinnix for drafting.

News of the strategy was held to a small circle. Fraser concurred with the decision. Heinselman was relieved, but still concerned about what the details would be. Dick Conlon from the Democratic Study Group was pulled in to help manage the public relations; he and Rapson opened a discussion with *Minneapolis Tribune* reporter Al McConagha about the angle he would emphasize. Burton and Vento began preparations for a mid-March announcement.

Burton and Vento unveiled their proposal, dubbed the "Burton-Vento bill," on March 16th.[33]

Heinselman could take satisfaction from the bill's heavy reliance on his work the past fall.

Taking its lead from Heinselman, the Burton-Vento bill's boundaries were expansive: the bill included about twenty small additions to the wilderness totaling about 45,000 acres and followed the Carter Administration's recommendation to establish a 227,000-acre National Recreation Area outside the wilderness.[34]

The bill adopted the approach of permitting ten-horsepower motors on those lakes on the perimeter of the BWCA. It expanded Heinselman's list to include Brule, Little North, North Fowl, South Fowl, Magnetic, and Little

It's kind of a zone defense

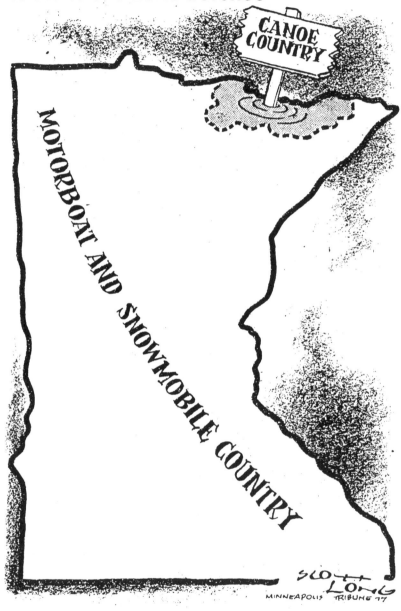

(*Reprinted with permission from the* Minneapolis Star Tribune)

Gunflint Lakes. It also provided a five-year phase out of motorboat use during peak fishing seasons on Seagull Lake east of Three Mile Island and on Newton Lake and Pipestone Bay of Basswood Lake.

The bill called for the end of logging after a one-year phase out. It authorized the Forest Service to compensate loggers for existing contracts, and to offset the loss of BWCA timber by managing a twelve-million-dollar fund for the intensification of forest management practices outside the wilderness.

The bill permitted snowmobiling on only two corridors necessary to make Canadian residential properties accessible from the United States side of the border (Saganaga Lake and Little Vermilion Lake).

Finally, the bill adopted Fraser's so-called ameliorative measures, which authorized the Forest Service to purchase those resorts that no longer wanted to continue operations and to provide funding to help remaining resorts convert to a wilderness-oriented clientele.[35]

The proposal was successful in being seen as a new effort, not simply a dressing up of the Fraser bill. The major media praised its conciliatory tone, and the environmentalists conceded that it was a fair accommodation to the interests of northern Minnesota.[36]

The real test, however, was Oberstar. Much of the impetus for the bill was to enlist his acquiescence in a more moderate approach. The bill had, more-

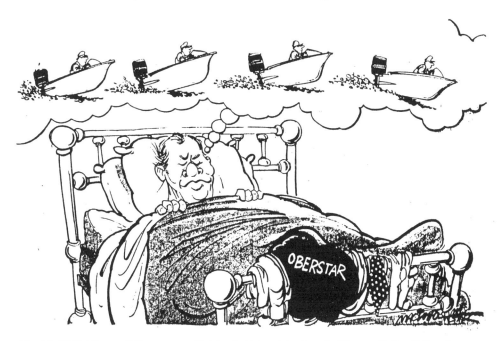

May 14, 1978 *Minneapolis Star* cartoon. (*Reprinted with permission from the* Minneapolis Star Tribune)

over, left him ample room to extract further concessions on behalf of his constituents. Burton and Vento, who had not shared the draft with him before its release, waited for his reaction.

That reaction was not exactly what the two men had hoped.

To say that Oberstar came out with both guns blazing would be an understatement. It was more like he was armed with three SCUD missiles and an antiaircraft gun.

Oberstar reserved his most incendiary comments for a crowd in Ely, capping a description of the new bill with the statement, "That's not a compromise. That's an execution."[37]

Local residents picked up the cue. The *Ely Echo* headlined, "Rep. Burton Hurls Bomb At Ely Area Resorts," and later editorialized that "Big Brother will getcha!"[38] "It's another disaster," claimed Grand Marais activist Gene Groth. "It takes away all the rights of the local people [and puts] the entire Gunflint Trail under the thumb of the federal government."[39] About fifty Gunflint Trail residents met with Vento on March 30 to register their opposition.[40]

Oberstar's reaction was ominous in its implications.

It revealed a level of personal investment that would not permit even the slightest appearance of appeasement to the environmentalists generally and Fraser in particular. The bad blood ran deep. This was now personal.

It underscored how much weight the hardline view within his constituency carried in his political calculations. The consistent public opinion majority against the Fraser bill within the Eighth District was a significant understatement of the fervor of the hard-core wilderness opponents.[41] And Oberstar believed that these hardliners would determine his political future.

It suggested that he had made the strategic decision to fight Burton rather than join him and that he believed he could win—either by engineering support for his own bill or, at the least, by bottling up the legislation in the House. Many months earlier, Oberstar had said to Rapson, "I don't understand you. You don't have a chance to pass this bill. Why don't you just give it up now?"[42] In a district that had been served for a quarter century by one of the masters of protecting local prerogatives, his district assumed that Oberstar would have his way. His reputation as an effective strategist and legislative tactician was, therefore, on the line.

So the line was drawn. Burton was apoplectic when he learned of Oberstar's rejection. He had miscalculated, something he rarely did. "That bastard had a chance, and he blew it," he roared at Rapson, who had the misfortune of delivering the news. "And that's the last chance he'll get. I am going to cook his ass."[43] Not particularly artful, but he made his point.

The Subcommittee Moves

Burton began his barbecue by scheduling the subcommittee's line-by-line markup of the BWCA legislation for April 3 and 4.

A normal congressional markup session furnishes an element of suspense about what amendments will be offered, whether the debate will change members' positions, and, ultimately, whether the bill will emerge from the subcommittee at all. But Burton's markup sessions were anything but normal.

Burton was not about to subject a bill about which he cared to an uncertain fate.

The day before the markup, Burton called Heinselman, Conlon, Rapson, and a handful of other key allies into his office to explain how the session would go. The key element was proxies. Burton had collected the proxies of each of the Democrats on the subcommittee, guaranteeing that he would control enough votes to prevail on any issue raised, even if only he and all of the Republicans attended. As a safeguard, he had extracted from the Democratic members who might attend a commitment to follow his lead.

The Alliance had seen Burton's considerable charm and skill as a chair

Phillip Burton (center), presided over the subcommittee markup. Bruce Vento and Larry Romans are seated on Burton's left. (*Photo by Kevin Proescholdt*)

played out the previous fall. They were about to witness a less adorned side.

As it turned out, almost a dozen of the subcommittee members attended the April 3 markup.[44] Burton again permitted Oberstar to ask questions, debate the merits, but not vote or offer amendments.

The first day was filled with a reading of the entire bill, a process that permitted Oberstar to engage the subcommittee on each controversial issue. It was not a comforting process for the Friends. This was Oberstar at his best—well prepared, forcefully persuasive, and intellectually nimble. Oberstar launched major assaults on the intrusive regulatory aspects of the National Recreation Area, the unnecessarily restrictive controls on motorboat use, and the economically crippling effects of the proposed logging ban. The subcommittee members appeared sympathetic; it was not at all clear that Burton's careful orchestration was playing out.[45]

The discussion about the National Recreation Area illustrated this. Oberstar pointed out to the more conservative members of the panel that the National Recreation Area carried with it strong zoning controls, injecting yet another unwanted federal bureaucratic presence into the lives of northern Minnesotans. Georgia's Lamar Gudger appeared to be particularly moved by the argument. Sensing the risk, Burton quickly moved that Gudger head up an ad hoc working group to examine the issue in greater detail. Gudger agreed. Oberstar was satisfied. But Gudger likely understood full well what Burton's stratagem had accomplished: it had diffused the moment while loading onto the back of an already over-committed congressman from another state a task that would immediately fall to the bottom of his priority list. Indeed, the working group never met.[46]

Burton closed the first day's session after each of the bill's provisions had been reviewed and debated. The next day would be reserved for amendments and subcommittee action.

The next day's session began with Oberstar on the offensive.[47] Working through Representatives Clausen and Lagomarsino, he put one amendment after another on the table. But one after another, the amendments failed to overcome the proxies in Burton's hip pocket. It was one thing for Oberstar to score the debating points he had the day before; it was another to have Clausen and Lagomarsino carry water on issues about which they were only superficially informed. Burton and Vento's preparation showed—they were able to force the arguments into corners that left the California Republicans with little room to maneuver.

As the pattern repeated itself throughout the day, Oberstar grew more and more frustrated. The insidiousness of Burton's civility was dawning on him: Oberstar had been permitted to strut all he wanted, but had been rendered impotent to make a single significant change in the bill.[48]

BWCA

(*Reprinted with permission from the* Minnesota Daily)

Rather than withdrawing, however, Oberstar grew increasingly aggressive and caustic, escalating a rhetoric that could only be seen as prodding Burton.

He accused Burton of seeking to impoverish northeastern Minnesota and turn it into a "junior Appalachia." He said that NRA provisions "literally scare the hell out of the people of northern Minnesota—they have had it with federal regulations. You are putting another yoke on their necks." He attacked the resort assistance provisions by sarcastically asking Burton whether outfitters would be helped "if they have to move elsewhere and open a hula hoop factory?"[49]

Burton knew better than to rise to the bait. As Oberstar became more provocative, Burton became more dismissive.

Burton responded to Oberstar's continued pounding on the creation of an NRA by assuring him that he had little reason to worry: Oberstar would have plenty of time during the bill's path through Congress "to lop three or four hundred thousand acres out of the wilderness."

When Burton noted that he had not been swayed by the great amount of mail he had received, Oberstar interrupted and said, "I see from your refusal to note the amount of mail that you don't want to hear what the people think, do you?" Burton curtly replied that the letters would be tallied; he later informed Oberstar that the subcommittee's mail ran about fifteen to one against Oberstar's approach.

Oberstar and the Alliance were fuming by day's end. After two full days of consideration, they hadn't made a dent in the Burton-Vento bill. Burton moved that the subcommittee adopt the bill and report it to the full Interior Committee. The motion was approved on a voice vote; the only voice heard was Burton's.[50]

Appendicitis

The Friends were buoyant. After the frustration of a five-month wait, events seemed to be back on track. But once again, their optimism would prove short-lived. It all began with a case of appendicitis.

Burton wasted no time in seeking to capitalize on the subcommittee's action. He announced that he would bring the bill to the full committee the very next day, April 5. Tactically, this would prevent Oberstar from being able to group his forces. Personally, it was Burton's way of reminding Oberstar that their swords remained crossed.

The point wasn't lost on Oberstar. He called the press in to denounce the move as a "Pearl Harbor attack on northern Minnesota."[51] Burton relented, putting off action for one week.

It was a costly decision.

That afternoon, Rapson received an urgent call from Fran Sheehan, the committee staff to Morris Udall. "Udall's going into the hospital," Sheehan said. "I don't know what this means for you and the Boundary Waters." Udall was diagnosed with an inflamed appendix and underwent an emergency appendectomy.

Udall's prognosis was positive; he would be able to resume his duties in a number of weeks. That potential delay had serious implications for the Friends, however. If the committee waited for its chair to return, it might delay the markup for a month, and the BWCA clock was ticking. If the committee proceeded without Udall, the Friends would lose one of their most reliable and respected allies and a chair who could be counted on to direct the panel's session with a minimum of rancor.[52]

The prospect of delay was the determining factor for the Friends. That and the fact that the next most senior member of the committee would preside in Udall's absence. And that member was Phil Burton.

Burton relished the thought of taking the reins. After conferring with Udall, he announced that he would chair the markup and that the committee would convene within a week.

The announcement was a disaster for the Alliance, who realized that as long as Burton was in charge, Oberstar would be marginalized. But neither was it unmitigated good news for the Friends, who recognized that Burton would not build the kind of bridges coming out of committee that Udall would have.[53]

But Burton it would be, and the Friends took up where they had left off with the subcommittee, setting up a schedule of meetings with those members of the full committee whom Burton targeted as the key votes.

Congressman Bruce Vento emerged as a key proponent of strong BWCA wilderness legislation. (Photo by Gordon Oschwald)

The Fraser office resumed its role as command central, scheduling meetings, preparing materials, and coordinating the Friends' activities with those of the national environmental lobby. The whir of activity began rebuilding the Friends' confidence that Udall's loss would not be a serious setback.

A phone call from their staunchest ally, however, threatened to break that confidence. Just as the Friends' lobbying effort was shifting into high gear, Larry Romans, Vento's aide, called Rapson with a note of panic in his voice. Vento had been approached by Tip O'Neill's office to let up on Oberstar: "We've got huge trouble," Romans explained. "The Speaker's leaned on Bruce really hard. I don't know what Bruce is going to do."[54]

Rapson understood how serious the threat was. Vento was a particularly vulnerable target for the House Speaker: a freshman bucking the congressional convention of deference to a well-connected local representative. Oberstar had played an important card. Romans described exactly what had happened.

O'Neill's senior aide, Spencer Smith, had told Vento that the House Speaker wanted Vento to investigate compromises: "The Speaker doesn't like to see three Democrats fighting in public. You're the one who can put an end to it." Rapson realized that this new pressure was about much more than the fight among Fraser, Oberstar, and Vento. The repercussions of Burton's leadership duel with Jim Wright, O'Neill's Majority Leader, were still being felt. O'Neill was pulling in the leash on Burton the only way he could. Wilderness politics had been joined not only with Minnesota DFL politics, but with the high stakes and "rarified atmosphere of [House] leadership politics."[55]

Rapson asked Romans to check Vento's schedule for an opening. He then called Heinselman. They agreed that a one-on-one meeting between Vento and Heinselman was their only hope of reaffirming Vento's commitment.

Heinselman and Vento talked for three hours.[56] Vento was uncharacteristically nervous. He wavered between guilt, defiance, and confusion. He told Heinselman that the pressure from the House Speaker's office had been compounded by Burton's lack of support for his work. His voice cracking, he angrily pounded the table and exclaimed: "Burton is just not helping me on this! I'm not going to get hung out to dry because of him!"

Heinselman reminded Vento that the entire national environmental community stood behind him. Vento waved him off: "What does it matter Bud? They don't take any of the pressure. They don't have to answer to Tip O'Neill."

Vento then jumped to a series of ideas about how the environmentalists could make concessions on motorboat routes and logging that would probably satisfy Oberstar and his constituents. Heinselman was stunned. Not only were those concessions a deep violation of everything the Friends had fought for, they would likely only open the door to more far-reaching concessions once the bill reached the Senate.

Vento flushed deeply, got up, and turned his back on Heinselman. When he turned back, he was shaking. Heinselman had clearly touched a nerve. "You just don't understand. This is not a Sierra Club annual meeting, it's the United States Congress. We have to meet them part way."

Heinselman broke down and wept. He got up and left the office. He feared that Vento had been lost to the cause.

Rapson tried to settle Heinselman down and to reassess what might be done.

He reminded Heinselman that Vento's commitment to the environment ran deep.[57] Vento would not lightly take a step that violated that commitment and threatened his growing reputation as a young legislator of principle and vision. The BWCA, Rapson reasoned, was Vento's first trial by fire in Washington. He needed some assurance that the pressures of the moment would pass.

The first step was to let Burton know that he needed to check in with Vento and to acknowledge that he had cast Vento into a fray that had proved far more controversial than even Burton could have imagined.

The second step was to get to the heart of O'Neill's pressure. Rapson suspected that O'Neill had no intention of breaking Vento's career over this issue. But that needed to be confirmed and conveyed to Vento.

Rapson tracked down Conlon and Burton to enlist their help. They agreed.

He then conferred with the Sierra Club's Brock Evans and Trish Record about getting to the heart of Spencer Smith's conversations. Evans and Record met with Smith to walk him through the points of the controversy. They came away believing that they had been able to correct a series of misconceptions he had received from his conversations with Oberstar. They told Vento that they believed the conversation would help pull O'Neill away from the controversy.

Vento took all of this in. Whether through his own soul-searching, Heinselman's passion, Burton's renewed support, or O'Neill's softening, Vento concluded that he needed to stay the course. When Heinselman next talked to him, he was his old self: focused, energetic, and committed. He had faced down a personal crisis and had emerged stronger than ever. He was now braced for the escalating pressure that the committee and full House deliberations promised.

All of this activity had spanned only a very few days. The committee markup was scheduled to begin on Monday, April 10, just four days away. Vento's crucible had reminded Burton and the Friends that some of the issues were far from locked up.

Primary among them was logging.

To the House Interior Committee members, issues like what size motorboats would be permitted on which lakes seemed esoteric and remote. But logging was an issue they had confronted in controversies throughout the country: the old-growth forest debates of the Northwest, the redwoods controversies of northern California, the land set-asides of Alaska, and countless others. The BWCA would open the same timber industry pressures each of these others had.

Matters were complicated by a Forest Service report that had been released a number of months earlier.[58] The report sought to quantify the economic impact of a BWCA logging ban. It concluded that such a ban would, over a twenty-year period, drain thirty million dollars annually from the state's economy and result in the loss of up to 1,190 jobs.

Unrefuted, these numbers would be deadly in the committee's deliberations, no matter how many proxies Burton held. The Friends needed an antidote. It came in two forms.

The first was an analysis by the State of Minnesota. The DNR, speaking through Commissioner Bill Nye, had repeatedly stated its belief that the BWCA harvest could be replaced by forests outside the area. But it took some first-rate detective work by the DNR's forestry director, Rod Sando, to make the argument stick.

Sando had taken the same numbers the Forest Service used and run an analysis of timber stands of like size and quality outside the BWCA. He demonstrated that the supply of these stands could not only meet the demand created by the withdrawal of BWCA timber, but would exceed it.[59]

The second antidote came, however reluctantly, from the Forest Service itself.

Heinselman and Evans suspected that the Forest Service had not cleared its analysis through the assistant secretary's office. They were right. They visited

Cutler at week's end.[60] He was infuriated that the Forest Service was working, in effect, to undermine the Carter Administration's logging position: "Those bastards work for me!" he stated in exasperation. He then grinned and picked up the phone.

The call went to Max Peterson, deputy chief of the Forest Service for Programs and Legislation. Cutler got right to the point: "Max, this is Rupe. I've read the report on timber availability in northeastern Minnesota. Doesn't it say there would really be no effect on the cut if Portal Zone logging ended? [Yes] Good. I'm sending Bud Heinselman over to see you with some questions—be helpful to him."

As he hung up, Cutler told Heinselman to prepare two documents: a letter from Vento to the Forest Service asking a series of questions about the availability of timber outside the BWCA and a set of Forest Service responses to each of the questions.

Heinselman happily obliged. He drafted the letter and the Forest Service response that afternoon and walked it over to Peterson. Peterson had already cleared Cutler's directive with John McGuire, chief of the Forest Service. The formal letter from Vento and McGuire's formal response were in Vento's hands by midday Friday.[61]

With Burton set to preside, Vento's commitment rekindled, and the logging arguments prepared, the Friends had done all they could to prepare for Monday's markup. But their internal crises had drawn them out of touch with an event that would fundamentally reshape the course of events to come.

The Alliance had been planning a large Wild Game Feed rally and fundraiser since February. It was scheduled for Friday, April 7, in the mining town of Virginia.

The Alliance had held large rallies before, probably one reason this one came in under the Friends' radar. But this promised to be an altogether different affair.[62]

Following the subcommittee's passage of the Burton-Vento bill, Duluth pizza magnate Jeno Paulucci offered to provide $25,000 to fight the Burton-Vento bill in court to any organization that could match his contribution.[63] The Alliance saw in the Wild Game Feed the vehicle to raise that kind of money. They faced a daunting task, however: attracting 2,500 people at ten dollars apiece.[64]

But on Friday night, almost exactly that many people stood shoulder to shoulder in the Miners Memorial Auditorium to eat a dinner of pheasant, venison, moose, bear, lake trout, and walleyed pike. It was a politician's dream, and the politicians responded accordingly.

Doug Johnson, Lessard, Begich, Grahek, and other local politicians each made his way to the microphone to ratchet up the frenzy an additional notch.

When Oberstar moved forward, the crowd roared. He was in his element, preaching fire and brimstone to the converted.

When he stepped down, only one figure remained. As Wendy Anderson strode to the podium, the crowd quieted. He was an unknown quantity. With an ease and humor that had been his trademark as governor, he started slowly and then settled in for business:

> I oppose the Fraser bill. I oppose the Burton bill. And I want you to know that I oppose them not just in Virginia, Minnesota. I oppose them in the Twin Cities, I oppose them in Minneapolis and St. Paul, I oppose them in southern Minnesota, and I do it because you are right. You are right and they are wrong.

The crowd was momentarily stunned—it had expected equivocation, not such bald support. But it raised the roof as Anderson continued:

> I serve on the Parks Subcommittee of the Energy and Natural Resources Committee on the Senate side, and I am going to see to it that no bill gets through the Senate that the people of northeastern Minnesota can't live with.[65]

Anybody who wasn't already on his or her feet, got on them to give Anderson a thunderous standing ovation.

The news hit the Friends like a thunderbolt. Not unlike the crowd in Virginia, they had expected at worst a noncommittal posture from Anderson until the bill hit the Senate. Never had they imagined such a precipitous move.

The Friends had to react quickly to minimize the impact of Anderson's statement.

Knowing that Anderson would use his influence to block the Burton-Vento bill meant that the House might well have second thoughts about sending the Senate a bill that would be pronounced dead on arrival. This would play into Oberstar's hand in orchestrating floor amendments that would water the bill down.

Anderson's rhetoric in Virginia also ensured that the BWCA bill would become a polarizing issue not only in Fraser's Senate bid, but in Anderson's. It was one thing for the Range to target Fraser for political retribution. It was quite another for the BWCA bill itself to become a political litmus test for other state-wide candidates.

Fraser was not prepared to issue a statement, but encouraged the Friends to respond as they saw fit. Rapson, Heinselman, and Proescholdt gathered a small working group in Fraser's office on Saturday to hammer it out.

They included Dick Conlon, who had reviewed the events with Burton earlier in the day. The group agreed on the basic points they wanted to make and sent Heinselman into a side office to draft the language. When Heinselman brought back his first effort, Conlon shook his head: "It's not strong enough Bud. It's got to be tougher. Wendy can't be allowed to get away with this. We have to hurt him politically."[66]

Heinselman winced and ran his fingers through his hair. The group heatedly discussed the implications of creating a statement so critical of Anderson that any possibility of cooperation might be destroyed. But Conlon was adamant. He argued that this was the opening gambit in a negotiation that would extend over months; Anderson had to be convinced that he was dealing with people who were not afraid to stick to their guns. Heinselman took another cut at the language.[67]

The process repeated itself two or three times. Finally Heinselman read a version that met with Conlon's approval. It characterized Anderson's statement as "an outrageous betrayal of the principle of wilderness preservation." It then got a bit more personal, charging that Anderson "is not a man of his word and cannot be trusted." He had backtracked on his commitment to end logging and to work for speedy Senate resolution of the issue. And to make sure the point was not lost, it concluded:

> He has stuck a knife in the back of the BWCA bill. He has indicated that he is willing to gut our wilderness heritage for the sake of his own political advantage. He has thus aligned himself unequivocally with an intransigent fringe of the 8th Congressional district. He has bowed to their extreme and unyielding demands in an attempt to salvage his crumbling political campaign.[68]

The room was quiet. This represented a much more militant stand than the Friends had ever taken before. Conlon broke the silence. He reminded the group that this was politics and that the politics of the moment required not appeasement, but a forceful response in kind. Heinselman was dispatched to deliver the press release to the Minneapolis newspaper.

Minneapolis Tribune reporter Al McConagha looked up at Heinselman after reading the release: "Are you sure you want to say this, Bud?" Heinselman gritted his teeth and nodded. The story hit the streets the next day.[69]

The reaction from Anderson's staff was immediate. Anderson staffers Susan Martell and Andy Kozak got on the phone to Heinselman within minutes of reading the newspaper account. Furious, they demanded a meeting with Heinselman and Heinselman alone. When they got him face-to-face, they were still livid. They could not believe that the environmentalists had not checked with them before issuing so damaging a statement. They fumed that Anderson's position had been misrepresented—that he had not really endorsed the Oberstar bill and that there was ample room to work out a compromise. They strongly intimated that the Friends would not be welcome partners in shaping a bill from here on out. Heinselman stood his ground. The meeting adjourned abruptly with smoke still coming out of Martell and Kozak's ears.[70]

The Alliance was, of course, ecstatic. On the eve of a probable Friends' victory in the House Interior Committee, the entire applecart had overturned. There would be new political momentum, new financial support, and new energy for their work. Oberstar suddenly seemed less isolated.[71]

The House Interior Committee

The tumultuous weekend behind them, the Friends turned to the markup in full committee on Monday, April 10.

The similarities to the subcommittee markup were pronounced. Again, Burton came prepared with a pocketful of proxies. Again, Oberstar was permitted to participate. Again, Burton walked the members line-by-line through the bill, explaining each section's significance.

A few things were different, however.

Burton had concluded that the power of the federal government to promulgate zoning regulations for the National Recreation Area was an easy target. He moved they be removed.[72] They had already served their purpose of drawing attention from the key issues within the BWCA's boundaries to measures that affected land outside the BWCA. Their removal would enable Oberstar to claim a small victory.

Oberstar was sufficiently astute to see through Burton's ploy. He spoke in opposition to removing the controversial language: "I'd like to see this turkey go to the House with this tin can tied to its tail," he groused to Burton. Burton smiled, nodded his head, and cast his proxies for the removal of the zoning language.

The second point of departure was the extent of the logging discussion.

In a committee filled with members skeptical of any effort to shrink the availability of timber supplies, Oberstar saw an opportunity to pierce through Burton's veil of control. He hauled out the Forest Service memo that estimated the annual economic loss of withdrawing BWCA timber at thirty million dollars and 1,200 jobs.[73] That got Steve Symms' attention, who proposed an amendment to increase the logging phase-out from one year to twenty.

This was Vento's cue. He stood primed and energized to destroy the timber argument once and for all. He explained to the committee that the Forest

Service had acknowledged that its analysis had been incomplete. He further noted that he had taken the liberty of clarifying their position through a letter to the Chief. He then read from his letter and McGuire's response:

> [Vento]: If I understand [the Forest Service] correctly, there .
> . . is already enough softwood timber under contract outside the Portal Zone of the BWCA so that . . . the current harvest levels could be maintained for at least ten years.[74]
>
> [McGuire]: Your interpretations of the facts . . . are correct. The current softwood cutting rates on the Superior National Forest could be maintained for ten years and still have nearly a two-year's supply of softwoods under contract, even if all Portal Zone logging is terminated.
>
> Existing volumes under contract and potential sales which can be made elsewhere on the Superior National Forest are adequate to sustain current employment levels in the timber industry.
>
> Any additional softwood timber that the State of Minnesota can make available during the coming decade would provide wood for the expansion of paper mill production or for the maintenance of a somewhat larger backlog of National Forest timber.[75]

Vento then sealed his case by quoting from Sando's analysis that the State of Minnesota could in fact make available the timber supply McGuire referred to.[76]

No reductions in the supply. No decreases in employment. Indeed, the possibility of industry expansion. Case closed. The Symms amendment was defeated on a voice vote.

The advocates for BWCA logging would never recover from those few moments. It was, as well, a moving moment for Heinselman in particular, who had spent his professional life studying and seeking to protect the BWCA forest. When Rapson joined a Friends dinner that evening, he proclaimed: "There will never be logging in the BWCA again. And it is because of you, Bud."

The rest of the markup was anti-climactic. Burton's proxies passed the bill out of committee on an unrecorded voice vote. The next stop was the floor of the House.[77]

Notes

1 See John Earl Haynes, *Dubious Alliance: The Making of Minnesota's DFL Party* (University of Minnesota Press: 1984).

2 Early in 1977, Fraser, Quie, and Rapson walked back together from a meeting at the Capitol. Quie, who had served even longer than Fraser, noted that it was time for him to move on. Fraser, always a supporter of term limits, replied that he had increasingly been considering the same thing. Rapson realized that he was probably the first person to learn that the two senior members of the Minnesota delegation would pack up and perhaps move their political tents. Rapson Recollections, December 1983.

3 *Minneapolis Star*, Nov. 4, 1977, "Fraser Finds Senate 'Water' Warm."

4 Zabinski Interview, Dec. 21, 1987.

5 The Alliance's loss may have been a blessing on one important front. Buckler was able to convince the timber industry not only to continue the Alliance's funding, but to increase it. Zabinski Paper, p. 22.

6 *Ely Echo*, Jan. 4, 1978, p. 1, "Ed Zabinski Heads BWCA Drive"; Zabinski Paper, pp. 1 and 22; Edward Zabinski Interview, Dec. 21, 1987.

7 The Alliance also began using special events as vehicles for building support. For example, it for the first time operated a booth at the popular Annual Minnesota Sportsman's Boat, Camping, and Vacation Show in January in St. Paul.

8 Zabinski Paper, p. 22; Zabinski Interview, Dec. 21, 1987; see also *Minneapolis Tribune*, Oct. 6, 1977, p. 2B, "Fraser Picketed for Stand on BWCA"; and *Minneapolis Star*, Oct. 6, 1977, p. 11A, "Release Critical of Fraser Senate Bid Printed in Oberstar's Office."

9 Cutler explained his reasoning in a letter to Oberstar: "After our thorough review and evaluation, we feel that to temporarily suspend the administrative ban on snowmobile use and allow use on the routes in your legislation would invite demands for reconsideration of the entire BWCA Management Plan." See *Duluth News-Tribune* (editorial), Feb. 10, 1978, p. 12B, "Bum public relations"; *Ely Miner*, Feb. 15, 1978, p. 1, "Feds say no to BWCA snowmobiles"; *Duluth News-Tribune* (Letter to Editor by James L. Oberstar), Feb. 21, 1978, p. 10B, "Oberstar's request not tied to protest."

The Alliance had also sought the governor's intervention in permitting snowmobiling to continue during the winter of 1977/1978. See Edward M. Zabinski to Governor Rudy Perpich, Jan. 5, 1978; Burnham Philbrook to Judy Heaton (Governor's Appointments Secretary), Feb. 21, 1978, Re: "Governor's Briefing File: March 1, 1978, Boundary Waters Conservation Alliance"; copies in possession of authors.

10 See *Duluth News-Tribune*, Jan. 15, 1978, p. 1A, "15 snowmobilers face charges after protest ride into BWCA"; *Mesabi Daily News*, Jan. 16, 1978, p. 1, "Snowmobilers heading for court"; *Ely Echo*, Jan. 18, 1978, p. 1, "Forest Service Grabs 15 In Tower Blitz"; *Ely Echo* (editorial), Jan. 25, 1978, "'Big Brother' is here"; *Duluth News-Tribune* (editorial), Feb. 10, 1978, p. 12B, "Bum public relations."

11 All fifteen violators lived in Tower; four were Native Americans. See *Duluth News-Tribune,* Jan. 15, 1978, p. 1A, "15 snowmobilers face charges after protest ride into BWCA"; *Mesabi Daily News,* Jan. 16, 1978, p. 1, "Snowmobilers heading for court"; *Ely Echo,* Jan. 18, 1978, p. 1, "Forest Service Grabs 15 In Tower Blitz"; *Ely Echo* (editorial), Jan. 25, 1978, "'Big Brother' is here"; *Duluth News-Tribune* (editorial), Feb. 10, 1978, p. 12B, "Bum public relations."

12 Friends vice chair Dan Engstrom responded, "We feel the demonstration shows these people do not have the patience and tolerance to let the political process work in Congress." *Duluth News-Tribune,* Jan. 10, 1978, p. 1A, "Snowmobilers mobilize to defy ban; plan caravan to BWCA"; *Ely Echo* (editorial), Jan. 11, 1978, p. 4, "The Snowmobile Protest Ride"; *Ely Echo,* Jan. 11, 1978, p. 1, "Snowmobilers To Ride In Saturday Protest."

The fifteen pleaded not guilty in federal court on January 20. On April 18, Federal Magistrate Patrick McNulty fined each $210, but suspended all but ten dollars, which the Alliance paid. *Ely Miner,* Jan. 25, 1978, p. 1, "Snowmobilers plead not guilty in Duluth court, trial date set"; *Duluth News-Tribune,* April 19, 1978, p. 2A, "BWCA snowmobilers found guilty in protest"; *Minneapolis Tribune,* Apr. 20, 1978, p. 2B, "Duluth: 15 found guilty of riding snowmobiles in BWCA; 13 fined"; *MLH Chronology,* Apr. 20, 1978.

On February 10, 1978, Judge Miles Lord also upheld Larry Haapala's earlier ticket from the "Ely Ten" snowmobile ride the previous February in which the Forest Service had charged ten Ely men with snowmobile use on Thomas Lake. The other nine had pleaded no contest to the original charge; Haapala had appealed his ticket. *Ely Echo,* Mar. 2, 1977, p. 1, "Ely Snowmobilers Back in Court"; *Duluth News-Tribune,* Mar. 12, 1977, p. 1, "Vehicle Use in BWCA Cited"; *Ely Miner,* Feb. 15, 1978, p. 1, "Feds say no to BWCA snowmobiles"; *Minneapolis Tribune,* Feb. 11, 1978, p. 12A, "Conviction of Haapala Upheld for Snowmobiling in BWCA."

13 Zabinski Paper, pp. 27-28; *Ely Echo,* Mar. 8, 1978, "Wait for Action on Burton BWCA Bill."

14 Even as the fall hearings were being conducted in Washington, the loggers were making preparations to resume cutting on their BWCA timber sales. The Superior National Forest office of the Forest Service was not helping matters—they encouraged Harry Fischer of Grand Marais to proceed with cutting on his East Tofte timber sale. Vento and Oberstar finally persuaded McGuire that moving forward on this track would serve little purpose. McGuire ordered a halt to the sales on November 8 for all but Fischer's sale. By the middle of November, Fischer's sale was brought within the coverage of the moratorium. *Duluth News-Tribune,* Nov. 9, 1977, p. 1, "5 BWCA logging moratoriums extended"; *MLH Chronology,* Nov. 17, 1977.

15 Olson, Fraser, Les Blacklock, and other wilderness notables (Paul Clement, Adolph Anderson, Arnold Bolz) attended. Olson spoke of passing the torch to younger generations to carry on the fight. He noted that if any of the past battles had been lost, there would be nothing to fight about now: "I won't be here forever. I may only be around for another five years, or ten years [laughter], or twenty years [more laughter]." After the for-

mal program, two authors sold and autographed their new books: Blacklock's *Meet My Psychiatrist* with its introduction by Sig Olson and Newell Searle's *Saving Quetico-Superior*. *MLH Chronology*, Dec. 10, 1977; see *St. Paul Pioneer Press*, Dec. 12, 1977, p. 21, "Wilderness Champions Gear Up for Battle."

16 For example, Heinselman, Rapson, and IowaPIRG's Kevin Proescholdt met in early January with Iowa Senator John Culver, a strong supporter of Fraser's wilderness approach. A close friend of Burton, Culver agreed to put some pressure on to move the BWCA legislation soon so the Senate would have the chance to consider it.

17 Zabinski Paper, p. 26.

18 *Ibid.* at pp. 26-27.

19 See generally *MLH Chronology* 10/22-11/4/77.

20 The Roadless Area Review, RARE-II, was being undertaken by the Carter Administration atthe same time the BWCA was being discussed.

21 Vento aide Larry Romans and Burton Subcommittee Staff Director Cleve Pinnix were also drawn in selectively.

22 Rapson Recollections, December 1983.

23 *Ibid.* See also Chuck Dayton, "Completing Bud Heinselman's Dream," *BWCA Wilderness News*, Spring/Summer 1993, p. 7.

24 "Proposed Substitute Bill," Nov. 1977, 18 pp., copy in possession of authors.

25 Nye also indicated his support. *MLH Chronology*, Jan. 5, 1978; see *St. Paul Pioneer Press*, Jan. 6, 1978, p. 13, " Compromise on BWCA Worked Out."

26 Bill Magie to Sigurd F. Olson, undated (circa April 1978), Sigurd F. Olson Papers, BWCA 1974-1977 Folder, MN Historical Society Archives.

27 *Ely Echo*, Jan. 25, 1978, p. 2, "Republican Hopefuls visit Ely."

28 Quie supported the 1964 Wilderness Act; during the debate, he had inserted into the *Congressional Record* a statement from Magie calling for the reclassification of the BWCA as a wilderness. *Congressional Record*, Aug. 20, 1964, 20631-20632.

29 Quie took time during his January trip to Ely to meet with Olson. Quie confirmed to Olson that he intended to run for governor. The two men discussed spiritual values and the relevance of Quie's born-again Christianity to the BWCA. *MLH Chronology*, Jan. 22, 1978; Albert H. Quie to William H. Magie, Jan. 25, 1977, copy in possession of authors.

30 See generally *MLH Chronology*, Jan. 31, 1978, and Feb. 10, 1978.

31 February 28, 1978. Rapson Recollections, December 1983.

32 Rapson Recollections, December 1983.

33 *St. Paul Pioneer Press*, Mar. 17, 1978, p. 27, "BWCA proposal finally reached";

Minneapolis Tribune, Mar. 17, 1978, p. 2B, "New BWCA compromise put forward"; *Minneapolis Star,* Mar. 17, 1978, p. 4, "New BWCA bill could end impasse"; *Duluth News-Tribune,* Mar. 17, 1978, p. 2A, "BWCA Bill would Allow Wilderness, Recreation."

34 The Burton-Vento bill provided for federal zoning authority over lands and structures in the NRA.

35 Subcommittee Draft BWCA Bill, copy in possession of authors.

36 See, e.g., *Duluth News-Tribune* (editorial), Mar. 18, 1978, p. 10B, "Good BWCA bill"; *Hibbing Daily Tribune* (editorial), Mar. 23, 1978 "BWCA compromise"; *St. Paul Pioneer Press* (editorial), Mar. 26, 1978, p. 2, "BWCA compromise"; *Minneapolis Tribune* (editorial), Mar. 28, 1978, p. 4A, "A constructive compromise for the BWCA"; *Milwaukee Journal* (editorial), Mar. 30, 1978, "Preserving a Splendid Wilderness."

37 See *Ely Echo,* Mar. 22, 1978, p. 1, "Rep. Burton Hurls Bomb At Ely Area Resorts"; *Ely Echo,* Apr. 5, 1978, p. 1, "Ely People Speak Out At Oberstar Meeting."

38 *Ely Echo,* Mar. 22, 1978, p. 1, "Rep. Burton Hurls Bomb At Ely Area Resorts"; *Ely Echo* (editorial), Mar. 29, 1978, p. 4, "Big Brother will getcha!"; *Ely Echo,* Apr. 5, 1978, p. 1, "Ely People Speak Out At Oberstar Meeting."

39 *Minneapolis Tribune,* Mar. 27, 1978, p. 2B, "Angry reactions greet BWCA 'compromise.'"

40 *Minneapolis Tribune,* Mar. 31, 1978, p. 2B, "Rep. Vento hears BWCA complaints."

41 This split had been registered in pubic opinion polls in the Eighth District up until this this time. See, for example, *Minneapolis Tribune,* Aug. 14, 1977, p. 13B, "Minnesotans split over uses of BWCA," which showed that northern Minnesotans favored multiple use over wilderness for the BWCA by a fifty-four to forty-two margin. But by the summer of 1978, even northern Minnesotans favored the more restrictive BWCA wilderness bill by a narrow fifty to forty-nine percent margin. See *Minneapolis Tribune,* July 16, 1978, p. 1A, "58% back BWCA limits."

42 Rapson Recollections, December 1983.

43 *Ibid.*

44 On the Democratic side, Paul Tsongas, Mo Udall, Bruce Vento, John Krebs, Lamar Gudger of Georgia, and Peter Kostmayer and Austin Murphy of Pennsylvania attended. On the Republican side, Joe Skubitz of Kansas, Robert Lagomarsino of California, Phillip Ruppe of Illinois, and Don Clausen of California attended.

45 Burton also permitted DNR Commissioner Nye to address the subcommittee. Nye indicated the state's approval of both the mining and logging prohibitions in the bill.

46 Recollections of Brock Evans: Boundary Waters Campaign, (Oct. 1978, 46 pp.), pp. 1-2, (subsequently cited as "Brock Evans Recollections.") See also *Minneapolis Star,* Apr. 4, 1978, p. 9, "Oberstar criticizes compromise plan for BWCA"; and *MLH Chronology,* Apr. 3, 1978.

47 See generally Brock Evans Recollections; *MLH Chronology*, Apr. 4, 1978.

48 Oberstar certainly knew some of this in advance. Just before the markup began, he half-joked to Rapson: "Well, here comes the Fraser/Burton/Vento juggernaut all ready to roll, I see." Rapson Recollections, December 1983.

49 "Will they use hardwood to make hula hoops?" Burton retaliated. "They will have to," Oberstar retorted. "There won't be any softwood."

50 *Minneapolis Tribune*, Apr. 5, 1978, p. 1A, "Vento BWCA plan backed"; *Duluth News-Tribune*, Apr. 5, 1978, p. 1A, "Panel Passes BWCA Bill"; Brock Evans Recollections, pp. 1-2; *MLH Chronology*, Apr. 4, 1978.

51 *Minneapolis Tribune*, Apr. 6, 1978, p. 2B, "House committee's session on BWCA bill set, scratched."

52 See Brock Evans Recollections, p. 3.

53 *Ibid.*

54 Rapson Recollections, December 1983.

55 See generally Brock Evans Recollections, pp. 4-5.

56 The meeting was held in Vento's office on April 5, 1978. See *MLH Chronology*, Apr. 9, 1978.

57 A science teacher by training, Vento had served in the Minnesota Legislature for five years before his election to Congress. He had served on the House Environment Committee, learning from the ardent environmentalism of the committee's chair, Willard Munger of Duluth.

58 The report was released in December of 1977. See *Minneapolis Tribune*, Dec. 9, 1977, p. 2B, "Report says ban on BWCA logging would be costly"; *MLH Chronology*, Dec. 9, 1977.

59 The DNR sent the report to the Governor in late March. The State released it to the public during the week of the subcommittee markup. Burton's handling of the markup made extensive discussion of the DNR report unnecessary. *Minneapolis Tribune*, Apr. 3, 1978, p. 2B, "DNR: No need to log in BWCA"; *MLH Chronology*, Apr. 1, 1978.

60 Brock Evans Recollections, p. 5; MLH Chronology, Apr. 6, 1978.

61 *MLH Chronology*, Apr 6-7, 1978; Brock Evans Recollections, p. 6.

62 The event was also fueled by a controversy that had surfaced the week of April 3rd.
    The controversy centered on a rumor that the Burton-Vento bill would ban motors on Lake Vermilion, a large and popular resort and fishing lake outside the BWCA. The rumor was credible only because the BWCA wilderness boundary had for decades followed a section line that nicked the northern tip of a small bay of the lake. Local residents reasoned that this small nick would give the federal government an excuse to treat the

entirety of Vermilion as a wilderness lake, causing motors to be eliminated and home-owners and resorters to be bought out by the federal government. The *Ely Echo* wrote, for example, that "[s]ome lakes would be motorless by January 1979, which includes Lake Vermilion." *Ely Echo*, Apr. 12, 1978, p. 10, "Attention: Vento-Burton Foes."

The Friends tried to combat the rumors by sending copies of the subcommittee bill and accompanying maps to newspapers in northeastern Minnesota. On hearing about the dispute, Burton ordered that the problem be corrected immediately. But the rumors spread wildly. The Friends were concerned that the rumors might be part of an intentional campaign of misinformation timed to distract attention from the subcommittee and com-mittee actions. Even the Duluth newspaper editorialized "that some demagogues have greatly exaggerated the effects of this proposed new BWCA law." *Duluth News-Tribune*, Apr. 5, 1978, p. 2A, "Vermilion Stormy for Fraser Canoe." See also *Duluth News-Tribune* (editorial), Apr. 12, 1978, "BWCA Clarifications."

The rumors were finally put to bed only after the Wild Game Feed. Indeed, hold-ing the feed in Virginia, close to Lake Vermilion, poured fuel on the fire. See Zabinski Paper, p. 32; Zabinski Interview, Dec. 21, 1987.

63 *Duluth News-Tribune*, Apr. 6, 1978, p. 1A, "Paulucci's BWCA Offer Eyed"; *Minneapolis Tribune*, Apr. 7, 1978, p. 2B, "Duluth: Paulucci offers $25,000 to fight U.S. proposals for BWCA."

64 Zabinski Paper, p. 31. See also *Ely Echo*, Apr. 12, 1978, p. 10, "Attention: Vento-Burton Foes."

65 Transcribed Remarks, Senator Wendell R. Anderson, Miner's Memorial Hall, Virginia, Apr. 7, 1978, copy in possession of authors. See also *Duluth News-Tribune*, Apr. 8, 1978, p. 1A, "Paulucci's BWCA Pledge Matched"; *St. Paul Pioneer Press*, Apr. 8, 1978, p. 3, "Wendy Supporting Oberstar BWCA Bill."

66 See generally *MLH Chronology*, Apr. 8, 1978.

67 Rapson Recollections, Dec. 1983.

68 "Friends Respond to Anderson Support for Oberstar Bill," Friends Press Release, Apr. 8, 1978.

69 *Minneapolis Tribune*, Apr. 9, 1978, p. 1A, "Environmentalists say Anderson has 'stuck knife' in BWCA bill."

70 See generally *MLH Chronology*, April 9, 1978.

71 Zabinski would later note that "Anderson was the hero of the moment." Zabinski Paper, p. 33; Zabinski Interview, Dec. 21, 1987.

72 The Vermilion Lake controversy contributed to his decision. See discussion supra. During the markup, Burton removed from the proposed wilderness boundaries the tiny bay of Lake Vermilion that had generated the controversy.

73 "The 22 million board feet of allowable annual cut of softwoods in the Portal Zone thus represents a potential annual loss of about $30,000,000 and approximately 1,190

jobs." See John R. McGuire to Phillip Burton, Sept. 12, 1977; copy in possession of the authors.

74 Bruce F. Vento to John R. McGuire, Apr. 7, 1978; copy in possession of authors.

75 John R. McGuire to Bruce F. Vento, Apr. 7, 1978; copy in possession of authors.

76 Sando stated that sixty percent of the softwood cut in the BWCA could be made up from "surplus" capacity on state lands in five counties. In addition, Sando wrote, there was evidence that county-owned softwood supplies were also available to meet demand: these supplies had recently been put on auction in St. Louis County, but had not been sold. Rodney W. Sando to Bruce F. Vento, Mar. 6, 1978; copy in possession of authors.

77 Brock Evans Recollections, pp. 8-9; *Minneapolis Tribune,* Apr. 11, 1978, p. 2B, "Panel passes BWCA bill"; *Duluth News-Tribune,* Apr. 11, 1978, p. 1A, "New BWCA Bill Clears House Unit."

Chapter Five

The House Floor Fight

The shift to the House floor meant that the days of tight control by Phil Burton had passed. In a body of 435 members, Oberstar would be far freer to build alliances among colleagues less versed in the subtleties of wilderness preservation than in the more straight-forward proposition of respect for local prerogative.

And over all of this hovered the cloud of Senate politics that had blown in with Anderson's speech in Virginia.

The Political Temperature Rises

That cloud covered not only the House deliberations, but the Minnesota political landscape. Dick Conlon was worried enough to make a trip to Minnesota after the Interior Committee markup to assess the situation. He returned full of misgivings. In a sobering memo to Burton, Heinselman, and Rapson, he wrote:

> Wendy Anderson's BWCA speech in Virginia on April 7 has set off a chain reaction which jeopardizes the election chances of both Anderson and Don Fraser, as well as hurting chances for passage of the BWCA bill in the House. The [political situation] is now festering and will get worse with the passage of time. Thus the only solution is to get a bill enacted into law as quickly as possible and get the BWCA issue behind us.[1]

Conlon was not one to overreact. His comments increased the sense of urgency among the Friends, who were worried that they had only months in which to navigate not only the House, but an increasingly complex Senate, all in the middle of local political turmoil.

By mid-April, Burton too had begun laying plans for the floor debate.

Burton's reconnaissance had uncovered the possibility that Al Quie was preparing a floor amendment that would thrust him into the center of the debate.

Burton called together Conlon, Rapson, and Pinnix on April 19 to fix on a strategy to co-opt Quie.[2]

Burton feared that the electoral realities of Quie's gubernatorial bid—having to cut into Perpich's base in the Eighth District—would drive him into alliance with northern Minnesota and Oberstar. "If Quie succeeds, Perpich loses," Burton flatly predicted. "Perpich fries in his own grease."[3] Burton also suspected that Quie would try to fashion a middle ground position as a way of uniting Republicans and conservative Democrats, both on the House floor and back in Minnesota. Burton directed Conlon and Rapson to develop some ideas that would prevent either scenario from playing out.

Burton met again the next day with Rapson. Burton had sounded out Senator Jim Abourezk of South Dakota on the BWCA. Abourezk chaired the Senate subcommittee that would first take up the BWCA bill. Like Burton, Abourezk was a strong-willed, unpredictable political maverick. He was not intimidated by the argument that a local senator should control the destiny of legislation that had national significance. And he had developed a deep respect for Fraser's work on international human rights issues.

As Burton had begun filling Abourezk in about the BWCA, Abourezk cut him short: "Oberstar is screwing over Fraser. Fraser would be a damn good Senator, and Oberstar's trying to ruin him. I don't like it."[4] Burton had discussed the possibility of Abourezk's subcommittee holding hearings on the BWCA as a way of diffusing Anderson's influence. Abourezk said he would consider it.[5]

The following day, Burton and Rapson met again.[6] Burton reported that Oberstar had tried to have the bill referred to the Agriculture Committee before it reached the House floor, a so-called "sequential referral." Rapson was horrified —this would would almost certainly kill the bill.

Burton read the expression on Rapson's face and let out a bellowing laugh: "Oberstar doesn't understand that nobody sneezes in this place without my knowing about it." Burton had paid a visit on the House's junior parliamentarian, the official who assigns bills. Burton waited until phones were ringing and people were walking in and out of the man's office before approaching him and pressing his case that the bill not be referred to Agriculture. Overwhelmed by the frenzy of the moment and the weight of Burton's presence, the man relented. There would be no referral to Agriculture.

The same day, Rapson learned that Chuck Dayton's law partner, John Herman, had spoken at length with Tom Kelm, a long-time political strategist for Anderson.[7] Kelm had stated that Anderson wanted the House to produce a strong BWCA bill, which Anderson could then revise, enabling him to put his own stamp on the bill. Although Anderson was not able to admit this publicly, he wanted the Friends to understand that he needed as much flexibility as possible in the Senate.

The call of the wild

April 6, 1978, *Minneapolis Tribune* **cartoon.** (*Reprinted with permission from the* Minneapolis Star Tribune)

Unknown to the Friends, yet another meeting was held on Friday, April 21. Vento met with Oberstar at the latter's request to explore how the motorboat and snowmobiling issues might be resolved.

Oberstar believed that a compromise on these issues would break the impasse. He had announced a day earlier his willingness to throw in the towel on logging; the exchange in the Interior Committee mark-up had broken the back of the timber argument.[8] He laid out to Vento a proposal that called for motorboats to be permitted on all the major perimeter lakes, on the international boundary, on the major bays of Basswood Lake, and on four major lake chains.[9] The proposal also called for continued snowmobile use on two major routes.[10]

Vento told Oberstar he would think carefully about the proposal. He reported the discussion to Fraser and suggested that the two of them sit down with Oberstar and discuss it in a few days.[11]

The pressure for compromise began building in other quarters as well.

Democratic party leaders in Minnesota were increasingly nervous about their likely Senate candidate being branded an extremist by the most potent political electorate in the state. Voters in the Eighth District, particularly the Iron

Range, turned out in disproportionate numbers for democratic candidates. Fraser threatened to undo that and to bring other statewide candidates down with him.

AFL-CIO leader David Roe was the first to weigh in. He told Dayton that if there was going to be a compromise, Fraser should be the one identified with it, not Burton and Vento. Fraser needed to get the issue solved and do it in a way that he got credit for.[12]

Fraser was well aware of the pressure that was building on him to make a politically expedient move. It made the meeting with Vento and Oberstar all the more difficult.

Oberstar reviewed the list of compromises he had discussed with Vento earlier. Fraser asked a few questions, but told Oberstar he would have to reflect on the meeting before giving him a response. He was more forthcoming with Vento as they walked back to their offices together: "[Oberstar] wants to throw in not only the kitchen sink, but all the related plumbing."

Vento was agitated. He was under pressure from all sides.

He told Fraser about a call he had received the previous day from Dick Moe, one of Mondale's chief staff advisers, following up on a meeting between Oberstar and the vice president. Moe reported that Mondale, in an unknowing echo of Humphrey's failed attempt a year earlier, wanted to convene a grand meeting of the principals to broker a compromise. Vento also relayed a conversation with Anderson in which Anderson had said that he would push something through the Senate if only Vento could get a House bill over to him.

Fraser remained silent. Vento wasn't through. Vento had come to see

Congressmen
Bruce Vento
(left) and Don
Fraser conferred
on the BWCA.
(*Photo courtesy of
Don Fraser*)

that Oberstar could and would hold the BWCA bill hostage to Fraser's Senate race. Oberstar believed that, to be a viable candidate, Fraser would have to bend. Once Mondale convened his summit meeting, Oberstar was convinced that Fraser would have no choice but to bend. Hence Oberstar's overture to Vento and Fraser: better to shape the compromise quietly than to have it imposed on you by the vice president.

Vento urged Fraser to think carefully about whether Oberstar wasn't correct. This might be the time to act.

Fraser stopped and turned to Vento. "This is all extremely troubling, Bruce," he said in a quiet, slow voice. "The last thing I want is to put you in the middle of a bad situation. But you need to understand that I simply will not agree to taint this issue with my political ambition."[13] They finished their walk in silence.

In a meeting the next day with Conlon, Vento appeared deflated and aloof. Unaware of the meeting with Oberstar or the conversation between Fraser and Vento, Conlon proposed to Vento that Fraser again be pushed to the forefront of the debate. To Conlon's surprise, Vento was cool to the idea. Conlon was disturbed by Vento's response. He could only guess that Vento had come to enjoy his leading role and was not inclined to fall back to the part of a supporting actor.

That was not the first discouraging conversation Conlon had had that day. He had spoken in the morning with Mondale staffer Moe to enlist the vice president's help in nipping in the bud the Senate candidacy of businessman Bob Short, a long-time friend of Mondale.[14] During the course of the conversation, Moe told Conlon that the only way to settle the BWCA issue was through the grand summit that he had discussed with Vento. Conlon dismissed the idea. Fraser and Oberstar could never sign on to the same bill, he argued. Someone has to lose, and the DFL party had the responsibility to step forward to buffer the consequences. Moe replied curtly, "Then Fraser has to be the one to lose."[15]

Conlon checked in with Burton in midmorning. Burton agreed that any middle-ground bill should bear Fraser's imprint. Burton made the case that this was not the time to cut a deal, however. It was one thing to consider floor amendments that would strengthen the bill's prospects by giving the appearance of reasonableness. It was another thing to suggest in any way that Fraser was cutting a deal with Oberstar. Whatever deals needed to be cut would better be done on the Senate side. Anderson and Fraser could eventually find common ground—they would be running on the same ticket and were temperamentally not the oil and water that Oberstar and Fraser were.

Conlon paid a second call on Burton late that night after his conversation with Vento. Burton wasn't surprised by Vento's reaction. Vento was not accustomed to this kind of political pressure cooker and probably could not fathom why Fraser would insist on a purist position when palatable alternatives were lying on the table. But Burton had almost lost Vento once before. He was not about to do it again. He told Conlon he would come up with something by the end of the week.[16]

He did. He called the troops together on Friday, April 28: Conlon, Pinnix, Fraser, Rapson, Vento, Romans.

Burton realized that his task was to deflect attention from internal tensions and refocus on a common strategy. That strategy had three components: managing the bill once it got to the floor, preempting Al Quie as a mediating force, and ensuring that the bill came to the floor soon.

Burton indicated that the particulars of their floor strategy could be ironed out later. What they needed to agree on was their bottom line. He ticked off his: buffering the BWCA from mining even if the NRA had to be abolished[17]; holding to the logging ban and providing incentives for increased timber management outside the BWCA; conceding only temporary routes for snowmobiling; and resisting the sweeping motorboat provisions of Oberstar's proposal. There was no disagreement. Vento in particular seemed to have his spirit back and voiced support for each of Burton's points.

Burton shifted the group's attention to Quie. Burton had spoken with Quie a number of times, each time becoming more nervous that Quie would take the middle ground and preempt it from Fraser. Two things were working in their favor, though. First, Quie had not conveyed the kind of energy Burton felt would be necessary for the fight. Second, any position Quie took could harm him politically; he wanted to distance himself from Fraser without appearing to carry Oberstar's water. A delicate balance. Burton agreed to continue conversations with him.

The process of getting the bill to the floor threatened to be the most significant obstacle of all.

Burton reminded the group that once the Alaska bill reached the floor, it would preempt any other natural resources legislation for weeks, particularly one as controversial as the BWCA. The House Rules Committee, the traffic cop for when bills would be considered on the floor, had scheduled the Alaska bill for May 15. That gave the group a window of only two weeks.

Several obstacles would make it difficult to squeeze through that window.

First, the Committee Report documenting the Interior Committee's actions had to be written. Once written, the report had to "lie on the table" for two days before being eligible for floor consideration. Pinnix had already anticipated the problem by preparing a rough draft of the report and characterizing it to House officials as a "final" report in order to start the two-day clock ticking. This literary license would not prove a problem if he and Rapson could prepare the final version over the weekend and file it on Monday.[18]

Burton's finessing of the bill's attempted referral to the House Agriculture Committee posed the second obstacle. Committee Chair Tom Foley of Washington was not pleased to learn of Burton's scheming. Grinning from ear to ear, Burton reported to the group, however, that he and Foley had come to an "accommodation." They had agreed that the Agriculture Committee would insist on a twenty-four hour sequential referral. After the bill sat in Agriculture for one working day—no more and no less—it would be freed for floor action. This would preserve the committee's institutional prerogatives to retain jurisdiction over Forest Service matters while not delaying significantly the bill's passage to the floor.

The third obstacle would not be overcome so easily. The House Rules Committee had wide berth in determining when a bill would make it onto the House's calendar. It was a conservative panel, populated with members who delighted in the internal machinations of House politics. It was also home to a number of Oberstar's closest allies, most importantly Tip O'Neill. If Oberstar requested a delay, which he almost certainly would see to his advantage, it would be hard for the panel to deny him that courtesy.

Burton had calculated that he had to turn the tables a bit. As the acting chair of the committee that had reported out the bill, he would be accorded some deference. He would formally request a date-certain for floor consideration and then spend time with his friends on the committee. He also handed out assignments to Fraser and Vento.[19]

As the meeting broke up, Fraser suggested that it was time to bring the Friends and the national environmental community back into the loop. They needed to know what strategies were taking shape. It was also time to get their help.

Fraser brought a large group together the next week. After walking through the floor strategy, Fraser described the mounting political pressure of the last few weeks. He asked for people's reactions.

Sierra's Brock Evans jumped in immediately.[20] From where Evans sat, it looked like Oberstar was engaged in an elaborate bluff. Oberstar did not have the votes to prevail on the floor. Burton could be depended on to out-maneuver him in the Rules Committee. Anderson was interested in pushing forward a solution in order to avoid the impression of legislative impotence.

Evans softened for a minute. The best thing Fraser could do, he said, was to remain statesmanlike. The politics of principle would ultimately be the best legislative politics and, Evans believed, the best electoral politics. Fraser had shown himself to be a legislator of rare integrity. That image would stand him well from here on out.

Fraser smiled. He agreed with Evans. This was not a political fire sale. But that did not mean that certain concessions might not be necessary to get the bill through Congress. It was a delicate balance: how the Friends could show their willingness to be reasonable without setting in motion a chain reaction of compromises that would ultimately go too far.

The Friends and environmental community agreed to work with Rapson to scope out how that balance might be struck.[21]

Guerilla Warfare

The DFL did not have a corner on the market of political heat. From the moment of Anderson's speech in Virginia, the Alliance had begun to flex its organizing muscle.

The Alliance had seen in the speech an opportunity to isolate Fraser and Vento within the state's party structure. In a caustic press release following the speech, the Alliance trumpeted the growing rift: "[Anderson's] position indicates an understanding of the issue and the problems of the people of Northern Minnesota, an understanding Twin Cities Congressmen Bruce Vento and Don Fraser lack."[22]

It shifted quickly into other channels of public relations as well.

In mid-April, almost six hundred Alliance sympathizers marched on the Forest Service building in Grand Marais. With full approval of the City Council, they turned off the building's electricity and ushered the Forest Service staff outside. As the television cameras rolled, they taped a four-foot wide cardboard eviction notice to the front door and attached a giant wooden padlock. The event was intended to symbolize the Burton-Vento bill's lockout of northern Minnesotans from their own homes and places of recreation.[23]

The Alliance organized another protest march in Duluth two weeks later. The protesters marched from the Duluth Arena Auditorium parking lot to the downtown Federal Building, where they met with Superior National Forest Supervisor Robert Rehfeld.[24]

They were back at it two days later, picketing a Fraser fundraiser in Minneapolis. The demonstrators passed out a mock dinner menu that included such items as "Cold Heart of Burton," "Don's Tiny Minority Casserole Service With Malice," and "Marshmallows Miron Over a Dayton Nut Pudding."[25]

The train kept rolling. The May 3rd edition of the *Ely Echo* devoted its entire edition to the BWCA. To read the *Echo*, nothing had changed over the last year's debate. "Jeep" LaTourell discussed why local wilderness guides needed motorboats. An editorial resurrected statements Sig Olson had made in 1964 that were at odds with his current purist approach. A profile of a floatplane operator suggested that bush pilots would be made extinct by the Burton-Vento bill. An interview with a former Forest Service employee made the case that the BWCA forest would die off without managed logging.[26]

Two weeks later, the Alliance used the fishing opener as a way to bring their message to thousands of potentially sympathetic outdoors enthusiasts. Setting up checkpoints along highways leading to Ely, Tower, and the Gunflint Trail, the Alliance gathered 10,000 signatures in a single day expressing opposition to the Burton-Vento bill and the curtailment of motorboat use. They held a protest rally the next day at the Ely Voyageur Visitor Center to deliver the petition to the Forest Service.[27]

The crescendo of the Alliance's activities was intended to build to the DFL endorsing convention in early June.[28] The Alliance had left no doubts that it could organize effectively the discontent local residents felt about the emerging House bill.

April 2, 1978, *St. Paul Pioneer Press* cartoon. (*Reprinted with permission from the* St. Paul Pioneer Press)

The Friends took a sheet from the Alliance's score in organizing a protest of an Anderson fundraiser shortly after his Virginia speech. In part to demonstrate his environmental credentials, Anderson had lined up John Denver to perform a fundraising concert. Carrying picket signs like "Wendy Waffled Wrong" and "Rocky Mountain High-pocrisy," the Friends drove home a message they hoped would haunt Anderson: a commitment to the environment that was spotty at best and opportunistic at worst.[29]

A month later, in mid-May, the Friends took their cause to the state capitol. Fraser, Vento, and a host of wilderness supporters addressed a crowd of 1,000. It was a less glitzy performance than those arranged by the Alliance, but it reminded the media, the public, and state lawmakers that the environmental community remained a potent organizing force.[30]

A Case of Triple Vision

Two thousand miles away, the dynamics were taking only a slightly more polite form.

If all eyes in Minnesota were focused on the June 4th endorsing convention, the eyes in Washington were having trouble with double and triple vision. There was the DFL convention to be sure. But there was also the Alaska lands bill and the growing immovability of the Rules Committee.

A week after Burton's grand strategy session, Fraser, Vento, Conlon, Rapson, and Romans met to follow-up. They spent much of the meeting discussing how to impress on Oberstar the need to soften his hard-line approach. A second session between Fraser and Oberstar was ruled out: the personal chemistry had grown too volatile. Approaching Mike Berman of Vice President Mondale's staff was similarly put on the back burner; Mondale appeared hostile to Fraser's position.

Rapson suggested that they approach Ric Scott, the state DFL party chair, as an intermediary. Scott had the advantage of being friendly with Oberstar, closely connected with organized labor, and not publicly associated with any side to the dispute. Scott had also been in touch on a regular basis with the Fraser Senate campaign organization to coordinate its efforts with those of the party.[31]

Rapson and Conlon called Scott that evening, filling him in on their side of the story. They urged him to think about how Fraser could become more visible in the process of a compromise on the BWCA while not appearing to have capitulated to political pressure. They reminded him that all the pressure thus far had been directed at Fraser; Conlon relayed that Dick Moe of Mondale's staff had essentially threatened Fraser's campaign manager, Janet Shapiro, by intimating that unless Fraser gave in, Mondale would probably not see his way to making campaign appearances on Fraser's behalf.[32]

Scott heard them out. He agreed that Fraser had to reassert his leadership. He reminded them, however, that Oberstar's constituency was far more directly affected by the dispute that was Fraser's. Oberstar had to receive substantial credit for coming up with the solution.

Scott confided that he had talked with Oberstar about what that solution would be. Oberstar's bottom line would start from a permanent motorboat presence on Trout Lake, Lake Saganaga, Seagull Lake, Basswood Lake and its bays, and, most likely, Lac La Croix. Snowmobiles would have to be allowed on Trout Lake, the Moose to Knife route, and perhaps the Poplar to Brule route. Scott added that Anderson had given his commitment to accept a package that looked like this.

Rapson and Conlon were skeptical. They expressed doubt that either Oberstar or Anderson would be content with this. They feared that Oberstar would keep pushing the ante up and that Anderson would not permit an Oberstar-engineered set of concessions to be the last word. Scott replied that it was his job to sound that out. He reminded them that the exchanges could be made confidentially and could be withdrawn at any time. Conlan wanted a greater assurance than that. "We don't trust Oberstar," Conlon said. "He is contemptuous of Fraser and may think he can take Fraser to the cleaners on this."[33]

After they hung up, Conlon and Rapson decided they had to play out Scott's advice.[34] The compromise that Oberstar had proposed to Fraser and Vento would soon be introduced in bill form and would be offered as a compromise amendment during the floor debate.[35] Fraser's failure to put something of his own on the table would keep Oberstar in a controlling position.

Rapson and Conlon agreed on the key points. Rapson drafted a memorandum to Burton, Fraser, and Vento the next day, outlining three compromise points and five steps that had to be taken to put the compromise in play within the next few days. Time was of the essence: debate on the Alaska lands bill was still scheduled to begin on May 15.

The memorandum gave three visible issues enough of a twist to appear significant, but not so much of a twist as to prevent further movement if that became necessary.[36]

First was the nettlesome National Recreation Area. Local residents could stomach an NRA as long as it was, as Oberstar proposed, drawn within existing BWCA boundaries. But the prospect of creating a new regulatory overlay outside the BWCA irritated local residents to distraction. Rapson proposed eliminating the NRA and substituting for it a Mineral Protection Zone that would bar mining and mineral exploration within its boundaries.

Second were the lakes that apparently constituted Oberstar's bottom-line: Saganaga, Seagull, Trout, and the bays of Basswood. Rapson proposed permitting motorboating to continue for twenty years, but not during the peak canoeing months of July and August.

Third were the smaller lakes on the perimeter of the BWCA on which homes and resorts were located: Snowbank, Fall, East Bearskin, Magnetic, and South Farm Lakes. Rapson proposed raising the permissible motor size from a comfortable fishing capacity of ten horsepower to a more recreational capacity of twenty-five horsepower.

The memorandum then proposed a process for enacting the package. Burton would make final arrangements to prevent Quie from emerging as a spoiler and continue pressuring the Rules Committee for a fixed floor date. Rapson and Conlon would ask Scott to get a general reading from Oberstar about his willingness to consider something less than his avowed bottom line. Even if Oberstar were not receptive, Fraser and Vento would present the package to him and then unveil it publicly. Once on the House floor, the package would provide an alternative to Oberstar's substitute bill.[37]

It was a sensible approach. There was one problem: Oberstar was no longer interested in talking.

On May 4, Scott reported back to Rapson that Oberstar was not inclined to negotiate. Oberstar told Scott that he would introduce his new bill on May 8 and would spend the time until then lining up support.[38] It did not take much reading between the lines to detect Oberstar's confidence. Despite having received negative editorial comment on his working draft,[39] Oberstar was confident that the pressure was on the environmentalists, not on him, to show movement.

Conlon fumed that Mondale was at the heart of the problem, working through his aides to bolster Oberstar and undercut Fraser. He confronted Oberstar days later about taking a serious look at the Fraser compromise. Oberstar dispensed with the usual courtesies:

> Just let it go to the floor. It's the same silly-ass proposal about phase-outs. If Fraser really wants to be helpful, he should get Burton to drop it all.[40]

Oberstar's confidence was likely buoyed by his belief that he could stymie Burton and Fraser's efforts to move the bill out of the Rules Committee. That created a number of possible scenarios, each favorable to Oberstar. The bill might never make it to the floor. If it did, it was increasingly likely to follow in the wake of the Alaska bill. Members would be eager to see in the Oberstar compromise a way to avoid repeating the bitter and divisive debate that was virtually certain to characterize the Alaska wilderness discussion. And all of this could occur either immediately before the DFL endorsing convention—which would increase the pressure on Fraser to compromise lest he be cast as an inflexible ideologue[41]—or shortly after—which would, Oberstar suspected, weaken Fraser dramatically.[42]

The next week dragged by, with Alaska looming larger and larger on the horizon. Oberstar's office finally called on May 15, appearing to reverse fields. They told Rapson that Oberstar would acquiesce to a floor debate within the next week.[43] The Friends relief lasted only a little longer than the phone call. Two days later, they learned that Oberstar had quietly persuaded two key Rules Committee members to delay the measure; the House Speaker had subsequently been brought on board.[44] The House leadership agreed to remove the Burton-Vento bill from their agenda for two weeks, pushing the date into early June.

That was enough of an opening, as Oberstar almost certainly knew, for the Alaska bill. The bill came to the floor in what was arguably the largest mobilization of environmental and counter-environmental activism in history. Hundreds of lobbyists from the conservation community locked horns with even greater numbers of oil, mining, logging and development operatives in a highly-charged showdown that would have repercussions for years to come. When the bill passed the House on May 19, the environmental movement had scored a monumental victory but was exhausted and its political capital depleted.

Fraser, Burton, and the Friends were facing the prospect not only of trying to navigate in the wake of Alaska, but of being capsized by a party convention that was barely two weeks off. That was precisely what Oberstar had hoped. He was proving a tactical foe worthy of Burton.[45]

Fraser realized that the only way to neutralize Oberstar's design was to force the House leadership to confront it directly.

His first instinct was to send Oberstar an open letter laying out the compromise points of Rapson's memo.[46] He and Vento drafted the letter,[47] but were convinced by Burton that this was too roundabout—the real challenge at hand was not to move Oberstar, but to move the Rules Committee.

Fraser shifted gears and the next day, May 19, hand delivered a blunt, very personal letter to Rules Committee Chairman James Delaney of New York. Fraser asked for a rule that would bring the bill before the House on May 31, less than a week before the DFL convention. He laid bare Oberstar's intentions:

> [T]here is being planned by the people backing Jim Oberstar's substitute a large demonstration directed against me. Moreover, these same people have claimed that they now have enough votes to block my endorsement.
>
> The obvious purpose is to put the political squeeze on me, even though three of Minnesota's four Democratic members support the BWCA bill as reported from committee. They believe that I am vulnerable to this pressure because of my intention to make a statewide

race. If the bill is delayed now, it will appear to be related to the political pressures which the opponents are attempting to develop against me. I have no problem about facing these pressures, but to have the timing of this bill set in such a way as to maximize this problem hardly seems reasonable.

I have not asked for too much from the Rules Committee, only a reasonable break so that the timing of this bill does not become intertwined with the efforts of people back in Minnesota who are attempting to defeat me in my race for the U.S. Senate.[48]

Udall and Burton also sent a short letter to Delaney asking for the same rule.[49]

Delaney responded three days later, saying that the earliest that the Rules Committee could hear the BWCA bill would be on May 31.[50] An aide to Majority Leader Jim Wright then called Rapson to confirm categorically that the BWCA bill would come up on the House floor on June 5, the day after the DFL convention.[51] Oberstar had won another round.

The setbacks were a form of shock therapy for the environmental coalition. They turned their attention from procedural plotting to substantive work. Burton, Fraser, and Vento had to agree on whether to use Rapson's compromise package and, if so, when. The environmental community had to be re-energized. And, almost four hundred House members had to be educated. All in a matter of two weeks.

The first decision was the compromise package. Its initial purpose as a negotiating tool for Oberstar was supplanted by its role in demonstrating to the full House membership that Burton, Fraser, and Vento had reasonably and significantly met the concerns expressed by northern Minnesota residents. Burton was adamant that the package Fraser and Vento had come within a hair of sending to Oberstar should be offered preemptively by the three of them, alerting House members to the compromise position well in advance of the floor debate.

Before that could be done, however, Fraser needed to bring the environmental community into the fold. The changes in the Burton-Vento bill contemplated by the Rapson memo had never been discussed with the national conservation organizations. Rapson and Heinselman asked them to a briefing session on May 30.

It was the first time in months that the Sierra Club, the Ikes, National Audubon, the Wilderness Society, and the other members of the Friends' national coalition had gathered to discuss the BWCA. After exchanging anecdotes about the Alaska campaign, the group rolled up its sleeves for what everybody knew would be a difficult session.

Rapson went right to the point. He laid out the political pressures arising from the Senate race, Oberstar's apparent procedural victories, and Burton's judgment about the need to float a compromise before the floor debate. He closed by walking through the three compromise points.[52]

Nobody interrupted. But it was clear that the family reunion was about to turn hostile. There was a lot of red faces, shuffling chairs, and head shaking.

Little by little, the tone of the questions became more aggressive. Each of the national organizations weighed in against the compromise, often cutting Rapson's responses short. There was no need to act precipitously, they felt. The votes would be there on the House floor. Let Anderson do his worst in the Senate; there was no need to make his job easier by gutting the bill.

Rapson bristled. There was no intention of gutting anything, he said. The logging ban was intact. Protection against mining was strengthened by the buffer area. Snowmobiles were banished. Motorboats on the larger lakes would disappear by the turn of the century.

But his departure from a characteristic even temper ignited the discussion. Maitland Sharpe of the Ikes stood and angrily jabbed his finger for emphasis: "You can't take us for granted. You can only push us so far. This is not just Don Fraser's issue!"

It was a pregnant moment. Rapson realized that he was not the one to diffuse it. He looked at Heinselman and nodded. Heinselman stood, and the agitation in the room quieted.

Rapson was respected in the environmental community. But Heinselman was loved. Every person in the room understood that his or her work ultimately was grounded on Heinselman's unparalleled knowledge of the BWCA, his lifetime of dedication to its preservation, and his abiding personal integrity.

As he began, Heinselman's voice was shaky and his eyes teary. No fingers running through his hair. Just a direct statement from his depths.

He spoke of how Fraser had refused to capitulate, knowing full well that the consequences could be the end of his political career. He reminded people that Rapson had become the touchstone for every important decision that had been made over the last year. He recalled how the environmental community's unity had transformed this issue from a local dispute over narrow issues into a national debate about the role of wilderness. He compared their effort on Alaska to the challenges they still faced on the House floor and in the Senate.

And finally, he became personal:

> You know me, you know how much I care about the Boundary Waters. You know I don't like these compromises any more than anyone else. You don't think I could support this if I didn't think this was the right thing to do.[53]

Brock Evans stood, put his hand on Heinselman's shoulder, and said, "All right, we must stick together and support this then." There was a general nodding of heads. The meeting was over. One by one, each person approached Heinselman and Rapson to recommit themselves to the work ahead.

Rapson and Heinselman were shaken, but relieved. They went back to the Fraser office to fashion a formal declaration of the compromise proposal. It was released to the public the next day in a "Dear Colleague" letter to the full House membership from Fraser, Vento, and Rick Nolan.[54] The letter positioned the proposal as the second compromise to the original Fraser bill: the first had been the provisions of the Burton-Vento bill itself.[55]

In the next two days, Rapson prepared four more "Dear Colleague" letters emphasizing different aspects of the dispute: a "national interest" letter signed by twenty-three House members from throughout the country; a "Committee" letter signed by House Interior Committee members; a "New York" letter signed by members of that state's congressional delegation, enclosing a pro-wilderness editorial that had appeared in the May 21st *New York Times*; and a "Republican" letter signed by Republican members.[56] Friends volunteers walked from office to office, talking with staff members and ensuring that the offices had seen the letters.

Bud Heinselman, at the microphone, kept the Friends together throughout the legislative process. Don Fraser is standing near the center, and Sigurd Olson is seated at the right. (*Photo by Mary Olson*)

Heinselman fully anticipated that the Fraser-Vento-Nolan compromise would be met in Minnesota with some of the same shock that had accompanied the national environmental community's first exposure to it. He and Chuck Dayton wrote press statements that sought to soften the impact.

"We are disappointed that circumstances are such that this additional and substantial weakening was necessary," Dayton was quoted. He continued:

> But we recognize that if Congress is to pass a bill this year, some further accommodation on motorboats had to be made. We know that Fraser, Vento, and Nolan would not have taken this action otherwise. This means that large portions of the wilderness area will remain open until the next century—not only our children but our children's children will be grown before the lakes are quiet again.[57]

Heinselman urged supporters "to understand the need for compromise and reconciliation with citizens of northeastern Minnesota who insist on continued motorboat use in even larger areas than these amendments would allow."[58]

Friends members nevertheless deluged the Friends' local office with calls. A number of supporters angrily wanted the Friends to convey their anger at Fraser's having sold out. Others said they would no longer write checks to the Friends. Between the prospect of a tough DFL convention that weekend and an even tougher floor debate on Monday, the Friends were at a low ebb.

Democracy At Work

The DFL state convention began on Friday, June 2, and would continue through Sunday. It promised to be supercharged and acutely divisive. Abortion. Gun control. The Boundary Waters. Senate candidates that engendered deep loyalties and fierce hatreds. The party was on trial.

The party's unspoken leader was neither Don Fraser nor Wendy Anderson, but Fritz Mondale. The party would hold at the seams only through his influence.

Mondale had sought to bring that influence to bear even before the convention was gaveled to order. After his overture to serve as a mediator among the parties fell flat, he had decided that the Carter Administration would not issue its formal position on the Burton-Vento bill until after the convention.[59] Although the administration's support of the bill was a mere formality, Mondale understood that an announcement would be seized by the media and the Alliance as a way of casting in even brighter relief the schism between Fraser and Anderson.

Mondale had hoped through a variety of pressures—the offer of mediation, the calls from Moe—to convince Fraser that his position was untenable and

Vice President Walter Mondale came to the DFL convention seeking party unity. (*Photo by Kevin Proescholdt*)

destructive.[60] The convention provided one last chance.

During the course of the convention, Mondale and his aide Mike Berman met with Ed Zabinski and three other members of the Alliance in Mondale's hotel room in St. Paul. He met them in shirt-sleeves, smoking a big cigar. "What can I do; how can I help this?" he asked. If he hoped for a breakthrough, the Alliance was not about the provide it: "Get Fraser to back off the bill." Mondale agreed to talk with Fraser. There was little else he could do.[61]

The action was concentrated in the endorsements, which would occur Friday night (including the governor, who was running without opposition), the formal acceptance of nominations, scheduled for Saturday, and the adoption of the party platform on Sunday.

The Friends concentrated their energies on organizing an environmental caucus that would keep communications open among neophytes and party regulars alike. Coordinated by the Friends' Dan Engstrom and Sierra Club's Carol Lee, the caucus phone-banked, operated a hospitality room, and circulated issue papers on the floor.[62]

The Alliance played to their strength. At the party convention in Duluth two years earlier, more than 3,000 northeastern Minnesotans had packed the galleries to protest then-Governor Wendell Anderson's attempt to force Reserve Mining Company to begin on-land disposal of taconite tailings or shut down. If it worked once, try it again. The Alliance arranged for a thousand local residents to caravan to St. Paul in buses. They were united by the theme "Blow the Whistle on Fraser." One suspected that small devices emitting shrill sounds would figure somewhere in their strategy.

Oberstar and Doug Johnson greeted the group on their arrival. Oberstar would be the conductor, providing cues about when to make noise and for how long.[63]

The problem was that they would not arrive until Saturday, and the endorsement of their arch-demon Fraser was scheduled for Friday night. The Alliance was rebuffed in an attempt to change the rules to delay the endorsement balloting. They would have to be content with making their presence felt during the speeches on Saturday.

Anderson was the first up on Friday night. He had encountered some turbulence when he had informed the Endorsements Committee that he would not oppose a constitutional amendment banning abortions and would not support a platform plank endorsing the Burton-Vento bill.[64] But not enough to prevent his endorsement on the first ballot over a little-known St. Paulite named John Connolly.

That was the good news for the Anderson camp. The bad news was that Anderson had reached the required sixty percent endorsement threshold with just twenty-three votes to spare: 753 to 467. The Fraser wing of the party had defected, contributing only 75 or 80 votes to Anderson's total. Anderson's supporters were furious. They had been embarrassed not so much by a political unknown as by their likely Senate running mate.[65]

Fraser was next up. Anderson supporters were primed to return the favor.[66]

They were given a substantial boost by Doug Johnson, who had announced nine days earlier that he would challenge Fraser as a favorite son from northern Minnesota. Before the Anderson balloting, Johnson likely aspired only to throw sand in the Fraser machine. After it, he stood a good chance of blocking Fraser's nomination.

Johnson pulled no punches. He made clear that his was an anti-Fraser candidacy, not a pro-Johnson candidacy. He attacked Fraser as an "opportunist," a candidate without "sensitivity."[67]

Johnson blocked Fraser on the first ballot, gathering forty-two percent of the vote. Fraser's 698 votes fell thirty-four short of the required sixty percent. The question remained whether the anti-Fraser alliance would be content with having made their point or would instead hold tight in an attempt to prolong Fraser's discomfort.

They chose to keep the pressure on. Fraser picked up votes on the second ballot but still fell four votes short of endorsement. The Fraser floor organizers were deflated. Fraser would go over the top on the next ballot, but his endorsement had come with a steep price. In both the Fraser and Anderson camps, supporters would carry feelings of bitterness toward the other Senate candidate into the election season. It would affect everything from fundraising to get-out-the-vote efforts. And it would scar the party for years to come.

Mondale sought to smooth over these feelings in an address to the convention on Saturday. He urged the delegates to leave the convention unified, to recognize that their real foes were not sitting across the room, but were organizing a campaign for Republican candidates.[68] That the appeal came too late was demonstrated not just by the catcalls that met his remarks, but with the reception Fraser received shortly afterward.

By the time Fraser stepped to the rostrum to formally accept the endorsement, the northern Minnesota contingent had arrived, been briefed by Oberstar and Johnson, and packed the galleries. They had spent the earlier proceedings warming up for Fraser's appearance, responding to any mention of Fraser with with booing, catcalls, and whistleblowing.

Fraser began—or tried to. His first words were drowned out by a deafening cacophony of hoots, shouting, stomping, and whistleblowing. As the vice president of the United States and a United States senator sat passively by, making no attempt to quell the rage, Fraser waited for the noise to subside. It didn't. For eight interminable minutes, Fraser stood alone, abandoned by the party leadership, dignified in his resolve not to back down.

Oberstar finally gave his conductor's cue to the demonstrators. The din stopped. "It's good to be in hot water now and then," Fraser ad-libbed. "It keeps you clean."[69] He got through the rest of his speech, but few in the convention hall could later remember what he said; the impression that endured was the isolated figure on the stage.[70]

There was still one day to go.

Sunday was reserved for consideration of the party's platform, normally a relatively routine, sparsely attended affair. The BWCA saw to it that there would be nothing routine about it. There was very little attrition from Saturday's attendance: 1,200 delegates had voted Saturday night on Fraser's endorsement; 1,219 voted on the BWCA plank.

The platform delineates those positions for which the party stands. Engstrom and Lee's environmental caucus had proposed a party plank supporting the Burton-Vento bill. Adopting such a plank would be highly inconvenient for Oberstar and Anderson, who would have to explain why they could pick and choose among the party's official positions. After a good deal of huffing and puffing, however, the delegates did just that, reaching the sixty percent threshold with five votes to spare.

Anderson's advisers concluded that this was an intolerable situation. Keith Ford and Tom Kelm of the Anderson staff circulated among the delegates to generate support for a motion to reconsider the BWCA plank, arguing that removing any reference to the BWCA would aid party unity.[71] They realized that delegates would begin an exodus as the day wore on. If hard-core interest groups —particularly the Pro-Life Caucus and northern Minnesota delegates—could be convinced to stay and lend their support to Anderson's effort, a second vote late in the day might overturn the BWCA result.

Ford and Kelm's strategy was right on the mark. By the afternoon, Engstrom and Lee had flown back to Washington for the next day's House debate, leaving the environmental caucus without leadership. The motion to reconsider passed. The BWCA plank was again before the convention. This time around, the staying power of the Anderson coalition made the difference. The

June 4, 1978, *St. Paul Pioneer Press* cartoon. (*Reprinted with permission from the* St. Paul Pioneer Press)

plank failed to gather the required sixty percent.[72] The party platform would not include any reference to the BWCA.

Whatever room remained after the endorsement process for ill will between the Anderson and Fraser camps had just been filled. An Anderson floor worker summed up his camp's attitude: "Some of the Fraser delegates are the kind who would sacrifice a Senate seat for a couple of lakes."[73] A Fraser supporter retorted that actions like this would ensure that environmentalists would work for Anderson's defeat.[74]

The only faction to emerge intact from the convention's wreckage was the Alliance. The liberal wing of the party might not have appreciated the barnyard tactics, but the Alliance had successfully shaped a riveting, disturbing image of a party torn apart by BWCA politics. The Alliance could not help but believe that this image of discord would play into Oberstar's hands in the next day's House vote.[75]

In the Pit

Monday, June 5. The Burton-Vento bill was scheduled for two hours of floor debate.[76]

While Oberstar was directing the political carnage in St. Paul, Burton had spent the weekend reviewing every possible twist and turn of the House debate. He had calculated that attendance would be high—between 340 and 375 of a possible 435.[77] That meant that he needed 200 votes to be safe—he counted 175 in his corner. The swing votes that would make the difference were not likely to be reached on ideological grounds or on the basis of personal loyalties. He had to figure out some way to prevent Oberstar from pulling them into his orbit through a compromise amendment.

When Rapson filled him in on the course of the convention, Burton slammed his desk and began pacing back and forth in his office. He stopped abruptly, took a cigar out of the drawer, and smiled. "We're gonna crush the bastards," he exclaimed. "And I just figured out how."[78]

The how was deceptively simple.

Oberstar had assumed from the fanfare that had accompanied the announcement of the Fraser-Vento-Nolan compromise that Burton would introduce the measure as a way of putting his compromise into play first, preempting Oberstar. That was just fine with Oberstar, who would then offer his bill as a substitute, forcing the House to vote on his bill, not Burton's. For members unfamiliar with the conflict, it would be easier to vote *for* an amendment that seemed to represent a reasonable middle ground than to vote *against* it. Such a strategy would also make Oberstar, not Burton, the focal point of the debate.

But Burton had decided to play a little poker. He would sit on his hand, letting Oberstar make the first move.

The Burton-Vento bill would automatically be the measure before the House as the bill reported out of the Interior Committee. If, as Burton suspected, Oberstar waited for the Fraser-Vento-Nolan bill to be moved as a substitute, Burton would let him wait. He would not introduce it. Oberstar would face a vote on Burton-Vento, gambling that House members would find the committee bill too extreme to support.

It was a risky strategy on Burton's part. All of the agonizing over whether to propose the Fraser-Vento-Nolan compromise had arisen because Burton and the Friends had concluded that Oberstar could well defeat the committee bill unless it was tempered. But Burton was willing to risk that. He had concluded that his ability to swing the twenty-five votes he needed depended less on whether Burton-Vento or Fraser-Vento-Nolan was before the House than on whether the vote was one for his bill, not against Oberstar's.

If he had miscalculated the importance of the vote-for-my-bill-not-his strategy, the entire BWCA war would be lost in a matter of minutes.

So the House debate began with the two protagonists headed directly toward a procedural OK Corral.

The debate opened with the now obligatory prickly exchange between Burton and Oberstar. Burton asked Oberstar whether he had not been given the opportunity to participate in the subcommittee and committee hearings and markups. Oberstar shot back that members should not overstate the importance of Burton's gesture since "the chairman had all the votes locked up in his pocket."[79] Thereafter, the debate proceeded predictably.[80]

Vento sought to remind the members how narrow the range of differences was: "The issue of motorized use within the BWCA is the major remaining controversy. Indeed, in one area there ought to be an opportunity where someone can go and have some solitude, where someone can go and have an experience that is different."[81]

Oberstar sought to turn Vento's argument on its head. If the only dispute is over motorboats, the House membership should embrace a reasonable middle ground position on that issue:

> Under my substitute, the Boundary Waters will be preserved from any ecological damage from mining and logging. There will be no question the Boundary Waters is a unit of the wilderness system. The committee bill accepts motors in the BWCA. Their position is not inconsistent with the Wilderness Act of the 1964 in this respect. It is inconsistent and an abrogation of the Wilderness Act in that it does not recognize motorized recreation is an integral part of the BWCA and that the way of life of the people of my district depend upon it.[82]

John Sieberling, who had sat through the committee sessions, and whose father once accompanied Sig Olson on a Quetico-Superior canoe trip, provided a few moments of eloquence:

> A wilderness experience such as one might find in the Boundary Waters Canoe Area is not something which can be easily described. Sigurd Olson, who is considered the poet laureate of the Boundary Waters, and the most eloquent proponent of preserving it as a wilderness area, said in a recent interview that when people go into the wilderness today, they are looking for spiritual values and inspiration which are almost impossible to define. In wilderness, such seekers can find a rejuvenation of the spirit, and a sense of harmony and oneness with all living things. The preservation of this spirit is one goal of the Boundary Waters Wilderness bill, and I urge my colleagues to vote for the passage of this important legislation.[83]

Burton had taken on the responsibility for making sure that Al Quie did not play a pivotal role in shaping the floor strategy. Whatever Burton did, worked. Quie offered no amendments, had assembled no coalitions, and offered only an uninspired statement about the harmlessness of motorboats.[84]

Quie was a beacon of rationality compared with the rest of the Minnesotan Republican delegation. "[T]here is plenty of land, air, and water up there," Bill Frenzel observed. "Whatever the local people need in order to prosper, and whatever the resorts need to prosper and, indeed, whatever people need to enjoy a wilderness experience is available."[85] Shades of Rudy Perpich.

Fortunately for the Republican Party, New Jersey's Millicent Fenwick, the patrician Republican after whom Doonesbury modeled a comic strip character, rose to answer her colleagues from the midwest:

> Why should there not be one place in which there are no motors? Why can we not have that quietness? I see no reason not to keep this wilderness area quiet and peaceful and what a wilderness area ought to be.[86]

The debate had proceeded without amendments. As the time ticked on, Oberstar waited for the expected appearance of the Fraser-Vento-Nolan compromise. Burton made no move. Neither did Oberstar.

With very little time left on the clock, Oberstar was the first to blink. He rose and offered an amendment: he sought to substitute his bill for the Burton-Vento bill. For a split second, it appeared that Burton's calculation had failed.

But it was a short split second. Burton gave Rapson a friendly thump on the arm and the right side of his mouth curled up in a smile. He signalled to Vento, who rose almost before the last words were out of Oberstar's mouth.

"Mr. Chair, I move a substitute," Vento boomed. Oberstar looked over in a horrified and immediate recognition of what Burton had done. Whereas Oberstar had only one bill to work with, Burton had two. Burton would have been content with a vote on the Burton-Vento bill. But he would be downright pleased with a vote on the Fraser-Vento-Nolan bill. That was what Vento had substituted for Oberstar's bill. The vote would, after all, be on a pro-wilderness measure.

The voting bells were sounded. Members would have twenty minutes to cast their electronic vote.

Many of the members streaming into the chamber were confused by the tactical maneuvering. But Burton had prepared well. Well-known faces from the national environmental community were positioned at the entrances to the floor to buttonhole friendly members. Burton, Fraser, Vento, and Nolan spread throughout the floor to talk to colleagues.

The wisdom of Burton's approach became clear as at least a half-dozen members approached Rapson to say that they would vote "yes" for the compromise, but was it the Fraser compromise or the Oberstar compromise?

April 24, 1978 *St. Paul Dispatch* **cartoon.** (*Reprinted with permission from the* St. Paul Pioneer Press)

As a "yea" or "nay" light went on next to a name on the large electronic board behind the House Speaker's chair, Heinselman would check them off on his list, groaning or yelping in pleasure as the vote accorded or failed to accord with the Burton projections. The early tally did not look good—many of Oberstar's allies had joined the debate and accordingly voted early.

But as the bell signalled the close of voting, the totals stood: 213 in favor of substituting the Fraser-Vento-Nolan bill for the Oberstar bill, 141 against. Procedurally, that meant that Fraser-Vento-Nolan would be substituted for the Oberstar bill, which would have substituted for the committee bill. The rest was a formality. Without further debate or amendment, the Fraser-Vento-Nolan bill was adopted on a vote of 324 to 29.

Oberstar fumed later that he had not been permitted a direct vote on his bill.[87] But that of course was the whole idea. Burton had not wavered one iota from his strategy. He had predicted accurately the number of members who would vote (he estimated 340-370; 354 did), the number of votes he would need (200; he got 213), and the process by which he would get them. Lyndon Johnson could not have done it better.

Notes

1 See Dick Conlon memo, "Political Impact of BWCA Controversy and Resolution Thereof," Apr. 17, 1978. See also *Minneapolis Tribune*, June 11, 1978, p. 18A, "Minnesotan Helps Democratic Group Achieve New Focus."

2 Rip Rapson Notes, DMF Papers, Apr. 19, 1978.

3 Rip Rapson Notes, DMF Papers, Apr. 19, 1978. See also *St. Paul Pioneer Press*, Apr. 21, 1978, p. 1F, "Quie, Oberstar Offering BWCA Bills"; and *Minneapolis Star*, Apr. 21, 1978, p. 13A, "Oberstar Offers 'Last' Compromise on BWCA; Quie Readies His Own."

4 Rip Rapson Notes, DMF Papers, Apr. 20, 1978.

5 Abourezk announced that he would hold hearings on the BWCA if "Minnesota really wants it." See *St. Paul Pioneer Press*, Apr. 22, 1978, p. 18F, "Senate Ready for BWCA Case."

6 They were joined by Chuck Dayton and Larry Romans of Vento's staff. Rip Rapson Notes, DMF Papers, Apr. 21, 1978.

7 *Ibid.*

8 See *Minneapolis Tribune*, April 21, 1978, p. 1A, "Oberstar Offers BWCA Compromise"; and *Minneapolis Tribune*, April 23, 1978, p. 1A, "DFLers Vary in Enthusiasm for Oberstar's BWCA Revision."

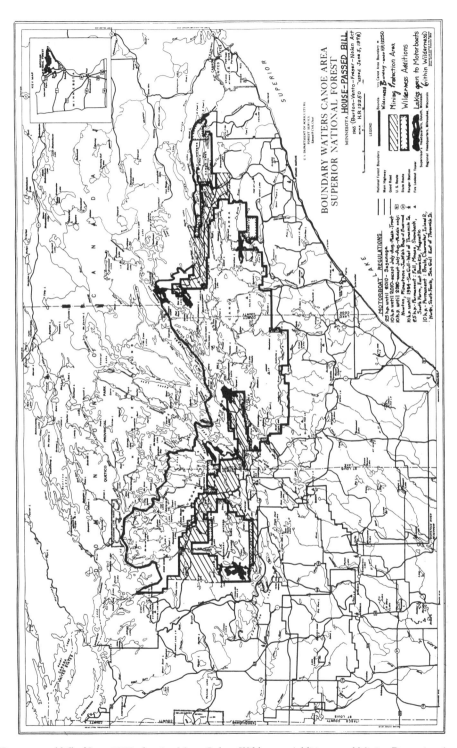

House-passed bill of June 1978, showing Motor Lakes, Wilderness Additions, and Mining Protection Area.
(*Map by M. L. Heinselman*)

9 The proposed motorboat routes were as follows:
>Fall, Moose, and Snowbank;
>Saganaga;
>Seagull open permanently east of Three Mile Island;
>Trout;
>Jackfish, Pipestone, and Back Bays of Basswood for 20 years;
>New Found and Sucker Lakes open 10 years;
>La Croix;
>the Lake One-Insula-Thomas-Ensign route;
>the international border route from Sucker to Saganaga;
>the international border route on the eastern Caribou unit;
>the Brule Lake to Poplar Lake route; and
>the East Bearskin to Pine Lake route.

Oberstar did call for the immediate closing of Four Mile Portage. Rip Rapson Notes, DMF Papers, Apr. 24, 1978, Apr. 25, 1978.

10 Snowmobiles would be allowed on the Vermilion to Trout route, and on the Moose to Knife Lake route. *Ibid.*

11 *Ibid.*

12 *Ibid.* The same sentiment emerged at a meeting in St. Paul among Ronnie Brooks of Perpich's staff, Senate Majority Leader Nick Coleman, Oberstar aide Jody Kauchik, state senator Doug Johnson, and environmentalist Jan Green. Brooks asked Kauchik and Johnson why Oberstar had waited so long to back off on the timber issue; it was pulling the DFL apart. Johnson replied that the northerners couldn't compromise on motor routes. Coleman said it looked like Anderson was willing to sell off the wilderness to the highest bidder; Brooks added that Fraser looked unwilling to compromise and that both DFL Senate candidates looked bad. Brooks and Coleman both came away from the meeting with the advice that another compromise had to emerge on the BWCA, and Fraser had to have his name on it.

13 Rip Rapson Notes, DMF Papers, Apr. 25, 1978.

14 Specifically, Conlon wanted Moe to ask Mondale to dissuade former Representative John Blatnik from endorsing Short over Fraser. Rip Rapson Notes, DMF Papers, Apr. 26, 1978.

15 *Ibid.*

16 Rip Rapson Notes, DMF Papers, Apr. 26, 1978, Apr. 27, 1978.

17 "The mining protection zone stays as long as Heinselman wants it," Burton declared. Rip Rapson Notes, DMF Papers, Apr. 28, 1978.

18 House Report 95-1117, Part 1, May 4, 1978.

19 Rip Rapson Notes, DMF Papers, Apr. 28, 1978.

20 See Brock Evans Recollections, p. 12. See also *MLH Chronology*, April 22-28, 1978.

21 Rapson had prepared a memorandum that laid out a step-by-step negotiating strategy with Oberstar. The Friends knew that Oberstar would offer on the House floor a compromise package that would likely appear reasonable to House members who had not been following the dispute. Rapson proposed that Fraser anticipate this offer by putting a proposal on the table that would increase the number of lakes on which motorboat use could continue for a period of years. When Oberstar responded with his proposal, Fraser could add seasonal motorboat use.

This approach would come into play quite soon. See Brock Evans Recollections, p. 12. See also *MLH Chronology*, April 22-28, 1978; and *Minneapolis Tribune*, May 2, 1978, "Fraser Still Looks for Compromise in BWCA Dispute."

22 *Cook County News-Herald*, Apr. 20, 1978, p. 1, "Alliance Happy With Wendy"; *Ely Echo*, April 12, 1978, p. 1, "DFL In-Party Fight as BWCA Issue Heats Up."

23 *Duluth News-Tribune*, Apr. 15, 1978, p. 1, "Grand Marais Shuts Down"; *Minneapolis Tribune*, Apr. 15, 1978, p. 15A, "City Cuts Off Electricity to Protest BWCA Bill"; *St. Paul Pioneer Press*, Apr. 15, 1978, p. 1, "Marchers in Grand Marais Protest 'Sellout' of BWCA"; *Cook County News-Herald*, Apr. 20, 1978, p. 1, "County Says to the Feds: You do it to Us and We'll do it to You," and "City Council Throws Full Weight Behind Protest." See also Zabinski Paper, p. 29, although this paper mistakenly places the protest in March following initial release of the Burton-Vento measure. For a more in-depth of the Gunflint-area members of the Alliance at this time, see *Minneapolis Tribune*, Apr. 16, 1978, p. 1A, "Boundary Waters Feelings Run Deep."

24 *Ely Echo*, April 26, 1978, p. 1, "BWCA March Set For Friday"; *Minneapolis Tribune*, April 29, 1978, p. 1A, "Marchers in Duluth Support Multiple Use for BWCA."

25 *Minneapolis Tribune*, May 1, 1978, p. 4B, "Group Protests Fraser's BWCA Stand at Minneapolis Fundraiser"; *Ely Echo*, May 3, 1978, p. 3, "Fraser Picketed In Twin Cities."

26 The Alliance subsequently used the issue as a lobbying piece. *Ely Echo*, May 3, 1978, p. 1, "Ely Guides, Resorters Fight for Public Use"; *Ely Echo*, May 3, 1978, p. 1, "What Did Sig Say in 1964?"; *Ely Echo*, May 3, 1978, p. 3, "Veteran Bush Pilot Faces Ouster"; and *Ely Echo*, May 3, 1978, p. 4, "Former Ranger Disputes Wilderness Theories."

27 *Ely Echo*, May 17, 1978, p. 1, "Highway Pickets Get 10,000 Signatures"; *St. Paul Pioneer-Press*, May 14, 1978, p. 1, "10,000 Sign BWCA Petition for Multiple Use"; and *Minneapolis Star*, May 15, 1978, p. 9A, "10,000 Signatures Collected—Support Motorboats in BWCA."

28 They opened a new office in Ely in late May to supplement their office in Duluth. *Ely Echo*, May 31, 1978, "BWCA Battle Moves to Washington, St. Paul. . . . Alliance Office Opens Here."

29 *Minneapolis Tribune*, April 22, 1978, p. 1A, "200 Picket Denver for Backing Anderson."

30 Among the wilderness supporters was Paul Clement, at eighty-six one of the founders of the Minnesota wilderness movement. Clement finished his remarks by raising his

clenched fist and crying, "Fight On!" The demonstration featured signs, adorned canoe paddles, and a thirty-six-foot voyageur canoe. *Minneapolis Tribune*, May 22, 1978, p. 2B, "Friends of BWCA Wilderness Rally at Capitol"; *St. Paul Pioneer Press*, May 22, 1978, BWCA Rally Staged"; *Minneapolis Star*, May 22, 1978, p. 3A, "Supporters of Burton-Vento Wilderness Bill Rally in St. Paul"; *Minnesota Daily*, May 22, 1978, "BWCA Defenders Rally for Burton-Vento;" see also Herb Johnson, "Paul Clement—Still in the Fray," *BWCA Wilderness News*, Mar. 1982, pp. 14-15.

31 Rip Rapson Notes, DMF Papers, May 3, 1978.

32 Rip Rapson Notes, DMF Papers, May 3, 1978. See also *Minneapolis Tribune*, May 2, 1978, "Fraser Still Looks for Compromise in BWCA Dispute."

33 Rip Rapson Notes, DMF Papers, May 3, 1978.

34 Rapson had previously urged a process that took this tack. See note 21 *supra*.

35 H.R. 12609, 95th Congress, 2nd Session (May 8, 1978); see also *Congressional Record*, May 31, 1978 (House floor amendment).

36 See Rip Rapson Notes, DMF Papers, May 3 and 4, 1978.

37 Rip Rapson Notes, DMF Papers, May 4, 1978.

38 Rip Rapson Notes, DMF Papers, May 4, 1978.

39 *Minneapolis Tribune*, May 5, 1978, p. 8A, "BWCA: Oberstar Doesn't Go Far Enough"; *St. Paul Pioneer-Press*, May 4, 1978, p. 8, "No Canoes For Wendy"; *Duluth News-Tribune*, May 7, 1978, p. 2D, "Final BWCA Draft." For an analysis of the BWCA controversy after Oberstar announced his new bill, see *Minneapolis Tribune*, May 14, 1978, p. 1B, "BWCA Dispute Hangs on Resorts, Motors."

40 Rip Rapson Notes, DMF Papers, May 12, 1978 (conversation of May 11, 1978).

41 Brock Evans Recollections, pp. 15-17.

42 Rip Rapson Notes, DMF Papers, May 12, 1978.

43 Rip Rapson Notes, DMF Papers, May 15, 1978.

44 Representative John Moakley of Massachusetts and Morgan Murphy of Illinois. *MLH Chronology*, May 17, 1978.

45 *MLH Chronology*, May 19, 1978.

46 See "Possible Fraser-Vento Package to Resolve Boundary Waters Canoe Area Controversy," Rip Rapson Notes, DMF Papers, May 19, 1978.

47 Donald M. Fraser and Bruce F. Vento to James L. Oberstar, May 18, 1978 (not sent), DMF Papers; copy in possession of authors.

48 Donald M. Fraser to James Delaney, May 19, 1978, DMF Papers; copy in possession of authors.

49 Morris K. Udall and Phillip Burton to Jim Delaney, May 19, 1978, DMF Papers; copy in possession of authors.

50 James J. Delaney to Donald M. Fraser, May 22, 1978, DMF Papers; copy in possession of authors.

51 Rip Rapson Notes, DMF Papers, May 24, 1978. See also *Minneapolis Tribune*, June 1, 1978, p. 2B, "BWCA Bill Cleared for Floor Action; 2-Hour Debate Set"; *Minneapolis Tribune*, May 26, 1978, "BWCA Bill Expected to reach House Floor during Week of June 4"; *St. Paul Pioneer-Press*, June 1, 1978, p. 19, "BWCA Debate Slated."

52 See *MLH Chronology*, May 31, 1978; Brock Evans Recollections, pp. 18-19.

53 Brock Evans Recollections, pp. 18-19.

54 Donald M. Fraser, Bruce Vento, and Richard Nolan to Dear Colleague, May 31, 1978, DMF Papers, copy in possession of authors. See also *Minneapolis Tribune*, May 31, 1978, p. 1A, "House Offered BWCA Changes"; and *Duluth News-Tribune*, May 31, 1978, p. 1, "Another BWCA Pact Offered."

55 "The committee bill is itself a major compromise and our amendments represent a second major compromise designed to resolve this issue in a manner that is fair to local residents while at the same time preserving the BWCA as a true wilderness." Donald M. Fraser, Bruce Vento, and Richard Nolan to Dear Colleague, May 31, 1978, DMF Papers; copy in possession of authors.

56 See Anthony Beilsenson and Don Fraser *et al* to Dear Colleague, June 1, 1978; Morris K. Udall and Phillip Burton *et al* to Dear Colleague, June 1, 1978; Jonathan Bingham *et al* to Dear Colleague, June 1, 1978; and Silvio Conte *et al* to Dear Republican Colleague, June 1, 1978. See also the editorial in *New York Times*, May 21, 1978, "Making Change: The Wild Ones."

57 See *Minneapolis Tribune*, May 31, 1978, p. 1A, "House Offered BWCA Changes."

58 *Ibid.*

59 *Minneapolis Tribune*, June 3, 1978, p. 1A, "Mondale Linked to U.S. Delay on BWCA Measure."

60 *Ibid.*

61 Zabinksi Paper, p. 37; Zabinski Interview, Dec. 21, 1987. See also *Minneapolis Tribune*, June 4, 1978, p. 1A, "Seek Unity, Mondale tells DFL."

62 Dan Engstrom Interview, Nov. 17, 1987.

63 Observation by Herbert C. Johnson, June 3, 1978, St. Paul Civic Center. See also Jim Klobuchar's column in *Minneapolis Star*, June 1, 1978, p. 1B, "One Way to Buy Loyalty for the DFL."

64 *St. Paul Pioneer-Press*, June 2, 1978, p. 17, "Wendy Won't Endorse Support for Vento Bill." See also *Minneapolis Tribune*, June 2, 1978, p. 1A, "Anderson Won't Take a Stand

on Constitutional Abortion Ban"; and *Minneapolis Star*, June 2, 1978, p. 11A, "DFL Delegate is Agonizing Over Supporting Anderson."

65 *Minneapolis Tribune*, June 3, 1978, p. 1A, "DFLers Join Forces to Endorse Anderson, Fraser, and Perpich."

66 There is no evidence that Anderson or his staff organized any such effort. See generally *Minneapolis Tribune*, June 3, 1978, p. 1A, "DFLers Join Forces to Endorse Anderson, Fraser, and Perpich." See also *St. Paul Pioneer-Press*, June 3, 1978, p. 1, "DFL Endorses Wendy, Fraser."

67 *St. Paul Pioneer-Press*, June 4, 1978, p. 1, "Candidates Ask for Unity Amid Catcalls."

68 *Minneapolis Tribune*, June 4, 1978, p. 1A, "Seek Unity, Mondale Tells DFL."

69 *St. Paul Pioneer-Press*, June 4, 1978, p. 1, "Candidates Ask For Unity Amid Catcalls"; *Minneapolis Tribune*, June 4, 1978, p. 1A, "Seek Unity, Mondale Tells DFL"; and *Duluth News-Tribune*, June 4, 1978, p. 1A, "DFLers Unity Theme Pushed by Mondale."

70 Rapson Recollections, December 1983.

71 See Dan Engstrom Interview, Nov. 17, 1987.

72 The vote was 672 to 534 in favor of the plank, fifty votes short of sixty percent. Dan Engstrom Interview, Nov. 17, 1987; *Duluth News-Tribune*, June 5, 1978, p. 1, "Burton-Vento Bill Loses DFL Convention Support."

73 *St. Paul Pioneer-Press*, June 5, 1978, p. 1, "DFL Sidesteps Stand on BWCA." See also Jim Klobuchar's column in *Minneapolis Star*, June 5, 1978, p. 13A, "Anderson Gives Them What They Want."

74 *Minneapolis Tribune*, June 6, 1978, p. 1A, "BWCA Plank Passed, Reversed by DFL"; *Minneapolis Tribune*, June 6, 1978, p. 1A, "Fragile DFL Unity Comes Unglued."

75 Zabinski Interview, Dec. 21, 1987; Zabinski Paper, p. 38.

76 See *Minneapolis Star*, June 5, 1978, p. 1A, "Law Won't Settle Age-Old BWCA Issues."

78 *Ibid.*

79 *Congressional Record*, June 5, 1978, H4945.

80 The floor debate cast Rick Nolan into his first public role on the bill. Nolan devoted a significant part of his remarks to debunking the idea that the Burton-Vento bill would deny access to persons with disabilities:

> I should like to briefly describe an organization whose expressed mission is to provide access to such wilderness areas to the handicapped. This organization calls itself the Wilderness Inquiry II and is one of three affiliate groups under the parent organization, the Wilderness Inquiry Association. Wilderness Inquiry II is designed to meet the recreational needs of the handicapped by providing access into such areas. It is intended that such excursions may be employed to assist

handicapped individuals in coping with their disabilities by using the Wilderness as a means of developing self-confidence in themselves. *Congressional Record*, June 5, 1978, H4953.

82 *Congressional Record*, June 5, 1978, H4948.

83 *Congressional Record*, June 5, 1978, H4954.

84 "The only thing that stands in the way of the present motorboat routes being accepted by people is that canoeists do not like the sound of a motor," Quie stated. And because snowmobiles "stay on the lakes . . . they are not damaging to the wilderness area." *Congressional Record*, June 5, 1978, H4949.

85 "The denial of access to the BWCA for these people far outweighs, in my opinion, the miniscule, largely psychological advantages that might accrue to those [who seek a wilderness experience,]" Tom Hagedorn sputtered. *Congressional Record*, June 5, 1978, H 4952-H4954.

86 Congressional Record, June 5, 1978, H4949.

87 See generally *Congressional Record*, June 5, 1978, H4960-H4967; *Minneapolis Tribune*, June 6, 1978, p. 1A, "House Passes Strict BWCA Bill"; *St. Paul Pioneer-Press*, June 6, 1978, p. 1, "DFL House Trio Succeeds on BWCA Bill"; *Duluth News-Tribune*, June 6, 1978, p. 1, "House Passes BWCA Restrictions."

Chapter Six

The Senate

The House had sent the Senate a BWCA bill. But the bill's future in the new forum was riddled with uncertainty. Where Fraser, Vento, and Burton had been able to unite to overcome the institutional deference to home-district prerogative, Anderson was likely to play that prerogative to the hilt. Where there had been room in the House to compromise without doing severe violence to the basic principles of the bill, the Senate would have far less of that luxury. And where the House process had been able to absorb delays, the Senate had only four months in which to complete its work.

A New Cast

The Friends were strangely subdued after their victory on the House floor. They understood the magnitude of their accomplishment. But they also recognized that the Senate was a different world, an institution in which home-state senators were rarely denied on issues affecting them directly. With Muriel Humphrey likely to defer to Anderson, and Anderson committed to supporting only that which the residents of northern Minnesota could accept, the Friends feared the worst. It was conceivable that Anderson would push a bill so unacceptable to the environmental community that even a conference committee's reconciliation of the House and Senate bills would not be enough to produce a result the environmentalists could support. They might then be put in a position of seeking to kill a bill they had spent years developing.

That fear prompted the Friends executive committee to meet ten days after the House vote to discuss whether they should participate in the Senate process or resign themselves to doing nothing this session and starting over again after the fall elections, when they hoped Fraser would be in the Senate to advance a new bill.[1] In a straw vote, the majority supported abandoning the effort until the next year.[2] Although Heinselman was later able to convince the group that

Senator Wendell Anderson (left) had enjoyed a popular tenure as governor. (*Photo by Kevin Proescholdt*)

they could not afford to wait, the vote was a measure of the depth of their distrust of Anderson.

That distrust illustrated just how far Anderson had fallen from grace not just with the environmental community, but with Minnesota voters generally.

Young and energetic, an Olympic hockey star turned lawyer, Anderson had enjoyed widespread popularity as governor.[3] His administration seemed to have been captured in a picture on the cover of *Time* in 1973 extolling the "good life in Minnesota." A lake and pines in the background, the plaid-shirted governor displayed a smile from central casting and a large, recently-caught northern pike:

> Like the state itself, Anderson can sometimes seem almost too good to be true. [He] has athletic dash and youthful charm that make many of his constituents think of a Midwestern Kennedy.[4]

The article observed that in Anderson the national Democrats had a likely 1976 vice presidential candidate.

That was before he arranged to resign and have newly ascended Governor Perpich appoint him to the Senate seat vacated by Mondale in 1976. Overnight, he was seen in a new light: opportunistic, shallow, a creature controlled by political insiders like Kelm.

By early spring of 1978, this image had solidified. Jim Klobuchar, a widely read *Minneapolis Star* columnist, drew the following portrait:

> In fright and exasperation, [Anderson] has shown us glimpses of a kind of campaign that seems borrowed from the pool hall grifter. [His self-appointment arises from] the gluttony of ambition. He [gives the impression of] demagoguing pol [seeking] to counter the imagery of the man of caution and indecision [from] a forum he didn't win, but seized.[5]

Whether this new characterization was any fairer than the more flattering depictions of his governorship is an open question. But it stuck. His staff

April 11, 1978, *St. Paul Dispatch* cartoon. (*Reprinted with permission from the* St. Paul Pioneer Press)

became more and more the mirror image of the senator: protective, closed, defensive. The Friends had received a particularly strong dose of this treatment after their press release attacking Anderson's speech in Virginia. They had little direct access to Anderson, and were increasingly brushed off by his staff.

Anderson's early handling of the BWCA did little to inspire confidence that this was a man of principle who knew what he was doing. The first clear articulation of his position appeared to many to be pandering—an over-the-top statement made before the highly partisan, intimidating crowd in Virginia. His only statement following passage of the House bill was to respond to a *Minneapolis Tribune* editorial urging his prompt action.[6] And, in contrast to Burton, he failed to outline publicly how the Senate would go about its business—which committees would hear it, what provision would be made for public testimony, what the timeline would be, and the like.

Given Muriel Humphrey's affection for Anderson and her desire to encourage his leadership on the BWCA, it was a cruel irony that Anderson's image was frequently contrasted with hers. In the same article in which he so mercilessly skewered Anderson, Klobuchar noted that Humphrey seemed motivated not by personal gain—she had announced in April her intention not to run for the seat in the special election—but by a desire to promote party unity:

She walked away from all of it, with a bearing that was almost majestic in the best sense because it was so free from mawkishness or any suggestion of personal sacrifice. In giving up a hugely prestigious position she could have had by asking for it, she seemed to be responding to a fundamental instinct for the right deed and word that have earned her the veneration of millions in this state.[7]

On the BWCA issue, however, Humphrey gave no indication that she considered the right deed anything other than giving Anderson the latitude he needed to work matters out.

The Friends and Alliance waited anxiously to see how Anderson would do just that.

Maneuvering for Position

The Friends had tried to build support for a wilderness bill in the Senate even before the House completed its work.

Their principal ally was Iowa's Dick Clark. Clark's constituency had weighed in heavily with the entire Iowa congressional delegation; both Democrats and Republicans on the House side had become sponsors of the Fraser bill. Clark had made up his mind even before the pressure began to mount. In cooperation with Fraser's staff, he had introduced the Fraser bill in the Senate a full year before the House acted.[8] Although his action irritated Anderson's staff, it provided Clark with an opening to begin talking to his colleagues about the issue.[9]

Clark was helpful in encouraging many of his colleagues to talk with Heinselman. In the early spring, Heinselman quietly paid visits on the Senate offices to prepare the ground.

Far more than in the House, however, Heinselman's pitch was met with a polite noncommittal: the Senate offices firmly indicated that they would be guided by Anderson and Humphrey—they could not imagine anything emerging from their body without the blessing of both Minnesota senators.

Toward the end of June, Anderson was ready to announce his intentions. The night before his public statement, he asked the Friends' leadership to meet with him when his plane arrived at the Minneapolis/St.Paul airport.

Heinselman, Dayton, and others drove to the airport encouraged by this act of courtesy. Their optimism soon turned to bitterness.[10] Anderson had done Oberstar a turn better. He had accepted the cessation of logging, the creation of a mining buffer zone, and the expansion of the wilderness but had otherwise ignored the House bill. Not only had he incorporated each of Oberstar's motorboat and snowmobile routes, but he had included almost two dozen departures from the House document, each of which diluted the strength of the bill's overall approach to wilderness management.

April 28, 1978, *Minneapolis Tribune* cartoon. (*Reprinted with permission from the* Minneapolis Star Tribune)

This was calculating, hard-ball politics. It now became clear why Anderson had sought the meeting. By proposing a bill so fully the creature of northern Minnesota pressures, he had boxed the environmentalists in: they would either have to swallow their rage and go along with his proposal or be forced to work for its defeat, throwing the entire dispute back to ground-zero—reinstituting the current regimen of motorboating, logging, snowmobiling, and mineral exploration. Heinselman, with tears streaming down his face, told Wendy that the proposal was unacceptable.[11]

Anderson introduced the bill the next day, June 23.[12] In a surprise move, he also announced that he would bring members of the Senate Parks and Recreation Subcommittee to northern Minnesota to tour the BWCA in mid-July.

The reaction had the intended effect. Oberstar praised Anderson's work: "[This is] a solid, constructive proposal. I am very hopeful now that we will be able to resolve the BWCA dispute this year." The Alliance's Ed Zabinski did the same, although it was evident that many of his members still had reservations about a bill that changed current management in any way at all.[13]

The environmentalists struggled to see their way clear to a strategy. They took their obligatory public swings at the proposal,[14] but quietly tried to understand what they could do to stop Anderson's train from crushing their work.

220 / Troubled Waters

Fighting the new bill was challenge enough. Coping with a tour of the BWCA arranged on short-notice and with little Friends input intensified the problem.

Anderson was not a member of the subcommittee. By becoming the subcommittee's tour guide, he would neutralize that. To the subcommittee members, he would be the person orchestrating the show. To the media, he would be the source of a series of tantalizing stories. To the public at large, he would be the center of action, demonstrating a style of leadership at which he excelled.

There was also a subtlety of purpose that was not lost on the Friends. Anderson was, in effect, circumventing the normal process of legislative deliberation. These were not hearings. This was not a markup. It was a free ride: a way of positioning an argument without any of the attendant accountability.

That argument was rooted in accommodating the needs of local residents. There was no better way to showcase those needs than to permit residents to tell their stories face-to-face, on-site to the senators who would decide their fate.

It was a brilliant piece of wiliness. But it didn't adequately cover one small detail: the feistiness of Jim Abourezk, Phil Burton's close friend and the chair of the subcommittee.

The Road Show

Preparations over the next three weeks came to resemble advance work for a papal visit.[15]

Anderson had lined up three of the subcommittee's members to visit: Abourezk, Howard Metzenbaum of Ohio, and Dale Bumpers of Arkansas. Muriel Humphrey would also join them. Oberstar would not—Anderson was not about to share the stage. Anderson arranged with Mondale to have "Air Force 2," the vice president's DC-9, fly the delegation into the Ely airport.

Peter Gove of Anderson's staff had choreographed every minute of the visit, now set for July 16 and 17. Rapson was designated as the Friends negotiator, but made little headway in steering the event toward neutral ground. Rapson was able to give the Friends a role in the initial and concluding briefing sessions, to place Friends' representatives on the tour boats, and to secure himself a seat on the plane with the senators and their staff. But he was otherwise unable to make a dent in who and what the senators would see. Anderson would be in charge from start to finish.

On the afternoon of Sunday, July 16, Ely was dressed to the nines, its residents awaiting the most prestigious air cargo likely ever shipped to that locale.

They weren't disappointed. On a cloudless day, the plane made a spectacular entrance, casting a ground-shadow as it circled the midsection of the BWCA. The senators were treated to a rare panorama, a labyrinth of glistening blue lakes and emerald-green trees stretching for miles in all directions.[16]

As Air Force 2 taxied to a stop on the runway, cameras from throughout the state began what would become a media fest over the next two days. The delegation was met by the political royalty of the north and ushered to the Ely City Hall for an opening briefing.

The Alliance and the Friends each had been allotted thirty minutes to make an overview presentation. The Alliance went first.[17]

The Alliance spokesman was Lee Hotaling, the owner of a resort on Snowbank Lake. Signalling a theme that would be carried throughout the visit, Hotaling drew a distinction between the extremism of "professional environmentalists" and the moderate requests of local residents: "the loudest voices often come from those who seldom used the BWCA."[18]

Carl Gawboy, a Chippewa artist and Ely native, hammered the theme home:

> Only slowly have we come to realize that the Boundary Waters is a victim of a national campaign by wilderness preservationists who do not recognize the distinctive qualities that make it one wilderness area that can be enjoyed by all—regardless of age or limited time, material affluence, or physical abilities.[19]

The Friends countered with Heinselman; Dick Flint, Chair of the Sierra Club's North Star Chapter; and Becky Rom, a Minneapolis lawyer who also was an Ely native and seasoned bush pilot.[20] They emphasized that for all the stories of personal hardship they would hear, the senators should see the BWCA through the prism of its status as a unique national resource.

The reception to both sides was reserved. The arguments were familiar, and the senators had come not to be briefed but to look around.

Their hosts had resolved to make sure that they got a good look at more than the natural beauty of the place. The next stop was an open house at the Ely Community Center. Anyone expecting a tasteful coffee and desert reception in the meeting room was disappointed. The senators entered an auditorium stuffed full with more than 1,000 local residents. Fearing a little more deja vu than would be comfortable after the Ely field hearings of a year ago, the Friends were represented only by Rapson. It was probably a wise decision. Each senator in turn was beckoned to the microphone. It was a difficult place to be impartial. Fed by the carnival-like atmosphere, the senators gave the crowd a reason to cheer, generally praising the local community and its forceful leader in Washington, Senator Anderson.

The next morning, the visitors were delivered to the landing at Fall Lake. For the rest of the day, they would be treated to every kind of motorized transportation the Friends were battling: a bus and jeep carrying them over the "truck portages," motorboats, high-speed "towboats," and float-planes.

A parking lot of motorboats (top) provided part of the senators' tour of the wilderness. A school bus on the Four Mile Portage transported the senators and media entourage. (*Photos by M. L. Heinselman*)

The entourage, which included the senators, Alliance members, Friends members, and the media, began by boarding motorboats for the trip up Fall Lake to Basswood Lake. Rapson had unsuccessfully argued with Gove about the boat arrangements. Each boat was guided by three or four Alliance representatives, who provided a running narrative on what the senators were seeing. Rapson, Heinselman, Dayton, and Jan Green were distributed in four separate boats to provide a modicum of balance.

The group was transferred to a full-size school bus at the Four Mile truck portage. As the bus slowly bumped its way along the full four miles, the Alliance commentators asked the senators to image how difficult it would be to portage a canoe over such a distance. Heinselman pointed out that canoeists would take alternative routes. The driver responded that this was exactly the point: the portage was meant for motors, not for canoeists—there was plenty of room in the wilderness for both.

At the end of the bus ride, the travelers were transferred to motorboats for a quick trip to Basswood's Wind Bay. On such a clear day, the motorboats made good time. The Alliance guide in Rapson's boat pointed out the difficulties a canoeist would have on such big expanses of water. Rapson countered that Basswood, as the centerpoint of the international boundary, was a lake canoeists navigated with regularity—they just took their time doing it. Moreover, the lake was full of campsites in case the going got rough. When Rapson finished, the boat veered sharply to the left and took a series of rocky leaps against the wake left by the boat in front of them. "You want to navigate this lake in a windy day without a motor?" the guide asked. "It gets a lot worse than this."[21] Metzenbaum, looking slightly green around the gills, nodded in agreement.

Much to Metzenbaum's relief, they docked soon afterward at Wind Bay. Twenty canoes sat on the shore, piled with sandwiches and soft drinks. For the next hour, the delegation took turns paddling in the calm inlet in the company of Heinselman, Dayton, and Green. Rapson stayed on shore to monitor the lunchtime conversation of those who chose to eat rather than paddle.

Their wilderness experience dispensed with, the group was loaded back into motorboats for a trip to the Prairie Portage truck portage. After crossing the short portage, they received their first exposure to towboats—vehicles whose twin eighty-horsepower motors and canoe racks enabled canoeists to get a jump-start on their trip by being "towed" deep into the wilderness. Eager to demonstrate their product, the towboat operators roared the Washington delegation down the Moose Lake chain at forty miles per hour.

The Friends had anticipated this show of technological bravado. In a staged, but effective, contrivance, a fleet of a half-dozen canoeists rocked their canoes in feigned concern about being swamped by the passing towboats' wake.

Float planes flew the senators to Seagull Lake for the next leg of their tour. (*Photo by M. L. Heinselman*)

At the end of Moose Lake, the multi-modal transit experience continued with a transfer to a few float-planes. The delegation was pared to just the senators, a few Alliance members, and Rapson and Heinselman. They were soon on route to Seagull Lake near the end of the Gunflint Trail.

For the first time that day, the senators could sit back, look out the window, and not worry about cameras or a political pitch. The beauty of the day had held. The airspace ban had been waived for the trip, making the crystalline quality of the lakes even more evident than it had been from Air Force 2. Heading northeast, the senators could look across the international boundary into Canada, the water and the trees spreading to the horizon line. As they began their descent to Seagull Lake, Metzenbaum leaned over to Rapson and said over the drone of the plane, "Good God, it's really worth all this trouble, isn't it?"[22]

The group was welcomed at Seagull by a huge crowd of almost four hundred people. This was the Gunflint Trail's answer to the "open house" in Ely the night before. Displays describing the lakes along the Gunflint were tacked onto trees. An outdoor, sit-down lunch of walleye was served on placemats depicting an alligator (i.e., the federal government) poised to devour the BWCA. A reception with the full crowd waited inside Seagull Lodge for the delegation to finish their second lunch. All told, the Seagull stopover lasted three hours.[23]

After flying back to Ely in the late afternoon, the senators had a final

"Good God, it's really worth all this trouble, isn't it?" said Senator Howard Metzenbaum as he looked down at the BWCA. (*Photo by Rip Rapson*)

The Alliance reception at Seagull Lake. (*Photo by M. L. Heinselman*)

working session on their itinerary. Rapson had extracted one large concession from Gove: after the full day of Alliance-driven images and messages, the Friends would be given an opportunity to put the events into perspective. Gove and Anderson had agreed, provided the Alliance would be invited to observe.

The long day had taken a toll. Anderson informed the Friends that the senators were weary and would be able to listen only for fifteen minutes. The Friends quickly concluded that only one person would leave the impression they sought: Sig Olson.

Just as he had during the Ely hearings the summer before, Olson appealed to the higher values of the lawmakers. He described how wilderness helped shape the spiritual make-up not just of individuals, but of a nation. Looking directly into Metzenbaum's eyes, he reminded the senators that theirs would be an act of stewardship—of the land, of its history, of its spiritual power.[24]

The effect was to pierce the web Anderson had woven. The senators had been brought back full circle. They came bearing the responsibility for exercising fair judgment on an issue with national overtones and local implications. During the tour, they had been caught up in the power of the latter. Olson had called them back to the former. There was an awkward silence.

Abourezk broke it.

He asked a few questions of each side. The answers exasperated him— the parties clearly were not talking the same language. He finally pounded the table and said, "Look, I'm not going to be able to figure out and Congress isn't going to figure out which of these lakes should be motorized and which of them should not be motorized. You simply have to work it out."[25]

When he still got nothing but shaking heads and blank stares, he sat back for a moment. He then leaned forward and signalled to Dayton, Hotaling, and Anderson. "Come talk with me in private for a minute," he said, directing the small group into a side room. The rest of the group stayed where they were, making sparse, nervous conversation.

Abourezk sat the group down and turned to Anderson. "Wendy, you and I both know that there is no way our friends in the Senate will tolerate our spilling blood over whether five or fifteen lakes should have motorboats zooming around," he began. "Let's give these gentlemen the authority to try to work something out."[26] Abourezk proposed that the two sides enter a formal mediation under the auspices of the Senate Energy and Natural Resources Committee. The sessions would proceed with all the resources the Senate had to offer. "Is that okay with you?" he asked Anderson; Anderson nodded.

They rejoined the larger group. Abourezk outlined his plan: "It makes no sense for us to devise motor regulations for the BWCA. We don't know the area. You know the area," he said, pointing at people from both sides. He made clear that as chair of the subcommittee that would consider the legislation, he was not asking for cooperation, he was demanding it. Looking at Dayton and Hotaling, he clarified that the Friends and the Alliance would each select a negotiating representative and begin talks in the presence of a committee mediator within ten days. Anderson announced his willingness to incorporate any agreement that was produced into his pending Senate bill. In a flurry of thank-yous and good-nights, the meeting was adjourned.

It was as if Anderson had been hit by lightning. He had walked into the City Council chambers triumphant after the political and public relations coup of the last twenty-four hours. He had walked out less than an hour later stripped of his control over the situation. He was at the mercy of a process that would occur in private, guided by Abourezk's subcommittee rather than by him.[27]

The Friends and the Alliance gave the appearance less of being struck by lightning than of being caught in headlights. The Friends were being drawn further and further away from the structured legislative process they understood and felt they could influence. The Alliance failed to see the point of wasting time negotiating away their position of strength.[28]

Neither side believed there was any real chance of a negotiated outcome. But neither side was willing to antagonize Abourezk by saying so. Both made their plane reservations for Washington.[29]

In the Basement of the Russell Office Building

Their skepticism about the outcome did not prevent the Friends and the Alliance from beginning preparations immediately.

The first matter at hand was selecting a lead negotiator.

The Friends concurred with Abourezk's assumption that Dayton would represent them. The alternative was Heinselman, who, despite his encyclopedic knowledge, was unlikely to summon the dispassion that would be required as compromises were batted back and forth.[30]

Dayton was ideally suited for the role. His knowledge of BWCA issues was second only to Heinselman's. He had represented the environmental community in two BWCA logging lawsuits, in administrative appeals of Forest Service BWCA management plans, and in the BWCA snowmobile lawsuit. His family had operated Dayton's Canoe Base just outside the BWCA on Jasper Lake for years. He was a founding member of the Friends.

More than anything, however, Dayton was known for his incisive intelligence and deep integrity. He had practiced law for fifteen years, developing a penchant for detail and thoroughness. He enjoyed the trust of the entire Friends leadership.

Attorney Chuck Dayton had worked for years to protect the BWCA. (*Photo by Kevin Proescholdt*)

Abourezk had assumed that Hotaling would represent the Alliance. But Hotaling was not an attorney, and the Alliance had a healthy respect for Dayton's skills. They decided instead on the Ely City Attorney, Ron Walls.

It was a good match-up. The parallels with Dayton's experience were striking. He was familiar with the disputes that had engulfed the area, representing Kainz Logging during the BWCA logging lawsuits and local residents in the snowmobile litigation. He knew the terrain, having lived in Ely for years and guided wilderness canoe trips for the boy scout base on Moose Lake. He was respected as a competent attorney and honest public official.[31]

Unlike Dayton, however, Walls had kept an arm's length distance from the inner circle of his new client. Partly because of this and partly because of the Alliance's deep distrust of the idea of negotiating with the enemy, Walls was kept on a very short leash. His instructions from the Alliance were clear: talk, but don't agree to anything; bring home any deal you make and the Alliance membership will look it over. As the Alliance's Zabinski explained, "Walls was not enthralled with his limitations, but accepted the assignment."[32]

The second order of business was pulling together the back-up teams that would support the negotiators with information and political advice and that would relay information between Washington and Minnesota.

The Friends team would be Bud and Fran Heinselman, Rapson, Green, Kathy Dayton, and Larry Romans.[33] The Alliance team would be be larger: Gunflint resorters Bruce Kerfoot, Luanna Brandt, and Al Danielson, logger Wes Hedstrom, Ely representatives Lee Hotaling, John Smrekar, Leon Ping, and George Scott, and Alliance Director Ed Zabinski.

The negotiators and the teams in place, the Friends began piecing together a strategy.

While Dayton poured through maps and potential areas of negotiation with Heinselman and Green,[34] Rapson prepared a fall-back strategy in the event the negotiations broke down. He opened a conversation with Anderson's Republican senatorial opponent, Rudy Boschwitz, to solidify Boschwitz's commitment to a more moderate position than Anderson's. He cleared with the committee staff the possible introduction of two sets of amendments prepared by Dayton, one friendly to Anderson, one for the use of Senate Republicans to put Boschwitz's ideas into play. He ironed out with the Majority Leader's office the procedures for amendment on the Senate floor.[35]

Rapson also spoke at length with DFL Party Chair Ric Scott to assess the political context of the negotiations.[36] The party had been completely frozen out of the senate tour and been given no role in the negotiations. Noting that Anderson had dropped completely from sight in the ten days since the trip, Scott asked Rapson whether Anderson knew what he was doing in acquiescing to the negotiations. "Not at the time but probably now," Rapson replied. That fits, Scott said: "His campaign has circled the wagons. No information goes in or out without it being approved by Kelm. We can't talk to them; nobody can."[37] "What advice would you give them," Rapson asked. "Use the mediation as an excuse to move off center. It would be good politics in Minnesota," Scott responded. It would also be sound legislative strategy insofar as Anderson could probably not count on the usual senatorial courtesies in the aftermath of Abourezk's initiative.

The ten days passed quickly. On Thursday, July 27, the negotiations began.

The third leg of the negotiating stool was Tom Williams, a member of the Senate Energy and Natural Resources Committee staff and a personal favorite of both its Chair, Henry "Scoop" Jackson of Washington, and Abourezk.

Williams hardly looked the part of a diplomat. Bearded, burly, and informal, he looked more like a logger than the skilled bureaucrat he was. He had served before as a troubleshooter for the committee on park and wilderness issues. He had already boned up on the BWCA issues, accompanying the subcommittee members on their tour.

Abourezk and Jackson had decided that they wanted the negotiators close enough to be accessible, but removed enough to avoid the normal interruptions of the Senate's daily chaos. They agreed on a bare-bones conference room in the basement of the Russell Senate Building.

Williams greeted Dayton and Walls by informing them that the conference room was where Senate wives had rolled bandages during the Civil War and that he fully anticipated that the three of them would need some of those bandages by the time they were through. His instructions were, he said, to keep them there until they had produced an agreement. If that was five days, fine, but he would rather get home for the weekend.[38]

The ground rules were simple. Williams was in charge. Dayton and Walls would leave the room only by mutual agreement. The support teams would not be permitted in the room for any reason. Meetings with the support teams would be subjected to time limits to encourage the sharing of information, but not the

"Okay! We grab the BWCA away from those people up north so that we can tell them exactly what they can and cannot do with their lives."

(Reprinted with permission from the Minneapolis Star Tribune)

extended hashing out of positions—that would be left to the two negotiators. The sessions would go as long into the evening as appeared fruitful, but would begin again early the next morning regardless.

Williams preemptively acknowledged that neither side could envision a negotiated compromise. But he reminded them that they were now in the middle of a political whirlpool that they would have great difficulty controlling.

He chided Dayton not to put any stock in the possibility of revisiting the issue the next year. The Friends would simply not get this far again. House members would be highly unreceptive to repeating the divisive and complicated process of taking a BWCA bill through their chamber. The Senate, even were Fraser elected, would give equal weight to his colleague, and neither Anderson nor Boschwitz was likely to fall on his sword for a bill once the election season had passed. And there was always the possibility that Fraser would not win.[39]

Williams next took aim at Walls. The Alliance cannot sit back and assume Congress will permit nothing to happen, he observed. Congress will do something, and it is very likely that that something will look a lot like the House-passed bill. Even if Anderson's bill passed intact, and it almost certainly would not, it would be sent to a conference committee. And nobody, nobody, was better in conference committees than Phil Burton. He will, Williams said, jabbing in the air for emphasis, have you looking for your wallet by the time you're through.

Williams let this sink in a bit. The three then went to work. Using a six-foot map tacked on the wall, piles of briefing papers, and the competing bills, they first moved through the dispute item by item to see where there was agreement, where there was disagreement, and where there might be room for middle ground.

All the while, the support teams sat in nearby offices, waiting for the word that they might be needed. The day passed without it coming.

At the end of the first day, Williams, Dayton, and Walls had covered a lot of ground, but had failed to identify any substantial area of potential agreement. It left the Friends discouraged and the Alliance more convinced than ever that this was an empty exercise.[40]

They began again on Friday morning. Williams began mixing in different formats for discussion. He tried individual sessions with Dayton and Walls, trying to probe ideas each would not discuss in the presence of the other. He tried floating ideas through a form of shuttle diplomacy, first getting a reaction from Dayton and then from Walls. He tried bundling issues to avoid letting one issue block progress.

During the day, the discussions had come to focus on Basswood Lake. Neither Dayton nor Walls was willing to move to secondary issues until he had a reading on how the use of Basswood would be resolved.

Both sides agreed that Basswood was the heart of the BWCA. It was the passageway of the international boundary, through which canoeists and motorboaters alike passed to the north into Quetico, to the west to Lac La Croix, and to the east to Knife and Saganaga. For the canoeist, it epitomized a wilderness lake, full of bays, inlets, and islands. For motorboaters, it was the ultimate big water, where the vast distances did full justice to a motor trip. For the resort and outfitting industries, it was the anchor of the economy, the destination of towboats and fishing expeditions. For the Ely area, Basswood symbolized all the frustrations with the historic advance of wilderness regulations pushed by environmentalists and the federal government; for wilderness advocates, Basswood symbolized all that the wilderness might one day become.

It was a classic deadlock. Walls would not accept Basswood as a nonmotorized lake; Dayton would not accept it as a motorized lake. All the shuttling, packaging, and private discussions Williams could devise were powerless to break the impasse.[41]

Williams encouraged Dayton and Walls to visit with their support teams to get a fresh perspective. It only served to cement the positions further.

Frustrated, Williams pulled one of his trump cards. Later in the day, the negotiators were paid a visit by Scoop Jackson. Jackson was a larger-than-life figure in the Senate, a powerhouse on national defense issues and a constant presence in national presidential politics. He did not like to waste his time.

Jackson impressed on Dayton and Walls that they were doing the nation a service—rarely had the Senate vested so much authority in the good judgment of two partisans. They needed to rise to the occasion by leading their respective constituencies in a new direction. If they simply parroted inflexible, tired positions, they would be wasting everyone's time. Congress had already spent a hell of a lot of time on this issue. Get it over with.[42]

It was a powerful appeal that appeared to sink in. The Friday session nevertheless adjourned without a breakthrough. Williams would not, it turned out, make it home for the weekend.

Saturday started as a mirror image of the previous two days. The Alliance back-up team decided that enough was enough: they made reservations to fly back to Minnesota that afternoon and left for the hotel to pick up their bags. Only George Scott stayed to accompany Walls to the airport as soon as the session was called off.

The Friends had a slightly different take. Dayton had prepared a series of ideas about how Basswood might be seen as a series of lakes, rather than as a monolithic problem. Sometime in the early afternoon, the strategy appeared to be paying off. In the late morning, Walls disappeared. Dayton and Williams only hoped he had not hopped a plane with his companions. It turned out that he was using the time to check through some of Dayton's ideas with Oberstar. When he returned, the discussions began to move slightly.[43]

About that time, the Alliance delegation checked in from the airport. Walls reported that although there was a little progress, it was not enough for them to miss their flight. They didn't. They fully expected to meet up with Walls on the late connecting flight from Minneapolis to Duluth.[44]

Dayton's device was to isolate those portions of Basswood most heavily used by motorized fishing parties. If Walls would agree to remove motors from the sections of Basswood most frequented by canoeing parties, they might have something with which to work.

Dayton knew that a concession on Basswood would be further than the Friends would be comfortable in moving. Whereas the Friends had always stated their willingness to accede to motorboat use on peripheral lakes, they had been unequivocal in their refusal to open up the interior lakes, particularly Basswood. Dayton was taking Scoop Jackson's advice to heart: he was pushing beyond the comfort zone. But he also understood that making the first concession on Basswood would leverage a bucketful of concessions by Walls on other critical lakes.

Walls immediately understood the significance of Dayton's gambit. Walls would be able to protect a significant amount of the commercial resort and local fishing interests. Walls agreed to pursue Dayton's line of thinking.

Every bit as thorough as his reputation would have it, Dayton tied other compromises by the Alliance to the Basswood concession, placing a highly choreographed succession of proposals on the table. All of a sudden, this was a real negotiation.

The dynamics were transformed that afternoon. There were constant breaks as Walls traveled the hallway to Scott and Dayton to Heinselman, Green, and Rapson. Both Scott and Heinselman were initially taken by surprise, expressing disbelief that their principals could even discuss what was being proposed. Rapson increasingly played the role of a buffer, letting Heinselman vent his frustration and anger and conveying back to Dayton his impression of when the discussion needed to be reined in.

By dinner time, the tension was unbearable. Heinselman was beside himself with the swirl of trade-offs. The parties agreed to a dinner break.

Hauling boats across portages on trucks is not usually the stuff of stimulating dinner conversation. It was that night, however. Dayton reported to his team that Walls was insisting that three so-called "truck portages" be kept open for easy motorboat access: Four Mile Portage and Prairie Portage into Basswood and Trout Portage into Trout Lake. For Heinselman, that would break any deal: he simply refused to sanction trucks, jeeps, and school buses pulling machines into the wilderness. Dayton grimly agreed.

When Dayton and Walls returned to the Russell basement, they agreed on the outlines of a Basswood package, sidestepping for the moment the truck portages. Motorboats would be permitted on a number of large, long bays— Jackfish, Pipestone, Back, Hoist, and Wind—extending south from the heart of Basswood. Motorboats would also be allowed on a portion of the international border stretching from Prairie Portage west to Washington Island. In exchange, the rest of Basswood would become motorboat-free after a five-year phase-out. Two-thirds of the international border would accordingly be reserved for canoeists: from Basswood Falls east to U.S. Point, and from there south to Washington Island.

If Dayton was thorough, he was also crafty. As the parties turned back to the truck portages, Dayton proposed that the portages could be kept open if the motorboaters could demonstrate that there was no "feasible" alternative to the truck portages for getting their boats into Basswood and Trout Lakes. If they failed to make this showing to the satisfaction of the Secretary of Agriculture, the portages would be closed after five years. This held out for Walls the possibility that local residents would be able to show that pushing boats and motors across difficult terrain on wheelbarrow-like contraptions just would not work. He extracted from Dayton some basic standards for determining how to test feasibility, including the use of three able-bodied persons as the standard crew. They had an agreement.

There were two concealed traps in Dayton's language. First, the burden of proof would lie with those who wanted to keep the portages open, not those who wanted them closed. Second, the term "feasible" was a term of art in the environmental law field, designating something that was possible from an engineering standpoint—it could take longer, be less convenient, and even be downright tortuous and still meet the courts' definition.[45] Dayton was relatively sure that Walls had attached a layman's interpretation to the language, not the narrower definition that would be imposed by the courts. "Candidly," Dayton recalled, "I doubt whether Ron as a general practitioner in a small town knew that. And I didn't tell him about it."[46]

The negotiators put Basswood to one side and opened more fully some of the sticky issues Basswood had preempted. A series of relatively small issue tied them up for hours.

The first was Brule Lake, a spectacular 5,200-acre lake to the west of the Gunflint Trail. A single road led to the only private parcel on the lake, Sky Blue Water Lodge. As early as the 1930s, wilderness proponent Bob Marshall had targeted Brule for special protection against the encroachment of logging and roads. Brule was a personal priority for Dayton. Within hiking distance of Eagle Mountain, the highest point in the state, and with direct road access, the lake provided an opportunity to transform a motorized lake into an incomparably beautiful wilderness experience.

The obstacle was a very entrenched resort owner, Mark Janssen. Walls resisted condemning an existing property. Dayton countered that a single person should not be permitted a monopoly on a lake of such unique qualities. Perhaps knowing of Janssen's reputation for toughness,[47] Walls held his ground. But neither would Dayton relent. He proposed giving Janssen rights to operate the resort for fifteen years, or as long as he owned it, whichever came first; once Janssen offered the property for sale or passed away, it would revert to the federal government for management as wilderness. That extricated Walls from his duty to Janssen. He agreed.

The second small, but vexing, issue was the chain of lakes linked to East Bearskin Lake off the Gunflint Trail. East Bearskin was home to the beautiful and popular Bearskin Lodge. It connected via land portages into a string of small, narrow lakes ideal for both paddling and fishing with small motors: Alder, Canoe, Pine, and McFarland Lakes. Following his standard approach throughout the negotiations, Dayton proposed permitting motors on the peripheral lake, East Bearskin, but closing the motor route at lake's end, making the rest a paddle-only route.

This time Williams, not Walls, intervened. Williams informed Dayton that Dave Tuttle, the owner of Bearskin Lodge, had been the college roommate of the son of Kentucky Senator Wendell Ford. Ford was one of the Energy and Natural Resources Committee's most senior and powerful members. He would see to it that Tuttle's interests were protected, and that meant keeping most of the chain of lakes open to motors:

> Senator Ford's only going to want to know about this one thing. And if we take care of this one thing, that's all he'll want to know about. So we're going to have to take care of this one thing. You won't like it, but we'll have to do it.[48]

That settled that. Adding insult to injury, Dayton was forced to accept snowmobiles on the route for another five years as well.

It was now after midnight and some of the most contentious issues remained. The negotiators decided to press on. Heinselman, Green, Rapson, and Dayton's wife Kathy sat outside; Scott was in a room down the hall. But for a small, forward mouse Rapson nicknamed Phil, in honor of Burton, the basement was deserted.

The next three hours became increasingly tense as Dayton and Walls moved through some of the thorniest ground: Lac La Croix, Saganaga and Seagull, smaller canoe routes, towboats, the length of motorboat phase-outs. Heinselman was running his fingers through his hair non-stop.

Particularly excruciating was Lac La Croix, a long, meandering picture-book lake of hundreds of bays and islands. The site of some of the BWCA's best preserved native pictographs and of pine stands dating to the 1600s, La Croix was Rapson's Achilles' heel, his vision of the perfect canoe country. He and Heinselman instructed Dayton that La Croix should not become a bargaining chip—it needed to be considered on its own merits.

Dayton was confronted with a tough situation on La Croix. Immediately to its western-most reach lay Crane Lake, a huge, heavily motorized lake that served as a magnet for sports fishermen with an interest in traveling to La Croix. That was compounded by the recent decision of the Ontario government to permit motors on the Canadian side of La Croix. And to top it off, the Lac La Croix Indian Tribe operated a motorized fishing guiding business on the Canadian side. He explained to Rapson that there would have to be some give.

The solution came in a Basswood-like approach of designating the west-ern-most bays most heavily used by the fishing guides as motorboat routes, while preserving the northern and eastern two-thirds of the lake, particularly its seclud-ed bays, for canoe-only routes. As difficult as this way for Rapson to swallow, it brought Scott to tears. When Walls informed Scott of the preliminary agreement to limit motorboat use to the western edge, Scott broke down. He evidently shared Rapson's passion for the lake.

The negotiators then turned to the other end. Seagull and Saganaga Lakes were large, island-specked, and heavily-used lakes at the end of the Gunflint Trail. Seagull had many of the qualities of La Croix, Saganaga many of the qualities of Basswood. At this point in the negotiations, both Dayton and Walls realized they had to yield ground. They got out U.S. Geological Survey maps and began to explore where they might divide the lakes into motorized and non-motorized zones.

Seagull presented a relatively easy solution. A large island, aptly called "Three Mile Island," was a logical divide. Motors of no more than ten horsepow-er would be allowed in the substantial water area to the east of the Island; beyond that motorboat use would be phased out after twenty years.

Saganaga defied such a ready divide. Consulting extensively with Heinselman, Green, and Rapson, Dayton finally could move Walls only to elimi-nating motors west of American Point. He used Walls' major victory on Saganaga as leverage, however, for a five-year phase out of the noxious tow-boats not only on Saganaga, but on the Moose Lake chain leading to Basswood.

The final major maneuvering was over the many smaller lakes on the edge of the wilderness. Dayton generally adhered to a standard that would permit motorboat use on those lakes on which homes and resorts were located: Moose, Snowbank, Fall, Clearwater, and others. In return, he prevailed on the removal of motors from a group of small lakes without private homes or businesses on them: the Moose River/Nina Moose/Agnes route, the Lake One/Insula/Alice route, the North and South Kawishiwi Rivers, Gabbro and Bald Eagle Lakes, Isabella Lake, the Sawbill/Cherokee/Temperance River route, Tuscarora and Alpine Lakes, the South/Rose/Mountain/Moose chain, and others.

It was now 3:00 A.M. Dayton came out for one final housekeeping detail. He told Heinselman that the compromise would provide for the Forest Service to maintain in functional order any man-made dams in the wilderness. He was stunned by the violence of Heinselman's reaction.

"That's it, Chuck. We're finished! You've been pushing me all night, and this is just too much." Heinselman exploded, venting some twenty hours of pent-up emotions and tensions. No less tired and tense, Dayton shot back, "Then find yourself another lawyer," and walked away.[49]

The inconceivable was about to happen. After finding common ground on issues so intractable they had divided a state for generations, the deal was about to be undone by whether a few dozen modest wooden structures could be repaired by the Forest Service to preserve the water levels they held back.

Rapson caught up with Dayton and asked him for a half-hour break. "It's three in the morning," Dayton barked. "So what difference will 3:30 make?" Rapson replied. "We're not about to get ourselves another lawyer. Give me a little time to calm Bud down."

Rapson then took Heinselman on a long walk through the darkened hallways. They stopped and sat at the top of a stairway. Heinselman was distraught, but not irrational. It was the principle of wilderness that bothered him more than anything, he explained:

> At some point, Rip, you have to ask yourself whether you are being true to the spirit of the land. We have eroded that spirit with every compromise we have made tonight. And we are choosing to do it, a handful of us, in private, without the chance to reflect on the consequences of what we do. It is the height of arrogance. It is worse than being asked to accept a Senate vote that is at least taken with full debate and in full public view.
>
> In some way the dams are more important than Basswood or La Croix. At least with the lakes, we have talked about the possibility of splitting the baby. There is at least an argument about the need to reconcile conflicting uses. But there is no reason to compromise the integrity of wilderness for a bunch of damn dams. They are completely out of place in a wilderness—without them, water will re-find its natural level, and we will adapt to the condition nature prefers.
>
> It simply offends me. And like it or not, I am the person this negotiation has put in the position of being a steward of when enough is enough. This is enough.[50]

There was nothing more to say. Rapson left Heinselman at the stairway and went back to speak with Dayton. Dayton, too, had calmed. He listened carefully to Rapson's explanation and slowly nodded in agreement. They would leave the dams to work out until after the negotiations were complete.

The interlude had taken a half-hour. At 3:30 A.M., Williams, Dayton, and Walls began the process of documenting the points to which they had agreed. It took more than four hours to fill in omitted details, tighten loose understandings, and reargue ambiguous provisions.

But at 7:45 A.M. Sunday, July 30, after twenty-three hours of continuous negotiation, the three initialled a hand-written memorandum of understanding. They got up from their chairs and took the document to Williams' office to be typed. A short time later, Walls and Dayton signed the formal version and agreed to recommend to their respective constituencies that it be adopted.[51] They concurred that they would keep the provisions of the agreement quiet until after those constituencies had been briefed. They then left to get a few hours of sleep.[52]

It was an extraordinary accomplishment, achieved in an overwhelming atmosphere of skepticism. It was attributable in large part to skills each of the three principals brought to the table: the tenacity of Williams, who through a combination of toughness and sensitivity was able to hold the negotiators' feet to the fire; the careful preparation and quick thinking of Dayton, who had been able to produce fresh approaches when deadlock had appeared certain. And the integrity of Walls, who chose to serve his constituency not by stonewalling, as they had expected, but by negotiating in good faith.

The hard labor that gave birth to the agreement may not have been enough, however. The question remained whether the Dayton/Walls compromise, as it was soon dubbed, would be stillborn.

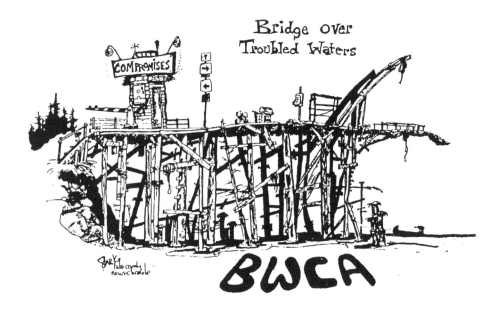

(Reprinted with permission from the Lake Country News-Chronicle)

A Compromise that Suited Nobody

The negotiating teams flew back to Minnesota the next day to brief their constituencies.

Almost two hundred members of the Arrowhead Chapter of the Alliance met Monday night at Kerfoot's Kove in Grand Marais to hear Walls describe the package.

Walls took the tack that the compromise more fully protected the recreational and economic interests of the Gunflint Trail than did the House-passed bill.[53] Walls knew it would be a tough sell. He was right. The crowd remained unconvinced of the necessity for any compromises. Walls walked them through the difficulties they would face in the Senate and in a conference committee. He urged them to be realistic: "If you think we're going back to 1964, it isn't in the cards. Sooner or later, we've got to budge in some direction."[54] Two hours of heated discussion and questioning only hardened the group's resistance to the message. It rejected the compromise on a 101 to 13 vote.

That was the highpoint of his evening. He was couriered to Ely via small airplane. The discussion was even more heated there. Again, Walls pointed out that rejecting the compromise might come back to haunt them: "To say you can sit back and fight denies reality. You have to have the votes." If Grand Marais was a rout, Ely was an obliteration: all two hundred ten people present voted to reject the compromise.

Neither Grand Marais nor Ely needed any help to make up their minds about the wisdom of the Dayton/Walls agreement. But there was speculation that Oberstar had supported them in their resolve, holding out the possibility that he could secure for them a better deal in the following Congress.[55] Whatever his role, Oberstar made his distaste for the compromise plain.[56]

The Friends were not aware of the events to the north. They had gathered at the Heinselman home in St. Paul to be briefed by Dayton, Heinselman, and Rapson.[57] Never had so many bodies been squeezed into the Heinselmans' modest living and dining rooms. Never had so many cameras and microphones squeezed onto their front porch, waiting word about the details of the compromise and the Friends' attitude toward it.

The trio from Washington anticipated that the mood in St. Paul was likely to be antagonistic. They decided on a three-part strategy. First, describe in detail the background and process of the negotiations, to remind people of the stakes and the context. Second, prepare detailed explanations of each compromise provision to demonstrate the reason it was adopted and its relation to other concessions. Third, have Rapson make the presentation to take the pressure off of Dayton and Heinselman.

Rapson spoke with two maps tacked to the wall behind him. They were shrouded, to avoid drawing fire before their provisions had been explained fully. As planned, he began with a broad overview of the politics and the process. He then stepped provision-by-provision through the compromise. Finally, he uncovered the two maps, one depicting in bright red current motor routes, the other depicting in blue the Dayton/Walls compromise.

The room exploded.

Barely had one speaker finished than another picked up a different refrain. There was no justification for yielding on the international border—it cut the area into multiple zones, rather than preserving it as a unit. The total amount of permanent motorboat use was far more than could be justified on the grounds of meeting the economic needs of local residents. The compromise backed down on most of the big victories in the House-passed bill, and that was a shell in contrast to the original Fraser bill.

And so it went. Rapson could sense the growing frustration of Heinselman and Dayton, but kept the hostility directed toward him. This was a tight-knit group that deserved to vent their frustration and explore their options.

But he also kept the discussion alive to buy time. He believed that the Friends would ultimately approve the accord. If they did not, however, the last thing they wanted was to be the first on record as repudiating the work of Dayton and Walls. If anybody was going to torpedo the accord, let it be the Alliance.

The problem was the silence from the north. Rapson impatiently asked for status checks every quarter hour from the news reporters and Friends' sources on the Range.

The word finally arrived. Grand Marais' vote was in. Dayton shook his head in disappointment. Still no Ely.

The internal argument was getting more difficult to control. People began demanding a vote. Right before 10:00 P.M., the media told Rapson that word had come in from Ely. The discussion inside came to an abrupt halt as a TV was hauled in. The lead story on each channel was northern Minnesota's defiant rejection of the compromise. The work of Dayton and Walls, the stories went, was for naught.

By avoiding a vote on the compromise, the Friends could, and did, take the high ground. They were able to say truthfully that they were exploring a very thoughtful and balanced proposal when the Alliance had made the entire conversation moot. They deplored an attitude of intransigence at a time reasonable minds needed to weigh in. They indicated their willingness to work with Senator Anderson to find a way out of the situation.

Once the media left, the Friends continued their conversation. It was apparent that there would have been enough votes to ratify the compromise. The

(*Reprinted with permission from the* Minneapolis Star Tribune)

question was how to keep Anderson from using the Alliance's actions as an excuse to kill the bill altogether. They divided responsibility for calling or visiting anyone who might influence Anderson. They finally broke up after midnight, as one after another congratulated Dayton on his effort. Most, however, left their optimism in the Heinselman living room.

The next day was August 1. Not a word from Anderson.

On Wednesday, Dayton received a call from David Lebedoff, a professional colleague and one of Anderson's most trusted advisers. Lebedoff characterized the call as a friendly check in after the grueling events of the previous days. He asked generally about the compromise and the Friends' attitude toward it. It was only after Dayton hung up that he realized that Lebedoff had been on a reconnaissance mission and that Anderson was exploring the possibility of resurrecting the compromise if it had support among environmentalists.[58]

A day later, that is exactly what Anderson did. In an announcement that displayed the kind of leadership that had eluded him throughout his senatorial tenure, Anderson declared that he would incorporate the Dayton/Walls compromise into his BWCA bill and move for passage of the measure before congressional adjournment in October. "This is the bottom line," he stated. "The time for controversy is over. To continue this discussion in anger and animosity serves no purpose."[59]

Anderson doubtless had enjoyed considerable counseling from Lebedoff, Kelm, Gove, and others. One of the others was Vice President Mondale. "Wendy and I discussed it," Mondale explained, "and we agreed together that the compromise probably is the best way of resolving this issue."[60]

The Alliance was flabbergasted. They had learned the hard way that there are no friends in politics, only allies: "A man made a promise to us, and he reneged on that today," said the Gunflint's Bruce Kerfoot. He reported that some of the Alliance members were "very, very, very, very hot" over the decision.[61]

Hot was too mild a term to describe the reaction. On Saturday, the Alliance set up a blockade on six popular BWCA entry points to prevent anyone from going in.[62] As one ugly confrontation followed another, Lake County sheriff's deputies stood by and watched.

"You're punishing me for going into the wild," a woman who had traveled from Ohio yelled at Ely resident Jay Salerno. "This is the last chance we've got," Salerno replied. "All we want is to keep the BWCA open to everyone." She hadn't come all that way for nothing:

Alliance supporters reacted angrily to Anderson's support of the Dayton/Walls Compromise. (*Photo by M. L. Heinselman*)

You're infringing on my rights. I can't believe you will take away my day
from me to prove something to the government. It's totally irrational.
I've never had another citizen do this to me in 53 years.[63]

One hoped she found another way to get into the wilderness because
Salerno didn't back down.

When the Alliance realized that Anderson meant what he had said, they
recognized that their most potent weapon was the ballot box. Anderson and
Fraser would be on the ballot in early September. Increasingly, all the Alliance's
organizing savvy and strength would be focused on those two elections. A local
resident captured the sense of renewed purpose many Alliance members felt:

I hate to say this, but if we lose that election, you're never going to see
anything like it. There's going to be utter destruction. We have the feeling that if we can't use the area, nobody can.[64]

After a year of paddling in opposite directions, Anderson and Fraser were
now in the same boat.

Notes

1 MLH Chronology, June 15, 1978.

2 Voting in the minority were Engstrom, Dayton, and Erika Sitz. Heinselman was in
Washington but expressed his strong belief that the Friends should push forward. MLH
Chronology, June 15, 1978.

3 Five years previous, in 1973, Minnesotans gave Anderson a two to one favorable to
unfavorable rating. Time, Aug. 13, 1973, pp. 34-35.

4 Time, Aug. 13, 1973, pp. 34-35.

5 Minneapolis Star, Apr. 10, 1978, Jim Klobuchar, "A View of Two Senators."

6 Minneapolis Tribune, June 7, 1978 "Anderson Should Follow House on BWCA";
Minneapolis Tribune, June 12, 1978, p. 8A, "Anderson Responds." ("I also said I would not
support the elimination of the present use of motorboats from the area. . . . I intend to
move forward and attempt to pass a BWCA bill in the Senate this year, even though only
four months remain in the session.")

7 Minneapolis Star, Apr. 10, 1978, Jim Klobuchar, "A View of Two Senators."

8 S. 1769, Congressional Record, June 24, 1977, pp. 20773-20774.

244 / Troubled Waters

244 / Troubled Waters

244 / Troubled Waters

Clark's colleague from Wisconsin, Senator Gaylord Nelson, soon joined that effort. A co-sponsor of the 1964 Wilderness Act, Nelson was considered one of the staunchest environmentalists in the Senate. Trish Record of the Sierra Club had suggested to Heinselman that someone like Nelson might introduce a "killer bill" that would go beyond the Fraser bill. This would make the Fraser/Clark bill seem less extreme and reduce the pressure for compromise.

In the fall of 1977, Heinselman had prepared a killer bill for Nelson's introduction. But the strategy was aborted before the bill was introduced. After reviewing the bill, Sierra Club's Evans, Conlon, and Rapson convinced Heinselman and Record that it might backfire by provoking Anderson to lock into a position the Friends might not like. Rapson Recollections, December 1983; MLH Chronology, Dec. 14, 1977.

9 Rapson Recollections, December 1983.

10 MLH Chronology, June 22, 1978.

11 MLH Chronology, June 22, 1978.

12 S. 3242, Congressional Record, June 23, 1978, S9637-43; see also the fact sheet prepared by Fraser's office entitled "Changes the Anderson-Humphrey BWCA Bill Makes in the House Bill," 5 pp., copy in possession of authors.

13 Duluth News-Tribune, June 24, 1978, p. 1, "'Motorized' BWCA Bill Introduced"; Ely Miner, June 28, 1978, "BWCA Leaders React to Anderson's Bill."

14 Steve Payne of the Wilderness Society blasted the measure, saying, "The plan is absolutely unacceptable and unrealistic." Dan Engstrom of the Friends claimed, "This proposal is absolutely unacceptable to the environmental community and to the majority of BWCA users who desire a quiet, non-mechanized wilderness." Duluth News-Tribune, June 24, 1978, p. 1, "'Motorized' BWCA Bill Introduced."

15 On the eve of the Senate visit, the Minnesota Poll found that state residents were increasingly comfortable with a dramatic reduction in motorized use in the BWCA: fifty-eight percent of all Minnesotans statewide supported a sharp curtailment of motors; thirty-eight percent favored greater motorboat use. The poll revealed that northern Minnesotans favored more restrictions on BWCA motor use by a narrow fifty to forty-nine percent margin. Minneapolis Tribune, July 16, 1978, p. 1A, "58% Back BWCA Limits."

16 See generally Minneapolis Tribune, July 17, 1978, p. 2B, "Senators Fly Over BWCA Area"; Minneapolis Tribune, July 18, 1978, p. 1A, "Senators in BWCA Seeking Accord"; Ely Echo, July 19, 1978, p. 1, "Senators Order Parlay To End BWCA Conflict"; Ely Echo, July 19, 1978, p. 2, "Sunday Sessions Enlighten Senators"; Minnesota Daily, July , 1978, p. 2, "Senators Tour BWCA, Solicit Revised Proposals for Use."

17 See Itinerary, Boundary Waters Canoe Area Tour, Senate Energy and Natural Resources Committee; copy in possession of authors.

18 See Minneapolis Tribune, July 17, 1978, p. 2B, "Senators Fly Over BWCA Area"; Ely Echo, July 19, 1978, p. 2, "Sunday Sessions Enlighten Senators"; Voices In The Wilderness,

Boundary Waters Conservation Alliance, July 1978 Newsletter, p. 1, "1500 Impressed Senators"; *MLH Chronology*, July 16, 1978.

19 *Ibid.*

20 *Ibid.*

21 Rapson Recollections, December 1983.

22 *Ibid.*

23 *Cook County News-Herald*, July 27, 1989, "U.S. Senators Hear Local Reaction in BWCA Debate."

24 Rapson Recollections, December 1983.

25 Charles K. Dayton Interview, Nov. 13, 1989; Rapson Recollections, December 1983; *MLH Chronology*, July 17, 1978.

26 Rapson Recollections, December 1983 (contemporaneous conversation with Charles Dayton).

27 Anderson was not the only one to be cut out of the process. Abourezk had previous-ly informed Joe Alexander, Bill Nye's successor as commissioner of the Department of Natural Resources, that the State of Minnesota would have no role in the subcommittee's deliberations. Alexander was not allowed to fly in Air Force 2 with the senators, though he had attempted to insist on it, and Abourezk refused to allow Alexander or the state a part in the compromise negotiations. "The state has no involvement in the matter," Abourezk told Alexander, "It's before Congress." See *Minnesota Daily*, July 18, 1978, p. 2, "Senators Tour BWCA, Solicit Revised Proposals For Use."

28 See Edward M. Zabinski, "A Narrative History of the Boundary Waters Conservation Alliance," Plan B Paper, Hubert H. Humphrey Institute of Public Affairs, University of Minnesota, December 1983; *Ely Echo*, July 19, 1978, p. 1, "Senators Order Parlay to End BWCA Conflict."

29 Charles K. Dayton Interview, Nov. 13, 1989; *Minneapolis Tribune*, July 18, 1978, p. 1A, "Senators in BWCA Seeking Accord"; *Minnesota Daily*, July 18, 1978, p. 2, "Senators Tour BWCA, Solicit Revised Proposals for Use"; *Ely Echo*, July 19, 1978, p. 1, "Senators Order Parlay To End BWCA Conflict."

30 See Charles K. Dayton Interview, Nov. 13, 1989; *MLH Chronology*, July 18, 1978.

31 See generally Edward M. Zabinski, "A Narrative History of the Boundary Waters Conservation Alliance," Plan B Paper, Hubert H. Humphrey Institute of Public Affairs, University of Minnesota, December 1983, at p. 43.

32 *Ibid.*

33 Rip Rapson Notes, July 20, 1978.

34 As he proceeded, Dayton stayed in close touch with the broader circle of Friends'

activists. On July 25, for example, the Friends patched together a long conference call involving Heinselman and Rapson from Washington, canoe outfitter Jon Waters from Ely, and a large group including Dayton from Minneapolis. The call had two purposes: (1) to revisit and put to rest the argument that the Friends should work for legislation this year rather than delay and hope for better legislation next year; and (2) to agree on guidelines for use in the upcoming negotiations. *MLH Chronology*, July 25, 1978.

35 Rip Rapson Notes, July 24-25, 1978; Charles K. Dayton to Rip Rapson, July 21, 1978.
The Boschwitz proposal called for motorized use on Jackfish Bay of Basswood, but not Pipestone Bay. Such an arrangement would have required access to Jackfish Bay from Jake Pete's property on the Range River, an area slated as a wilderness addition under the House-passed bill. In his proposed amendments, Dayton added Pipestone Bay to the list of motorized lakes to allow motorboat access to Jackfish Bay by way of Pipestone. This would prevent the institutionalizing of permanent motor access on the Range River.

36 Rip Rapson Notes, July 26, 1978.

37 *Ibid.*

38 See generally Charles K. Dayton Interview, Nov. 13, 1989; *Minneapolis Tribune*, July 28, 1978, p. 2B, "D.C. Negotiations on Future of BWCA Begin amid Secrecy."

39 Charles K. Dayton Interview, Nov. 13, 1989.

40 See *St. Paul Pioneer Press*, July 28, 1978, "No Progress Reported in 1st BWCA Session."

41 Charles K. Dayton Interview, Nov. 13, 1989.

42 *Ibid.*

43 *Ibid.*

44 Zabinski Paper, p. 44.

45 The term had been defined not only in a series of federal decisions, but also in the Minnesota Environmental Rights Act of 1971 and the Minnesota Environmental Policy Act of 1973, both of which Dayton had had a hand in drafting.

46 Charles K. Dayton Interview, Nov. 13, 1989.

47 Janssen and Fraser had met early in the dispute. When asked by Fraser how he would react to being bought out, Janssen responded, "And how would you like looking down the barrel of a gun?" Fraser didn't pursue the issue further with him. Rapson Recollections, December 1983.

48 Charles K. Dayton Interview, Nov. 13, 1989.

49 *Ibid.*

50 Rapson Recollections, December 1983.

51 The full Dayton-Walls agreement included the following provisions:
- Permanent, unlimited horsepower motorboats on Little Vermilion Lake, Loon River, Loon Lake, and Wilkins Bay of La Croix, all at the west end of the BWCA.
- Permanent, twenty-five-horsepower motors on Trout Lake, the Moose Lake chain, Snowbank Lake, South Farm Lake, East Bearskin Lake, Magnetic Lake, the Fall/Newton chain, nearly all of Saganaga Lake, and, on Basswood, Jackfish Bay, Pipestone Bay, Back Bay, Hoist and Wind Bays, and the international border from Prairie Portage west to Washington Island.
- Permanent ten-horsepower motors on Clearwater Lake, North and South Fowl Lakes, Alder and Canoe Lakes, Island River, and Seagull Lake east of Three Mile Island.
- 1984 phase-outs of twenty-five-horsepower motorboats for Birch Lake and the two stretches of international border of Basswood Lake from Basswood Falls east to U.S. Point and south to Washington Island.
- 1984 phase-outs of ten-horsepower motors for Crooked Lake, Basswood River, Knife Lake and River, and Carp Lake.
- A 1994 phase-out of 10 horsepower motorboats on Brule Lake, or until Janssen's Sky Blue Waters Lodge ceased operation, whichever came first.
- A 1999 phase-out of ten-horsepower motorboats on Seagull Lake, but only for that portion of the lake generally west of Three Mile Island.
- Snowmobiles were re-introduced on five routes. Three were subject to a 1984 phase-out, on Trout Lake, the Moose to Saganaga route, and East Bearskin to Pine Lakes. Permanent snowmobile use was allowed on the Saganaga "corridor" and a short route between Crane Lake and Little Vermilion Lake.
- A 1984 phase-out of towboats of unlimited horsepower on the Moose Lake chain and on Saganaga Lake. Towboat use was to end under the phase-out.
- A 1984 phase-out of truck portages at Trout Lake, Prairie Portage, and Four Mile Portage. Truck portages could continue only if the Secretary of Agriculture determined that no feasible nonmotorized alternative existed.
- The following motor routes immediately closed to motor use: Little Indian Sioux River north of the Echo Trail to Loon Lake, the Moose River/Nina Moose/Agnes route, the northern and eastern two-thirds of the United States half of Lac La Croix, Bottle and Iron Lakes on the international border, Oriniack and Pine Lakes near Trout Lake, Fourtown Lake, Wind Lake, the Lake One/Insula/Alice/Thomas/Ima/Ensign route, the Parent/Disappointment/Ima route, the North and South Kawishiwi Rivers and Clear Lake, Gabbro and Bald Eagle Lakes, Isabella Lake, Perent Lake, the Sawbill/Cherokee/Temperance River/Flame loop, the Brule/Winchell/Poplar route, Tuscarora Lake, Alpine Lake, Ottertrack Lake on the international border, the Granite River route on the international border, the South/Rose/Mountain Moose chain on the international border, and Pine Lake.

52 Word leaked out that there had been an agreement, but the details were kept secret. *Minneapolis Tribune,* July 31, 1978, p. 1A, "Two Sides Tentatively Agree on BWCA."

53 He acknowledged that Brule Lake was the exception: "Brule was the only place where we changed from something that was more beneficial to the local people to something which was less beneficial." See *Cook County News-Herald*, Aug. 10, 1978, p. 1, "Local Alliance Rejects Walls/Dayton Agreement."

54 *Ibid.*

55 See *Minneapolis Tribune*, August 1, 1978, p. 1A, "State Group Rejects BWCA Compromise"; *Minneapolis Tribune*, Aug. 2, 1978, p. 1A, "Compromise Rejection puts BWCA Future in Flux."

56 *Ibid.*

57 See generally *MLH Chronology*, July 31, 1978.

58 Charles K. Dayton Interview, Nov. 13, 1989.

59 *St. Paul Pioneer Press*, Aug. 4, 1978, p. 17, "Wendy to Submit BWCA Compromise to Senate"; *Minneapolis Tribune*, August 4, 1978, p. 1A, "Anderson to Push BWCA Compromise"; *Duluth News-Tribune*, Aug. 4, 1978, p. 1A, "Wendy Backs BWCA Compromise"; *Cook County News-Herald*, Aug. 10, 1978, p. 1, "Wendy Pushes for Compromise BWCA Solution."

60 *Ibid.*

61 *Minneapolis Tribune*, Aug. 4, 1978, p. 1A, "Anderson to Propose BWCA Compromise."

62 The blockade was set up at Lake One, Snowbank Lake, Fall Lake, Moose Lake, Trout Lake Portage, and Loon Lake from 5:00 A.M. until 4:30 P.M. on August 5. *Minneapolis Tribune*, August 5, 1978, p. 1A, "Residents of BWCA to Stage Protest"; *Minneapolis Tribune*, Aug. 6, 1978, p. 1A, "Angry BWCA Area Residents Block Roads, Vent Frustration"; *St. Paul Pioneer Press*, Aug. 6, 1978, p. 1, "Ely-area Residents Block BWCA"; *Ely Miner*, Aug. 9, 1978, p. 1, "BWCA Lockout Stays Non-violent."

63 *Ibid.*

64 *Ibid.*

Chapter Seven

The Race to the Finish

Anderson's embrace of the Dayton/Walls compromise charged the state's political atmosphere. It heightened the visibility of the BWCA positions of Anderson's likely Republican opponent, Rudy Boschwitz, and of Fraser's opponents, Republican Dave Durenberger and Democrat Bob Short. It energized the Iron Range to work against the two endorsed Democrats. And it spilled over into the governor's contest between Rudy Perpich and Al Quie.

There was a little over a month to the September 12 primary. For Anderson, who had only nominal primary election opposition, it was a month to push his compromise position through the Senate and to begin positioning himself against Boschwitz. For Fraser, it would become five weeks of fending off some of the most crass political campaigning in Minnesota history.

The Challengers

Like his opponent, Boschwitz could look beyond September to the November general election. The owner of Plywood Minnesota, a popular home-improvement store chain, Boschwitz had been the Republican front-runner since January.[1]

Early on, he had seen in Anderson's vacillation and softness on the BWCA an inroad to moderate and liberal Democrats, who were also alienated by Anderson's anti-abortion position. He was helped along by Friends member Herb Johnson, a fellow businessman to whom Boschwitz had looked for advice on environmental issues. Working with Johnson, Boschwitz proposed in May his own plan for the BWCA.

The Boschwitz plan closely resembled the Fraser/Vento/Nolan compromise that would pass the House a month later. It banned mining, logging, and snowmobiling, and limited motors largely to the peripheral lakes.[2] Even if the

'HERE, WENDY, TRY AGAIN'

(*Reprinted with permission from the* Minneapolis Star Tribune)

environmental community would quibble with some of his lake choices, it saw in
his overall commitment that of a strong ally. Boschwitz explained:

> Since the BWCA is the second largest wilderness area in the U.S., the only
> canoe wilderness and one of the largest tracts of virgin forest anywhere, an
> acceptable boundary waters plan must put a primacy on non-motorized use in the
> BWCA itself.[3]

Boschwitz's position was partisan to be sure: it stood in strong contrast to
Anderson's indecision during May and June. But that partisanship worked to the
environmentalists' advantage.[4] Boschwitz briefed many of his hoped-to-be Republican colleagues on his proposal, building both awareness of the issue and a recep-
tivity to a more environmentally sensitive approach than many of them would
have supported had they been left to their own devices.

The other Republican in the Senate derby also adopted Boschwitz's tactic of placing the longest possible distance between between himself and his opponent's BWCA position. Dave Durenberger castigated Fraser's approach:

'SEEMS THE KID IN THE MOTORBOAT IS FROM ELY AND HE OBJECTED
TO BEING FOLLOWED BY A CANOE. WELL, THE OTHER KID SAID IF HE HAD HIS WAY
THERE WOULDN'T BE ANY MOTORBOATS ON THE RIDE. AND THEN...'

(Reprinted with permission from the Minneapolis Star Tribune)

The disaster in the Fraser approach is that he insists on doing things whether people like it or not. He lacks the patience Hubert Humphrey had to work at it and bring people along with him, and everybody in northern Minnesota is mad because they distrust government.[5]

Coming from a former corporate counsel to the H.B. Fuller Company and the chief of staff for Republican Governor Harold LeVander, this might not have been a surprise. But coming from someone who had served on the Hennepin County Park Board, the Metropolitan Parks and Open Space Commission, and the board of Project Environment Foundation, it came as a shock. At least one columnist decried that politics could undermine a life's commitment to the environment.[6]

Durenberger had intended to run for governor, but had been dissuaded by Al Quie's early strength within the party. Durenberger switched to the race against Fraser in April.[7] He announced his BWCA position, indistinguishable from Oberstar's, in May.

Don Fraser's United States Senate race intertwined with the volatile BWCA issue. (*Photo by Gordon Oschwald*)

It appeared to gain him little at first; his campaign was slow to get rolling, and proceeded in fits and starts throughout the spring and summer. At low tide, he trailed Fraser in public opinion polls by a whopping thirty-six percentage points.

By the end of August, Durenberger had found his feet. He had climbed to within eighteen points of Fraser in the public polls, within eight in his own polling.[8]

At this point, however, the real thorn in Fraser's side was Bob Short. Short was a highly successful businessman, the owner of several hotels and a trucking firm. He had established a name for himself when he had moved the Washington Senators baseball team, which he owned, from the nation's capital to

Minnesota in 1960 to become the Minnesota Twins. He was a veteran political actor, Karl Rolvaag's running mate as lieutenant governor in a losing effort in 1966 and treasurer of the national Democratic party during Humphrey's 1968 run for the presidency.

Short had announced his challenge to Fraser in May, indicating that he would by-pass the party's endorsing process.[9] With a poor labor relations track record, he was anathema to labor. Strongly anti-abortion, he was the bane of the pro-choice community. Endorsed by the National Rifle Association, he had alienated much of the rest of the DFL's progressive wing. He topped it off with an unapologetic parroting of Oberstar's BWCA position.

This combination, barely aberrational in the 1990s, was unprecedented in 1978. Here was an arch-conservative pro-business maverick, running against a well-known, highly-respected, well-financed, party-nominated candidate. The person for whose seat they were running, Muriel Humphrey, strongly endorsed Fraser, despite her husband's close ties with Short. Short appeared to be looking at long odds.

But two things happened on the way to the dance that changed all that.

The first was Short's aggressive campaign style. He hammered out three issues: abortion, gun control, and the BWCA.[10] He was focused, tough, and amply underwritten with his own money.[11] He took to the airwaves with a series of blunt contrast ads:

> Here's how they compare: Big government, Fraser. Reducing government, Bob Short. Expanding federal government, Fraser. Reducing government, Bob Short. Expanding federal taxing system, Fraser. Reducing federal taxing system, Bob Short. Increased federal spending, Fraser. Decreased federal spending, Bob Short. Increased federal control of your personal lives, Fraser. Decreased control, Short.[12]

That was the highpoint. The campaign turned more and more personal, bitter. Fraser found himself consistently on the defensive, finding it difficult to get his own message out in the midst of Short's continuous barrage of attack ads.[13]

By the last week before the primary, Fraser was fighting at least three rear-guard actions. He was combatting a NRA mailing depicting him as "one of the anti-gun, anti-hunting crowd."[14] He was countering a Short ad in the *Minneapolis Tribune* accusing him of voting in favor of using tax dollars to permit babies who had survived abortion to be used as experimental research subjects, opposing penalties for distributors of child pornography, and suggesting a return to the draft and military intervention in Cambodia. And he was scrambling to overcome a Fraser-kills-babies, anti-abortion literature drop in the parking lots of Catholic churches.

"I don't like being told I'm a one-issue voter. I'm also against fluoridation!"

September 15, 1978 Minneapolis Tribune cartoon. (*Reprinted with permission from the* Minneapolis Star Tribune)

Short also tapped into the demonization of Fraser on the Iron Range. The Alliance may not have known what to do in an Anderson/Boschwitz race, but a Short/Fraser match up was a dream come true. The Alliance, joining cause with the gun lobby, the pro-life lobby, and the followers of Sun Myung Moon,[15] mobilized with a fervor. They plastered "DUMP FRASER" bumper stickers to anything that moved, or didn't for that matter. They phone-banked. They rallied. The turnout in northeastern Minnesota was always high; this year it promised to be astronomical.

The second activity that changed the course of the election was Short's appeal to cross-over voters from the Republican party.

With the Durenberger and Boschwitz primary races essentially uncontested, the Republicans were ripe for an interesting place to cast their ballots on September 12. They could always, and would, vote within their own party when it counted in November. Short saw the opportunity and exploited it with a vengeance, at one point sending out a half-million pieces of campaign literature urging Republicans to cross the line. It was a shrewd, but pivotal decision.

The Primary

September 12 was a nasty, cold, rainy day—six inches of rain in Rochester, two in the Twin Cities. Political observers immediately raised red flags for the Fraser camp: the true mettle of the Fraser organization would be tested by whether it could turn out the vote in sufficient strength in Minneapolis, St. Paul, and Rochester to overcome the wave that was expected to roll in from the eighth district.

The early returns were ambiguous, but favorable to Fraser. Turnout was low, but Fraser was piling up comfortable margins in the Twin Cities. No word from the north, where it would take hours to tabulate in the many areas that still used paper ballots.

By midnight, the scenario had changed little. Fraser was hovering around fifty-five to sixty percent. He went to bed to prepare for the next day's activities thinking he had beaten back Short's challenge. Even if northern Minnesota came in with its usual Democratic vote totals, he would be comfortable.

The Heinselmans and others in Washington were still too nervous to go to bed quite yet. At 12:15 A.M., they received word that Fraser's condition had been downgraded from good to fair—the northern Minnesota votes were still largely unreported.[16]

At 1:00 A.M., they learned that with sixty percent of its precincts reporting, Duluth was going for Short, but by a relatively small margin of 3,800 to 3,300 or fifty-three to forty-seven percent. Not enough for panic. Statewide, Fraser still clung to a fifty-eight to forty-two lead.

Forty-five minutes later, another call. With thirty-five percent of the vote tallied, Fraser held the same fifty-eight to forty-two spread. The eighth district and southern Minnesota, a Republican stronghold, were still being counted.

At 2:15 A.M., the numbers began coming in more quickly. With fifty-eight percent of the precincts reporting, Fraser's lead had been cut slightly to fifty-six to forty-four. At 2:45 A.M., with sixty-six of the precincts in, it had narrowed a bit more to fifty-five to forty-five.

In drips and drops, the Iron Range and southern Minnesota votes began to come in. Fraser's margin diminished with each new precinct to report. By breakfast time, it was a dead heat, too close to call.

Finally, at 8:30 A.M., Larry Romans of Vento's staff called Heinselman. All the precincts were in. Of more than 500,000 votes cast, Fraser had fallen 3,400 votes shy. Short had won.[17]

Part of it was beyond anybody's control: the weather. Voter turnout in the Twin Cities was a relatively low thirty percent.

But two big parts had been fully within Short's control.

The first was the Republican cross-over. Short's strategy had paid off, coupled with a likely perception among Republicans that Durenberger would have an easier time with Short than with Fraser. Almost 100,000 votes in the Democratic primary, one in five, had been cast by a Republican. Fraser was the beneficiary of very few of them.[18]

(Reprinted with permission from the Minnesota Daily*)*

The second was the anti-Fraser BWCA vote in northern Minnesota. The numbers out of the Range were staggering, providing many times the margin of Short's victory:[19]

Cook County (Grand Marais):
Short: 1,273 — Fraser: 125

Lake County (Two Harbors):
Short: 2,554 — Fraser: 486

St. Louis County (Duluth, Ely, and the Iron Range):
Short: 38,090 — Fraser: 14,062

In Ely alone, Short amassed two-thirds of his margin of victory, carrying the town 2,265 to 110. The *Ely Echo* was not shy about claiming credit on behalf of northeastern Minnesota for Short's success: it ran a front-page editorial cartoon of the "Little Guys of N.E. Minnesota" shooting down the Fraser jet with a sling-shot.[20]

The Alliance believed that they had made the Fraser race a referendum on the BWCA. Their joy in having defeated Fraser was rooted partially in a collective sense of personal vindication, of having pulled down someone they viewed as typifying the arrogance of the environmental movement.[21] It also derived from a sense that they were again relevant to the discussion in Washington, that they should now be permitted to influence the course of events in Congress.[22] Their preferred result was delay. With either Durenberger or Short in one seat come January 1, they would have an ally who would ensure that the next session produced, if anything at all, an approach far more sensitive to their needs. Their task thus became to block Anderson for the four or five weeks left until adjournment.

The depth of the anti-Fraser sentiment was reflected in more than rejoicing in the streets of Ely and Grand Marais. While Ely and other Range towns were celebrating on Wednesday night, three residents of Cook who had supported Fraser, including former state legislator Alpha Smaby, received threatening phone calls. Two days later, both Fraser's United States Senate campaign headquarters and his Minneapolis congressional office were evacuated after a bomb threat. On the following Sunday, there was a serious fire in the Fraser's apartment in Washington, a blaze suspected to be arson.[23]

Fraser reacted with a characteristic reserve and acceptance. The Friends, however, were badly shaken. They understood that, to a large extent, the Alliance was right: Fraser's defeat was a referendum on the BWCA and could send a message to Congress that it would be better to wait until next year to act. More fundamentally perhaps was the Friends' realization that they had extinguished the aspirations of a rare public personality. Fraser had been with them from the start and had never permitted his political agenda to distort the wilderness agenda. He had compromised only when the conservation community and Burton had concluded it necessary to the bill's survival. He had not backed down to the pressure of Vice President Mondale, the state party, or the political muscle of the eighth district. He had put his political career on the line for a matter of principle.

Lost Momentum

The personal sadness of the loss was compounded by the practical difficulties it posed. The Friends would be increasingly vulnerable to the vicissitudes of Anderson's judgments about how to move forward, particularly if he concluded that he needed to reverse field in order to stave off Fraser's fate. They also had lost the safety valve of coming back next year—they needed the Dayton/Walls compromise to be adopted this session.

The Friends had also to cope with the departure of Rapson just two weeks before the primary to begin law school in New York.[24] Heinselman and Rapson had become virtually inseparable; Heinselman was devastated by the one-two punch of Fraser's loss and Rapson's departure. The Friends were losing their chief tactician outside of Burton.

Before he left in late August, Rapson had a series of meetings with Burton and Conlon to develop strategies for moving the Senate process forward. Burton identified the members of the Senate Energy and Natural Resources Committee with whom he had influence—he had a working majority of the panel. Conlon was not so sure. He pointed out that the process still hinged on Anderson—his willingness to stick out the tough politics of his choice to push the Dayton/Walls compromise, his ability in the midst of a Senate campaign to focus on the work that needed to be done, and, ultimately, his skill in shepherding a bill through the Senate and conference committee in less than a month. He urged Burton to be more aggressive: "We're relying on Wendy and they're relying on Oberstar. Damn it Phil. Who would you put your money on?"[25] Burton told Conlon to keep an eye on Oberstar; Burton would make sure the Senate did its job, with or without Anderson.

June 7, 1978, *Minneapolis Star* cartoon. (*Reprinted with permission from the* Minneapolis Star Tribune)

Burton's ability to make good on his commitment held more than passing interest. Congress was scheduled to adjourn on October 14. More than six weeks had passed without any substantial movement from Anderson.

Anderson had convened a subcommittee hearing on August 17 to take testimony from Rupert Cutler and other members of the Carter Administration on the Dayton/Walls compromise. Cutler reiterated the administration's continuing support.[26] The hearing was over in fifteen minutes.[27]

Beyond the hearing, however, nothing had happened. Anderson had not redrafted his bill to incorporate the Dayton/Walls provisions. He had not scheduled a subcommittee or committee markup session. He was increasingly subject to the usual end-of-the-session logjam, with tens of major and minor bills queuing up for their place on the Senate floor schedule.[28]

A huge tax bill. A comprehensive energy bill. The Alaska Lands bill. Each demanding considerable floor time. Each pushing smaller bills out of their way. For those, like the Sierra Club's Brock Evans, who had been through the year-end rush before, the situation was growing critical. He wrote in his journal:

> Last days, last days. Everyday it gets more intense as the pressure builds toward the end of the session . . . I walk into the office in the morning, and it is a whole hour before I can even get back to my room, on the phone constantly out in front, with one call after another. Calls from Los Angeles—trying to find out what happened to the Santa Monicas; Boundary Waters calls; Endangered Species Act up soon; RARE I . . . the pressure gets more and more enormous . . . Wheeling, dancing, spinning . . . racing from one place to the next, no time to think; just drawing on reservoirs of past experience and instinct, hoping I'm right.[29]

The Friends pushed as many buttons as they could. They met with Bob Herbst, a friend of Anderson and Mondale and an assistant secretary of the Interior.[30] Fraser spoke with Mondale.[31] Burton discussed scheduling with Scoop Jackson.[32] The days ticked by, with no progress.

The first breakthrough came on September 27, when the Anderson office announced that it had completed a revised bill that included the Dayton/Walls provisions.[33] They had been faithful to the compromise, weakening only two technical provisions concerning the government's right of first refusal when property on peripheral lakes was offered for sale and the process by which the government would acquire mineral rights.

The readiness of the Anderson bill cleared the way for Scoop Jackson to schedule a markup session for the Senate Energy and the Environment Committee. It was set for October 3.

There were ten days until adjournment. There could be no further side trips or delays. Anderson would need to choreograph the final steps with real skill.

Committee Markup

The first test was the committee markup. Unlike the deliberate, almost leisurely, pace Burton had set in the House, the Senate would have very little time to spend on the BWCA. Anderson could not afford extended debate or surprise moves.

He got both.

The hearing was immediately sidetracked by a long discussion about snowmobiles, begun by a liberal Republican from Oregon, Mark Hatfield. What was unnerving was that Hatfield was appearing to argue the environmental side of the case, questioning why the compromise had included snowmobiling when the environmental community had recently fought so hard to ban them in the Gospel Hump Wilderness in Idaho.

Hatfield continued at length, insisting that Anderson was being granted greater latitude than the committee had extended for the Idaho members of the committee, Frank Church and Jim McClure. McClure and Church had no objection to the Anderson approach,[34] but Hatfield persisted nonetheless. To the horror of the Friends, who had counted on Hatfield as an ally, he observed, "I feel so strongly about this I may have to carry it to the floor. Did I understand that the Sierra Club, the Wilderness Society, and the others are for this snowmobile use? I thought they were purists."[35]

Anderson had clearly not paved the way prior to the markup. Neither was he able to steer Hatfield back into the fold. Jackson finally rescued the situation when it threatened to consume the entire time allotted for markup. He directed Anderson and Hatfield to come to a meeting of the minds before the floor debate. Hatfield's needling done for the moment, the committee would move on.[36]

The environmentalists' relief lasted about forty-five seconds. Not only had Anderson not laid the groundwork with the Republican members, he had apparently not laid it within his own party either.

Kentucky's Wendell Ford, the same senator whose son had roomed with Bearskin Lodge's Dave Tuttle, was not content with the Dayton/Walls provisions permitting motorboats on the string of lakes starting with East Bearskin. He proposed exempting home owners, resort owners, and their guests from the quotas regulating the number of persons who could begin their trip from a particular entry point. He also proposed setting the quotas at a fixed number based on use in 1976 to 1978, eliminating the previous language that would gradually reduce the quotas. He completed the Dave Tuttle memorial amendment package by proposing that snowmobiles be permitted to groom cross-country ski trails.[37]

Anderson acquiesced to each. The committee adopted the amendments.

The Friends held their breath for another shoe to drop. Mercifully, there were no further surprises, and the committee approved the bill as amended on an eighteen to zero vote.[38]

Grateful that the bill could now move to the Senate floor, the Friends nevertheless were apprehensive. Anderson had shown himself to be no legislative strategist; he seemed incapable of anticipating problems, shaping strategies, or lining up votes. The committee's chipping at the bill had weakened a number of management policies that would strike the public as minor, but that would affect BWCA management significantly. The Friends suspected that Anderson had himself engineered some of the Ford amendments to further weaken the bill. And the ease with which the amendments had been offered and adopted suggested that a similar process might take hold on the Senate floor and spin out of control.

The Senate Floor

October 4. The ten-day countdown had begun. There remained the floor action, a conference committee, and subsequent approval of the conference report by both houses.

Just as the Friends began to sift through the endless details necessary for the floor debate, they were stopped dead in their tracks by yet another tactical oversight.

A "hold" had been placed on the bill. In the House, the Rules Committee controlled the flow of traffic to the floor. In the more ceremonial Senate, a member had the prerogative of subjecting a bill to a hold, preventing it from coming to the floor.

The source was Bob Packwood of Oregon, who had evidently acted at the request of a constituent and in conjunction with Senators Hatfield and McClure. Rudy Boschwitz intervened to try to straighten things out with his fellow Republican. The national environmental lobbyists quickly drummed up pressure. After days of frantic meetings, calls, and briefings, Packwood backed off.[39]

Anderson had failed to see the hold coming and had not contributed to its removal. The delay had consumed five precious days. It was now Monday, October 9. Adjournment was scheduled for Friday. A severe case of panic was setting in.[40]

With the hold removed, however, responsibility for tactics passed from Anderson to Senate Majority Leader Robert Byrd, a supremely competent legislative strategist.[41] The BWCA now joined Byrd's dance card, and he would make sure that it received its proper turn on the floor.

Byrd waited until late Monday evening to make his move. With floor attendance even sparser than normal—some thirteen senators were spotted throughout the chamber—Byrd injected the BWCA bill into a collection of routine business matters at 11:15 P.M. There was no debate. There were no amendments. There was no recorded vote. Not even Wendy Anderson, who missed the entire affair. Just a simple voice vote ratifying the Senate's work and appointing conference committee members.[42] In skilled hands, the BWCA had been sprung loose from the Senate, a "'blip' in the night."[43]

The Alliance was caught completely unawares. The group cried foul, accusing the Senate of railroading a bill that deserved the full exposure that a Senate floor debate would have afforded. Anderson received the brunt of their wrath.[44]

It was ironic. Apart from holding the line on his commitment to incorporate the Dayton/Walls compromise into his bill, Anderson had been almost invisible at every stage of the Senate process. What the Friends lamented as political paralysis, the Alliance lambasted as "insensitivity to the citizens of Minnesota."[45] He lost coming and going. And all the campaigning in the world wouldn't change that.

The Conference Committee

Tuesday, October 10. Four days to go.

Not only did the bill need to pass to a conference committee, where its provisions would be reconciled with the House-passed version, it had to make one final stop in the House. The Friends dreaded giving Oberstar one more shot.

Their concerns were justified.

Both Bob Short and Jeno Paulucci had played on personal relationships to encourage Tip O'Neill to do what he could to derail the bill.[46] And in a move reminiscent of the Senate, Republican Representative Robert Livingston of Louisiana objected to Morris Udall's request that the House appoint conferees by unanimous consent. Livingston's objection bumped the bill into a contested matters calendar, preventing the conference committee from meeting.

Once again, the Friends scrambled to determine what motives were at play. They traced Livingston's action to Al Quie, who had sought to kill the bill surreptitiously through a surrogate. The Friends dispensed with niceties. They laid out the story to the *Minneapolis Tribune*, which the next day identified Quie as the source of the delay.[47] Quie immediately arranged with Livingston to have the objection lifted.

Quie's maneuver had consumed one more day. The conference committee was not able to meet until Wednesday, October 11.[48]

Despite the press of business in both chambers, both the House and Senate were well-represented. Udall, Burton, Skubitz, Seiberling, and Vento from the House. Abourezk, Weicker, Anderson, and Jackson from the Senate. The small room in the Capitol was stuffed with Friends and Alliance members, congressional staff, and the press. Much to the irritation of the Alliance, the atmosphere was informal and light. Burton needled Abourezk about holding up his Omnibus Parks bill. Abourezk grunted back a series of soft insults.

The real work of the conference committee waited while each of its members praised Anderson's statesmanship in breaking the impasse. With a knowing grin on his face, Burton then moved that the House accede to the Senate version of the bill, obviating the need to hash out differences between the two. The motion passed without objection.[49]

Eleventh-Hour Shenanigans

Thursday October 12. The conference committee report had been signed, printed, and filed by morning. Its next stop was the House floor. Back to Burton's lair.

The quickest way to clear the conference committee bill would be to proceed under a procedure termed suspension of the rules. Suspending the rules, which foreclosed debate, required a two-thirds majority. Burton concluded that this was too risky—the Friends' vote counts suggested they could fall short.

Burton opted instead to bring the bill up on the normal calendar. That gave Oberstar the opening he needed. He asked Tip O'Neill for a twenty-four hour delay, removing the bill from a very crowded floor calendar. O'Neill agreed. The bill would not be brought up until Friday, the 13th. Oberstar and the House Speaker realized they could not get away with dropping the bill off the calendar altogether, but thought that pushing it into the last hours of a frenetic closing session might do the trick.[50]

It looked like they were right. The bill was restored to the calendar on Friday, but was placed well down a hefty list. All day, Burton, Vento, and Fraser made unsuccessful attempts to move the bill up. It would have to wait its turn.

Fraser finally got through to O'Neill late Friday night. He called Heinselman at midnight to report that O'Neill was inclined to take a vote on the bill Saturday afternoon, but had been dissuaded by Oberstar, who told him that he had an obligation to spend Saturday with his children. As Heinselman groaned in disbelief, Fraser chuckled. Jim Oberstar was a good family man—maybe he could bring his kids to the House galleries for the half-hour it would take to complete something he had been working on for five years.[51]

O'Neill made good on his commitment to permit Oberstar time with his family: the BWCA stayed buried in a mound of unfinished business throughout Saturday afternoon. Fortunately for the Friends, the depth of that mound forced

Congress to stay in session throughout the night and morning. Unless O'Neill was turned around, however, the House could stay in session for weeks with the same result.

Burton couldn't do it. O'Neill's actions were likely as much motivated by his antipathy toward Burton as they were by loyalty to Oberstar. The job fell to others. Vento vowed to camp alternatively in O'Neill's and Majority Leader Jim Wright's offices until he shook the bill loose. Heinselman also arranged for Mondale's friend Bob Herbst to have the vice president call O'Neill.

Their persistence finally made a dent. When Rick Nolan collared the House Speaker on the House floor, O'Neill relented: "Vento has been camping on my doorstep for two days. Tell him I'm going to get that goddamned bill out for him."[52]

The Final Hours

The House deliberations moved at a snail's pace through the dinner hour and into the evening. Heinselman and others kept a vigil in Vento's office, listening to the debate drone on.

The monotony was broken after midnight by a report from one of the Friends' observers that the House would adjourn after passing two large bills that were next up on the docket. Heinselman sent panicky notes into Burton, Fraser, and Vento on the floor.

All three came out to meet Heinselman. The report proved to be only a rumor. With a big smile, Burton put his arm around Heinselman and said, "Don't worry, Bud, there are dozens of important bills we've got to pass after the BWCA bill. We won't adjourn until they're all passed. Your bill will come up, and we're going to pass it!" Fraser and Vento didn't seem so sure, but they recommended a few hours of sleep.[53]

Heinselman did not, of course, take their advice. He stayed glued to Vento's speaker box. A little after 8:30 on Sunday morning, the time had come: the BWCA conference report was next up. Heinselman led the Friends group to the gallery.

At 9:00 sharp, the BWCA debate began.

Perhaps it was the all-night session. Perhaps it was the cumulative impact of two years of frustration with Fraser. Or perhaps it was the recognition that his back was finally to the wall. Whatever the reason, Oberstar unleashed a mean-spirited floor speech that equated Fraser's defeat with a referendum on the BWCA:

On September 12 a referendum of sorts was held in my district on the merits of this so-called Walls/Dayton, now Anderson "compromise." The people did not feel this proposition had any merit whatever. They voted overwhelmingly in that primary election against the terms of the bill now before the House. . . . At this early hour of the morning we are kind of bleary-eyed and weary. Our minds are nearly wrung out. We are considering a bill that has been rushed through under the pressure of a supercharged emotional and political atmosphere in Minnesota. I think we ought to take a little time and consider it more thoroughly in due season.[54]

Burton moved quickly to Fraser's defense:

[Don Fraser] stood for the full protection he knew this resource deserves, and he has never strayed from that commitment despite personal attacks and terrible damage to his own political career. His one mission throughout this entire battle has been to see this unique water wilderness passed unimpaired to future generations. Don Fraser will not be back in the 96th Congress, but his legacy for future generations will endure.[55]

Fraser then asked to be recognized. This would be the last speech of his sixteen-year of service in Congress. Even the Republicans took their seats to listen as Fraser began:

There is no question that the BWCA was a "deciding factor" in my defeat—as Congressman Oberstar has been pleased to advertise over the past month. Nor is there any question that the atmosphere is "emotionally supercharged"—particularly in Congressman Oberstar's district where . . . some of my supporters have been subjected to threats and intimidation, usually by way of anonymous telephone calls suggesting personal violence and burning of homes.

But to argue that these are reasons to defer action on the BWCA is to continue to miss the point. The Boundary Waters Canoe Area is a national resource, not a state or local resource as Congressman Oberstar and some of his constituents seem to believe. It is—and has been—Federal property that we are talking about, and it is used by people from all over the United States—not simply by the people of Mr. Oberstar's district . . .

Thus, Mr. Speaker, the fact that Mr. Oberstar's supporters are "emotionally supercharged" and the fact that I was defeated are irrelevant insofar as the Boundary Waters issue is concerned. To take these factors into consideration would be to permit the actions of a local minority to determine national policy. It would be tantamount to have permitted the people of Philadelphia, Mississippi, to determine national civil rights policy in the 1960s.[56]

Realizing that Oberstar's forces had him outnumbered on the floor, Burton called for a roll call vote. As one bleary-eyed member after another entered the chamber, coming past Friends members and representatives of the national environmental organizations giving the thumbs-up signal to urge a yes vote, the months of Friends lobbying finally paid dividends. The final tally: 248 in favor of the conference report, 111 against.[57]

Completely carried away by the emotional moment, Heinselman reached over and gave his wife Fran the first smooch anyone in the environmental movement could remember seeing the two exchange. They were quickly reprimanded by a guard for behavior unbecoming to the House galleries.

The Friends spilled outside into a sunny and crisp October morning. They walked to Vento's office for an impromptu celebration and to wait for word on when the conference report would be taken up by the Senate, which had been forced to stay in session until they had disposed of the House-passed actions.

Bruce Vento (left) and Phil Burton (right) celebrated with Bud and Fran Heinselman after the final passage of the BWCA Wilderness Act. (*Photo by Kevin Proescholdt*)

The celebrants in Vento's office thought nothing of the passage of the first hour. But as hour after hour ticked by with no word from the Senate, there was a growing apprehension that yet something else had gone wrong.

Indeed it had.

A call to the Senate clerk turned up nothing: the report, which should have been automatically forwarded from the House to the Senate, had not arrived. The Clerk advised the Friends to move quickly—the Senate was getting ready to adjourn.

A flurry of calls to Speaker O'Neill's office, the House clerk, and others turned up nothing. The report had disappeared.

The Friends spread in all directions, trying to reconstruct a paper trail. Iric Nathanson, Fraser's administrative assistant, offered to go to the House floor. It was a wise choice. Nathanson, who had a good working relationship with the clerk's staff, methodically searched every nook and cranny in which the bill could have been placed.

The scenario could not have been more implausible. No matter how busy the last hours in the House were, there were clear procedures that governed what went where, and who had responsibility for what. As Fraser would later note, "Never in my sixteen years in the House of Representatives have I ever seen this happen."[58] Given the bill's history, the Friends were convinced that they were not looking at an accident.

Nathanson kept pouring through reams of paper. Just as he was about to give up, he saw the word "Boundary" peeking out from one of the piles destined for the White House for signature. He grabbed it. It was the conference report.

He didn't bother to let anyone know. He ran through the Capitol hallway to the Senate, tracked down the Senate clerk, watched as he recorded having received the document and as he entered it onto the Senate agenda. He then rushed back to bring the others to the Senate galleries.

Nathanson's heroics had gotten the conference report to the Senate. But the tortuous trip was still not over.

Minutes after the Friends arrived at the gallery, the conference committee report was announced on the consent calendar. But routine was not a word in the BWCA bill's vocabulary. Republican Ted Stevens of Alaska, reserving the right to object to the bill, rose to ask a series of questions with a decidedly negative edge. The collective blood pressure of the Friends rose as they had visions of a virulently anti-wilderness senator throwing sand in the works. But it was more a case of being ill-informed than of being hostile—a fellow senator put a list of the conference committee members in front of him, apparently satisfying Stevens that his interests had been represented. He sat down.[59]

After Stevens, the Friends were relieved to see the Senate's staunchest

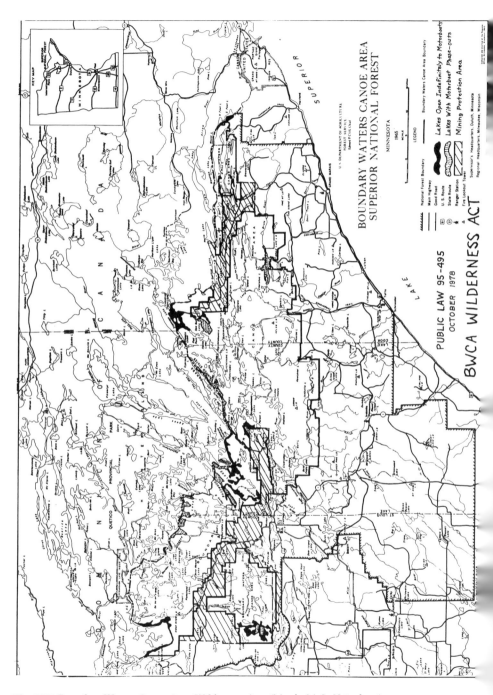

The 1978 Boundary Waters Canoe Area Wilderness Act. (*Map by M. L. Heinselman*)

wilderness advocate rise to address the issue, Gaylord Nelson of Wisconsin. Unprompted, and certainly unbriefed, Nelson also reserved the right to object, expressing concern that the Senate might be approving with little reflection a bill that did not enjoy the support of the environmental community. The gallery sat stupefied. They quickly scanned the floor to locate Anderson, who could reassure his colleague. But Anderson was again missing in action. That he had neglected to bring Nelson into the fold was one thing. That he hadn't been sufficiently tuned in to even be present for the floor action was unthinkable.

Jonathan Ela, a regional staffer for the Sierra Club and a personal friend of Nelson, raced down the stairs, joined by Nathanson and Heinselman. They were able to pull Nelson from the floor before he went any further. As he listened to their explanation, Nelson turned red, apologized and returned to the floor to withdraw his objection.[60]

With Nelson's objection removed, the Senate approved the conference report without further debate. It was 12:15 P.M. By 3:00 that afternoon, the 95th Congress would adjourn. After more than two years or almost ten thousand hours of congressional captivity, the BWCA bill had escaped with virtually no time left on the clock.[61]

Public Law 95-495

The president still had to sign the bill. And Oberstar and Short weren't through.

Oberstar publicly urged the president to veto:

> [I urge you] not to trade off life styles, livelihoods and legitimate desires of the people of northeastern Minnesota for equitable treatment in favor of the vague and ill-defined interests of other, perhaps more clamorous constituencies far removed from the BWCA.[62]

Not to be outdone, Short telegrammed President Carter, staking out the same turf.[63]

The appeals played back to Carter a controversial statement he had made during a late September campaign swing though Minnesota. Carter had attributed Fraser's loss to an inattentiveness to the electorate's feelings about local issues.

> If a candidate like Don Fraser, who is a very fine person, is not as sensitive about the issue of, say, snowmobiles in northern Minnesota...[he] cannot expect the issue to be decided on the basis of international statesmanship or past voting records in Congress.[64]

Oberstar's final ploy misjudged the president. The Carter Administration had been stalwart in its support of stronger BWCA wilderness protection. Carter was not about to undercut Bob Bergland and Rupe Cutler. Nor was he about to embarrass his vice president, who had encouraged Anderson to bring the issue to a close.

On Saturday, October 21, 1978, without fanfare, the president of the United States signed the BWCA bill.[65] After generations of uncertainty and turmoil, the BWCA had become the Boundary Waters Canoe Area Wilderness in practice as well as in name. Public Law 95-495 was now the law of the land.

Notes

1 *St. Paul Dispatch*, Jan. 24, 1978, p. 22, "Quie, Boschwitz Top I-R Straw Vote for Governor, Senator"; *Minneapolis Star*, Jan. 24, 1978, p. 4A, "Quie-Boschwitz Top IR Hopeful in Moorhead Straw Vote."

Boschwitz won his party's June endorsement with an eighty-percent vote on the first ballot. His two opponents both favored the Alliance's "multiple-use" approach. Cook County Board Chairman Chester Lindskog, nominated by Ely's Duane Krause, placed a distant second with only 208 votes; former Governor Harold Stassen limped in with 148 votes. *St. Paul Pioneer Press*, June 24, 1978, p. 1, "I-R Party Endorses Boschwitz"; *Ely Echo*, July 26, 1978, p. 1, "Harold Stassen Visits Here."

2 The Boschwitz bill would have permitted twenty-five horsepower motors on Fall, Trout, Clearwater, Moose, Brule, South Farm, Snowbank, East Bearskin, Magnetic, Long [Pine?], Jackfish Bay of Basswood, the Island River east of Isabella Lake, and on the eastern portions of Seagull and Saganaga. Boschwitz proposed 1984 phase-outs for the western portions of Seagull and Saganaga, and no additions of land to the wilderness. Text of the Boschwitz Statement on the Boundary Waters, May 5, 1978, 3 pp., copy in possession of authors. See *Minneapolis Star*, May 5, 1978, p. 1A, "Boschwitz Proposes Restrictive BWCA Bill"; *St. Paul Dispatch*, May 5, 1978, p. 27, "Boschwitz Joins BWCA Fray"; *Minneapolis Tribune*, May 6, 1978, p. 17A, "Boschwitz Proposes New Plan for BWCA"; *St. Paul Pioneer Press*, May 25, 1978, p. 3, "Boschwitz Pushing Own BWCA Bill"; *Minneapolis Tribune*, June 18, 1978, p. 1A, "Senate may get Boschwitz BWCA Bill."

3 *Ibid.*

4 Needless to say, the Boschwitz approach did not sit well in northern Minnesota. When he traveled to Grand Marais and Ely in early June, he got an earful. John Chelesnik, the Alliance official in charge of advertising, told him:

I just want to tell you that next week the newspaper ads are going in even stronger than before. We are going to put our money into this and defeat you at the polls, and you will not get a vote in the 8th District.

Ely steelworker Jack Meskill threatened that his 20,000-member union would oppose Boschwitz and support Anderson unless Boschwitz changed his BWCA plan. *St. Paul Dispatch,* June 5, 1978, p. 1, "Boschwitz Foresaw BWCA Trouble; Boy Was He Right"; *Minneapolis Tribune,* June 5, 1978, p. 2B, "Boschwitz Plan Spurned in BWCA-Land"; *Ely Echo* editorial, May 10, 1978, p. 1, "More BWCA Bunk"; *Ely Echo* editorial, June 14, 1978, p. 1, "Rudy Can't Get His Act Together."

5 *Minneapolis Star,* May 11, 1978, p. 15A, "Durenberger Backs BWCA Multiple-Use"; *Minneapolis Star,* May 12, 1978, p. 13A, "Not Everybody Is Raging Up North" (Jim Klobuchar column); *Ely Echo,* Aug. 30, 1978, p. 1, "Durenberger BWCA Stance Favors Broad Use."

6 *Minneapolis Star,* May 12, 1978, p. 13A, "Not Everybody Is Raging Up North" (Jim Klobuchar column).

7 *St. Paul Pioneer Press,* Apr. 7, 1978, p. 19, "Durenberger May Run for Senate Instead"; *Minneapolis Star,* Apr. 7, 1978, p. 1A, "Durenberger Urged to Run for Humphrey Senate Seat"; *Minneapolis Tribune,* Apr. 23, 1978, p. 1A, "Durenberger Confirms He will Run for Senate"; *St. Paul Pioneer Press,* Apr. 23, 1978, p. 1, "Durenberger to Run for Senate Opening."

8 Durenberger faced several relatively unknown candidates in the September primary, the most well-known of whom was former University of Minnesota President Malcom Moos. *Minneapolis Star,* Sept. 5, 1978, p. 1B, "Dave Durenberger."

9 He had actually begun in February, but stated he would not challenge Muriel Humphrey. When she decided not to run, he entered the race. *Minneapolis Star,* Feb. 8, 1978, p. 6A, "Short to Start Senate Drive"; *St. Paul Pioneer Press,* Feb. 9, 1978, p. 34, "Robert Short to Announce Candidacy for U.S. Senate"; *St. Paul Dispatch,* April 11, 1978, p. 3, "Short Officially in Senate Chase."

10 *St. Paul Dispatch,* April 11, 1978, p. 3, "Short Officially in Senate Chase."

11 Short reportedly spent $700,000 of his own money just through the primary. See *Minneapolis Star,* June 16, 1978, p. 1A, "DFL Unity to be Tested in Battle for Senate."

12 *Minneapolis Star,* June 16, 1978, p. 1A, "DFL Unity to be Tested in Battle for Senate."

13 See generally Fraser Interview, Oct. 25, 1991.

14 *Minneapolis Star,* Sept. 8, 1978, p. 11A, "Fraser-Short Fight Roars to Bitter End." See also Fraser Interview, Oct. 25, 1991.

15 The so-called "Moonies" were apparently dispatched to Minnesota in retaliation for Fraser's role in investigating Moon through Fraser's Subcommittee on International Organizations and Movements of the House Foreign Affairs Committee. See Fraser Interview, Oct. 25, 1991.

16 *MLH Chronology*, Sept. 12, 1978.

17 *MLH Chronology*, Sept. 12, 1978. The other races produced no surprises. Boschwitz, Durenberger, and Anderson won handily, as did Quie and Perpich in the governor's race. *Minneapolis Tribune*, Sept. 13, 1978, p. 1A, "Anderson, Boschwitz Defeat Challengers."
The governor's race, although not tied as directly to the BWCA as the Senate races, nevertheless became embroiled in the controversy. Quie recognized that his only chance for siphoning votes from Perpich's base on the Range was to take an Oberstar/Short-like stand on the BWCA. He did, and it appeared to pay dividends. The Alliance endorsed him. *Duluth News-Tribune*, Oct. 3, 1978, p. 1A, "Cook Alliance Endorses Quie."

18 *Minneapolis Star*, Sept. 13, 1978, p. 1A, "Short Rallies, Takes 3,747 Lead"; *Minneapolis Star*, Sept. 13, 1978, p. 9A, "Crossovers Played Big Role in Short Support, Poll Says."

19 Minnesota Legislative Manual 1979-1980, pp. 472-473.

20 *Ely Echo*, Sept. 20, 1978, p. 1 (editorial cartoon). Short, recognizing the role northeastern Minnesota had played, visited the area immediately after his victory. *Minneapolis Tribune*, Sept. 14, 1978, p. 1A, "Thankful Short at Home on 'Range'"; *Ely Echo*, September 20, 1978, p. 1, "Bob Short Thanks Ely for Voter Support."

21 See *Minneapolis Star*, Sept. 14, 1978, p. 1A, "They're Whooping it up in Ely, Gloating in the Defeat of Fraser"; *Minneapolis Tribune*, Sept. 14, 1978, p. 1A, "Thankful Short at Home on 'Range'"; Zabinski Paper, pp. 46-49.

22 See generally Zabinski Paper, pp. 46-49.

23 *Minneapolis Tribune*, Sept. 19, 1978, p. 2B, "Fire in Fraser's Home called 'Suspicious'; Backers Grow Edgy."

24 Confident that Fraser would be soon joining the Senate, Rapson had left the office when the BWCA seemed on a reliable track. Fraser had emphasized in a long conversation with Rapson that much of the work would now fall to Anderson's staff and to Burton; it was a good time to pursue his graduate studies. Rapson Recollections, December 1983.

25 *Ibid.* These concerns about Anderson dominated subsequent strategy sessions as well. See *MLH Chronology*, numerous entries, e.g., September 15, 17, 18, 21, 26, 1978, October 4, 1978. And indeed, the Alliance was relying more and more on Oberstar. At the Alliance's second annual meeting in mid-September, the organization seemed unsure of its direction and tried to look ahead to 1979 and whether to "move to other issues and concerns" like "timber wolf, zoning, [Coastal Zone Management for Superior's North Shore], Voyageurs National Park, copper-nickel mining, peat harvesting, and wild and scenic river designation." See Zabinski Interview; *Voices in the Wilderness*, Boundary Waters Conservation Alliance newsletter, Aug./Sept. 1978, p. 1.

26 "Although portions of [the Dayton/Walls compromise] differ in some respects from the Department's original recommendations to the House, we feel that it achieves a workable compromise on the motorboat and snowmobile issues." Statement of M. Rupert

Cutler, Publication No. 95-148, Senate Energy and Natural Resources Committee, August 17, 1978, p. 64.

27 Cutler, who was accompanied by Deputy Forest Service Chief Max Peterson and Superior National Forest Supervisor Bob Rehfeld, told the Subcommittee on Parks and Recreation that the Carter Administration believed strongly that it was desirable to produce a bill during the current Congress. Publication No. 95-148, Senate Energy and Natural Resources Committee, August 17, 1978; *Minneapolis Tribune*, Aug. 18, 1978, p. 1A, "Carter Endorses BWCA Compromise"; *Minneapolis Tribune* editorial, Aug. 19, 1978, "BWCA: A Push from the Administration."

28 See *Minneapolis Tribune*, Oct. 1, 1978, p. 4B, "Adjournment Date Called Threat to BWCA Bill."

29 Brock Evans Recollections, October 11, 1978, p. 41.

30 *MLH Chronology*, Sept. 18, 1978.

31 *MLH Chronology*, Sept. 21, 1978.

32 *MLH Chronology*, Sept. 22, 1978.

33 *Minneapolis Tribune*, Sept. 27, 1978, p. 2B, "Action is Near on BWCA Measure"; *MLH Chronology*, Sept. 28, 1978.

34 Heinselman had earlier explained the differences in the two situations to McClure's staff; McClure's office assured Heinselman they would not object to the approach taken in the BWCA bill. *MLH Chronology* Sept. 28, 1978.

35 See Brock Evans Recollections, October 3, 1978, p. 38.

36 *Ibid.*

37 Ford Amendment to Anderson Compromise on Boundary Waters Canoe Area, copy in possession of authors; Brock Evans Recollections, Oct. 3, 1978, pp. 38-39.

38 Senate Report No. 95-1274; ; *Iowa State Daily*, October 4, 1978, p. 1, "BWCA Bill Gets Nod"; *Minneapolis Tribune*, Oct. 4, 1978, "Panel Advances BWCA Measure."

39 *MLH Chronology* Oct. 6, 7, 8, 1978.

40 *MLH Chronology* Oct. 6, 7, 8, 9, 1978.

41 *MLH Chronology* 10-6-78 thru 10-9-78; *Minneapolis Tribune*, Oct. 10, 1978, p. 1A, "BWCA Bill Passes Senate, Goes to House."

42 *Congressional Record*, Oct. 9, 1978, S17885-91; *Minneapolis Tribune*, October 10, 1978, p. 1A, "BWCA Bill Passes Senate, Goes to House"; *St. Paul Pioneer Press*, Oct. 10, 1978, p.1, "BWCA Compromise Bill's Chances now up to House."

43 *Friends of the Boundary Waters Wilderness Newsletter*, Oct., 1978, p. 3.

44 See *St. Paul Pioneer Press*, Oct. 11, 1978, "BWCA Bill Vote Called 'An Insult.'"

45 *Ibid.*

46 Dick Conlon conversation with Bud Heinselman. *MLH Chronology*, Oct. 6,7 1978.

47 *Minneapolis Tribune*, Oct. 11, 1978, p. 1A, "House Hits Snag on BWCA Bill"; *MLH Chronology*, Oct. 10, 1978.

48 *Congressional Record*, Oct. 11, 1978, H12255; Brock Evans Recollections, p. 41.

49 Despite the wishes of Burton and the Friends to improve upon the Dayton/Walls Senate bill in a conference committee deliberation, Burton quickly recognized that not enough time remained to compromise between the House and Senate bills. Brock Evans Recollections, Oct. 11, pp. 41-42; *Minneapolis Tribune*, Oct. 12, 1978, p. 1A, "House Conferees Agree to Accept Senate BWCA Bill"; *St. Paul Pioneer Press*, Oct. 12, 1978, p. 1, "Quick Vote Could Pass BWCA Bill."

50 *Minneapolis Tribune*, Oct. 14, 1978, p. 3A, "House Action on BWCA Plan Uncertain in Drive to Adjourn."

51 *MLH Chronology*, Oct. 13, 1978.

52 Brock Evans Recollections, Oct. 14, 1978, p. 44; *MLH Chronology*, Oct. 14, 1978.

53 *MLH Chronology*, Oct. 15, 1978.

54 *Congressional Record*, Oct. 14, 1978, H13440-41.

55 *Congressional Record*, Oct. 14, 1978, H13439. Vento spoke to the merits of the conference committee report.
> While the Senate motorized use provision is admittedly less restrictive than we would have wished for, it does cut back considerably in the number of lakes that will be open to motorboats. . . . We have done our homework, hearings have been held and the House and the Senate conducted comprehensive deliberations to produce this measure which will preserve this resource for future generations.
Congressional Record, Oct. 14, 1978, H13440.

56 *Congressional Record*, Oct. 14, 1978, H13443.

57 *Congressional Record*, Oct. 14, 1978, H13436-44.

58 Fraser Interview, Oct. 25, 1991.

59 Brock Evans Recollections, Oct. 15, 1978, p. 45.

60 *MLH Chronology*, Oct. 15, 1978; Brock Evans Recollections, Oct. 15, 1978, pp. 44-45.

61 *Congressional Record*, Oct. 14, 1978, S19195; *Minneapolis Tribune*, Oct. 16, 1978, p. 1A, ". . . Compromise Bill on BWCA Limits."

62 *Minneapolis Tribune*, Oct. 17, 1978, p. 2B, "Oberstar asks Carter to Listen to People and Veto BWCA Bill."

63 *Ibid.*

64 *Minneapolis Tribune*, Sept. 28, 1978, p. 1A, "Carter says Fraser lost by Slighting Local Issues."

65 P.L. 95-495; 92 Stat. 1649; *Minneapolis Tribune*, Oct. 24, 1978, p. 1A, "Carter Signed BWCA Bill Saturday."

Chapter Eight
Epilogue

The Boundary Waters Canoe Area Wilderness Act did not shut off the spigot of controversy. Indeed, for years after the bill became law, the controversies flowed virtually unabated.

There was first of all the immediate politics of the November election. Two weeks after President Carter signed the act, the November elections produced the "Minnesota Massacre," in which Democrats were trounced at every level. Short, whom Fraser had refused to endorse and whose cross-over strategy now came back to bite him, was swamped by Durenberger almost two to one, 64% to 36%.[1] Anderson was clobbered by Boschwitz, 58% to 42%.[2] Perpich ran a little closer, but not much, losing the governorship to Quie 54% to 46%.[3] The Minnesota House was transformed from a ninety-nine to thirty-five Democratic majority to a sixty-seven to sixty-seven stalemate.

The BWCA did not solely account for all of these defeats. But it had certainly contributed to the campaign dynamic of each.

Then there was the spirit of the Alliance, carried forth by State Senator Doug Johnson. Early in 1979, Johnson and Representative David Battaglia of Two Harbors were able to push through the Legislature a seventeen-member BWCA Citizen's Advisory Task Force, complete with a $40,000 budget. The Task Force would be authorized to study BWCA issues and bring recommendations back to the legislature, a tactic northern Minnesota residents had used effectively in creating anti-Voyageurs National Park agitation.[4]

The Task Force remained in operation for several years, not living up to Johnson's expectations of troublemaking. It passed quietly out of existence when its authority expired in 1983.

Finally, there were the legal challenges to the act. It was in this arena that the Friends and northern Minnesota locked horns most directly.

The Lawyers' Turn

Northern Minnesotans had repeatedly given notice that they would take their case to the courts, if necessary. The Sierra Club had begun assembling a volunteer legal team in anticipation of these challenges.[5] Brian O'Neill from Faegre and Benson and Chuck Dayton took lead responsibility. The team didn't have to wait long to start work.

Three separate lawsuits were ultimately filed in federal court challenging the act.

The first was filed in July 1979 by the Texas-based National Association of Property Owners (NAPO), an organization that shopped around the country for private property interests to represent in challenges against the government.[6] Through its representative Ben Wallis of San Antonio, it found a receptive audience in the Ely/Winton Boundary Waters Conservation Alliance, related to, but not the same as, the old Alliance.[7]

Wallis would tie up a lot of court time and put the Friends through their legal paces before he was done. But he was not F. Lee Bailey. At one hearing scheduled months in advance, he submitted an affidavit saying he could not meet the deadline because of a bout of food poisoning. He filed a second NAPO action based on a case the Supreme Court had overturned months before; he refused to dismiss it when informed that his precedent had disappeared. Dayton and O'Neill would have found his behavior amusing had the stakes not been so high.[8]

The NAPO suit challenged the BWCA law on five fronts.

First, Congress unlawfully delegated authority to the Secretary of Agriculture to draw the new wilderness boundaries. Second, the Act unconstitutionally discriminated against handicapped people by limiting motorboat and snowmobile use. Third, the sections limiting motorboat use and providing the government a right of first refusal on properties adjacent to the wilderness infringed on the Ninth Amendment property rights of landowners and violated due process of law. Fourth, the act violated the Webster/Ashburton Treaty of 1842 by prohibiting access to the international boundary waters by the Lac La Croix Indian Band. Fifth, the Forest Service's enforcement of the act was selective.

By filing a motion in Washington, D.C., with no notice to the Friends, Wallis almost succeeded in obtaining a temporary restraining order prohibiting the Forest Service from implementing the act. Dayton happened to be in Washington representing the National Audubon Society on another matter when he learned of Wallis' pending motion; although he was not admitted to the federal court in D.C., he called the Sierra Club's Brock Evans to move his admission. It was a wise move. The Justice Department attorney knew little about the suit or the act. Judge Harold Greene advised him to take an hour and collect his thoughts. Dayton was able to step in, take over much of the argument, and persuade the court after the break not to enter the restraining order.[9]

Wallis withdrew the action from the D.C. court and refiled it a week later in Minnesota. Wallis used the opportunity to call for a congressional investigation of the improper relationship between the Sierra Club and the Forest Service, claiming that the federal government was represented at the court hearing by the Sierra Club's Dayton. The Alliance picked up the tune, sending telegrams to members of Congress calling for an investigation of the "cozy" relationship between the Forest Service and the Sierra Club.[10]

Undeterred by the apparent lack of congressional interest in exploring that relationship, Wallis argued his motion for a temporary restraining order on August 7 before Federal Magistrate Patrick McNulty of Duluth.[11] O'Neill, Dayton, and an assistant United States attorney responded. The arguments consumed almost four hours.

Magistrate McNulty denied Wallis' motion and granted the motion of ten environmental organizations to intervene in the suit.[12] The district court concurred with McNulty and formally denied the motion for a restraining order on August 28.

On August 7, the environmental organizations had also moved to dismiss the NAPO case for failure to state a claim or, in the alternative, for summary judgement. A series of other motions and counter motions subsequently flew back and forth.[13] On September 10, Magistrate McNulty heard the arguments and took the matters under advisement.[14] By October, all the parties agreed that all necessary motions had been filed.[15]

The second challenge to the act was filed by the State of Minnesota right before Christmas of 1979. Acting against the advice of the state attorney general's office, the state challenged the right of the federal government to preempt state jurisdiction over BWCA waters. This was the same argument that Wallis had advanced earlier that fall and that the state had unsuccessfully trotted out two years before in challenging the federal government's jurisdiction over the waters of Voyageurs National Park.[16] The governor's decision to press ahead with the lawsuit appeared to be part of a political strategy to bolster his standing in northern Minnesota.[17]

The third suit came in January of 1980, again courtesy of NAPO.[18] It claimed that the act should be enjoined because no environmental impact statement had been prepared. Although devoid of substantial legal precedent, the suit combined with the pending NAPO and State of Minnesota actions to present a significant draw on the environmental legal community's time and talent. O'Neill and Dayton needed all sixteen of their volunteer attorneys just to keep up.

The federal district court consolidated the three actions and set them for hearing before Chief Judge Miles Lord on April 17 and May 2, 1980.

Lord was intimately familiar with the BWCA; he had presided over the logging lawsuits in the early 1970s. He was unpredictable and controversial.

In remarks the first day, Lord telegraphed to Wallis a small indication of what to expect. Referring to Wallis' environmental impact statement action, Lord observed: "I don't even have to look in a lawbook to tell you that you don't need an environmental impact statement to leave something natural alone."[19] It would not be the last time the judge would make Wallis look like a beginning law student.

The May 2nd hearing became a six-hour marathon. Each of the five causes of action NAPO raised in its first suit, the state's water jurisdiction arguments, even Wallis' impact statement allegations were all briefed, argued, and taken under consideration by Chief Judge Lord.[20]

On July 24, 1980, Lord dismissed all three lawsuits in a lengthy, carefully crafted opinion. He gave short shrift to the NAPO lawsuits, leaving no doubt that he viewed Wallis' legal theories as little more than nuisance actions.

He devoted more time to the state's arguments but was ultimately persuaded by the argument that the state and federal governments enjoyed joint jurisdiction:

> The new Act does not divest the state of jurisdiction over the surface waters within the Wilderness. The only extent to which the state's jurisdiction is restricted by the new Act concerns the situation where Minnesota would wish to open more surface water for motorized use—this the state cannot do. The state, however, could issue regulations restricting motorized uses which are more stringent than the federal restrictions; under the Act, the state could close all the surface waters of the Wilderness to motorboats and snowmobiles. . . . Nothing in the Act divests the state of its authority to regulate mining in the BWCAW. The Act contemplates that both the state and the federal government will retain equal control in the Wilderness.[21]

O'Neill captured the relief of the environmental community, calling the decision "a sweeping victory. The opinion preserves the wilderness."[22]

The state appealed within the month.[23] After oral argument in mid-June of 1981,[24] the Court of Appeals for the Eighth Circuit upheld Lord's ruling in a unanimous opinion issued September 30.[25]

The governor, despite receiving advice to the contrary from the Attorney General's office and having already spent more than $100,000 on the case, chose to appeal to the United States Supreme Court.[26] The Supreme Court denied the petition for review on March 8, 1982.[27] The legal process had finally been exhausted.

Pecking Away

The series of defeats in the courts only increased the resolve of the Alliance and others to find other ways of undercutting the act. One small guerrilla action followed another.

In September of 1981, just before the Court of Appeals ruling, the *Ely Echo* printed a seven-point plan for amending the act.[28] The plan was designed to coincide with the close of the comment period for the Forest Service's plan for implementing the new law. Taking no chances, the environmental community forwarded to the congressional delegation a twelve-page response. Nothing further came of the proposal.[29]

Just before its sunset in the spring of 1983, the BWCA Citizen's Advisory Task Force issued a six-point recommendation to Governor Rudy Perpich (elected after Quie had chosen not to run for a second term) that the state pursue changes in the federal law.[30] Vento acted quickly to stave off any ideas the state might have; in a letter to the House Interior Committee, he warned Chair Morris Udall about the proposal and stated his strong opposition to it.[31] The proposals went no further.

The act provided for a series of phase-outs of some motorboat routes in 1984. It was to that cause that northern Minnesota turned next.

When the BWCA Citizen's Advisory Task Force went out of existence in 1983, a state agency called the Iron Range Resources and Rehabilitation Board (IRRRB) formed a Border Lakes Tourism Task Force to carry on the previous task force's work. Heavily dominated by Alliance activists, the IRRRB Task Force proposed extensive amendments to the BWCA law, including repealing most of the motor provisions.[32]

In the fall of 1983, Doug Johnson attempted to coerce the environmental community into accepting the IRRRB amendments. In an October meeting, he reminded a group of environmentalists of his support for the state Superfund Law governing the cleanup of hazardous waste dump sites; an effort to kill the bill at final passage earlier that spring would have succeeded had he not voted against it. Johnson suggested that environmental organizations in the state should accept at least some of the BWCA changes proposed by the IRRRB or risk not having the support in the future from Johnson and his allies on "real environmental issues" like Superfund. He stated that he would settle for modest changes: the reopening of all of Lac La Croix and the elimination of all phase-outs. The environmentalists politely declined the offer.[33]

The IRRRB Task Force was simultaneously trying to solicit Canada's help in pressuring the United States to lift motor restrictions on the international border lakes. In October, the Task Force had quietly arranged for an official in the Canadian Department of External Affairs to write a legal opinion that claimed that both the Ontario "Provincial Parks Regulation" which governs Quetico Provincial Park and the United States' BWCAW law violated two international treaties. The story was leaked to the Minnesota press in early November.[34] No sooner had the story hit, however, than a spokesman for the Department of External Affairs disavowed the legal opinion as not representing official departmental policy. The public relations boon had gone bust.[35]

Just to be sure, Vento met quickly with the Canadian ambassador, Allan Gotlieb, in Washington to clarify the status of the legal opinion. Vento followed up with a letter jointly signed by Morris Udall and John Sieberling expressing concern about any potential changes in motorboat policy within Quetico. The three reaffirmed their opposition to any changes on the American side of the lakes.[36]

Canadian officials were quick to respond, stating that the opinion was a "goof that was let out," that it was only "an opinion" and not policy, and that the entire affair was "an issue south of the border, not north of the border, and we won't let it whip us around."[37]

This exchange delivered the *coup de grace* to the IRRRB's recommendations.

Just as that issue died down, another raised its head. As the January 1984 phase-out date drew nearer, local residents began pressuring the Forest Service to allow the *possession* of motors within the BWCA, even if they could not be *used*. The theory was that motors could be lifted out of the water in paddle-only zones but could be reinserted once the boat entered a motorized zone.[38]

In January, the Forest Service partially capitulated, requesting public comment on whether to allow motor possession in three particular areas of the BWCA Wilderness: the eight miles of international border on Basswood Lake that had just been closed to motors that month, Lac La Croix, and the North Kawishiwi River from Farm Lake east to the first portage.[39]

The conservation community organized an extensive letter-writing campaign.[40] Nearly 500 people responded, the vast majority in opposition to the proposal. That was enough for the Forest Service. The agency announced in March that possession of outboard motors would not be allowed in nonmotorized portions of the BWCA Wilderness.[41]

Nearly a year passed before the next incursion, again led by Johnson.

In the spring of 1985, Johnson in the Senate and Dave Battaglia in the House introduced companion resolutions calling on the federal governments of the United States and Canada "to take prompt action to ensure that all travel on water routes between the United States and Canada by motorized watercraft be allowed." Never mentioning the BWCA or the BWCA Wilderness Act, the resolutions appeared innocuous.[42]

Environmental lobbyists Nelson French and Kevin Proescholdt spotted the resolution the day before its formal introduction and quickly spread word to allies about its true purpose. In the Senate, Gene Merriam and Bill Luther were able to arrange for the resolution to be referred to the Rules Committee, side-tracking it from its intended destination, the Committee on Veterans and General Legislation, which was chaired by resolution co-sponsor Bob Lessard. The resolution died a peaceful death in Rules.

Johnson and Battaglia were thwarted, but not defeated. In the session's final days, they circulated a similarly worded letter to President Reagan.[43] The letter was signed by 134 of the 201 members of the legislature.[44]

The president had his Forest Service chief respond. In August, Chief Max Peterson rejected Johnson's arguments, noting that they were largely a replay of legal contentions the courts had already resolved.[45]

Like a dog at a bone, Johnson kept gnawing. During the summer of 1985, Senator Durenberger had announced a plan to deal with various legitimate United States/Canadian border conflicts, such as hours of operation for customs crossings and fishing regulations on joint water bodies. Durenberger proposed the creation of a joint United States/Canadian commission to study and manage border area resources. A hearing was scheduled for August 23, 1985, in International Falls to solicit public input on the proposal.[46]

Unknown to Durenberger, Johnson intended to use the commission to weasel his issues back onto the agenda. Just prior to the hearing, the environmental community alerted Durenberger to Johnson's plans.[47] Durenberger pre-empted the subterfuge by announcing in his opening comments at the public hearing that "the Boundary Waters Canoe Area Wilderness Act will not be reopened, nor will legislation establishing Voyageurs National Park. These issues have been debated both here and in Washington for the last 75 years, and re-opening that debate is not an option the Commission will have."[48]

Johnson was livid at having been smoked out. He angrily interrupted Durenberger, saying it was his understanding that the proposed commission would discuss BWCA issues. He complained that he had been "desperately trying to get an audience for years" to deal with those issues. Durenberger held firm. Johnson, Battaglia, and several of their cronies then dramatically stormed out of the hearing in protest.[49]

Keepers of the Gate

The 1978 BWCAW Act had survived attempts to undo it in the courts and undermine it in the legislature. The environmental community faced a third set of challenges from an unexpected source, one that had been instrumental in bringing the law into being: the Forest Service.

From the very outset, the Forest Service sent messages that it would exercise wide professional discretion in implementing the act. This should have come as no surprise from an agency that traditionally saw its mission as *managing* natural resources for such commodities as timber or developed recreation, not stepping back and managing wilderness with a light hand. But the extent to which the the Forest Service sought to appease local residents and protect commercial interests was startling even to long-time critics of the agency.

The Friends first squared off with the Forest Service over the agency's 1981 implementation plan, where the agency announced numerous policies that subverted the intent of the law. But it was not until 1984 that a full confrontation began taking form.[50]

In 1984, the Minnesota Audubon Council produced a lengthy research study documenting the successes and failures of the law's implementation.[51] Among the failures: continuing the operation of the truck portages, maintaining and rebuilding dams within the wilderness, failing to remove the logging road crossing over the Isabella River, setting excessively high motorboat quotas, and permitting the continued operation of towboats on the Moose Lake Chain and Saganaga Lake.[52]

The Friends injected the concerns raised by the Audubon study into the preparation of the management plan for the Superior National Forest, which the Forest Service had been preparing at about the same time the study was released.[53] The plan was charged with providing specific ten-year management directions for the forest and the wilderness, as well as general management guidelines for the next half-century. The final plan was released in the spring of 1986.[54]

A coalition of conservation groups immediately challenged twelve aspects of the Plan.[55] The administrative appeal process that followed rivaled in length, formality, and technicality the previous BWCA lawsuits.[56]

The appeal included the key points identified by the Audubon study.[57] It dragged on for over a year. In December 1987, the Friends finally had the opportunity to present their appeal to the chief. He punted, requiring that the parties attempt to mediate before he made his decision. Beginning in January 1988, the environmental coalition, local interests who had intervened, and the Forest Service met monthly in Duluth to reconcile their differences.[58]

The parties were able to settle eight of the twelve issues, agreeing that:

- dams would no longer be maintained in the wilderness;
- the Isabella River logging road crossing would be removed;
- woodland caribou reintroduction in the BWCAW would be studied;
- additional safeguards governing the use of pesticides would be introduced;

• a minerals acquisition program would be developed for the BWCA Wilderness and Mining Protection Area;
• visitor use levels would be recalculated and justified by the early 1990s.[59]

Four of the major appeal issues, however, could not be settled: continued operation of the three BWCA truck portages, below-cost timber sales on the Superior outside the wilderness, the leasing of resorts purchased under the 1978 act back to commercial operation, and the potential addition of areas like the Homer/Brule region to the wilderness. These remained for the chief to decide.

The issue of truck portages, the heart of the Dayton/Walls compromise, was the most contentious of the four.

The Friends had anticipated that it would be. More than two years earlier, they had sent Heinselman, Friends Director Kevin Proescholdt, and O'Neill's colleague Rob Crawford to the BWCAW to document that the act's requirement of "feasible" alternatives to the truck portages had been met: they turned on a videocamera, attached portage wheels to a motorboat loaded with fishing gear, and wheeled the boat over the portages into the lakes served by the truck portages.[60]

Armed with the videotape and mounds of briefing materials, the chief's office issued a decision on the truck portages in March 1989. Written by Associate Deputy Chief David Unger, the opinion conceded the Friends' position:

> [A]ppellants are correct in their assertion that "feasible" does not mean "ideal" or "most practical." "Feasible" means "possible." Just because

The truck portage operation on Trout Lake inside the BWCA Wilderness. (*Photo by Kevin Proescholdt*)

motorized portages are easier does not mean that nonmotorized portages are not "feasible." The showing made by appellants casts doubt on whether the Forest's [earlier] determination was made in a nonarbitrary or noncapricious manner.[61]

Unger directed the Superior staff of the Forest Service to conduct trials of the feasibility of nonmotorized alternatives by October 1, keeping in mind that "there is a strong presumption in favor of wilderness values and against motorized use" under the act; in the meantime, the Four Mile and Trout Portages would be closed immediately.[62]

But a week later, Forest Service Chief Dale Robertson overturned his deputy, delaying the closings indefinitely. He had received a call from Oberstar urging that the other side of the argument be heard. He accordingly arranged to meet in April in Washington with Oberstar, Mayor Grahek, Doug Johnson,

The Friends' Rob Crawford (left), Bud Heinselman (center), and Kevin Proescholdt (right) pushed a loaded motorboat on portage wheels across one of the truck portages, 1986. (*Photo by Kevin Proescholdt*)

Governor Perpich, and others. O'Neill and Proescholdt were not allowed to attend, but were given a separate audience with the chief immediately following the meeting with the Ely contingent.[63]

The Ely interests won this round. Robertson announced that Four Mile and Trout Portages would remain open during the 1989 season while the Forest Service conducted serious trials of portage wheels at the contested routes.[64]

The trials, held in July, bore a passing resemblance to the episode in which Laurel and Hardy try to move a piano up a very narrow and steep flight of stairs. Forest Service management had located some of the heaviest boats they could find in northeastern Minnesota, loaded some of them with enough gear to equip a Desert Storm battalion (some loads were in excess of half a ton), and started off in one-, two-, and three-person crews (even though the Dayton/Walls compromise and the act's legislative history specifically referred to three-person crews as the standard). Despite the heavy loads, the crews successfully completed twenty of the twenty-four main trials (and twenty-six of thirty-four total attempts) over and back across the Trout, Prairie, and Four Mile Portages.[65]

Unfettered by the objective evidence, the Forest Service concluded that even though the tests demonstrated that it was "possible" to use portage wheels, it was nevertheless not "reasonable" to expect the public to use them.[66] Like Laurel and Hardy, the Forest Service crews had been forced to exert themselves too much.[67] The Forest Service's official position was, therefore, that nonmechanized means were not "feasible"—the truck portages could continue indefinitely within the wilderness.[68]

The Friends were not amused. In January 1990, they brought an action in federal district court to overturn the ruling.[69] Judge James Rosenbaum heard oral arguments in March 1991. In August he ruled in favor of the Forest Service, concluding that the agency had properly included physical exertion in its definition of "feasible."[70]

The Court of Appeals for the eighth circuit did not agree. Citing the act's legislative history and well-established legal precedent equating "feasible" with "capable of being done," it overturned Rosenbaum in November 1992 and ordered the truck portages closed.[71]

The City of Ely, Jim Oberstar, the Alliance's successor organization (Conservationists with Common Sense), and others appealed to the U.S. Supreme Court. The court refused to hear the case. In June 1993, fifteen years after passage of the act and nine years after the Forest Service should have acted in the first place, the battle over truck portages had come to a close.[72]

Planes, Rains, and Camper Strains

With every conceivable attack on the 1978 act exhausted, the wilderness should have enjoyed a reprieve. But other forces continue to put pressure on the area.

Military Fly-Overs. In 1976, the U.S. Air Force and the Minnesota Air National Guard had established a military flyover airspace above one-third of the BWCA Wilderness and much of Superior National Forest. Named the Snoopy Military Operations Area, it was little publicized and received scarce attention. By the mid-1980s, however, the number of flights in Snoopy had jumped nearly tenfold, increasingly replacing the sounds of waves, birds, and wind with the screech of afterburners and thunder of sonic booms.[73]

In 1988, the Friends and several other groups brought suit to redirect the flights.[74] The suit alleged that the effects of the flights on the wilderness had improperly escaped review by an environmental impact statement. After one day of trial, the military agreed to settle: they would redraw the boundaries of Snoopy to eliminate all overlap with the BWCA Wilderness.[75]

Acid Rain and Air Toxins. The BWCA, with its thin soils and softwater lakes, is among the most sensitive areas in the state to acid rain. In part because of this, the environmental community pushed through the 1982 legislature the Acid Deposition Control Act. Supported by highly technical rules, the act has produced the toughest acid rain standards in the world.[76]

The problem of air toxins, particularly airborne mercury, is just emerging as a problem of equal severity. In 1990, the Minnesota Pollution Control Agency discovered extensive mercury contamination in the lakes of northeastern Minnesota; fish consumption advisories were issued for all thirty-five lakes tested in the BWCA and ninety-nine of one hundred lakes in the Superior National Forest.[77] The main sources appeared to be coal-fired power plants, latex paints that utilize mercury, and garbage incineration. The 1990 Clean Air Act reauthorization failed, however, to limit mercury from power plants.[78] The problem is still with us.

Visitor Use. The 1978 act has changed the visitor patterns in the BWCA. In 1978, for example, thirty-eight percent of the visitors traveled by motorboat or snowmobile, and sixty-two percent traveled by nonmotorized means (canoe and hiking). By 1993, the percentages had shifted dramatically: only seven percent of the visitors used motorboats, while ninety-three percent traveled by nonmotorized means.[79]

The levels of visitor use have also increased. The number of overnight camping parties has increased more than fifty percent from 1983 to 1993, from 18,558 to 28,593. The BWCA remains the most heavily visited unit in the

National Wilderness Preservation System, receiving 200,000 visitors annually who account for approximately 1.5 million visitor days of use.[80] This in turn has not only placed greater pressure on the area's physical resources such as campsites and trails but has also made it more difficult to protect intangible wilderness qualities such as solitude, quiet, and a sense of remoteness.[81]

In part to implement the settlement agreement with the Friends on re-analyzing visitor use levels, the Forest Service completed a new wilderness management plan in 1993. The plan cut back on the number of overnight paddle permits, trimmed the number of overnight and day motor permits, and reduced the maximum group size from ten to nine.[82]

The plan pleased nobody. Local residents, canoe outfitters, counties, and others challenged most of the new regulations. The Friends also sued, claiming that the new plan allowed more motor use within the wilderness than is allowed under the 1978 law.[83] Both suits are pending.

The Future

If one thing is certain, it is that we have not seen the last threats to the BWCA Wilderness. Whether political, biological, economic, or otherwise, some new set of pressures appears all but inevitable.[84] But the BWCAW has endured such pressures before. And, for all its flaws, the 1978 Boundary Waters Canoe Area Wilderness Act has erected a framework and philosophy of wilderness protection and management that gives the BWCA a fighting chance to surmount such pressures again.

Missing from those fights will be a number of remarkable figures who dedicated much of their lives to the vision of a BWCA wilderness.

Ernest Oberholtzer died in 1977 at the age of ninety-three, just as the congressional debate over the future of the BWCA intensified. His friends and partners Frank B. Hubachek and Charles S. Kelly both died in 1987. Working against enormous odds beginning in the 1920s, their efforts in the infant years of the wilderness movement were instrumental in preserving the canoe country.[85]

Sig Olson passed away in 1982 while snowshoeing near his home in Ely. Before going out, he had taken one last walk to his "writing shack," where he typed his final, prescient words, found later in his typewriter: "A new adventure is coming up, and I'm sure it will be a good one."[86]

The same year, Bill Magie, who had finally given up guiding canoe trips at the age of seventy-nine, died at his home in Wisconsin. Colorful and sometimes irascible, Magie passionately guarded his wilderness as long as he could, attending acid rain conferences, sending out his usual barrage of letters to decision-makers, and carefully clipping articles and filing information on the wilderness.

Among his last words were "Save the North!"[87]

And finally, Bud Heinselman, who more than any individual was responsible for the 1978 act, died in 1993.[88] It is to Bud's memory that this book is dedicated. His life and his work are an inspiration to the following generations of people who believe that the BWCA Wilderness is well worth fighting for.

"IT'S A HOBBY OF MINE —— EVERY TIME THERE'S A CONTROVERSY ABOUT THE B.W.C.A., I GO OUT AND PLANT A TREE."

(Reprinted with permission from the Duluth News-Tribune)

Notes

1 Durenberger received 958,000 votes to Short's 539,000. Durenberger rolled up a seventy-one percent margin in the Twin Cities. See *The Minnesota Legislative Manual 1979-1980*, pp. 488-489.

2 *Ibid.* Anderson carried only two counties in the entire state, even losing the Eighth Congressional District. Michael Barone, Grant Ujifusa, and Douglas Matthews, *Almanac of American Politics 1980* (New York: E.P. Dutton, 1979), pp. 455-458.

3 Quie gathered 830,000 votes to Perpich's 718,000. Perpich carried the Iron Range and Duluth and many northern and western rural counties but failed to carry Democratic Ramsey County and Hennepin County. *The Minnesota Legislative Manual 1979-1980*, pp. 488-89. *See also* Michael Barone, Grant Ujifusa, and Douglas Matthews, *Almanac of American Politics 1980* (New York: E.P. Dutton, 1979), pp. 455-458.

4 S.F. 50, H.F. 55, 1979 Minnesota Legislature. The bill followed a tortuous path, at one point being given up for dead. But Johnson and Battaglia were able to append it to a bill creating Tettegouche State Park, which the environmental community was not willing to jeopardize. See *St. Paul Pioneer Press*, Jan. 19, 1979, p. 14, "Advisory committee for BWCA approved"; *Minneapolis Tribune*, Jan. 19, 1979, p. 5B, "Senate panel supports committee to advise U.S. on BWCA rules"; *Minneapolis Tribune*, Feb. 16, 1979, p. 2B, "Committee approves bill on BWCA citizen's board"; *Minneapolis Star*, Feb. 16, 1979, Jim Klobuchar column, "The wilderness gets a new committee"; *Minneapolis Tribune*, Mar. 21, 1979, p. 2B, "BWCA battle returns to Senate"; *Minneapolis Tribune*, Apr. 27, 1979, p. 2B, "Legislators drop BWCA council plan"; *St. Paul Pioneer Press*, Apr. 27, 1979, p. 31, "Committee for BWCA blocked"; *St. Paul Pioneer Press*, May 20, 1979, Sec. 3, p. 4, "Citizens get 'watchdog' in parks bill deal"; *Ely Echo*, May 28, 1979, p. 1, "BWCA Advisory Bill Passes In Legislature"; *Ely Miner*, May 30, 1979, "BWCA advisory committee bill a political trade-off."

5 The Sierra Cub's legal chair, Steve Snyder, put together a team that would eventually expand to include some of the finest legal talent in the Twin Cities: Chuck Dayton and Jim Payne from the firm Dayton, Herman, Graham & Getts; Brian O'Neill, Reid Carron, Charles Bohlen, James Ray, Charles Ferrell, James E. Nicholson, Rebecca L. Rom, and Betsy Taylor from Faegre & Benson; Stephen J. Snyder and Dick Flint from Gray, Plant, and Mooty; David P. Pearson and Marcia Gelpe from William Mitchell Law School. A first year law student named Rip Rapson joined the team as a summer intern at both Gray Plant and Dayton, Herman, Graham, and Getts.

6 *Duluth News-Tribune*, July 14, 1979, p. 1A, "9 groups sue to end BWCA motor ban"; *Minneapolis Tribune*, July 14, 1979, p. 11A, "Suit to challenge BWCA law."

7 See *Ely-Winton Boundary Waters Conservation Alliance Newsletter*, March, 1979, p. 2.
　　　The Ely-Winton Chapter of the Alliance incorporated separately as the Ely-Winton Boundary Waters Conservation Alliance and became far more active on the challenge to the 1978 BWCA law than did the main Alliance. See *Ely-Winton Boundary*

Waters Conservation Alliance Newsletter, March, 1979, p. 1. The Ely-Winton Alliance became a plaintiff in the legal action; the main Alliance did not. The Ely-Winton Alliance even had to remind its members, following a fund appeal from the main Alliance in Duluth, that "it is our ELY-WINTON GROUP, ONLY, that is responsible for the current litigation and the funding of attorneys." See *Ely-Winton Boundary Waters Conservation Alliance Newsletter*, Sept. 20, 1979, p. 5, "E-W B.W.C.A., INC. IS NOT THE SAME AS B.W.C.A., INC."

8 See *BWCA Wilderness News*, Spring 1980, pp. 1-2, "Battle Mounts; 3rd Suit Filed!"; Kris Sigford, "Boundary Waters Canoe Area," *Sierra North Star*, July-Aug. 1989, p. 5.

9 *Duluth News-Tribune*, July 18, 1979, p. 1A, "Judge rejects bid to halt enforcing of new BWCA act"; *St. Paul Pioneer-Press*, July 18, 1979, p. 19, "BWCA act foes lose bid in court"; *Minneapolis Tribune*, July 18, 1979, p. 2B, "BWCA injunction request denied."

10 *Minneapolis Tribune*, July 26, 1979, p. 2B, "Court suit seeking injunction in BWCA case is withdrawn"; *Ely Echo*, July 30, 1979, p. 1, "BWCA Lawsuit Postponed." See also *Boundary Waters Conservation Alliance Newsletter*, July 27, 1979, p. 4.

11 *Minneapolis Tribune*, Aug. 7, 1979, p. 2B, "U.S. Magistrate to consider restraining order on BWCA." Ten environmental and civic organizations sought to intervene in the suit, which named as the defendant the United States Forest Service. The ten included the Friends of the Boundary Waters Wilderness, Sierra Club, League of Women Voters of Minnesota, Izaak Walton League of America, Minnesota Rovers, Wilderness Inquiry II, Minnesota Environmental Control Citizens Association, National Audubon Society Chapters in Minneapolis, St. Paul, and Duluth; Minnesota Ornithologists Union, and the Wilderness Society.

12 *Duluth News-Tribune*, August 8, 1979, p. 2A, "Judge rejects bid to overturn BWCA act"; *Minneapolis Tribune*, Aug. 8, 1979, p. 2B, "Judge denies BWCA act restraining order"; *St. Paul Pioneer-Press*, Aug. 8, 1979, p. 9, "Court denies bid to block BWCA Act."

13 For example, NAPO moved to amend their complaint on September 28. It contended that because the Forest Service had no official map of the new BWCA boundaries, the selection of lakes for motor restrictions and for resort buy-outs was arbitrary and capricious. Although the court would later indicate little sympathy for this argument, it served to tie up everyone's energy.

14 See *Duluth News-Tribune*, Sept. 11, 1979, p. 1A, "BWCA law's validity challenged in court." See also Charles K. Dayton Memorandum to Intervenors and other interested parties in Boundary Waters Canoe Area litigation, Aug. 20, 1979, pp. 1-2; Charles K. Dayton Memorandum to Intervenors and other interested parties in Boundary Waters Canoe Area litigation, Sept. 18, 1979, pp. 1-3; and *BWCA Wilderness News*, Autumn 1979, p. 1, "BWCAW Lawsuit."

Wallis fell somewhat short of oratorical distinction during the hearing. At one point he rose to characterize the Act with all the eloquence the Friends had come to expect of him: "Quite honestly, it stinks."

15 Charles K. Dayton Memorandum to Intervenors and other interested parties in Boundary Waters Canoe Area Wilderness litigation, Oct. 10, 1979, pp. 1-2; *NAPO v. U.S.*, 499 F. Supp. 1223 (1980) at 1230.

16 *Minneapolis Tribune*, Dec. 22, 1979, p. 7A, "State sues U.S. over BWCA jurisdiction"; *St. Paul Pioneer-Press*, Dec. 22, 1979, p. 6, "Minnesota sues U.S. over BWCA waters." For a discussion of the 1978 act's regulation of the state waters under the property clause (which concludes that this regulation is constitutional), see Eugene R. Gaetke, "The Boundary Waters Canoe Area Wilderness Act of 1978: Regulating Nonfederal Property Under the Property Clause," *Oregon Law Review*, Vol. 60 (1-2) (1981):157-83.

The state lawsuit had long been in the works. The Alliance had urged the state early on to initiate legal action. On February 8, for example, Wallis and Alliance members met with Governor Quie to urge that the state file suit. A week and a half later, Quie and Oberstar met with Attorney General Warren Spannaus to discuss the possibility of a state suit to recover jurisdiction of BWCA waters. The governor asked the attorney general to prepare a memo on the merits of the suit. *Minneapolis Tribune*, Feb. 20, 1979, p. 4A, "Oberstar, Quie consider suit over BWCA control."

The attorney general's memo was presented to DNR Commissioner Joseph Alexander near the end of March. It concluded that a state BWCA suit would have to rely on the same arguments that were rejected in a legally indistinguishable lawsuit dealing with federal jurisdiction over waters in Voyageurs National Park. See *U.S. v. Brown.* 552 F.2d 817 (8th Cir.), *cert. denied*, 431 U.S. 949 (1977).

Nevertheless, a few days later, Wallis spoke to a crowd of 250 Ely Alliance members, counseling that the best way to elicit action from the state would be to sue Quie, Spannaus, and Alexander for failing to challenge the constitutionality of the Boundary Waters law. *Ely Echo*, Apr. 9, 1979, p. 8, "State Ponders BWCA Water Suit." Two weeks later, in mid-April, the Minnesota Department of Natural Resources announced the state's intentions of initiating litigation over the BWCA, using the same losing arguments before the same judges as it had in *U.S. v. Brown. Minneapolis Tribune*, Apr. 12, 1979, p. 2B, "State sues to retain jurisdiction in BWCA." See also *St. Paul Dispatch*, Apr. 12, 1979, p. 31, "Alexander Says Suit Not Political"; *Minneapolis Tribune*, Dec. 18, 1979, p. 2B, "Quie appears to be headed for fight over BWCA."

17 A long two-part investigative article in the *Twin Cities Reader* lent credence to this theory. *Twin Cities Reader*, Mar. 11, 1981, pp. 6-8, "Al Quie's BWCA Lawsuit: Winning Isn't Everything . . . Re-election Is"; *Twin Cities Reader*, Mar. 19, 1981, pp. 4-5, 24, "Governor Quie's BWCA Lawsuit: Part Two." See also *BWCA Wilderness News*, January, 1980, p. 1, "State Files Suit Over BWCA!"; *Duluth News-Tribune*, Apr. 13, 1979, p. 12B, "BWCA lawsuit? No"; *Minneapolis Tribune*, Dec. 23, 1979, p. 4A, "The state's ill-considered BWCA lawsuit"; *St. Paul Pioneer Press*, Dec. 27, 1979, p. 6, "Politics and the BWCA."

18 *Duluth News-Tribune*, Jan. 19, 1980, p. 1, "BWCA law opponents file new suit citing environmental act"; *St. Paul Pioneer-Press*, Jan. 20, 1980, Sec. 3, p. 5, "N. Minnesota groups challenge BWCA law"; *Ely Echo*, Jan. 21, 1980, p. 1, "Lawyers File 2nd BWCA

Suit Contesting '78 Law"; BWCA Wilderness News (Friends of the Boundary Waters Wilderness), Spring 1980, p. 1, "Battle Mounts: 3rd Suit Filed!"

19 Minneapolis Tribune, Apr. 18, 1980, p. 2B, "Judge Lord takes over 3 BWCA lawsuits."

20 The mining arguments, in particular, caught Lord's attention. The state sought to portray its interest in regulating activity on the water surface as a way of safeguarding against mineral exploration. Lord responded: "I think it [the BWCA] will be mined by the time my great-grandchildren come along. In another 100 years or so, the environmentalists may lose the battle." O'Neill countered that the jurisdiction for purposes of mining would be jointly exercised by the state and federal governments: the more restrictive regulations would control. He pointed out that the state's argument was a red-herring—their real interest was in removing motorboat restrictions. State attorney Wayne Olson admitted that the DNR would lift motorboat restrictions on thirteen BWCA lakes if successful in the suit. Minneapolis Tribune, May 3, 1980, p. 6A, "State may ease BWCA motor limits"; St. Paul Pioneer Press-Dispatch, May 3, 1980, p. 20, "BWCA court battle turns to mining."
   The Alliance was miffed by this emphasis in the argument—they were interested in motorboating, not mineral exploration. Alliance member Betty Salerno noted after the hearing: "We are very concerned. Much of the time was spent arguing about protecting the BWCA from mining. No mining interests are involved. It was established by both parties that there should be no mining in the BWCA. We are baffled by all this." Ely Echo, May 5, 1980, p. 1, "BWCA Lawsuits Under Study By Federal Judge Miles Lord."

21 National Association of Property Owners v. United States, 499 F. Supp. 1223 (D. Minn. 1980).

22 Minneapolis Tribune, July 25, 1980, p. 1A, "Lord dismisses 3 BWCA lawsuits"; St. Paul Pioneer Press, July 25, 1980, p. 1, "Court backs federal rule in BWCA." See also BWCA Wilderness News, Autumn, 1980, p. 2, "Lord Upholds 1978 BWCA Wilderness Act."

23 St. Paul Pioneer Press, Aug. 20, 1980, p. 25, "Appeal filed to challenge BWCA ruling"; Minneapolis Tribune, Aug. 21, 1980, p. 3B, "State appeals BWCA ruling." See also BWCA Wilderness News, Winter, 1981, p. 2, "Legal Battle Continues in St. Louis"; and BWCA Wilderness News, Spring, 1981, p. 3, "BWCA Lawsuit Hearing Scheduled for Mid-June."

24 Minneapolis Tribune, June 19, 1981, p. 3B, "State asks court to void BWCA motor limits"; St. Paul Pioneer Press, June 19, 1981, p. 27, "Judges study BWCA case."

25 State of Minnesota v. United States, 660 F. 2d 1240 (8th Cir., 1981). See Duluth News-Tribune, October 1, 1981, p. 1A, "U.S. may limit motors in BWCA, court rules"; Minneapolis Tribune, October 1, 1981, p. 1B, "Court upholds BWCA curbs on snowmobiles, motorboats"; St. Paul Pioneer Press, Oct. 1, 1981, p. 1, "Court backs BWCA limit on motor use"; Des Moines Register, October 1, 1981, "Court upholds limits in wilderness area." See also BWCA Wilderness News, Oct. 1981, p. 1, "1978 BWCA Act Upheld."

26 See Minneapolis Tribune, Oct. 24, 1981, p. 10D, "State will appeal limits on motor use in BWCA"; St. Paul Pioneer Press, Oct. 24, 1981, p. 1, "State's rights feud pops up over BWCA"; BWCA Wilderness News, Dec., 1981, p. 5, "Minnesota To Appeal BWCA

Lawsuit To Supreme Court"; *St. Paul Pioneer Press*, Oct. 4, 1981, Focus Section, p. 2, "State should drop its BWCA suit."

27 The petition is formally called a writ of certiorari. Only one justice, Sandra Day O'Connor, voted to hear the case. *Minnesota v. Block*, 102 S. Ct. 1645 (1982); *Minneapolis Tribune*, March 9, 1982, p. 1A, "Court backs U.S. right to regulate BWCA use"; *St. Paul Pioneer-Press*, Mar. 9, 1982, p. 1, "Minnesota demands a say-so over BWCA." See also *BWCA Wilderness News*, March, 1982, p. 5, "BWCA Act Upheld by the U.S. Supreme Court!"

28 *Ely Echo*, Sept. 14, 1981, p. 6A, "BWCA: The Plan And The Law." The paper's recommended changes in the law all dealt with motor provisions, including supporting truck portages, opposing the snowmobile phase-out, and continuing motorboat use on La Croix, Basswood, and Farm Lakes.

29 Brian O'Neill and Charles Ferrell, "Briefing Paper: The Fallacies of 'Reform' of the BWCA Act," [1981], 12 pp. plus appendices, copy in possession of authors.

30 See *Duluth News-Tribune and Herald*, Mar. 26, 1983, p. 2A, "Panel favors BWCA changes"; *Cook County News Herald*, Mar. 31, 1983, p. 1, "Task force urges changes in BWCA"; *Ely Echo*, Apr. 11, 1983, p. 7A, "Changes Sought In BWCA Management." Similar to the *Ely Echo's* proposals of a year and a half earlier, the recommendations proposed removing motor restrictions on La Croix, ignoring the 1984 phase-out for Basswood Lake, lifting the motor ban on the North Kawishiwi River from Farm Lake east to the first portage, ignoring the 1984 snowmobile phase-out between Moose and Saganaga Lakes, excluding the Fowl Lakes from BWCA management, and excluding the Blankenberg Peninsula on Saganaga from the BWCA boundaries.

31 Bruce F. Vento to Morris K. Udall, April 27, 1983. See also Bruce F. Vento to Erika Sitz, April 27, 1983; copies in possession of the authors.

32 Border Lakes Tourism Task Force, "Recommended Amendments to P.L. 95-495, the Boundary Waters Canoe Area Wilderness Act," July 20, 1983. The amendments would have eliminated all the phase-outs and re-opened all of Saganaga and Lac La Croix to motorboat use, as well as re-opened permanently to motors Pine, North Kawishiwi, Clear, Little Gabbro, Gabbro, Bald Eagle, Iron, Bottle, Lake One, Little Knife, Ottertrack, and Little Loon Lakes, as well as the South Kawishiwi, Little Indian Sioux, and Bottle Rivers. The amendments would have also re-opened for snowmobile use all lakes open to motorboats in the summer. See Kevin Proescholdt, "Analysis of Amendments to P.L. 95-495 from Border Lakes Tourism Task Force dated July 20, 1983," Nov. 1, 1983; copies in possession of authors.

33 The meeting was with Carol Lee Baudler of Sierra, Nelson French of Sierra's Project Environment, and Kevin Proescholdt of the Minnesota Audubon Council. Memo from Baudler, French, and Proescholdt to Sierra Club, Minnesota Audubon Council, and Izaak Walton League of America, Nov. 1, 1983; Memo from Baudler, French, and Proescholdt to BWCA Activists, Nov. 1, 1983. Copies in possession of the authors.

34 *Minneapolis Tribune*, Nov. 6, 1983, p. 21A, "Canada says motorboat ban violates treaties"; *Duluth News-Tribune*, Nov. 6, 1983, "Ban on motorboats in border waters illegal, says Canada"; *Ely Echo*, Nov. 7, 1983, p. 1, "Canadian Government Holds BWCA Law Not Valid."

35 *Minneapolis Star and Tribune*, Nov. 8, 1983, p. 3B, "BWCA motor ban opinion not official."

36 Morris Udall, John Sieberling, and Bruce Vento to Allan Gotlieb, Nov. 21, 1983; Gotlieb to Udall, Jan. 9, 1984. Copies in possession of authors.

37 Memo from Kevin Proescholdt to BWCA Activists, Jan. 24, 1984. Copy in possession of authors.

38 The proposal had been promoted as early as April 1983, when the Forest Service sponsored an Ely meeting involving environmentalists, outfitters, snowmobile groups, the DNR, and the Forest Service to discuss the upcoming motor phase-outs. The Ely outfitters requested a change in policy to permit possession of motors on nonmotorized routes. Clay Beal to Miron Heinselman, Apr. 6, 1983; Memo from Brian B. O'Neill to Stephen J. Snyder and John E. Grzybek, May 2, 1983. Copies in possession of authors.

39 Superior National Forest News Release, Jan. 25, 1984; *Minneapolis Star and Tribune*, Feb. 1, 1984, p. 2D, "BWCA motor possession rule may be eased."

40 Minnesota Audubon Council Action Alert, Jan. 27, 1984; Bruce F. Vento to Clay Beal, Feb. 7, 1984; Kevin Proescholdt to Clay Beal, Feb. 10, 1984; Bruce F. Vento to Kevin Proescholdt, Feb. 14, 1984; Charles K. Dayton to Clay Beal, Feb. 22, 1984; Erika Sitz to Clay Beal, Feb. 23, 1984. Copies in possession of authors.

41 Superior National Forest News Release, Mar. 27, 1984; *Minneapolis Star and Tribune*, Mar. 31, 1984, p. 8B, "Motor ban in BWCA includes possession"; *Ely Echo*, Apr. 2, 1984, p. 1, "Motors Not Allowed in BWCA Closed Areas"; *Cook County News-Herald*, Apr. 5, 1984, p. 5, "Forest Service Says No To Motors."

42 S.F. 1527 and H.F. 1657, 1985 Minnesota Legislature, May 6, 1985.

43 Douglas Johnson *et al* to President Ronald Reagan, May 8, 1985; *Minneapolis Star and Tribune*, May 19, 1985, p. 4A, "Lawmakers urge Reagan to lift ban on motorboats." The letter requested that the president "take immediate action to ensure that all water crossings between the United States and Canada by mechanically propelled watercraft be allowed and to remedy the harm caused by the restrictions which have been put into place and are contrary to the rights guaranteed by international treaty."

44 The letter played to unfavorable press reviews. See, for example, *Princeton Union-Eagle*, May 23, 1985, "Boundary Waters Canoe Area Alert"; *Red Wing Republican Eagle*, "BWCA/Wilderness protection is threatened by a fraudulent petition"; *St. Paul Pioneer Press Dispatch*, May 31, 1985, p. 12A, "Keep motorboat ban." The Friends wrote the Minnesota congressional delegation warning them about the resolution. Kevin Proescholdt to Rudy Boschwitz, May 25, 1985; Kevin Proescholdt to Bruce Vento, May

25, 1985; Dave Durenberger to Kevin Proescholdt, May 31, 1985. Copies in possession of authors.

45 R. Max Peterson to Douglas Johnson, Aug. 21, 1985; *Minneapolis Star and Tribune,* Aug. 24, 1985, p. 1B, "Reagan administration refuses to lift ban on motorboats in BWCA."

46 Dave Durenberger News Release, June 30, 1985; "An Assessment of U.S.-Canadian Boundary Waters Issues Along the Minnesota-Ontario Border," Donald D. Parmeter, May 16, 1985.

47 Ford M. Robbins to Dave Durenberger, Aug. 15, 1985; Herbert C. Johnson to Dave Durenberger, August 21, 1985.

48 Opening Remarks by Senator Dave Durenberger on the Border Waters International Commission, Subcommittee on Intergovernmental Relations, International Falls, Minnesota, August 23, 1985, p. 2. Copies in possession of authors.

49 *The Daily Journal* (International Falls), Aug. 26, 1985, p. 1, "Senator proposes border commission"; *Minneapolis Star and Tribune,* Aug. 24, 1985, p. 1B, "Reagan administration refuses to lift ban on motorboats in BWCA"; *Cook County News-Herald,* Sept. 19, 1985, p. 2, "Beyond the Breakwall."

50 *See* USDA Forest Service, "Plan to Implement the Boundary Waters Canoe Area Wilderness Act (Public Law 95-495)," Oct. 27, 1981.
  The Forest Service was also required to produce management plans for all national forests in the country, including the entire Superior National Forest, under the 1976 National Forest Management Act.

51 Kevin Proescholdt, *After the Shouting Stopped: Implementation of the Boundary Waters Canoe Area Wilderness Act,* (Minnesota Audubon Council: 1984), 155 pp.

52 *Ibid.* See also Proescholdt, "Implementing Environmental Legislation: the Boundary Waters Canoe Area Wilderness Act (Public Law 95-495)," *William Mitchell Environmental Law Journal* III (1985):1-41; Proescholdt, "Boundary Waters: More Obstacles for a Troubled Law," *Sierra* (July/Aug. 1984):18-21; and Proescholdt, "BWCA: The Embattled Wilderness," *American Forests* (July/Aug. 1989):28-33, 78.

53 A draft plan had been released for public comment in late 1984, and the Friends had helped solicit reactions to it from the environmental community. See Proposed Land and Resource Management Plan and Draft Environmental Impact Statement, Superior National Forest, November 24, 1984. See also *BWCA Wilderness News,* Winter 1985, pp. 1-2, "Superior National Forest Plan: Public Comments Needed."

54 Land and Resource Management Plan, Final Environmental Impact Statement, and Record of Decision, Superior National Forest, June 6, 1986. See also Kevin Proescholdt (for Friends of the Boundary Waters Wilderness) to Clay Beal, Mar. 14, 1985, 14 pp., and *BWCA Wilderness News,* Winter, 1985, pp. 1-2, "Superior National Forest Plan."

55 The Friends of the Boundary Waters Wilderness, the Sierra Club, Defenders of Wildlife, and the Wilderness Society.

56 Governed by detailed Forest Service administrative rules, the appeal was handled by Brian O'Neill, Rob Crawford, and Rick Duncan of the Faegre and Benson office. See administrative record of Forest Service Appeal No. 1628, especially appellants' Statement of Reasons, August 27, 1986; Forest Service's Responsive Statement, Feb. 5, 1987; appellants' Reply, Mar. 2, 1987. See also BWCA *Wilderness News*, Autumn 1986, pp. 1-3, "Friends Appeal Forest Plan."

57 The other issues raised by the appeal were:
    1. Prohibiting the use of pesticides inside the wilderness;
    2. Preventing an increase in road densities outside the wilderness—creating more roads in the habitat of the federally protected eastern timber wolf increases wolf mortality;
    3. Protecting and studying potential wild and scenic rivers outside the BWCA;
    4. Halting the practice of offering timber sales outside the BWCA to private interests at prices below the true cost to the Forest Service;
    5. Requiring the Forest Service to devise a minerals acquisition program;
    6. Barring the Forest Service from leasing resorts it had purchased under the act's authority back to commercial operators;
    7. Requiring the Forest Service to look at an area in the Homer/Brule region as a potential addition to the wilderness; and
    8. Reintroducing woodland caribou to the BWCAW.
Ibid.

58 See Transcript of Proceedings in Re: Appeal of Decision, Final Land and Resource Management Plan and Environmental Impact Statement for the Superior National Forest, Appeal No. 1628, by Sierra Club, Friends of the Boundary Waters Wilderness, Defenders of Wildlife, and the Wilderness Society, Hearing before the chief of the Forest Service, Dec. 16, 1987. See also BWCA *Wilderness News*, Winter 1988, pp. 1-3, "Superior Plan Appeal Continues: Six Issues Settled."

59 In addition the Forest Service agreed to protect and study six rivers as potential wild and scenic rivers, and to adopt a precedent-setting road density standard for Superior National Forest to protect the wolf population. See the following signed Statements of Agreement: for Issues II (Dams), III (Isabella River Road), VI (Wild and Scenic Rivers), VIII (Caribou), IX (Pesticides), and XII (Minerals), Feb. 8, 1988; for Issue VI (Wild and Scenic Rivers), Feb. 8, 1988; for Issue V (C & D) (Echo Trail Land Classification), Mar. 4, 1988; Issue XI (BWCA Visitor Use), Mar. 4, 1988; and Issue VII (Road Density), Mar. 4, 1988. See also BWCA *Wilderness News*, Spring/Summer 1988, p.4, "Forest Plan Appeal Awaits Chief's Decision"; BWCA *Wilderness News*, Autumn 1988, p. 5, "Friends' Forest Plan Appeal Protects Six Rivers!"; *Minneapolis Star Tribune*, Mar. 5, 1988, p. 3B, "Accord makes forest safer for wolves." See also Decision Notice and Forest Plan Amendments, Appeal #1628 and Appeal #1672, Superior National Forest, Sept. 27, 1988.

60 See Kevin Proescholdt's Affidavit Re: Motorized Portages within the Boundary Waters Canoe Area Wilderness, Aug. 1, 1986, and accompanying appendices documenting the use of portage wheels on May 28-29, 1986; see also videotape submitted as part of the administrative record in Appeal No. 1628 at Appellants Statement of Reasons, Appendix 1, p. 29.

61 David G. Unger to Brian B. O'Neill, March 10, 1989, (13 pp.), pp. 4-6. See also *Minneapolis Star Tribune*, Mar. 17, 1989, p. 6B, "2 portages in BWCA will be closed this summer for a watercraft study."

62 Unger ordered the two portages closed because the Forest Service, in its half-hearted 1981 attempt, only tried to cross Prairie Portage with portage wheels.

63 *Ely Echo*, Mar. 20, 1989, p. 1, "Closed portages not yet closed as first reported"; *Duluth News-Tribune*, Apr. 12, 1989, p. 1A, "Motorized portage battle travels to nation's capital"; *Duluth News-Tribune*, Apr. 13, 1989, p. 5A, "U.S. to rule on BWCA portages"; *St. Paul Pioneer Press Dispatch*, Apr. 13, 1989, p. 5D, "Ely portage ruling near"; *Ely Echo*, Apr. 17, 1989, p. 3, "Area leaders heartened by USFS meeting in Washington." See also David G. Unger to Brian B. O'Neill, Apr. 20, 1989.

64 *Minneapolis Star Tribune*, Apr. 21, 1989, p. 7B, "Two truck portages in BWCA will stay in use this summer"; *Duluth News-Tribune*, June 24, 1989, p. 8C, "Truck portages should be closed," (guest editorial by Kevin Proescholdt).

65 *Mesabi Daily News*, July 12, 1989, p. 1, "Portage tests produce mixed results at Trout Lake"; *Duluth News-Tribune*, July 12, 1989, "BWCA portage testing moves along"; *Ely Echo*, July 17, 1989, p. 1, "Prairie Portage test made with portage wheels"; *Duluth News-Tribune*, July 19, 1989, p. 2A, "Forest Service conducts BWCA portage tests"; *Ely Echo*, July 24, 1989, "Four-mile portage test not a tiptoe through the tulips." See also USDA Forest Service, Superior National Forest, "The Portage Report," Sept. 1989, 23 pp. and appendices.

66 USDA Forest Service, Superior National Forest, "The Portage Report," Sept. 1989. The Forest Service apparently forgot that there had been regulations on its own books for a quarter century authorizing the use of portage wheels.

67 *Ibid.*

68 F. Dale Robertson to Regional Forester, R-9, "Determination of Nonfeasibility—BWCA," Oct. 11, 1989; *Duluth News-Tribune*, Oct. 12, 1989, p. 1A, "Forest Service decides to keep portages in BWCA open"; *Minneapolis Star Tribune*, Oct. 12, 1989, p. 1B, "Forest Service allows 'motorized portages' in BWCA"; *St. Paul Pioneer Press Dispatch*, Oct. 12, 1989, p. 1B, "Boundary Waters portages to stay"; *Ely Echo*, Oct. 16, 1989, p. 1, "Motor portages stay open . . . at least for now." See also *BWCA Wilderness News*, Autumn 1989, pp. 1-3, "Forest Service Chief Keeps Truck Portages Open: Friends Announce Lawsuit to Enforce BWCA Law."

69 The other plaintiffs included Sierra Club, Wilderness Society, Defenders of Wildlife, Wilderness Watch, Wilderness Inquiry, Minnesota Public Interest Research Group, and

Izaak Walton League of America. See *Friends of the Boundary Waters Wilderness v. Robertson* Civ. No. 4-90-8 (D. Minn. 1990).

70 *Friends of the Boundary Waters Wilderness v. Robertson*, 770 F.Supp 1386 (D. Minn. 1991).

71 *Friends of the Boundary Waters Wilderness v. Robertson*, 978 F.2d 1484 (8th Cir. 1992). See *BWCA Wilderness News*, Autumn 1991, p. 4, "Friends Appeal Truck Portage Decision"; *BWCA Wilderness News*, Spring/Summer 1992, p. 3, "Appeals Court Hears Truck Portage Case"; *Duluth News-Tribune*, Nov. 7, 1992, p. 1A, "Portages in BWCA can't be motorized"; *Minneapolis Star Tribune*, Nov. 7, 1992, p. 1B, "Appeals court ruling bans motor vehicles from three BWCA portages"; *St. Paul Pioneer Press*, Nov. 7, 1992, p. 1E, "Court bans BWCA motor portages"; *Ely Echo*, Nov. 9, 1992, p. 1, "Decision on truck portages reversed"; *BWCA Wilderness News*, Winter 1993, p. 3, "U.S. Appeals Court Closes Truck Portages!"; and *BWCA Wilderness News*, Spring/Summer 1993, p. 1, "Ely Area Fights Truck Portage Closure."

72 See *Duluth News-Tribune*, June 15, 1993, p. 1, "Truck portages in BWCA will stay closed"; *Minneapolis Star Tribune*, June 15, 1993, p. 1B, "Decision on BWCA pleases environmentalists: Appeal to reopen truck portages declined"; *St. Paul Pioneer Press*, June 15, 1993, p. 1B, "Supreme Court upholds motorized portage ban"; *BWCA Wilderness News*, Autumn 1993, p. 3, "U.S. Supreme Court Denies Appeal to Re-Open Truck Portages!"

73 The number of flights in Snoopy MOA increased from 153 flights in 1983 to 1,425 in 1986. See *BWCA Wilderness News*, Winter 1987, pp. 1-2, "Military Aircraft Threaten Wilderness Airspace" and *BWCA Wilderness News*, Autumn 1987, pp. 1-2, "Wilderness Airspace Battles Continue."

74 *Friends of the Boundary Waters Wilderness, et al. v. Temple et al.*, Civil No. 3-88-423. The other environmental plaintiffs on the suit included the Izaak Walton League of America, Sierra Club, Wilderness Society, Help Our Wolves Live, and Friends of Animals and Their Environment.

75 See *BWCA Wilderness News*, Autumn 1988, pp. 1-2, "Friends Sue Over Jet Flights!"; *BWCA Wilderness News*, Spring/Summer 1989, pp. 1-2, "BWCA Military Overflights Trial Begins"; *Duluth News-Tribune*, Apr. 13, 1989, p. 1A, "Environmentalists taking jets to court"; *Minneapolis Star Tribune*, Apr. 15, 1989, p. 4B, "U.S. Forest Service backs lawsuit on flights over wilderness area"; *Duluth News-Tribune*, Apr. 15, 1989, p. 1A, "Military, environmentalists spar over flights in BWCA"; *Duluth News-Tribune*, June 9, 1989, p. 1A, "Guard to cease BWCA flights with agreement." The military continues to fly over other parts of northeastern Minnesota.

76 The law provides for an acid deposition standard of eleven kilograms per hectare per year and an acid deposition control plan for the state.

Unfortunately, the majority of the acid rain falling in Minnesota comes from sources outside the state. After eight years of opposition from the Reagan Administration and years of wrangling in the U.S. Congress, the United States House and Senate finally re-authorized the federal Clean Air Act in the fall of 1990, which included an extremely technical section on acid rain control. These provisions will require a ten-million-ton reduction in sulphur dioxide and a two-million-ton reduction in nitrous oxides, the principal precursors to acid rain.

The Friends had begun work on acid rain as early as 1977, when they asked Fraser and Oberstar to contact the U.S. State Department about plans to build an 800-megawatt coal-burning power plant—with no scrubbers—in Atikokan, Ontario, at the north edge of Quetico Provincial Park.

The Friends played a large role in pushing the issue of acid rain to the forefront of the national environmental agenda, sponsoring international conferences on acid rain, creating a professionally-produced acid rain slide-tape show which was sold around the nation, becoming involved in Minnesota state rulemaking, and providing early leadership to the National Clean Air Coalition. See generally Minnesota Acid Deposition Control Act, Laws of Minnesota 1982, Chapter 482, and Minnesota Statutes, Secs. 116.42-45; In the Matter of the Proposed Adoption of Minnesota Rules Parts 7005.4010-7005.4050 Relating to an Acid Deposition Standard and Control Plan, Minnesota Pollution Control Agency, Statement of Need and Reasonableness (1985) and Report of the Administrative Law Judge (June 27, 1986); 1990 Clean Air Act Amendments, Report 101-952, House of Representatives. For examples of the Friends articles on acid rain, see *Friends of the Boundary Waters Wilderness Newsletter*, Oct. 1978, p. 7, "The Future"; *Wilderness News*, May 1979, pp. 2-4, "Acid Rain Threatens Quetico and BWCA"; *BWCA Wilderness News*, Autumn 1980, p. 10, "Acid Rain Battle Comes Home to Minnesota"; *BWCA Wilderness News*, March 1982, pp. 8-9, "BWCA Lakes Showing Signs of Acidification," and p. 10, "APC-1 Hearings Closed—FOBWW Recommending Tighter Standards"; *BWCA Wilderness News*, Winter 1985, p. 3, "Minnesota Acid Rain Hearings: Will We Protect BWCA Lakes?"; Carol Garland, "MPCA Proposes Acid Rain Standard: Hearings Delayed Again Until January," *BWCA Wilderness News*, Autumn 1985, p. 3; Nelson French, "Acid Rain and Fish Mercury," *BWCA Wilderness News*, Autumn 1985, pp. 4-5; *BWCA Wilderness News*, Winter 1986, pp. 1-2, "Minnesota Acid Rain Hearings Finally Begin"; *BWCA Wilderness News*, Spring 1986, pp. 1-2, "The Acid Rain Front"; *BWCA Wilderness News*, Autumn 1986, pp. 6-7, "Minnesota Adopts Acid Rain Program"; Marilynne Roberts, "Acid Rain and West Germany's Waldsterben,"*BWCA Wilderness News*, Autumn 1987, p. 4; Carol Garland, "Dealing with Acid Rain: The Clean Air Act is Not Enough; State Action Provides a Temporary Umbrella," *BWCA Wilderness News*, Winter 1988, pp. 4-5.

77 See Minnesota Pollution Control Agency, "Assessment of Mercury Contamination in Selected Minnesota Lakes and Streams," December 1989; Minnesota Department of Health, "Minnesota Fish Consumption Advisory," May, 1989; Edward B. Swain and Daniel D. Helwig, "Mercury in Fish from Northeastern Minnesota Lakes: Historical Trends, Environmental Correlates, and Potential Sources," *Journal of the Minnesota Academy of Science*, Vol. 55, No. 1, 1989, pp. 103-109.

78 See *BWCA Wilderness News*, Autumn 1990, p. 7, "Passage of Clean Air Act Vital to Curbing Mercury"; 1990 Clean Air Act Amendments, Report 101-952, House of Representatives.

79 Superior National Forest, "1978 Boundary Waters Canoe Area Visitor Use Estimates," Aug. 1979, Tables 1-4; and Superior National Forest, "BWCA Wilderness Overnight Use Estimates—1993," p. 1.

80 Because of variations through the years in the keeping of visitor statistics, the Forest Service believes that the figures for overnight groups offer the best comparison from year to year for visitor use. See Superior National Forest, "BWCA Wilderness Overnight Use Estimates—1993," p. 1.

81 See, for example, BWCA Wilderness News, Spring/Summer 1990, pp. 1-2, "Wilderness Visitor Impacts: Are We Loving the BWCA to Death?"; "Visitor Use in the Boundary Waters Canoe Area (BWCA) Wilderness," a policy paper by the Friends of the Boundary Waters Wilderness, July 1992, 40 pp.

82 USDA Forest Service, Proposed BWCA Wilderness Management Plan and Implementation Schedule, and Draft Environmental Impact Statement, Nov. 1992; USDA Forest Service, BWCA Wilderness Management Plan and Implementation Schedule, and Final Environmental Impact Statement, Aug. 1993. The Friends of the Boundary Waters Wilderness produced a forty-page policy paper on visitor-use issues in the BWCA Wilderness and presented it to the Forest Service prior to the release of the draft plan. Friends of the Boundary Waters Wilderness, "Visitor Use in the Boundary Waters Canoe Area (BWCA) Wilderness," July 1992. See also BWCA Wilderness News, Autumn 1992, pp. 1-2, "Forest Service to Write New BWCA Plan"; BWCA Wilderness News, Winter 1993, pp. 1-2, "Intense Opposition Raised to Wilderness Protections in Proposed BWCA Plan!"; BWCA Wilderness News, Autumn 1993, pp. 1-2, "Final BWCAW Management Plan Released."

83 County of St. Louis et al. v. Jack Ward Thomas et al., United States District Court, District of Minnesota, Fifth Division, Civil No. 5-94-154. Friends of the Boundary Waters Wilderness et al. v. Jack Ward Thomas et al., United States District Court, District of Minnesota, Fifth Division, Civil No. 5-95-10. See also BWCA Wilderness News, Winter 1995, pp. 1-2, "Lawsuits Filed on BWCA Management Plan"; Minneapolis Star Tribune, Dec. 7, 1994, p. 3B, "Three Counties sue over BWCA Plan"; and Minneapolis Star Tribune, Jan. 18, 1995, p. 4B, "Forest Service Sued over Motorboat Use in BWCA."

84 Indeed, as this book goes to press, Congressman Jim Oberstar, Doug Johnson, Bob Lessard, and others from northern Minnesota have convinced U.S. Senator Rod Grams to hold congressional field hearings on their proposals to roll-back federal protections for both Voyageurs National Park and the BWCA Wilderness. See BWCA Wilderness News, Spring/Summer 1995, pp. 1-3, "BWCA and Voyageurs Face Attack!"; Press release from Sen. Rod Grams, June 9, 1995; Minneapolis Star Tribune, July 15, 1995 p. 3B, "Twin Cities hearing agreed to on Voyageurs use"; Ely Echo, Apr. 10, 1995, p. 1, "State DFL legislators ask for new legislation on BWCAW, Voyageurs."

85 Duluth News-Tribune, June 8, 1977, "Environmental pioneer dies"; Minneapolis Star and Tribune, Sept. 12, 1983, p. 13A, "'Ober.'"

86 *Minneapolis Tribune*, Jan. 14, 1982, p. 3B, "Wilderness advocate Sigurd Olson dies at 82"; *St. Paul Pioneer Press*, Jan. 14, 1982, p. 1, "Wilderness writer Sigurd Olson dies"; *Minneapolis Star*, Jan. 14, 1982, p. 1A, "Silence of the forest pays tribute to Olson"; *St. Paul Dispatch*, Jan. 14, 1982, p. 1C, "Olson dies in beloved wilderness."

87 *BWCA Wilderness News*, Fall 1982, pp. 4-5, "Save the North."

88 *Minneapolis Star Tribune*, Mar. 1, 1993, p. 4B, "Forest Service ecologist Miron Heinselman dies." See also the four articles about Bud in *BWCA Wilderness News*, Spring/Summer 1993: Kevin Proescholdt, "Bud Heinselman: Champion of the Boundary Waters Wilderness," pp. 4-5; Bruce Vento, "In Memory of Bud Heinselman," p. 6; John Pastor, "Bud Heinselman, Ecologist and Scientist," p. 6; and Chuck Dayton, "Completing Bud Heinselman's Dream," p. 7.

Appendix

The Legislative Chronology of the
Boundary Waters Canoe Area Wilderness Act

1. October 20, 1975, Oberstar Bill #1, H.R. 10247, 94th Congress, 1st Session.

2. June 28, 1976, Fraser Bill #1, H.R. 14576, 94th Congress, 2nd Session.

3. February 1, 1977, Fraser Bill #2, H.R. 2820, 95th Congress, 1st Session.

4. April 4, 1977, Oberstar Bill #2, H.R. 5968, 95th Congress, 1st Session.

5. June 24, 1977, Clark Bill, S. 1769, 95th Congress, 1st Session.

6. July 7-8, 1977, House Subcommittee Field Hearings, St. Paul and Ely.

7. August 3, 1977, Oberstar Bill #3, H.R. 8722, 95th Congress, 1st Session.

8. August 4, 1977, House Subcommittee Hearings, Washington, D.C.

9. September 12-13, 1977, House Subcommittee Hearings, Washington, D.C.

10. September 13, 1977, Administration Proposed Substitute Bill.

11. March 16, 1978, Burton-Vento Subcommittee Draft Bill.

12. April 20, 1978, Burton-Vento Committee Bill, H.R. 12250, 95th Congress, 2nd Session.

13. May 4, 1978, House Report 95-1117, Part 1.

14. May 8, 1978, Oberstar Bill #4, H.R. 12609, 95th Congress, 2nd Session.

15. June 5, 1978, House Passage.

16. June 23, 1978, Anderson-Humphrey Bill, S. 3242, 95th Congress, 2nd Session.

17. July 16-17, 1978, Senate BWCA Tour.

18. July 27-30, 1978, Dayton-Walls Compromise Negotiations.

19. August 17, 1978, Senate Subcommittee Hearings, Washington, D.C.

20. October 3, 1978, Senate Committee Markup and Passage.

21. October 4, 1978, Anderson Amended Bill, H.R. 12250, 95th Congress, 2nd Session; Senate Report 95-1274.

22. October 9, 1978, Senate Passage.

23. October 13, 1978, Conference Committee Passage. House Report 95-1770, Senate Report 95-1327.

24. October 15, 1978, Final Passage in House and Senate.

25. October 21, 1978, Enactment by President Carter.

Public Law 95-495
95th Congress

An Act

To designate the Boundary Waters Canoe Area Wilderness, to establish the Boundary Waters Canoe Area Mining Protection Area, and for other purposes.

Oct. 21, 1978
[H.R. 12250]

Be it enacted by the Senate and House of Representatives of the United States of America in Congress assembled,

Boundary Waters Canoe Area Wilderness, designation; Boundary Waters Canoe Area Mining Protection Area, establishment.

FINDINGS

SECTION 1. The Congress finds that it is necessary and desirable to provide for the protection, enhancement, and preservation of the natural values of the lakes, waterways, and associated forested areas known (before the date of enactment of this Act) as the Boundary Waters Canoe Area, and for the orderly management of public use and enjoyment of that area as wilderness, and of certain contiguous lands and waters, while at the same time protecting the special qualities of the area as a natural forest-lakeland wilderness ecosystem of major esthetic, cultural, scientific, recreational and educational value to the Nation.

PURPOSES

SEC. 2. It is the purpose of this Act to provide for such measures respecting the areas designated by this Act as the Boundary Waters Canoe Area Wilderness and Boundary Waters Canoe Area Mining Protection Area as will—

(1) provide for the protection and management of the fish and wildlife of the wilderness so as to enhance public enjoyment and appreciation of the unique biotic resources of the region,

(2) protect and enhance the natural values and environmental quality of the lakes, streams, shorelines and associated forest areas of the wilderness,

(3) maintain high water quality in such areas,

(4) minimize to the maximum extent possible, the environmental impacts associated with mineral development affecting such areas,

(5) prevent further road and commercial development and restore natural conditions to existing temporary roads in the wilderness, and

(6) provide for the orderly and equitable transition from motorized recreational uses to nonmotorized recreational uses on those lakes, streams, and portages in the wilderness where such mechanized uses are to be phased out under the provisions of this Act.

BOUNDARY WATERS CANOE AREA WILDERNESS DESIGNATION AND MAP

SEC. 3. The areas generally depicted as wilderness on the map entitled "Boundary Waters Canoe Area Wilderness and Boundary Waters Canoe Area Mining Protection Area" dated September 1978, comprising approximately one million and seventy-five thousand five hundred acres, are hereby designated as the Boundary Waters Canoe Area Wilderness (hereinafter referred to as the "wilderness"). Such designation shall supersede the designation of the Boundary Waters Canoe

16 USC 1132 note.

16 USC 1132.

Publication in
Federal Register.

Filing with
congressional
committees.

Area under section 3(a) of the Wilderness Act (78 Stat. 890) and such map shall supersede the map on file pursuant to such section. The map of the wilderness shall be on file and available for public inspection in the offices of the Supervisor of the Superior National Forest and of the Chief, United States Forest Service. The Secretary of Agriculture, hereinafter referred to as "The Secretary," shall, as soon as practicable but in no event later than one year after the date of enactment of this Act, publish a detailed legal description and map showing the boundaries of the wilderness in the Federal Register. Such map and description shall be filed with the Committee on Interior and Insular Affairs of the House of Representatives and the Committee on Energy and Natural Resources of the United States Senate. Such map and description shall have the same force and effect as if included in this Act. Correction of clerical and typographical errors in such legal description and map may be made.

ADMINISTRATION

SEC. 4. (a) The Secretary shall administer the wilderness under the provisions of this Act, the Act of January 3, 1975 (88 Stat. 2096; 16 U.S.C. 1132 note), the Wilderness Act of 1964 (78 Stat. 890, 16 U.S.C. 1131–1136), and in accordance with other laws, rules and regulations generally applicable to areas designated as wilderness.

Repeal.
16 USC 1133.

(b) Paragraph (5) of section 4(d) of the Wilderness Act of 1964 is hereby repealed and paragraphs (6), (7), and (8) of such section 4(d) are hereby redesignated as paragraphs (5), (6), and (7).

Motorboat use.

(c) Effective on January 1, 1979 the use of motorboats is prohibited within the wilderness designated by this Act, and that portion within the wilderness of all lakes which are partly within the wilderness, except for the following:

(1) On the following lakes, motorboats with motors of no greater than twenty-five horsepower shall be permitted: Fall, Lake County; Newton, Lake County; Moose, Lake County; Newfound, Lake County; Sucker, Lake County; Snowbank, Lake County; East Bearskin, Cook County; South Farm, Lake County; Trout, Saint Louis County; Basswood, except that portion generally north of the narrows at the north end of Jackfish Bay and north of a point on the international boundary between Ottawa Island and Washington Island; Saganaga, Cook County, except for that portion west of American Point; *Provided:* That, on the following lakes, until January 1, 1984, the horsepower limitations described in this paragraph shall not apply to towboats registered with the Secretary: Moose, Lake County: Newfound, Lake County; Sucker, Lake County; Saganaga, Cook County, as limited in this paragraph.

(2) On the following lakes and river, motorboats with motors no greater than ten horsepower shall be permitted: Clearwater, Cook County; North Fowl, Cook County; South Fowl, Cook County; Island River east of Lake Isabella, Lake County; Sea Gull, that portion generally east of Threemile Island, Cook County; Alder, Cook County; Canoe, Cook County.

(3) On the following lakes, or specified portions of lakes, motorboats with motors of no greater than ten horsepower shall be permitted until the dates specified: Basswood River to and including Crooked Lake, Saint Louis and Lake Counties, until January 1, 1984; Carp Lake, the Knife River, and Knife Lake, Lake County, until January 1, 1984; Sea Gull, Cook County, that portion generally west of Threemile Island, until January 1, 1999; Brule,

Cook County, until January 1, 1994, or until the termination of operation of any resort adjacent to Brule Lake in operation as of 1977, whichever occurs first.

(4) On the following lakes, or specified portions of lakes, motorboats with motors of no greater than twenty-five horse-power shall be permitted until January 1, 1984: Birch, Lake County; Basswood, Lake County, that portion generally north of the narrows at the north end of Jackfish Bay and north of a point on the international boundary between Ottawa Island and Washington Island.

(d) The detailed legal description and map to be published pursuant to section 3 of this Act shall contain a description of the various areas where the motorized uses permitted by this section are located. No provision of this section shall be construed to limit mechanical portages or the horsepower of motors used on motorboats in the following areas within the wilderness: **Exemptions.**

Little Vermilion Lake, Saint Louis County; Loon River, Saint Louis County; Loon Lake, Saint Louis County; that portion of the Lac La Croix, Saint Louis County, south of Snow Bay and east of Wilkins Bay.

(e) For the purposes of this Act, a snowmobile is defined as any **Snowmobile use.** motorized vehicle which is designed to operate on snow or ice. The use of snowmobiles in the wilderness designated by this Act is not permitted except that the Secretary may permit snowmobiles, not exceeding forty inches in width, on (1) the overland portages from Crane Lake to Little Vermilion Lake in Canada, and from Sea Gull River along the eastern portion of Saganaga Lake to Canada, and (2) on the following routes until January 1, 1984:

Vermilion Lake portage to and including Trout Lake; Moose Lake to and including Saganaga Lake via Ensign, Vera and Knife Lakes, East Bearskin Lake to and including Pine Lake via Alder Lake and Canoe Lake.

In addition to the routes listed above, the Secretary may issue special **Trail grooming,** use permits for the grooming by snowmobiles of specified cross- **special permits.** country ski trails for day use near existing resorts.

(f) The Secretary is directed to develop and implement, as soon **Motorboat use,** as practical, entry point quotas for use of motorboats within the **entry point** wilderness portions of the lakes listed in subsection c, the quota levels **quotas.** to be based on such criteria as the size and configuration of each lake, and the amount of use on that lake: *Provided,* That the quota established for any one year shall not exceed the average actual annual motorboat use of the calendar years 1976, 1977, and 1978 for each lake, and shall take into account the fluctuation in use during different times of the year: *Provided further,* That on each lake homeowners and their guests and resort owners and their guests on that particular lake shall have access to that particular lake and their entry shall not be counted in determining such use.

(g) Nothing in this Act shall be deemed to require the termina- **Boat portages,** tion of the existing operation of motor vehicles to assist in the trans- **motorized** port of boats across the portages from Sucker Lake to Basswood Lake, **assistance.** from Fall Lake to Basswood Lake, and from Lake Vermilion to Trout Lake, during the period ending January 1, 1984. Following said date, unless the Secretary determines that there is no feasible nonmotorized means of transporting boats across the portages to reach the lakes previously served by the portages listed above, he shall terminate all such motorized use of each portage listed above.

Motorized craft, authorizations.

Additional standards and criteria.

(h) The motorized uses authorized by this section shall be confined to those types of snowmobiles, motorboats and vehicles which have been in regular use in the Boundary Waters Canoe Area prior to the date of enactment of this Act. The Secretary may set forth additional standards and criteria to further define the type of motorized craft which may be permitted.

(i) Except for motorboats, snowmobiles, and mechanized portaging, as authorized and defined herein, no other motorized use of the wilderness shall be permitted. Nothing in this Act shall prohibit the use of aircraft, motorboats, snowmobiles, or other mechanized uses in emergencies, or for the administration of the wilderness area by Federal, State, and local governmental officials or their deputies, only where the Secretary finds that such use is essential.

RESORTS

Purchase, notice from owner.

Fair market value.

SEC. 5. (a) The owner of a resort in commercial operation during 1975, 1976 or 1977 and located on land riparian to any of the lakes listed below may require purchase of that resort, including land and buildings appurtenant thereto, by written notice to the Secretary prior to September 30, 1985. The value of such resort for purposes of such sale shall be based upon its fair market value as of July 1, 1978, or as of the date of said written notice, whichever is greater, without regard to restrictions imposed by this Act:

Fall, Lake County, Moose, Lake County, Snowbank, Lake County, Lake One, Lake County, Sawbill, Cook County, Brule, Cook County, East Bearskin, Cook County, Clearwater, Cook County, Saganaga, Cook County, Sea Gull, Cook County, McFarland, Cook County, North Fowl, Cook County, South Fowl, Cook County, Jasper Lake, Lake County, Ojibway, Lake County.

Residence retention.

(b) An owner requiring purchase of a resort under this provision may elect to retain one or more appropriate buildings and lands not exceeding three acres, for personal use as a residence: *Provided,* That the purchase price to the Government for a resort shall be reduced by the fair market value of such buildings and lands, with the same valuation procedures outlined above.

(c) With respect to any privately owned lands and interests in lands riparian to the lakes listed above, and if the Federal Government has been required to purchase a resort on said lake, said lands shall not be sold without first being offered for sale to the Secretary who shall be given a period of one hundred days after the date of each such offer within which to purchase such lands. No such lands shall be sold at a price below the price at which they have been offered for sale to the Secretary, and if such lands are reoffered for sale they shall first be reoffered to the Secretary: *Provided,* That, this right of first refusal shall not apply to a change in ownership of a property within an immediate family.

Appropriation authorization.

(d) There are authorized to be appropriated such sums as may be necessary for the acquisition of lands and interests therein as provided by this section.

TIMBER SALE CONTRACTS

Termination period.

SEC. 6. (a) The Secretary is directed to terminate within a period of one year after the date of passage of this Act, all timber sale contracts in the Boundary Waters Canoe Area Wilderness. There shall be no further logging of the virgin forest areas formerly enjoined from logging by the United States District Court on said contract areas during the termination period.

The purpose of said termination period is only to permit completion of the harvesting of timber within existing areas under contract that are not within the areas described above and permit the taking of ameliorative measures, including land and cover restoration that will, at the earliest feasible date, make the imprint of man's work substantially unnoticeable on the lands included as wilderness in this Act.

(b) (1) In the event that termination of timber sale contracts in subsection (a) reduces the total national forest volume which a purchaser has under contract on the Superior National Forest to less than two years cut based on the average volume of Superior National Forest timber harvested by the purchaser in the last three years, the Secretary may, with the consent of the purchaser, substitute, to the extent practicable, timber on other national forest lands approximately equal in species and volume to the timber sale contract affected. In offering substitute timber, the Secretary shall negotiate the substitution at a price that is mutually equitable considering such factors as species, volume, logging accessibility, and other terms of the agreement.

Substitution.

(2) The United States will pay just compensation for any timber contracts terminated or modified by this Act, consistent with amendment V to the Constitution of the United States. Losses due to costs incurred in directly fulfilling the terms of such contracts shall be paid by the United States. Any action for the recovery from the United States of cost as provided above shall be brought in a court of competent jurisdiction. Any such judgments shall be paid from the claims and judgments fund (31 U.S.C. 724a).

Compensation.

USC prec. title 1.

Recovery.

(c) Within the limits of applicable laws and prudent forest management:

(1) the Secretary shall, in furtherance of the purposes of subsection (a) of this section and of section 4 of the National Forest Management Act of 1976 (90 Stat. 2949), expedite the intensification of resource management including emphasis on softwood timber production and hardwood utilization on the national forest lands in Minnesota outside the wilderness to offset, to the extent feasible, the reduction in the programmed allowable timber harvest resulting from reclassification of the Boundary Waters Area, and the Secretary shall make a review of progress to date in 1983, and a forecast of planned achievements by 1985 and shall submit, as a part of the 1985 program under the schedule called for in the Resources Planning Act of 1974, a Plan and recommendations for 1985–1990. In administering the Superior National Forest, the Secretary is authorized and directed to engage in artificial and natural regeneration, release, site preparation, and other forms of timber production enhancement.

Resource management review and plan.
16 USC 1601.

Administrative provisions.

(2) The Secretary, in carrying out the requirements in section (c) (1), is authorized and directed to cooperate with the State of Minnesota and its political subdivisions to develop and implement a system of grants, for the development of renewable resources on State, County and private lands. He may also seek the cooperation of other Federal departments and agencies to assure a coordinated approach to renewable resources development.

Grants system, cooperation.

(d) There is authorized to be appropriated, in addition to such sums as may otherwise be appropriated for the Superior National Forest from existing authorities established by law, the following additional sums for the fiscal years 1980 through 1990 inclusive:

Appropriation authorizations.

(1) to carry out the purposes of subsection 6(c) (1) an additional $8,000,000 annually; and,

(2) to carry out the purposes of subsection 6(c)(2) an additional $3,000,000 annually: *Provided, however*, That the Federal share of any grant made pursuant to subsection 6(c)(2) shall not exceed 80 percent of the total cost of said grant.

(e) Funds appropriated pursuant to this section shall remain available until expended. Authorizations in excess of funds appropriated in a given fiscal year shall remain available for appropriation in subsequent fiscal years.

(f) In addition to those personnel who would otherwise be available, the Secretary is authorized to appoint and fix the compensation (not to exceed that of grade 15 on the General Schedule for Federal employees) of additional full-time personnel for the Superior National Forest to carry out the purposes of this Act.

5 USC 5332 note.

LAWS APPLICABLE TO CERTAIN LANDS AND WATERS IN THE SUPERIOR NATIONAL FOREST

SEC. 7. (a) The provisions of the Acts listed in paragraph (b) of this section shall continue to apply to lands and waters specified in such Acts notwithstanding the inclusion of any such lands and waters in the wilderness or mining protection area designated under this Act. For lands and waters to which such Acts listed in paragraph (b) apply which are also within the wilderness or mining protection area designated under this Act, any withdrawal, prohibition, or restriction contained in such Acts listed in paragraph (b) shall be in addition to any withdrawal, prohibition, or restriction otherwise applicable to such wilderness or mining protection area under any other law.

(b) The Acts referred to in paragraph (a) are as follows:

(1) The Act of July 10, 1930 (46 Stat. 1020; 16 U.S.C. 577a, 577b), herein referred to as the "Shipstead-Nolan Act".

(2) The Act of June 22, 1948 (62 Stat. 568, as amended, 16 U.S.C. 577c–577b), herein referred to as the "Thye-Blatnik Act".

(c) The provisions of the Shipstead-Nolan Act are hereby extended and made applicable to all lands and waters not otherwise subject to such Act which are within the wilderness designated under this Act.

(d)(1) The authorities contained in the Thye-Blatnik Act are hereby extended and made applicable to all lands and waters not otherwise subject to such Act which are within the wilderness designated under this Act.

(2) In applying the second proviso of section 5 of such Thye-Blatnik Act to the areas to which such Act is extended and made applicable under this subsection, the phrase "fiscal year 1980" shall be substituted for the phrase "the first full fiscal year after the approval of this Act" in such proviso.

16 USC 577g.

(3) There are authorized to be appropriated such sums as may be necessary to carry out the provisions of the Thye-Blatnik Act with respect to the lands and waters within the wilderness designated under this Act. Such sums may be used for the payment of court judgments in condemnation actions brought under the terms of the Thye-Blatnik Act without regard to the date such condemnation actions were initially instituted. Funds appropriated from the Land and Water Conservation Fund may be used for the acquisition of any lands and waters, or interests therein within such wilderness.

Appropriation authorization.

EXISTING AIRSPACE RESERVATION

SEC. 8. The provisions of Executive Order 10092 as made applicable to the Boundary Waters Canoe Area established by the Wilderness Act of 1964 shall be deemed incorporated into this Act.

16 USC 1131 note.

MINING PROTECTION AREA ESTABLISHMENT

Sec. 9. In order to protect existing natural values and high standards of environmental quality from the adverse impacts associated with mineral development, there is hereby established the Boundary Waters Canoe Area Mining Protection Area (hereinafter in this Act referred to as the "mining protection area"), comprising approximately two hundred and twenty-two thousand acres.

MAP AND BOUNDARIES

Sec. 10. The mining protection area shall comprise the area generally depicted as a mining protection area on the map entitled "Boundary Waters Canoe Area Wilderness and Boundary Waters Canoe Area Mining Protection Area" dated September 1978, which shall be on file and available for public inspection in the offices of the Supervisor of the Superior National Forest and of the Chief, United States Forest Service. As soon as practicable after this Act takes effect, the Secretary shall file a map and a legal description of the mining protection area with the Committee on Interior and Insular Affairs of the House of Representatives and the Committee on Energy and Natural Resources of the United States Senate. Such map and description shall have the same force and effect as if included in this Act. Correction of clerical and typographical errors in such description may be made.

Filing with congressional committees.

MINING AND MINERAL LEASING IN THE WILDERNESS AND MINING PROTECTION AREA

Sec. 11. (a) In addition to any other applicable prohibition or withdrawal from entry or appropriation under any provision of the Wilderness Act or under any other provision of law, no permit, lease, or other authorization may be issued by any agency or authority of the United States for—

Prohibitions.

(1) exploration for, or mining of, minerals owned by the United States within the Boundary Waters Canoe Area Wilderness and Boundary Waters Canoe Area Mining Protection Area; or

(2) exploration for, or mining of minerals within such areas if such activities may affect navigable waters; or

(3) the use of property owned by the United States in relation to any mining of or exploration for minerals in such areas which may materially impair the wilderness qualities of the wilderness area or which may materially impair the natural values and environmental quality of the mining protection area.

The prohibitions contained in this subsection and any withdrawal from entry or appropriation for mining of or exploration for minerals applicable to the Boundary Waters Canoe Area Wilderness and Boundary Waters Canoe Area Mining Protection Area shall not apply to the extent specifically provided in legislation enacted by the United States after the date of enactment of this Act pursuant to a national emergency declared by the President.

(b)(1) Consistent with the prohibitions and other requirements in subsection (a) of this section, no permit, lease, or other authorization shall be issued unless and until—

(A) the Secretary shall have approved a plan that details how mining will be conducted consistent with this Act and with other Federal, State, and local requirements, and that details how the area will be restored to its original condition or to a substantially equivalent condition, including the estimated cost thereof;

(B) the applicant has posted a bond for performance payable to the United States in an amount determined by the Secretary to be sufficient to assure completion of the reclamation plan if the work had to be performed by the United States;

(C) the applicant shall have obtained all permits, licenses, certifications, and approvals required by Federal, State, or local law; and (iv) the Secretary has determined that no permanent facility will be constructed nor alteration will occur that could render the area incapable of reverting to its original condition or to a substantially equivalent condition.

(2) The provisions of paragraphs (2) and (3) of section 4(d) of the Wilderness Act (78 Stat. 890; 16 U.S.C. 1133(d)(2) and 16 U.S.C. 1133(d)(3)) shall not apply to the area designated herein as the Boundary Waters Canoe Area Wilderness.

Minerals or mineral rights, acquisition.

(c) The Secretary is authorized to acquire any minerals or mineral rights within the wilderness and mining protection area alleged to be owned by persons other than the Federal or State governments in the following manner:

(1) The Secretary first may seek to acquire these minerals or mineral rights by donation. In seeking a donation, the Secretary shall inform the person alleging the ownership interest of the procedures and limitations to be followed in acquisition by purchase as set forth in paragraph (2) below.

(2) If the person alleging the ownership interest does not donate his minerals or mineral rights to either the Federal or State governments, the Secretary is authorized to acquire the rights by purchase, within the limits of funds appropriated for property acquisition in the Superior National Forest, and in an amount appropriately discounted for the following factors if existent in relation to the particular mineral interest:

(A) The original patenting from the Federal public domain was fraudulent. The patenting of lands in the Boundary Waters Canoe Area Wilderness and Boundary Waters Canoe Area Mining Protection Area is prima facie fraudulent if (1) the Act under which the patent was issued was one of the Acts intended to put settlers on the land, such as, but without limitation, the Cash Purchase Act of 1820 (chapter LI, Act of April 24, 1820, 3 U.S. Stat. 566, 567, as amended); the Preemption Act of 1830 (chapter CCVIII, Act of May 29, 1830, 4 U.S. Stat. 420, 421, as amended); the Homestead Act of 1862 (chapter LXXV, Act of May 20, 1862, 12 U.S. Stat. 392–394, as amended); and the Timber and Stone Act (chapter 150, Act of June 3, 1878, 20 U.S. Stat. 88, 89, as amended, particularly by chapter 375, Act of August 4, 1892, 27 U.S. Stat. 348); and (2) the land was patented after 1875 and before the establishment of the Superior National Forest by proclamation on February 13, 1909. The Secretary also shall consider any other evidence of fraud when determining the value of the minerals such as (1) the transfer by the entryman or patentee of whole or partial interests in the property during the patenting process or soon thereafter, (2) the appearance in the chain of title of persons known to have participated in land speculation as land brokers, entrymen, or in other capacities.

(B) The date of separation of the mineral or mineral rights from the surface interest, if the separation occurred after 1927, the year when the courts have determined that the roadless policy was established by the Secretary for the area.

(C) Any other factor, such as restrictions on mining within the area imposed by State or local government, or by operation of treaty.

(d) In the event any legal action or proceeding is instituted by or against the United States in relation to minerals or mineral rights where the patenting is prima facie fraudulent as described in subsection (c) of this section, the Attorney General of the United States shall assert the public's equitable right to constructive or public trusts, or to recover or offset damages including but not limited to those based on the value of land fraudulently acquired plus interest at 6 per centum per annum.

(e) Notwithstanding any requirement of this section, the Secretary shall have authority to acquire within the wilderness or mining protection area designated by this Act, existing mineral interests by donation, purchase, exchange, or through exercise of the power of eminent domain.

(f) There is authorized to be appropriated to the Secretary such sums as may be required to carry out the purposes of this section, to be available until expended. **Appropriation authorization.**

SEVERABILITY

SEC. 12. If any provision of this Act is declared to be invalid, such declaration shall not affect the validity of any other provision hereof.

EXISTING STRUCTURES

SEC. 13. Nothing in this Act or the Wilderness Act shall be construed to prohibit the maintenance of the Prairie Portage Dam (on the international boundary chain between Birch and Basswood Lakes), and the Secretary is authorized to perform such maintenance work as may be required to keep that dam functional at its present height and width. The Secretary is authorized to maintain other existing water control structures only where such structures are necessary to protect wilderness values or public safety. **16 USC 1131 note.**

JURISDICTION OVER FISH AND WILDLIFE

SEC. 14. Nothing in this Act shall be construed as affecting the jurisdiction or responsibilities of the State with respect to fish and wildlife in the wilderness and the mining protection area.

JURISDICTION OVER WATERS

SEC. 15. The Secretary is authorized to promulgate and enforce regulations that limit or prohibit the use of motorized equipment on or relating to waters located within the wilderness in accordance with the provisions of this Act: *Provided*, That nothing in this Act shall be construed as affecting the jurisdiction or responsibilities of the State with respect to such waters except to the extent that the exercise of such jurisdiction is less stringent than the Secretary's regulations promulgated pursuant to this section: *Provided further*, That any regulations adopted pursuant to this Act shall be complementary to, and not in derogation of regulations issued by the United States Coast Guard. **Regulations.**

Cooperative agreements.

The Secretary is authorized to enter into cooperative agreements with the State of Minnesota with respect to enforcement of Federal and State regulations affecting the wilderness and the mining protection area.

COOPERATION WITH STATE

Administration of mining protection area and adjacent lands.

SEC. 16. (a) The Secretary shall cooperate with the State of Minnesota and any political subdivision thereof in the administration of the mining protection area and in the administration and protection of lands within or adjacent to the mining protection area owned or controlled by the State or any political subdivision thereof. Nothing in this title shall deprive the State of Minnesota or any political subdivision thereof of its right to exercise civil and criminal jurisdiction within the wilderness and the mining protection area and impose land use controls and environmental health standards on non-Federal areas within the wilderness and the mining protection area, or of its right to tax persons, corporations, franchises, or other non-Federal property, including mineral or other interests, in or on lands or waters within the wilderness and the mining protection area.

(b) The Secretary is authorized to enter into cooperative agreements with the State of Minnesota with respect to enforcement of Federal and State regulations affecting the wilderness and the mining protection and shall consult with the State of Minnesota in an effort to enhance the multiple-use benefits to be derived from both State and national forest lands.

TREATIES

SEC. 17. Nothing in this Act shall affect the provisions of any treaty now applicable to lands and waters which are included in the mining protection area and the wilderness.

EXPANSION OF RECREATION PROGRAMS

SEC. 18. (a) The Secretary is authorized and directed to expedite and intensify the program of dispersed outdoor recreation development on the Superior National Forest outside the Boundary Waters Canoe Area Wilderness, as designated by this Act. The Secretary shall consider in such new program development the need for the following: additional snowmobile trails, particularly those now planned or under construction; remote campsites on lightly developed lakes; and lake access sites and parking facilities to provide motorized recreation experiences similar to those previously available in the Boundary Waters Canoe Area.

16 USC 1131 note.

(b) The Secretary, consistent with the Wilderness Act of 1964 and with this Act, is authorized to construct a system of new hiking, backpacking and cross-country ski trails within the Boundary Waters Canoe Area Wilderness as designated by this Act, and on appropriate adjacent Federal lands outside the wilderness. In constructing such a trail system, consideration should be given to locating portions of the system near existing resorts on the perimeter of the wilderness to provide additional outdoor recreation opportunities for resort guests.

(c) The Secretary is authorized and directed to develop an educational program for the recreational users of the wilderness which will assist them to understand the purpose, value, and appropriate use of wilderness lands and the functioning of natural ecosystems in wilderness.

Program for disabled persons.

(d) The Secretary in cooperation with the State of Minnesota and other appropriate groups, consistent with the purposes of this Act, is authorized and directed to develop a program providing opportunities for a wide range of outdoor experiences for disabled persons.

(e) There are authorized to be appropriated such sums as may be necessary for the Secretary to carry out the purposes of this section.

Appropriation authorization.

SEC. 19. (a) The Secretary, in cooperation with other appropriate executive agencies, is authorized and directed to develop a cooperative program of technical and financial assistance to resorts in commercial operation in 1975, 1976, and 1977, and outfitters in commercial operation in 1977 which are located within the mining protection area or which are located on land adjacent to any of the lakes listed in section 5 of this Act. There are authorized to be appropriated such sums as may be necessary for the purposes of this subsection.

Technical and financial assistance for certain commercial operations.

(b) There are authorized to be appropriated to the Secretary funds to be made available as grants to the Agricultural Extension Service, University of Minnesota, to provide over a three-year period educational and technical assistance to businesses and communities adjacent to the Boundary Waters Canoe Area Wilderness in order to improve economic opportunities for tourism and recreation-related businesses in a manner which is complementary to the management of the wilderness.

Grants.

MANAGEMENT STUDY

SEC. 20. The Secretary, acting through the Chief, United States Forest Service, shall, not later than October 1, 1981, submit to the Committee on Interior and Insular Affairs of the House of Representatives and the Committee on Energy and Natural Resources of the Senate, a comprehensive management plan setting forth the specific management procedures to implement the objectives of this Act. An interim report setting forth public involvement procedures, management alternatives, and a timetable for the remaining study actions, shall be submitted within one year from the date of enactment of this Act.

Submittal to congressional committees.

Interim report.

LIMITATION OF AUTHORIZATIONS

SEC. 21. All authorizations for any funds to be appropriated under the terms of this Act shall not be effective until October 1, 1979. Notwithstanding any other provision of this Act, authority to enter into agreements or to make payments under this Act shall be effective only to the extent or in such amounts as are provided in advance in appropriation Acts.

Approved October 21, 1978.

Sources

The authors utilized a great many sources for this book beyond the voluminous coverage by newspapers in Minnesota and around the country or in various magazines and journals. Many of the authors' special sources have never before been available to other scholars, and have helped provide invaluable insight and documentation for this book. Some of the more significant sources include:

Donald M. Fraser Papers. The official files of Congressman Donald M. Fraser on the BWCA controversy have never before been available. These files were primarily developed by his aide, Rip Rapson, one of the co-authors of this work. The files include copies of correspondence, background materials on various issues, files on the subcommittee hearings, floor strategy, and more. Of particular interest are the extremely detailed notes taken by Rapson during many of the key strategy meetings, which are cited in this book as "Rip Rapson Notes, DMF Papers."

Subcommittee Hearing Transcripts. The official transcripts from the hearings of the House Subcommittee on National Parks and Recreation during July, August, and September 1977, were obtained from the subcommittee in the late 1970s to assist in the defense of the BWCA law in the federal courts. These transcripts have also not been available before and were extensively utilized by the authors.

Subcommittee Testimony. The authors compiled the most complete known set of written testimony presented at the subcommittee field hearings in Minnesota and the subcommittee hearings in Washington, D.C. These written statements, from both sides of the issue, proved invaluable in researching and writing this book.

Miron L. Heinselman Chronology. Dr. Heinselman worked at the focus of the environmental forces working to pass wilderness legislation for the BWCA. He kept detailed telephone logs of all his phone conversations and meetings during the three-year period he served as Chairman of the Friends of the Boundary Waters Wilderness. From these phone logs, he developed a detailed chronology of events, meetings, intelligence gathering, strategy, and more, including many events, conversations, and details not documented in any other source. The authors made extensive use of this chronology and cited it as "MLH Chronology."

Brock Evans Recollections. Brock Evans directed the Sierra Club's Washington office during the BWCA fight. From April through October, 1978, he recorded his thoughts and accounts of the BWCA battle on a daily basis. His cassette tape dictation was later transcribed to written form, and cited by the authors as "Brock Evans Recollections."

Rapson Recollections. In the process of working on this book, Rip Rapson compiled a number of recollections, anecdotes, and events from his long, personal involvement with the BWCA controversy. These recollections are cited as "Rapson Recollections, December 1983."

Interviews. The authors also conducted a series of interviews with key people to fill in gaps and provide additional information on the Boundary Waters and the issues surrounding the area's management and protection. These interviews included:

Charles S. Kelly, September 24, 1985. Mr. Kelly served as a member of the President's Quetico-Superior Committee for more than forty years, from the 1930s until the 1970s, most of that time as chairman.

Dr. M. Rupert Cutler, October 5, 1986. Dr. Cutler served as Assistant Secretary of Agriculture during the Carter Administration, and formulated the administration's position on the BWCA in 1977 and 1978.

William Rom, March 25, 1987. Mr. Rom is a life-long resident of Ely who became the most successful canoe outfitter in the area, and who was involved with the issues of protecting the canoe country for many decades.

Dr. Daniel Engstrom, November 17, 1987. Dr. Engstrom served as vice chair of the Friends of the Boundary Waters Wilderness. He provided key leadership in organizing efforts in Washington, D.C., as well as at the tumultuous Minnesota DFL state convention in 1978.

Edward M. Zabinski, December 21, 1987. Mr. Zabinski served as the executive director of the Boundary Waters Conservation Alliance, the citizens group which opposed the wilderness designation for the Boundary Waters Canoe Area, during the pivotal year of 1978.

Robert Buckler, December 22, 1987. Mr. Buckler served on the staff of Congressman James Oberstar, later as the first executive director of the Boundary Waters Conservation Alliance, and still later in a position with the forest products industry during the BWCA controversy.

Charles K. Dayton, November 13, 1989. Mr. Dayton is an environmental attorney who worked on BWCA cases during most of the 1970s. He was a key player in the inner leadership of the Friends of the Boundary Waters Wilderness and represented environmental interests during the key Dayton/Walls negotiations on the BWCA in 1978.

Donald M. Fraser, October 25, 1991. Mr. Fraser represented Minnesota's Fifth Congressional District in the House of Representatives from his first election in 1962 until 1978. He first sponsored the BWCA wilderness legislation that bore his name in mid-1976, and was at the center of the congressional debate over the canoe country wilderness from then until late-1978. Don Fraser unsuccessfully ran for a U.S. Senate seat in 1978. From 1979 to 1994 he served as mayor of Minneapolis.

Minnesota Historical Society Archives. The Minnesota Historical Society maintains an excellent archival collection of materials dealing with the BWCA. The authors particularly utilized the papers of Sigurd F. Olson, William H. Magie, Senator Hubert H. Humphrey, Charles K. Dayton, the Ely-Winton Boundary Waters Conservation Alliance, and the Quetico-Superior Council papers of Ernest C. Oberholtzer. Also of great importance are the Society's microfilmed collection of historical records from the files of Superior National Forest.

Edward M. Zabinski Paper. In conjunction with graduate studies at the University of Minnesota, Mr. Zabinski wrote a sixty-page paper in 1983 entitled "A Narrative History of the Boundary Waters Conservation Alliance" (Hubert H. Humphrey Institute of Public Affairs, University of Minnesota). Although lacking documentation and footnotes, this paper provided an invaluable "insider's" view of this important BWCA advocacy group.

Burnham J. Philbrook Paper. Like Mr. Zabinski, Mr. Philbrook produced a Plan B paper for graduate studies at the University of Minnesota. (Burnham John Philbrook, "Portfolio of Papers Relating to State and Federal Legislation Affecting the Boundary Waters Canoe Area," Hubert H. Humphrey Institute of Public Affairs, University of Minnesota, 1981, 213 pp.) His paper consists of an extensive collection of documents, memos, and correspondence dealing with his involvement with the BWCA, beginning with his tenure in the Minnesota Legislature and continuing through his involvement during the congressional action in 1977 and 1978.

Searle Book. R. Newell Searle's book, *Saving Quetico-Superior: A Land Set Apart* (St. Paul: Minnesota Historical Society Press, 1977), provided an invaluable source of information and documentation on the history of efforts to protect the BWCA and Quetico Provincial Park. Searle's book is a particularly valuable reference for the wilderness preservation efforts which occurred from the 1920s through the 1950s.

Gladden Book. James Gladden, *Boundary Waters Canoe Area: Wilderness Values and Motorized Recreation* (Ames: Iowa State University Press, 1990). James N. Gladden wrote his doctoral dissertation on the same topic and later produced this book. He examined only the motorized use conflict from the BWCA battles of the 1970s, and believes that this conflict between the pro-motor and anti-motor forces represents a paradigm shift in environmental values in our culture. Gladden contends that the cultural view of the pro-motor forces represents an anthropocentric or utilitarian perspective, while the anti-motor culture represents a more biocentric viewpoint.

Backes Book. David Backes, *Canoe Country: An Embattled Wilderness* (NorthWord Press, 1991). David Backes covers essentially the same time period as did Newell Searle in *Saving Quetico-Superior*. But rather than detailing the conflicts over the canoe country, Backes constructs a framework for analyzing the continuing controversies over the area as the result of the clash of images that people held about the canoe country, and the role played by the mass media in spreading these ideas and images.

Newspaper File Collection. The authors, both in the course of personal involvement with the subject matter for this book as well as during the actual research for this book, developed an extensive newspaper file collection of BWCA articles, editorials, and editorial cartoons from newspapers around the country, which have been arranged in chronological order. Though certainly not a complete collection of all such pieces published in all newspapers across the nation or even in Minnesota, this collection has nonetheless provided an invaluable source of information and citations for this book.

Dr. Herbert E. Wright Papers. Dr. Herbert E. Wright, Jr., retired director of the Limnological Research Center at the University of Minnesota, played a key role in the BWCA issues of the 1970s. His work with the BWCA logging issue beginning around 1970 led to two lawsuits by MPIRG on that topic, and he worked as well with the Friends of the Boundary Waters Wilderness during the congressional controversy of 1975 and 1978. Dr. Wright also closely worked with and represented Friends of the Earth during the BWCA dispute. He compiled two volumes of his papers on the BWCA, including extensive correspondence not found in other collections, and made them available to the authors.

Personal Files. Dr. Heinselman and Mr. Proescholdt have both compiled extensive personal files on BWCA matters, particularly files related to the BWCA controversies described in this book. These files include lobbying materials used by both sides during the congressional controversy, background files on BWCA and Quetico matters, correspondence, position papers, newsletters, copies of legislation and other official documents, and more. Many of these materials are not found in other collections and were used extensively for this book.

For Further Information

The task of protecting the Boundary Waters Canoe Area (BWCA) Wilderness and the larger international Quetico-Superior Ecosystem will continue far into the future. Though many environmental organizations have played and continue to play a significant role in the efforts to protect the wilderness complex, the best by far is the Friends of the Boundary Waters Wilderness.

The Friends of the Boundary Waters Wilderness is the only conservation organization solely focused on the protection and preservation of the BWCA Wilderness and the Quetico-Superior Ecosystem, and as such, the organization is centrally situated in the on-going efforts to protect and manage the area. The Friends publishes a fine newsletter for its members, as well as other publications, and is engaged in a broad array of activities to protect the area and educate the public about it. The organization can be contacted at the following address for information on membership or current activities:

Friends of the Boundary Waters Wilderness
1313 Fifth Street SE, Suite 329
Minneapolis, MN 55414
(612)379-3835

Many other organizations, however, have helped protect the area and maintain great interest in the BWCA Wilderness and the Quetico-Superior Ecosystem. They include:

The Wilderness Society
900 17th St. NW
Washington, D.C. 20006
(202)833-2300

Sierra Club
730 Polk St.
San Francisco, CA 94109
(415)776-2211

Izaak Walton League of America
707 Conservation Lane
Gaithersburg, MD 20878-2983
(301)548-0150

National Audubon Society
950 Third Avenue
New York, NY 10022
(212)832-3200

National Parks and Conservation Association
1776 Massachusetts Ave. NW
Washington, D.C. 20036
(202)223-6722

National Wildlife Federation
1400 16th St. NW
Washington, D.C. 20036
(202)797-6800

In addition to these primarily U.S. organizations, several Canadian conservation organizations also work for the protection of Quetico Provincial Park in Ontario. These organizations include:

Federation of Ontario Naturalists
355 Lesmill Road
Don Mills, Ontario M3B 2W8
(416)444-8419

Wildlands League
401 Richmond Street West, Suite 380
Toronto, Ontario M5V 3A8
(416)971-9453

Quetico Foundation
48 Yonge Street, Suite 610
Toronto, Ontario M5E 1G6
(416)941-9388

Friends of Quetico Park
P.O. Box 1959
Atikokan, Ontario P0T 1C0

Index